Governing Shale Gas

Shale energy development is an issue of global importance. The number of reserves globally, and their potential economic return, have increased dramatically in the past decade. Questions abound, however, about the appropriate governance systems to manage the risks of unconventional oil and gas development and the ability of citizens to engage and participate in decisions regarding these systems. Stakeholder participation is essential for the social and political legitimacy of energy extraction and production, what the industry calls a 'social licence' to operate.

This book attempts to bring together critical themes inherent in the energy governance literature and illustrate them through cases in multiple countries, including the US, the UK, Canada, South Africa, Germany and Poland. These themes include how multiple actors and institutions – industry, governments and regulatory bodies at all scales, communities, opposition movements, and individual landowners – have roles in developing, contesting, monitoring, and enforcing practices and regulations within unconventional oil and gas development. Overall, the book proposes a systemic, participatory, community-led approach to achieve a form of legitimacy that allows communities to derive social priorities by a process of community visioning.

This book will be of great relevance to scholars and policy-makers with an interest in shale gas development, and energy policy and governance.

John Whitton is the Director of UCLan Energy and a Co-Director of the Research Institute of Citizenship, Society and Change at the University of Central Lancashire, UK.

Matthew Cotton is a Lecturer in Human Geography in the Environment Department at the University of York, UK.

Ioan M. Charnley-Parry is a post-doctoral research associate in UCLan Energy and the Research Institute of Citizenship, Society and Change at the University of Central Lancashire, UK.

Kathryn Brasier is an Associate Professor of Rural Sociology at Pennsylvania State University, USA.

Routledge Studies in Energy Policy

For further details please visit the series page on the Routledge website: www.
routledge.com/books/series/RSIEP/

Governing Shale Gas

Development, Citizen Participation and
Decision Making in the US, Canada,
Australia and Europe

Edited by
John Whitton, Matthew Cotton,
Ioan M. Charnley-Parry and
Kathryn Brasier

Routledge
Taylor & Francis Group

LONDON AND NEW YORK

from Routledge

First published 2018
by Routledge
2 Park Square, Milton Park, Abingdon, Oxon OX14 4RN

and by Routledge
711 Third Avenue, New York, NY 10017

Routledge is an imprint of the Taylor & Francis Group, an informa business

British Library Cataloguing-in-Publication Data
A catalogue record for this book is available from the British Library

Library of Congress Cataloging-in-Publication Data
A catalog record has been requested for this book

ISBN: 978-1-138-63930-0 (hbk)
ISBN: 978-1-315-63728-0 (ebk)

Typeset in Goudy
by Wearset Ltd, Boldon, Tyne and Wear

MIX
Paper from
responsible sources
FSC
www.fsc.org   FSC® C013056

Printed and bound in Great Britain by
TJ International Ltd, Padstow, Cornwall

Contents

Figures

Tables

Contributors

Doreen Atkinson is a Professor in Development Studies in the Karoo region of South Africa. She specialises in small town development, rural-urban dynamics, tourism, social development and heritage. She is a Trustee of the Karoo Development Foundation. Doreen was the Integrating Author of the Social Fabric chapter of the scientific assessment.

Tudor Baker has recently graduated from the University of Leeds with a BSc in Sustainability and Environmental Management. He has a particular interest in the underlying political dynamics of local contention and learning how local communities can use their power to address global environmental issues.

Tom Beckley has been working in the field of environment and natural resource sociology in Canada for 24 years. He teaches in the Faculty of Forestry and Environmental Management at the University of New Brunswick in Fredericton, in Canada. His PhD in Sociology and his Master's degree in Rural Sociology are both from the University of Wisconsin-Madison, USA. Prior to joining UNB in 2000, he worked for the Canadian Forest Service in Alberta and New Brunswick. His research topics have included: social problems and issues in forest-dependent communities, public participation in resource management and policy, criteria and indicators of sustainable development, community sustainability and adaptability, environmental values and environmentally supportive behavior. Recently Tom has branched out into explorations of energy (energy literacy and landscape effects of energy development), and climate change.

Michael Böcher is Professor of Political Science and Sustainable Development at the Otto-von-Guericke University, in Magdeburg, Germany. His main research interests are environmental policy analysis, regional governance and sustainable rural development, and scientific knowledge transfer in environmental and sustainability sciences.

Christian Brannstrom is Professor of Geography and Associate Dean for Academic Affairs in the College of Geosciences at Texas A&M University, USA. In addition to working on municipal policies for hydraulic fracturing, he has published on social and political aspects of wind power in Texas and in north-eastern Brazil. He teaches a course on Geography of Energy. His previous work has focused on land cover change, environmental governance, and environmental history.

Kathryn Brasier is Associate Professor of Rural Sociology in the Department of Agricultural Economics, Sociology, and Education at the Pennsylvania State University, USA. Her research and teaching programs focus generally on environment-society interactions at the community level and collective action related to agricultural and environmental issues. Her current research areas focus on describing community impacts of and response to unconventional energy development; public engagement in environmental issues; and gender and sustainable agriculture. She received her PhD in Sociology and Rural Sociology from the University of Wisconsin-Madison in 2002.

Kelly Bronson is a Canada Research Chair candidate in Science and Society at the University of Ottawa in Canada. She is a social scientist studying science-society tensions that erupt around controversial technologies and their governance, from GMOs to big data. Her research aims to bring community values into conversation with technical knowledge in the production of evidence-based decision-making. She has published her work in regional (*Journal of New Brunswick Studies*), national (*Canadian Journal of Communication*) and international journals (*Journal of Responsible Innovation, Big Data and Society*).

Ioan M. Charnley-Parry is a post-doctoral research assistant in the Energy and Society Research Group at the University of Central Lancashire, UK. His PhD explored the perceived social impacts and social sustainability of nuclear energy infrastructure on Anglesey, North Wales. He is currently involved in the European Commission's Horizon 2020 programme project 'HoNESt – History of Nuclear Energy and Society' as part of the Social Science work package, and has published on social sustainability, stakeholder engagement and public participation with regards to nuclear energy and shale gas developments in the UK and the US.

Matthew Cotton is a Lecturer in Human Geography in the Environment Department at the University of York, UK. His research examines the social and ethical dimensions of energy systems development and planning, specifically through the use of qualitative and participatory-deliberative research methods. He is the author of two monographs, *Nuclear Waste Politics* (Routledge) and *Ethics and Technology Assessment* (Springer). He has published on issues of shale gas in terms of discourse, public participation, stakeholder perceptions, and environmental justice in *Energy Policy, Energy Research & Social Science, Environment and Planning A* and *Local Environment*, respectively. His research on energy policy and environmental justice has been funded by a range of sources including the European Commission's Horizon 2020 programme, the UK Engineering and Physical Sciences

Research Council, the Department for Environment, Food and Rural Affairs, the Toyota Foundation and the Joseph Rowntree Foundation.

Matthew Dairon is a policy analyst with Environment and Climate Change Canada. His research interests focus on environmental sociology, particularly those areas that explore resource development and environmental justice.

Megan J. de Jager is undertaking her PhD at Carl von Ossietzky University in Oldenburg, Germany, looking at the relationship between hydrothermal carbonisation and soil productivity. Megan previously worked at the Council for Scientific and Industrial Research (CSIR) as an intern and was closely involved in the shale gas scientific assessment and stakeholder outreach programme. She co-edited the final assessment publication.

Andile Dludla has four years' experience in environmental management. He conducted his BSc thesis on water pollution risk and hydraulic fracturing at the University of the Western Cape. While employed at CSIR, he was appointed as the stakeholder engagement officer for the shale gas scientific assessment.

John Dzwonczyk is an Instructor of Geography in the Department of Geography and Environmental Engineering at the United States Military Academy, West Point, USA. His research interests include the water-energy nexus, political-industrial systems, and geographic education. He received his MS in Geography from the Pennsylvania State University in 2016.

Colter Ellis is an Assistant Professor of Sociology at Montana State University, USA. His research focuses on issues relevant to rural people such as agriculture, energy and natural resource extraction, and community trauma. His research has been published in *Rural Sociology*, *Energy Research and Social Science*, the *Journal of Interpersonal Violence*, and other peer-reviewed journals.

Surina Esterhuyse is a researcher whose research focuses on the regulation of unconventional oil and gas extraction for water resources protection in South Africa. She was a Contributing Author on the water chapter in the national shale gas scientific assessment. Surina also co-edited the book *Hydraulic Fracturing in the Karoo: Critical Legal and Environmental Perspectives* with Jan Glazewski.

Darrick Evensen is an environmental social-psychologist. He is currently an EU-funded Marie Curie Actions Research Fellow in the School of Psychology at Cardiff University, UK, where he is part of the Understanding Risk Research Group. Darrick's research predominantly focuses on public perceptions of and reactions to controversial energy and environment issues, with a focus on forwarding policy and regulation in these areas.

Matthew Fry is an Associate Professor of Geography at the University of North Texas, USA. His research into shale gas governance in Texas focuses on urban drilling, municipal distance ordinances, environmental justice, and land-use change. In addition, he has published research on urbanization and resource extraction, sustainability transitions, and historical land change in Mexico.

Julia H. Haggerty is Assistant Professor of Geography in the Department of Earth Sciences at Montana State University, USA. She holds a BA from Colorado College and a PhD from the University of Colorado-Boulder. Her teaching and research focus on resource geography and rural community development.

Paul Hardcastle is the Director of Planning and Policy Coordination in the Western Cape Department of Environmental Affairs and Development Planning, South Africa. Paul was a government representative who sat on the Executive Committee, overseeing and providing input into the shale gas scientific assessment. He was also closely involved in the public outreach and stakeholder engagements on the project.

Wendy Highby is an Associate Professor and Social Sciences Librarian at the University of Northern Colorado, in Greeley, Colorado, County of Weld, wherein 23,301 oil and gas wells were active, as of June 1, 2017, according to statistics maintained by the Colorado Oil and Gas Conservation Commission.

Douglas Jackson-Smith is a sociologist and Professor in the School of Environment and Natural Resources at the Ohio State University, USA. His research focuses on the drivers and consequences of technological and structural change in natural resource industries (agriculture, energy, and water). He uses social science theory and mixed methods to contribute to interdisciplinary studies of coupled human-natural systems.

Jeffrey B. Jacquet is an Assistant Professor in the School of Environment and Natural Resources at Ohio State University, USA. He holds degrees from the University of Wisconsin-Milwaukee, the University of Wyoming, and Cornell University. Dr Jacquet is formerly a resident of both Ithaca, Wisconsin, and Ithaca, New York.

Beth Kinne is an Associate Professor and Finger Lakes Institute Endowed Chair of Environmental Studies at Hobart & William Smith Colleges in Geneva, New York. She has degrees in biology from the University of Virginia, natural resource management from the University of British Columbia, and a J.D. and LL.M. in Asian and comparative law from the University of Washington, Seattle. Her research interests include development of water law in China, the regulation of hydrofracking in the United States, and the drivers of intermunicipal collaboration in watershed management. She is co-editor and author of *Beyond the Fracking Wars: A Guide for Lawyers, Public Officials, Planners and Citizens* (American Bar Association, 2013).

Hendrik Kotze is an expert dispute facilitator and manager. He is Product Development Executive with Nuvalaw, a LegalTech company, and Senior Researcher at the Africa Center for Dispute Settlement, South Africa. Hendrik acted as the independent facilitator during the scientific assessment, overseeing and designing engagement processes between stakeholders, the project team and the government.

Aleksandra Lis is an Assistant Professor at the Institute of Ethnology and Cultural Anthropology at the Adam Mickiewicz University in Poznań, in Poland. She holds a PhD degree in Sociology and Social Anthropology from the Central European University in Budapest. Her research interests focus on the social construction of carbon markets and on the politics of constructing large-scale energy infrastructures, such as CCS, nuclear power and shale gas extraction. She is interested in the politics of knowledge production on energy technologies and in the way different types of knowledge become part of governance processes. Aleksandra has worked on a number of national and international projects and published widely on these topics.

Paul A. Lochner is an environmental assessment practitioner at the CSIR in Stellenbosch. He has led a wide range of environmental assessment and management studies over the past 25 years. His sectors of experience include renewable energy, oil and gas, constructed wetlands and port development Paul co-led the South African shale gas scientific assessment and was one of the editors of the publication.

Hanabeth Luke is a Lecturer in the School of Environment, Science and Engineering at Southern Cross University, Australia. As a part of Southern Cross GeoScience research group, Hanabeth engages in science communication, and research, across the disciplines of science, geography and social-psychology. Her research interests lie in social dimensions of sustainable land use planning and management, with a focus on a social licence to operate.

John R. Parkins is a Professor in the Department of Resource Economics and Environmental Sociology, University of Alberta, Canada. His research encompasses topics in rural sociology and environmental sociology with a more recent focus on the challenges of renewable energy development in Canada.

Peggy Petrzelka is Professor of Sociology at Utah State University, USA. Her research interests focus on the interrelationships between the physical and social environment in a number of settings, from agricultural communities in the Midwest to towns experiencing hydraulic fracturing in Texas to rural communities in Morocco. Her research has been published in *Gender and Society*, *Rural Sociology*, *Society and Natural Resources*, *Land Use Policy*, and other peer-reviewed journals.

Imogen Rattle is a PhD student at the Sustainability Research Institute, at the University of Leeds, UK. Her work aims to explore the ways in which the public are using the internet to engage with environmental issues, and the effect this is having on environmental policy debates. Her research interests include the intersections between energy policy, climate, communities and the digital world.

William Rifkin is a Professor and Director of the Hunter Research Foundation Centre and Chair in Applied Regional Economics at the University of Newcastle, Australia. At the University of Queensland from 2012 to 2017, he led development of the UQ Boomtown Toolkit and socio-economic indicators effort, which publishes the *Annual Report on Queensland's Gasfields Communities* (https://boomtown-indicators.org). His focus is communication among experts and relative non-experts – engineers, scientists, medical specialists, lawyers, politicians, local residents, pub owners, farmers, etc. He has degrees from MIT, the University of California-Berkeley, and Stanford University.

Sarah T. Romano is an Assistant Professor of Environmental and Sustainability Studies at the University of Northern Colorado in Greeley, CO, USA. For more than a decade, her research has drawn together scholarship on social movements and environmental governance to examine strategies that politically marginalized actors use to gain inclusion in policy processes. Her book, *Rural Water Governance in Nicaragua: From Resource Management to Political Activism*, is forthcoming in 2019 with the University of Arizona Press.

Robert (Bob) J. Scholes is Professor of Systems Ecology at the University of the Witwatersrand in South Africa. He has participated in many IPCC Assessment Reports, in a range of capacities, co-chaired the Status and Trend working group of the Millennium Ecosystem Assessment, and co-chairs the IPBES Land Degradation and Restoration Assessment. He has led several national assessments, including the shale gas scientific assessment.

Gregory O. Schreiner is a Sustainability Scientist at the Council for Scientific and Industrial Research (CSIR). He is currently a full-time PhD student at the University of the Witwatersrand focusing his research on the value of scientific assessment in society. Greg co-ordinated and co-edited the South African shale gas scientific assessment and managed the day-to-day interactions between its participants.

Kate Sherren is an Associate Professor in the School for Resource and Environmental Studies at Dalhousie University, Nova Scotia, Canada. She researches sustainability transitions and landscape change in the context of climate adaptation, renewable energy, food systems, and biodiversity conservation.

Kristin K. Smith is a PhD Candidate in the Resources and Communities Research Group at Montana State University, USA. She draws upon the theories and methodologies of rural economic geography, community development, and political ecology to research the opportunities/challenges that rural areas grapple with due to restructuration, globalization, and late capitalism. Her dissertation analyses the socio-economic changes occurring in Montana and North Dakota due to the ebbs and flows of shale development.

Luanita Snyman-van der Walt is a registered Professional Natural Scientist focusing on Geographic Information System analyses for environmental assessment and decision-making. Luanita acted as the project officer on the shale gas scientific assessment and also co-edited the final publication.

Agata Stasik is Assistant Professor of Management at Koźmiński University, Warsaw, Poland, with a background in sociology and science and technology studies. Her research has focused on the dynamics of shale gas development, the impact of the internet on technological risk governance, and crowdfunding of technological innovation. Her current research interests include new forms of governance in energy innovations and practices and the impacts of future anticipation. She has been a visiting researcher at the University of Vienna and the University of Gothenburg.

Anna Szolucha is a Research Fellow at the Polish Institute of Advanced Studies, the Polish Academy of Sciences in Warsaw, Poland. Her research focuses on the history and impacts of shale gas developments in the UK and Poland. She wrote the first social impact assessment of shale gas projects in the UK entitled 'The Human Dimension of Shale Gas Developments in Lancashire, UK'. Her recent book is *Real Democracy in the Occupy Movement: No Stable Ground* (Routledge).

Gene Theodori is Professor of Sociology at Sam Houston State University, Texas, USA. He teaches, conducts basic and applied research, and writes professional and popular articles on rural and community development issues, energy and natural resource concerns, and related topics. A central feature of his work involves the design, implementation, and analysis of survey research. The findings from his survey research have been published in numerous journal articles, book chapters, research bulletins, and other professional reports.

Annette Elisabeth Töller is Professor of Public Policy and Environmental Politics at the FernUniversität in Hagen, Germany. Her main research interests are environmental policy, voluntary regulation and theories of the policy process.

James Van Alstine is Associate Professor of Environmental Policy at the Sustainability Research Institute at the University of Leeds, UK. With over 15 years of experience in the field of natural resource governance, he studies the political economy of the extractive industries and climate-compatible development with the aim of co-producing inclusive and pro-poor sustainable development outcomes in the contexts where he works. His work spans the Global North and the Global South, including Brazil, Ghana, Greenland, Uganda, the United Kingdom, Zambia and South Africa.

Kathryn Bills Walsh has a Bachelor's degree in Geography and Secondary Education from Keene State College, NH, and a Master's degree in Geography from the University of Victoria, Canada. Katie is a doctoral student in the Earth Sciences Department at Montana State University working in the Resources and Communities Research Group. She is completing an integrated human geography PhD, focused on energy development, landscape and reclamation in the US West.

John Whitton is Director of UCLan Energy, at the University of Central Lancashire. In his academic role, he works extensively with communities, carrying out social research on energy demand behaviour and the relationship between society and energy infrastructure. His work on developing a framework for social/community sustainability in energy communities and the representation of alternative conceptualisations of 'community' during major infrastructure developments is currently informing industry, the UK Government and EU policy. As a Director of Big Local Trust, his charity work brings him face to face with communities across the UK, to discuss a range of issues that are important to them. Big Local Trust is the overseer of the UK National Lottery 15-year resident-led community regeneration programme, Big Local.

Grace Wildermuth is a MS Candidate and Graduate Research Assistant in the Rural Sociology program in the Department of Agricultural Economics, Sociology, and Education at the Pennsylvania State University, USA, where she is also enrolled in the dual-title Human Dimensions of Natural Resources and the Environment program. Her research interests include environmental/ natural resource sociology, community impacts of energy development, and natural resource governance. Her latest research projects explore energy-related landowner coalitions and regional energy governance through River Basin Commissions.

Katherine Witt is a Research Fellow at the University of Queensland, Centre for Coal Seam Gas, in Australia. She has previously worked as an environmental scientist in the Queensland Government, and as a university lecturer. Kathy has an interdisciplinary PhD in environmental management/sociology. Her research focuses on: (1) the social (including psycho-social health) impacts of resource development for rural and regional communities; (2) multi-stakeholder collaboration in contentious issues; (3) public discourse and deliberative democracy; (4) communities as complex adaptive systems; (5) values frameworks and community capitals; (6) corporate/industry social responsibility; and (7) property/individual rights and social/ collective responsibility in resource management.

Jarrad G. Wright is a Principal Engineer based at the CSIR in Pretoria, South Africa. He has energy sector operations and planning experience in 11 African countries. He is a Commissioner on the South African National Planning Commission. He is currently pursuing his PhD at the University of the Witwatersrand.

1 Introduction

Governing shale gas

John Whitton, Matthew Cotton, Kathryn Brasier and Ioan Charnley-Parry

Introduction: the development of unconventional oil and gas resources

Unconventional oil and gas development (UOGD) from shales, coal beds and tight sands, has become one of the most important global energy policy phenomena of the twenty-first century. The demonstrable economic success of the so-called 'shale boom' in the USA since the early 2000s spurred national governments to develop their own domestic unconventional oil and gas resources. China, Argentina, Algeria, Canada, Mexico, Australia, South Africa, Russia and Brazil (in descending order of resource magnitude) are all embarking upon shale development programmes at various stages of maturity (U.S. Energy Information Administration, 2015), while smaller reserves in Europe (primarily the UK, Denmark and Poland) have estimated net profitability and demonstrable political support for extraction activities. At the national state-level, political support for shale gas (or in some cases coal-bed methane) is commonly motivated by a desire to ensure domestic energy security of supply, coal-to-gas transitions to reduce CO_2 emissions, (primarily rural) economic regeneration and taxation revenue generation (Rogers, 2011; Cooper et al., 2016). Yet, despite being potentially profitable, the technology invokes considerable socio-environmental controversy, prompts concerns over environmental injustice and stimulates political debate (see Neville et al., 2017). In response to this, public authorities have introduced new forms of energy governance across different cases and contexts throughout the world.

Social movements of opposition and non-governmental organizations (NGOs) have raised concerns primarily over the environmental impacts associated with unconventional hydrocarbon extraction. At the local level, this has centred on water availability and stress, surface (Burton et al., 2014) and groundwater (Montcoudiol et al., 2017) impacts, including methane and hydraulic fracturing, fluid contamination of water sources; seismic activity (Das and Zoback, 2011; Green et al., 2012); and local air, light and noise pollution primarily from drilling rigs and associated road traffic to and from the shale gas sites (Litovitz et al., 2013; Rich et al., 2014). At the global level, there has been increasing emphasis upon the risks associated with fugitive methane emissions and increased CO_2 emissions relative to renewable energy sources and the total impact that the unconventional oil and gas industry will have upon global anthropogenic climate change (Broderick *et al.*, 2011; Jenner and Lamadrid, 2013; Meng, 2017). This reflects the broadening of the scope of socio-environmental concerns within the environmental justice frame in recent years, concurrent with the diversification of definitions of 'environmental injustice' (Walker, 2009). Such considerations are of increasing importance within the field of energy research, with modern studies exploring the socio-environmental conflicts arising from international energy production from various energy technologies (e.g. Middleton, 2012; Weber and Cabras, 2017). With growing scientific evidence of the potential negative impacts of this otherwise profitable source of hydrocarbons, there have been ever-stronger calls for better quality assessments of the climate change (Few *et al.*, 2017; Partridge *et al.*, 2017) and public health implications (McKenzie *et al.*, 2012; Tillett, 2013; Adgate *et al.*, 2014) of development in different regional, national and international contexts.

As a challenge for the social sciences, many of the local-scale environmental risks associated with unconventional hydrocarbons (for a review, see Jacquet, 2014) are a direct result of the regional industrialization connected with resource development. These occur primarily on the surface (e.g. air pollution from lorry and other traffic required to service the wells) or from compressor plants along the pipelines that move the extracted gas to market (where applicable). As Christopherson and Rightor (2012) argue, these risks are evaluated differently from one community to another and from one country to another, making international comparisons an important aspect of their social scientific analysis, for example, in France, there is concern over wineries and tourism, in Lancashire, it is seismic activity, in Quebec, water contamination, in New York State, concerns were raised over the effect on human health and local community character; for a broad overview of the risks associated with unconventional shale gas development, see Small *et al.* (2014). As a question of social scientific concern, therefore, these environmental impacts have spurred a growth in the academic literatures on issues related to how shale gas is accepted or rejected among multiple stakeholder groups (including policymakers and publics), with growing empirical analysis of environmental discourse and framing effects (Cotton *et al.*, 2014; Jaspal and Nerlich, 2014; Wagner, 2014; Hilson, 2015; Williams *et al.*, 2017; Bomberg, forthcoming), the regulatory, legal aspects and political status of environmental activist and opposition movements (Cairney *et al.*, 2015; Nyberg *et al.*, 2017); or upon public and stakeholder perceptions of risk and social acceptance under different conditions (Brasier *et al.*, 2011; O'Hara *et al.*, 2013; Schafft *et al.*, 2013; O'Hara *et al.*, 2014; Cotton, 2015; Whitmarsh *et al.*, 2015; Evensen *et al.*, 2017; Lachapelle, 2017; Thomas *et al.*, 2017). At the level of policy and planning, there are repeated normative calls for greater and more involved public participation as part of planning, governance and regulatory processes to achieve social and environmental justice outcomes (Whitton *et al.*, 2017; Cotton, forthcoming). What is commonly identified is a lack of social licence to operate – essentially a trust gap between communities, industry and regulators (Cotton *et al.*, 2014; Bradshaw and Waite, 2017).

Collectively these different facets of risk, discourse, stakeholder perceptions, scientific and other forms of relevant knowledge (including lay expertise), environmental justice, political, planning and regulatory structures require sys-temic and multi-scalar analyses, looking across local, regional, national and transnational cases to identify the governance practices implicit within uncon-ventional hydrocarbon development. This book brings together critical themes inherent in the energy governance literature and illustrates them through cases in multiple countries. These themes include how multiple actors and institu-tions – industry, governments and regulatory bodies, communities, opposition movements and individual landowners – have roles developing, contesting, monitoring and enforcing practices and regulations within UOGD. The mul-tiple actors and institutions result in a fragmented regulatory system that cuts across many different environmental components (air, water, soil, climate). Further, new unconventional development is layered on top of existing political and regulatory systems, such as private property rights and trade protections, that create a complex network of actors, institutions and regulations. Scientific information infuses this system, though the knowledge is contested and incom-plete and may not translate easily into policy. The concepts of scale, place and space are socially constructed by different actors at different levels of govern-ance, and this affects the interaction between social movements of opposition and the planning process for shale gas development in Europe and beyond. The place-based nature of UOGD requires examination; how these governance and social systems affect the trajectory of development across nations, states/ provinces and communities. As discussed in several chapters in this volume, the specific context in which this governance system is enacted and the degree to which differing actors have capacity to influence the system are critical to the role and position of shale gas as an energy source. Comparative studies, as this book emphasizes, are essential to understanding how UOGD is governed within the context of unique political histories and geographies.

At the heart of this book is a concern with the subject of unconventional hydrocarbon development as a *governance* challenge. Governance has been described as 'a tool to identify solutions to problems created by neo-liberal glo-balization' (Biermann and Pattberg, 2008). Here, the concept of 'global environ-mental governance' relates to the myriad private, professional and public networks that threaten local-to-global communities – the term 'global' being used to define issues that a single state is unable to address alone. When framing governance in the context of this book, we recognize, through our chapter examples, the following components of contemporary governance: (1) the emer-gence of a new types of agency and actors, in addition to governments; (2) the emergence of new mechanisms and institutions of global governance; and (3) the increasing segmentation and fragmentation of the overall governance system across levels and functional spheres (ibid.).

Global energy governance

Of particular interest in the context of the research in this volume is the concept of 'global energy governance' – a concept which emerged as a policy priority at the 2005 G8 Gleneagles Summit in Scotland (Kirton, 2006). The concept of energy governance originally focused upon energy security of supply and risk identification and management, the term arising due to energy security concerns over rising oil prices, specifically relating to the first Russia-Ukraine gas dispute in 2006 and the relationship between non-renewable energy technology development and anthropogenic climate change (Van de Graaf and Colgan, 2016). Yet since this early framing of energy governance, the geopolitical emphasis on energy security has been challenged, particularly the 'myopic and erroneous presumption that global energy politics is necessarily a zero sum game in which one country's energy security is another's lack thereof' (Goldthau, 2016).

Researchers are increasingly exploring energy governance relating to: actors and structure relationships (Lesage and Van de Graaf, 2016; Van de Graaf, 2017); transnational standards (Sovacool *et al.*, 2016); the Global South perspective, in China (He, 2016) and Brazil (de Melo *et al.*, 2016); energy markets and institutions (Goldthau and Witte, 2010); energy infrastructure and industry (Edomah *et al.*, 2017); renewable energy (Mueller, 2016); climate change (Jänicke and Quitzow, 2017); and policy and regulatory frameworks (Andersen *et al.*, 2016). Increasingly, the role of individuals, communities and social networks on influencing energy governance is of interest to researchers, relating to: energy consumption behaviour (Bornemann *et al.*, 2017); renewable energy transition (Islar and Busch, 2016); community energy systems (Koirala *et al.*, 2016); energy communities (Campbell *et al.*, 2016); and community participation (Foran *et al.*, 2016). Also, there is a growing emphasis on energy governance and social justice, from spatial and social justice relating to 'mega-solar' developments and vulnerable communities (Yenneti *et al.*, 2016), to transnational agreements to curb carbon emissions in the wake of the Paris Agreement (Szulecki *et al.*, 2016).

Global energy governance fundamentally links the problem of anthropogenic climate change and energy transitions associated with decarbonising the economy. New governance structures are required to manage such transitions and their direct consequences – not only for national energy policy institutions and energy industries but also for communities that rely on coal and oil production for employment, economic development, regeneration and services. However, running in parallel to the low carbon energy transition is the additional disruption of shale gas and tight oil; seen either as a 'new era of energy abundance' by observers such as Rex Tillerson, the Chairman and CEO of Exxon Mobil (Tillerson, 2013), or as a sign that we are entering the 'Era of extreme energy' (Klare, 2011). As a result, unconventional hydrocarbon planning (specifically shale gas), exploration and operation are an area of emerging interest, for both academic researchers and policy-makers.

Clearly, for governance to be effective, culture, socio-economics and trust play a role if outcomes are to be considered fair and equitable, particularly in democracies where citizens expect to participate in influencing government energy decision making or for decisions to reflect their concerns. Beierle (2002) states that fairness in participation is achieved by broad representation and equalization of participants' power, while competence often involves the use of scientific information and technical analysis to settle factual claims. Other authors have disputed this equalization of participants' power as an ideal not always represented in deliberative practice. Van Stokkom (2005) emphasizes that deliberative processes to inform policy do not always meet equality and rationality ideals. Behind the ideal of rational dialogue between equal participants, the author finds an interplay of power and emotion dynamics that can aid or impede deliberation. Despite the significance of technological considerations and challenges, the process of UOGD is clearly not simply a technological issue (Centner, 2016). The core research questions for this book are, therefore, what is the human and social experience of shale gas energy planning, exploration and production? What similarities and differences in this experience emerge across different regional and national contexts? We require a greater understanding of the ways in which unconventional oil and gas are governed across different cases and contexts, with the capacity for learning from international experiences for a robust social scientific analysis. In the chapters that follow, our authors define shale gas governance in their own terms, exploring themes of knowledge, justice, policy, power, regulation and participation, each situating their analysis in the broader international picture – comparing their respective cases with those in similar and different countries.

The structure of the book

Part I Regulatory development and property rights

In Part I, we discuss regulatory development and property rights within the context of shale gas governance. This section provides initial glimpses into the history and evolution of the regulation of shale gas across multiple regions in the United States, Germany and Australia. The authors highlight how the political, regulatory, and statutory environments are fragmented across actors and agencies, challenged by the unique technology of high-volume hydraulic fracturing and its associated environmental risks, rooted in the unique histories and geographies of each country and region, and interwoven with existing inequalities in capacity and influence over decision-making at multiple scales. The chapters also highlight that this fragmentation has consequences for identifying and addressing environmental risks, creating inefficiencies and gaps in management, and opening space for innovations and new coalitions among actors.

In Chapter 2, Kinne provides a summary of the complex, fragmented regulatory system in the United States. As she notes, the locus of control over energy production in the United States is split across multiple scales, including the federal, regional, state and local levels, depending on the particular component of the complex extraction, production, distribution and waste management process (see also Warner and Shapiro, 2013). To illustrate the implications of this fragmentation, Kinne analyses the regulatory evolution of UOGD regulation through three examples, primarily in the Marcellus Shale region: (1) water withdrawals; (2) wastewater treatment; and (3) pipelines. Her chapter highlights how the onset of development, given the scale and pace of development and the new technology involved, challenged the existing system of energy regulation and led to adjustments and adaptation by regulators. The fragmentation across both issues and jurisdictions created opportunities for new collaborations and initiatives across sectors to address and monitor concerns. However, it also brought to the forefront a number of unintended consequences of these efforts, brought counter-actions by industry to protect their interests and highlighted gaps in the regulatory system. Together, these concerns frustrate the monitoring of health and environmental risks, limit public participation, exasperate the industry and create waste within the industrial and regulatory processes. This chapter provides an essential starting place for understanding the regulatory situation in the United States and an analytical approach that identifies the social, political and environmental consequences of this system.

In Chapter 3, Jacquet, Witt, Rifkin and Haggerty also provide essential groundwork for understanding the governance of oil and gas by examining the legal and cultural meaning of property rights in the United States and Australia. Property rights in both legal terms and popular discourse have evolved differently in the two countries but still drive the core of the debate about governance. Like Kinne, Jacquet and colleagues describe the governance system in both countries as highly fragmented and as tending to devolve to the most local level. They argue that landowners and municipalities, as institutions at the core of the governance system, have the least capacity to address issues when faced by a large-scale, powerful industry. Because of the use of private contracts, public participation is limited. Similar to Kinne, Jacquet *et al.* find that many topics and issues of concern, especially those that have impacts beyond the local level (e.g. climate change, water contamination) are missing from the broader regulatory framework. Consequently, these concerns lead to questions about inequity and justice and participation capacity, because of differences in who can negotiate or resist development.

In a further examination of the evolution and implementation of unconventional energy policy, in Chapter 4, Walsh and Haggerty argue that regulatory fragmentation and complexity limit policy effectiveness and lead to diminished environmental outcomes. Through an analysis of land reclamation policies in the coalbed methane industry in the US state of Wyoming, the authors identify three primary components of the governance system that limit the effectiveness of the policy. First, the science of reclamation has generally ambiguous findings that do not translate well into policy. Second, reclamation policy provides another example of jurisdictional complexity, with multiple regulatory systems at differing spatial scales leading to differing restoration policies across the landscape. Finally, they identify how the extractive history, political institutions and culture of Wyoming have led to a regulatory system that reacts slowly to a fast-changing industry. Walsh and Haggerty's analysis of coalbed methane reclamation policies reminds us that policy development and implementation processes and outcomes cannot be separated from the broader industrial, economic, geographic, scientific and political contexts in which they unfold.

The following chapter, Chapter 5, illustrates further the ways in which the context – the geography of deposits, the alignment of national and local politics and the formation of opposition movements – influences the formation of governmental regulations of unconventional oil and gas development. Töller and Böcher examine the evolution of German law governing UOGD between 2011 and 2016. They argue that three critical issues led to the strengthening of the legislation over time, particularly increasing environmental regulations, resulting in an indefinite ban on hydraulic fracturing adopted in 2016. First, the authors argue that the geographic distribution of shale deposits in Germany led to a constellation of interests among parliament members that did not necessarily follow party lines. Shale deposits are unevenly distributed over multiple regions, creating local pressure on members of parliament to provide environmental protections on shale gas development. The interests of the Conservative Party members joined together with the Social Democrats to strengthen the proposed legislation before passage in 2016. Second, the specific relationship between German states and the national government created opportunities for the individual *Länder* to enact strict rules or ban development prior to the enactment of national law. These political actors created pressure at the federal level to reconcile this patchwork of regulations. Third, Töller and Böcher argue that citizens' initiatives and the degree of organizing among these groups at a national level put additional pressure on the national government to enact strict legislation. This decision by the German federal legislature to substantially limit the development of shale resources reflects a more centralized, national level regulatory framework than the system in the United States, as described in Kinne's chapter. In effect, the national decision was intended to reconcile fragmented local laws, in opposition to the United States where states have primacy over most components of oil and gas development.

Töller and Böcher's work stands in stark contrast to Chapter 6 by Fry and Brannstrom, in which the reconciliation of local level rules and laws in Texas resulted in the encouragement of industrial development through state pre-emption of local regulations. Fry and Brannstrom examine the evolution of Texas law HB40, effectively pre-empting local ordinances to regulate well development. They argue that the key provisions of the bill – allowing only 'commercially reasonable' restrictions, use of 'prudent operator' as the standard for assessing operator practices, and a five-year window for establishing validity of local regulations – effectively limited the ability of municipalities to control well development. Because of the threat of lawsuits against local municipalities, many adopted the standards established by Dallas-Fort Worth in the years prior to expansive shale development (e.g. 600ft setbacks). Fry and Brannstrom find that HB40 effectively limited municipal authority, highlighted the role of industrial power in state rule-making and silenced local protests. This chapter reflects the broader questions in governing shale gas resources, as found in the chapters by Kinne and the Jacquet *et al.*, related to the capacity for meaningful public engagement among local participants in relation to powerful industrial actors.

The final chapter in Part I, by Wildermuth, Dwonczyk and Brasier, highlights another way in which regulatory fragmentation creates differing outcomes of development across the landscape. This chapter examines how two regulatory bodies, river basin commissions in the Marcellus region of the United States, created two very differing sets of regulations, despite sharing a border and having seemingly similar origins and enabling compacts. The Delaware River Basin Commission created draft rules on unconventional gas wells using high volume hydraulic fracturing (HVHF), which have not been finalized, leading to an effective moratorium; in contrast, the Susquehanna River Basin developed permitting and regulatory procedures that facilitated shale development. The authors argue that the river basin commissions differed in several critical dimensions. Echoing the findings of Töller and Böcher, Wildermuth *et al.* find that the geographic context influences the constellation of actors and alignment of interests, such that organized opposition was stronger in the Delaware River Basin Commission (DRBC) than the Susquehanna RBC. They also find that the interpretation of their respective mandates has evolved differently over time, to lead to the stronger regulatory presence of the DRBC and organizational structures which elevate the voices of organized environmental interests. In contrast, the SRBC developed a more limited authority, focusing heavily on developing scientific and technical information. The result of these decisions by river basin commissions is that neighboring landowners have very different opportunities to lease their development rights and limited decision-making and participation opportunities. This geographic and organizational fragmentation echoes that described by Walsh and Haggerty in their analysis of reclamation policy.

Part II Information, communication, scientific assessment and public participation

In Part II, the authors discuss shale gas governance within the contexts of information, communication, scientific assessment and public participation as they relate to the concept of unconventional oil and gas governance across a range of different local, regional, national and transnational cases.

In Chapter 8, Lis and Stasik explore the development of shale gas, primarily in Poland. Yet what Lis and Stasik's analysis does is to draw across different regional and governance boundaries to explore the multi-scale dimensions of social activism, discourse and environmental governance. Poland is, at a national level, notably enthusiastic about the prospect of shale gas exploration as a means to ensure the domestic security of the fuel supply (see Chapter 16 by

Szolucha and Chapter 14 by Whitton and Charnley-Parry later in this volume). Through a case study analysis of Chevron's exploration activities in Żurawlów, in South-eastern Poland, the authors examine issues regarding the relationship between social activism and movements of opposition at the local level, and their subsequent interaction with both national policy-making bodies (in Poland) and at the level of European Union policy-making. Using a range of qualitative methods including research interviews and secondary data analysis of online documentation, the authors explore the interactions between local actors and representatives of the anti-fracking movement at local and national levels. Also, how non-governmental organization representatives mediated connections between these sub-national level actors and international/global anti-fracking movements. When it comes to social movements of opposition, there is a high degree of integrated knowledge sharing and political empowerment across different regional-to-global scales. This contrasts with the inherent inability of the European Union to truly understand the relevance of the local scale in environmental policy, construing local planning issues as a concern for local-level administrations.

In Chapter 9, Evensen and Luke have produced a comparative qualitative study of shale gas cases in Northern Rivers in Australia, in New York and Pennsylvania in the USA and New Brunswick in Canada. They use a mixed method approach involving both ethnographic and interview research to explore the positions of activists, municipal officials, industry, academic and NGO stakeholders in these different cases. Drawing upon the social psychological approach of *social representations theory*, they examine the nuanced nature of shale gas discourse. What is notable in their chapter is that concepts of place and identity remain important, and that contrary to common representations of shale gas discourse in the media, they find less evidence of highly polarized for-or-against positions. Identities such as those of the activist have a small influence, whereas latent or perhaps covert opposition and reluctant acceptance of shale gas across different national case study contexts are more common than is currently understood. This study is, therefore, an important contribution to the unconventional oil and gas social scientific literature because it draws across the different national level contexts, finding greater similarity across countries at certain scales. It is interesting that in each case they find the federal (meso-level) scale of governance is worthy of further exploration and analysis, and this chapter proves useful in defining a new research agenda at this specific scale.

The third chapter in Part II is significant because it fills the research gap within the predominantly Anglo-American literature by looking explicitly at the development of shale gas in the Global South. In Chapter 10, Schreiner and colleagues focus upon the environmental assessment of unconventional oil and gas development in the Karoo Basin of South Africa. They begin by first presenting an overview of the South African energy policy situation. South Africa has two unique energy policy challenges. The first is the state-owned monopoly electricity market, and the second, the over-reliance upon coal for electricity generation. Many studies of shale gas discourse have identified the popularity of natural gas as a transition or bridge fuel to reduce carbon dioxide and particulate emissions when converting coal to gas for electricity production. This has potential climate change and air-quality benefits, though opposition activists commonly point to concerns over fugitive methane emissions, and local water, traffic, light and noise pollution impacts. Learning from the South African case, therefore, has specific relevance to Australia and the US where similar coal-to-gas transitions are likely to occur. The authors highlight one specific issue – that of inward investment as a dominant driver of shale gas development. Multinational firms such as Shell have acquired the majority of the exploration licences available. Given broader pan-African concerns with the market monopolization of natural resources by foreign corporate actors (specifically around the so-called 'resource curse'), this factor is highly significant in shaping shale gas policy discourse. By studying this case through the lens of environmental assessment, the authors then look deeper at issues around participation and community representation. Public participation is fundamentally built into the strategic environmental assessment and environmental impact assessment frameworks, but how it actually works in practice is a matter for debate. What is interesting about this chapter is that it identifies issues around different forms of participation through feedback within shale gas planning processes, for example, examining the role of scientific peer review. This chapter provides valuable information around the way in which extended peer communities are (or are not) directly involved, and the authors call for greater opportunities for the co-production of knowledge as a way to ameliorate many of the associated communicative challenges. This chapter is therefore of interest to those concerned with the relationship between knowledge, participation and development of the (potentially) post-normal science of fracking.

Continuing the theme of knowledge production, Chapter 11 by Romano and Highby looks at the role of universities in shaping deliberative democratic processes around energy governance. The portmanteau concept of 'frackademia' has become an important focus of activist action. This shares broader similarities with opposition movements against other socially and ethically controversial scientific developments (such as genetically modified organisms, for example). The involvement of academics in shale gas research is controversial because at times it becomes difficult for citizen actors to distinguish between independent research *of* shale gas (as a subject), and research *for* shale gas (and thus greenlighting a controversial industry). This is particularly true when industry funding is given to universities. Romano and Highby's chapter tells a detailed and complex story of frackademia across a number of different university campuses (UNCO, Allegheny, Ohio University and Bethany College). They explore university research as a source of *authority* in broader shale gas debates within civil society. They examine issues around shared governance, the corporatization of universities, top-down decision making within university administrations and the role of lay expertise. In terms of the broader contribution of these subnational-level cases to the international study of shale gas, Romano and Highby's work is valuable in evaluating the role that universities play in facilitating deliberative democratic dialogue, their capacity to open up spaces for co-produced knowledge creation and sharing, or else foreclosing discussion through top-down decision making.

Smith and Haggerty's Chapter 12 explores an important set of actors within unconventional fossil fuel regulation and governance, namely, the role of landowners associations. Their case study examines the issues surrounding unconventional fossil fuel development stemming from the Bakken boom affecting North Dakota and Eastern Montana, drawing comparisons with similar cases in Alberta and Queensland along the way. The study they present uses a mixed method approach: combining documentary and regional media analysis with stakeholder interviews focusing upon one group in particular – the Northwest Land Owners Association. The analysis draws out the stories that the members of these organizations have to tell, and what this means for the governance of the Bakken boom. One of the key findings is that the development of shale gas overlays the twin land uses of agriculture (namely, livestock rearing) and energy resource extraction. Landowners associations are found to be influential in negotiating these twin land-use objectives, and for bringing together the interests of landowners affected by oil and gas development (and in this case study, pipeline development) with industry, state officials and regulatory authorities. In that sense, this chapter is valuable to our understanding of shale gas governance in that it highlights the nature of these organizations in informal regulatory control, devolving governance, negotiating power dynamics and coalition-building among broader diverse interest groups affected by shale gas development.

The last chapter in Part II by Petrzelka, Ellis, Jackson-Smith and Theodori, Chapter 13, explores a regional-level case study of the Eagle Ford Shale play. The authors use a range of different qualitative methods including interviews with local residents and community leaders, as well as focus group activities. The main focus of their research is upon the quality of information, and the different outreach activities that shale gas industry representatives employ. They find that there is both a lack of information available and very poor-quality outreach. Issues such as corporate social responsibility and localized funding are discussed, but they also focus upon stakeholder involvement in detail. Specifically, they find that community leaders tend to be involved in decision making at specific downstream decision points, i.e. after licences have been established and efforts towards drilling have already taken place. This chapter explores the dynamics of engagement as *public relations*, that in this case study there is evidence of the highly discredited decide-announce-defend model, whereby industry governance provides no substantive opportunities for public involvement in decision making, and shale gas businesses focus instead upon trying to communicate a decision about a site that is already chosen, and then try to defend that decision in the absence of a social licence to operate. This chapter is therefore valuable in that it explores the complexities of this relationship between industry, community leaders and public stakeholders.

Part III   Actor networks, participation and social justice

The themes of actor networks, participation and social justice are explored further in Part III. To begin, Whitton and Charnley-Parry discuss the current state of shale gas governance (SGG) in the US, the UK, Poland and the Netherlands, comparing the approach to public participation of each and the implications for social justice. To support effective and fair governance, they propose a participatory framework based on the concepts of deliberative dialogue and social sustainability.

Public hearings, rather than participation, within governance structures have facilitated shale gas development in the US. In the UK, the government rhetoric of recent consultations and court rulings in the North of England highlight the UK approach to governance and the UK government's position. Despite a government policy commitment to 'localism', this has not been the experience of communities where decisions on shale gas and a rejection of shale gas locally have led to centralized decision making with a revised outcome in favour of shale gas nationally. The authors discussed the almost complete absence of public participation in shale gas decision making in Poland, perhaps in part due to a perceived widespread support for the technology. Here, economic realities of oil price fluctuations and an abundance of cheap coal rather than opposition see exploration in retreat. In the Netherlands, despite an early assumption by the Dutch government that the public would perceive shale gas exploration as they do conventional gas production, following public opposition, the authorities appear to have adopted a more considered and cautious approach to shale gas exploration. The implications for social justice highlighted in this and other chapters discussed here are profound; despite engagement rhetoric and associated processes, the public's influence on shale gas decisions is perceived to be either minimal or only considered in light of adverse public opinion or adverse economics. Thus, the authors provide a potential solution – the social sustainability framework aims to provide an approach to public participation, based on a range of local priorities. The framework highlights notions of transparency, accountability and social and procedural justice as key components, to contribute to a methodology of effective and legitimate governance.

Exploring further the relationship between social justice, power and participation in shale gas governance, in Chapter 15, Rattle, Baker and van Alstine carry out a qualitative thematic analysis of webcast proceedings associated with two planning hearing for shale gas drilling sites in the Fylde in Lancashire and Ryedale in Yorkshire in the UK. In this chapter, the authors describe and map the opportunities for public engagement within the English shale gas approval process. They highlight, with case examples, the limited impact of citizen engagement in energy planning and wider policy and the centralization of decision-making for the national infrastructure. They also discuss the importance of 'civic capacity', groups and networks that influence decision-making at the local and national scale – also termed 'social movements of opposition'. Here, organization and learning from experience count and can be deployed to exploration sites and communities that are perceived by organizers to lack the capacity to effectively resist shale gas developments.

Continuing this theme, in Chapter 16, Szolucha carries out ethnographic research in Lancashire, UK, and Grabowiec, Poland, and focuses on two questions: 'Is regulation robust enough to guarantee safety for those affected?'; and 'Is development carried out responsibly and according to the law?' The author examines how democracy and justice-based concerns have led to the amplification of risk perceptions by local residents and concludes that there is a discrepancy between how local residents, decision-makers and corporate stakeholders evaluate risk. This stems from how each actor assesses the adequacy of democratic arrangements that govern the development of shale gas. Szolucha highlights instances where the governance system has been manipulated, for example, in Poland where an environmental NGO was denied the right to participate in an engagement process as 'state bodies are solely responsible for controlling the planning process'. In the UK, the planning process is perceived by local residents as inadequate, as planners can only take into account planning and material considerations. This area of statutory UK law includes noise and traffic pollution, visual amenity and odour nuisance but not health, environment or climate. As Jacquet and colleagues discussed previously, the authors find that issues of concern, especially those that have impacts beyond the local level (e.g. climate change and water contamination) are missing from the broader regulatory framework. Also, as Lis and Stasik discussed earlier in this volume, this chapter highlights the concepts of multi-scale governance and the role of socially constructed narratives by different actors at different levels of governance.

In Chapter 17, Dairon, Parkins and Sherren use Q-methodology to identify energy and prosperity discourses on energy development (unconventional and renewable), including areas of consensus between groups, in the south-western region of Alberta, Canada. They do this to achieve the harmonious governance of energy resources (unconventional and renewable), within what the authors term an 'energy landscape', i.e. 'a large physical area comprising both natural and anthropogenic features, the most prominent of which is infrastructure for energy extraction or generation, which is a setting for resource decision making, visual and environmental impact, and sometimes conflict'. The authors define discourse as 'the avenues through which meaning is given to social and physical realities'. They identify two dominant (1 and 2) and two minority (3 and 4) discourses. The first is *Climate Concerned Citizens*, where energy development is perceived to be disrupting natural systems – energy and living natural systems are perceived to be interrelated. This group are not supportive of Canada's economy and prosperity relying on fossil fuel development. The second is *Energy and Prosperity*, where energy development is related to Canada's economic prosperity – based on affordable fossil fuels. This group embraces innovation and technological advances in general but specifically in the shale gas sector that has allowed this economic progress to continue but accept trade-offs to achieve this – such as siting energy developments in areas traditionally seen as off limits.

To exclude these areas would prioritize some communities above others, excluding them from the associated economic prosperity. The third is *Overconsumption and local sustainability*, a minor discourse where current rates of energy consumption are perceived as unsustainable. Interesting, this discourse has a weak link to climate change and a stronger link to local sustainability – a theme discussed earlier by Whitton and Charnley-Parry. Here, the perceived adverse effects of large-scale energy generation, such as transmission lines and other related infrastructure, are highlighted. Small and localized forms of energy production and distribution are seen as the way local communities can control and influence decision-making. The fourth and final discourse is *Power Inequality*, a minor discourse where participants recognize the benefit of energy and prosperity, but also express the view that energy resources are not distributed justly. This perception of injustice is directly related to the perceived lack of corporate responsibility for pollution and adverse impacts produced during energy production. This chapter neatly summarizes the multiple aspects considered by citizens to comprise energy governance.

Continuing the social justice theme, in Chapter 18, Bronson and Beckley discuss how governments fail to appreciate that many citizens view the development of shale gas as a moral and political issue, particularly, in the case of New Brunswick, First Nation residents. The authors use transcribed audio recordings of three formal public engagement sessions as an opportunity to carry out document and textual analysis on the proceedings. The analysis is compared against a broad government-level discourse in the US and the UK in particular, that promote shale gas as a facilitator of local and national economic prosperity and mitigating climate change. As is the case in other countries, the Canadian government also assumed citizens would accept the risk and nuisance associated with shale gas exploration and adopt the same values on the issue if they 'understood' the engineering and science associated with the process. This knowledge-deficit model is attributed to a broad government misunderstanding of the issue and ultimately an indefinite moratorium on shale gas exploration in New Brunswick. Following an outline of the 'fracking' narratives in New Brunswick, the authors identify moments where decision makers 'narrowly defined the limits of deliberations to overemphasize technical issues related to fracking at the expense of social, political and cultural concerns raised by activists in the province'. The authors highlight value-based and justice-based concerns raised by activists – similar to those narratives discussed previously by Szolucha, Rattle, Baker and van Alstine and others in this volume.

Conclusion

In the context of energy governance and the role and communication of science and engineering in energy policy decision making, we have demonstrated that the scientific reduction of debates on unconventional oil and gas exploration to the purely technical, choosing to ignore the social, cultural and value-based concerns held by members of an ever-distrustful public, is destined for failure.

Also, the exploitation of local community interests (the few) to meet the energy demands of the many without a sufficiently effective participatory role in decision making is considered to go against the principles of social justice expected by citizens within a modern democracy – despite generating tax revenues for national governments or profit for international corporations. As we have shown, this is not to say that economic prosperity is not important to citizens, however, we should and must question governance approaches demonstrating prosperity at any cost where the balance of influence or decision-making power is clearly removed from the hands of the public. The book reveals the complexity of governance, particularly in the context of energy; it is highly dependent on culture, politics, place and scale yet requires flexibility and must be responsive to changes over time. Rigid governance frameworks are likely to introduce conflict and ineffectiveness as opposed to sustainability and functionality.

Recommendations for future research include the degree to which governance systems progress, hinder or complement the trajectory of development and the effects of development on social and environmental sustainability. The degree to which energy governance systems are perceived to enhance local socio-economic and environmental conditions, rather than being a detrimental impact is also a recommended area of further inquiry.

References

Adgate, J., Goldstein, B. and McKenzie, L. (2014) Potential public health hazards, exposures and health effects from unconventional natural gas development. *Environmental Science & Technology* 48: 8307–8320.

Andersen, S. S., Goldthau, A. and Sitter, N. (2016) The EU regulatory state, commission leadership and external energy governance. In Godzimirski, J. M. (ed.) *EU Leadership in Energy and Environmental Governance: Global and Local Challenges and Responses*. London: Palgrave Macmillan, pp. 51–68.

Beierle, T. C. (2002) The quality of stakeholder-based decisions. *Risk Analysis* 22: 739–749.

Biermann, F. and Pattberg, P. (2008) Global environmental governance: Taking stock, moving forward. *Annual Review of Environment and Resources* 33: 277–294.

Bomberg, E. (forthcoming) Shale we drill? Discourse dynamics in UK fracking debates. *Journal of Environmental Policy and Planning*.

Bornemann, B., Sohre, A. and Burger, P. (2017) Future governance of individual energy consumption behavior change: A framework for reflexive designs. *Energy Research & Social Science* November.

Bradshaw, M. and Waite, C. (2017) Learning from Lancashire: Exploring the contours of the shale gas conflict in England. *Global Environmental Change* 47: 28–36.

Brasier, K. J., Filteau, M. R., McLaughlin, D. K., *et al.* (2011) Residents' perceptions of community and environmental impacts from development of natural gas in the Marcellus shale: A comparison of Pennsylvania and New York cases. *Journal of Rural Social Sciences* 26: 32–61.

Broderick, J., Anderson, K., Wood, R., *et al.* (2011) *Shale Gas: An Updated Assessment of Environmental and Climate Change Impacts*. Manchester: The Co-Operative and the Tyndall Centre Manchester.

Burton, G. A., Basu, N., Ellis, B. R., *et al.* (2014) Hydraulic 'fracking': Are surface water impacts an ecological concern? *Environmental Toxicology and Chemistry* 33: 1679–1689.

Cairney, P., Fischer, M. and Ingold, K. (2015) Hydraulic fracturing policy in the UK: Coalition, cooperation and opposition in the face of uncertainty. Paper presented at Political Studies Association Annual International Conference, Sheffield.

Campbell, B., Cloke, J. and Brown, E. (2016) Communities of energy. *Economic Anthropology* 3: 133–144.

Centner, T. J. (2016) Observations on risks, the social sciences, and unconventional hydrocarbons. *Energy Research and Social Science* 20: 1–7.

Christopherson, S. M. and Rightor, N. (2012) How shale gas extraction affects drilling localities: Lessons for regional and city policy makers. *Journal of Town and City Management* 2: 1–20.

Cooper, J., Stamford, L. and Azapagic, A. (2016) Shale gas: A review of the economic, environmental, and social sustainability. *Energy Technology* 4: 772–792.

Cotton, M. (2015) Stakeholder perspectives on shale gas fracking: A Q-method study of environmental discourses. *Environment and Planning* A 47: 1944–1962.

Cotton, M. (forthcoming) Fair fracking? Ethics and environmental justice in United Kingdom shale gas policy and planning. *Local Environment.*

Cotton, M., Rattle, I. and Van Alstine, J. (2014) Shale gas policy in the United Kingdom: An argumentative discourse analysis. *Energy Policy* 73: 427–438.

Das, I. and Zoback, M. D. (2011) Long-period, long-duration seismic events during hydraulic fracture stimulation of a shale gas reservoir. *The Leading Edge* 30: 778–786.

de Melo, C. A., Jannuzzi, G. D. M. and Bajay, S. V. (2016) Nonconventional renewable energy governance in Brazil: Lessons to learn from the German experience. *Renewable and Sustainable Energy Reviews* 61: 222–234.

Edomah, N., Foulds, C. and Jones, A. (2017) Policy making and energy infrastructure change: A Nigerian case study of energy governance in the electricity sector. *Energy Policy* 102: 476–485.

Evensen, D., Stedman, R. C. and Brown-Steiner, B. (2017) Resilient but not sustainable? Public perceptions of shale gas development via hydraulic fracturing. *Ecology and Society* 22.

Few, S., Gambhir, A., Napp, T., *et al.* (2017) The impact of shale gas on the cost and feasibility of meeting climate targets: A global energy system model analysis and an exploration of uncertainties. *Energies* 10: 158.

Foran, T., Fleming, D., Spandonide, B., *et al.* (2016) Understanding energy-related regimes: A participatory approach from central Australia. *Energy Policy* 91: 315–324.

Goldthau, A. (2016) Conceptualizing the above ground factors in shale gas: Toward a research agenda on regulatory governance. *Energy Research & Social Science* 20: 73–81.

Goldthau, A. and Witte, J. M. (2010) *Global Energy Governance: The New Rules of the Game*: Washington, DC: Brookings Institution Press.

Green, C. A., Styles, P. and Baptie, B. (2012) *Preese Hall Shale Gas Fracturing: Review and Recommendations for Induced Seismic Mitigation*. London: Department of Energy and Climate Change.

He, A. X. (2016) China in global energy governance: A Chinese perspective. *Vestnik Mezhdunarodnykh Organizatsii: International Organisations Research Journal* 11: 71–91.

Hilson, C. (2015) Framing fracking: Which frames are heard in English planning and environmental policy and practice? *Journal of Environmental Law* 27: 177–202.

Islar, M. and Busch, H. (2016) 'We are not in this to save the polar bears!': The link between community renewable energy development and ecological citizenship. *Innovation: The European Journal of Social Science Research* 29: 303–319.

Jacquet, J. B. (2014) Review of risks to communities from shale energy development. *Environmental Science & Technology* 48: 8321–8333.

Jänicke, M. and Quitzow, R. (2017) Multi-level reinforcement in European climate and energy governance: Mobilizing economic interests at the sub-national levels. *Environmental Policy and Governance* 27: 122–136.

Jaspal, R. and Nerlich, B. (2014) Fracking in the UK media: Threat dynamics in an unfolding debate. *Public Understanding of Science* 23: 348–363.

Jenner, S. and Lamadrid, A. J. (2013) Shale gas vs. coal: Policy implications from environmental impact comparisons of shale gas, conventional gas, and coal on air, water, and land in the United States. *Energy Policy* 53: 442–453.

Kirton, J. (2006) The G8 and global energy governance: Past performance, St Petersberg opportunities. In *The World Dimension of Russia's Energy Security*. Moscow State Institute of International Relations (MGIMO), Russia.

Klare, M. T. (2011) The era of xtreme energy: Life after the age of oil. *HuffPost*. Available at: www.huffingtonpost.com/michael-t-klare/the-era-of-xtreme-energy_b_295304. html: Huffington Post

Koirala, B. P., Koliou, E., Friege, J., *et al.* (2016) Energetic communities for community energy: A review of key issues and trends shaping integrated community energy systems. *Renewable and Sustainable Energy Reviews* 56: 722–744.

Lachapelle, E. (2017) The great divide: Public perceptions of shale gas extraction and hydraulic fracturing in Pennsylvania and New York. *Commonwealth* 19.

Lesage, D. and Van de Graaf, T. (2016) *Global Energy Governance in a Multipolar World.* London: Routledge.

Litovitz, A., Curtright, A., Abramzon, S., *et al.* (2013) Estimation of regional air-quality damages from Marcellus Shale natural gas extraction in Pennsylvania. *Environmental Research Letters* 8: 014017.

McKenzie, L. M., Witter, R. Z., Newman, L. S., *et al.* (2012) Human health risk assessment of air emissions from development of unconventional natural gas resources. *Science of the Total Environment* 424: 79–87.

Meng, Q. (2017) The impacts of fracking on the environment: A total environmental study paradigm. *Science of the Total Environment* 580: 953–957.

Middleton, C. (2012) Transborder environmental justice in regional energy trade in Mainland South-East Asia. *ASEAS, Austrian Journal of South-East Asian Studies* 5: 292–315.

Montcoudiol, N., Isherwood, C., Gunning, A., *et al.* (2017) Shale gas impacts on groundwater resources: Insights from monitoring a fracking site in Poland. *EGU General Assembly Conference Abstracts.* 7694.

Mueller, F. (2016) Encountering IRENA: Governance and global governmentalities of renewable energy. In Franziska, M. (ed.) *The WSPC Reference on Natural Resources and Environmental Policy in the Era of Global Change.* Singapore: World Scientific, pp. 279–302.

Neville, K. J., Baka, J., Gamper-Rabindran, S., *et al.* (2017) Debating unconventional energy: Social, political, and economic implications. *Annual Review of Environment and Resources* 42: 241–266.

Nyberg, D., Wright, C. and Kirk, J. (2017) Re-producing a neoliberal political regime: Competing justifications and dominance in disputing fracking. In Cloutier, C., Gond, J.-P. and Leca, B. (eds) *Justification, Evaluation and Critique in the Study of Organizations: Contributions from French Pragmatist Sociology.* Bingley: Emerald Publishing Limited, pp. 143–171.

O'Hara, S., Humphrey, M., Andersson, J., *et al.* (2014) *Public perception of shale gas extraction in the UK: The turn against fracking deepens.* Nottingham: University of Nottingham.

O'Hara, S., Humphrey, M., Jaspal, R., *et al.* (2013) *Public perception of shale gas extraction in the UK: The impact of the Balcombe protests in July–August 2013.* Nottingham: University of Nottingham.

Partridge, T., Thomas, M., Harthorn, B. H., *et al.* (2017) Seeing futures now: Emergent US and UK views on shale development, climate change and energy systems. *Global Environmental Change* 42: 1–12.

Rich, A., Grover, J. P. and Sattler, M. L. (2014) An exploratory study of air emissions associated with shale gas development and production in the Barnett Shale. *Journal of the Air & Waste Management Association* 64: 61–72.

Rogers, H. (2011) Shale gas: the unfolding story. *Oxford Review of Economic Policy* 27: 117–143.

Schafft, K. A., Borlu, Y. and Glenna, L. (2013) The relationship between Marcellus Shale gas development in Pennsylvania and local perceptions of risk and opportunity. *Rural Sociology* 78: 143–166.

Small, M. J., Stern, P. C., Bomberg, E., *et al.* (2014) Risks and risk governance in unconventional shale gas development. *Environmental Science & Technology* 48: 8289–8297.

Sovacool, B. K., Walter, G., Van de Graaf, T., *et al.* (2016) Energy governance, transnational rules, and the resource curse: Exploring the effectiveness of the Extractive Industries Transparency Initiative (EITI). *World Development* 83: 179–192.

Szulecki, K., Fischer, S., Gullberg, A. T., *et al.* (2016) Shaping the 'Energy Union': between national positions and governance innovation in EU energy and climate policy. *Climate Policy* 16: 548–567.

Thomas, M., Pidgeon, N., Evensen, D., *et al.* (2017) Public perceptions of hydraulic fracturing for shale gas and oil in the United States and Canada. *Wiley Interdisciplinary Reviews: Climate Change* 8.

Tillerson, R. (2013) Capitalizing on the coming era of energy abundance. Address to the Texas Alliance of Energy Producers. Houston, Texas, USA.

Tillett, T. (2013) Summit discusses public health implications of fracking. *Environmental Health Perspectives* 121: a15.

U.S. Energy Information Administration. (2015) *World Shale Resource Assessments.* Available at: www.eia.gov/analysis/studies/worldshalegas/

Van de Graaf, T. (2017) Organizational interactions in global energy governance. In Biermann, R. and Koops, J. A. (eds) *Palgrave Handbook of Inter-Organizational Relations in World Politics.* Berlin: Springer, pp. 591–609.

Van de Graaf, T. and Colgan, J. (2016) Global energy governance: A review and research agenda. *Palgrave Communications* 2: 15047.

van Stokkom, B. (2005) Deliberative group dynamics: Power, status and affect in interactive policy making. *Policy & Politics* 33: 387–409.

Wagner, A. (2014) Shale gas: Energy innovation in a (non-)knowledge society: A press discourse analysis. *Science and Public Policy* 42: 273–286.

Walker, G. (2009) Beyond distribution and proximity: Exploring the multiple spatialities of environmental justice. *Antipode* 41: 614–636.

Warner, B. and Shapiro, J. (2013) Fractured, fragmented federalism: A study in fracking regulatory policy. *Publius: The Journal of Federalism* 43: 474–496.

Weber, G. and Cabras, I. (2017) The transition of Germany's energy production, green economy, low-carbon economy, socio-environmental conflicts, and equitable society. *Journal of Cleaner Production* 167: 1222–1231.

Whitmarsh, L., Nash, N., Upham, P., *et al.* (2015) UK public perceptions of shale gas hydraulic fracturing: The role of audience, message and contextual factors on risk perceptions and policy support. *Applied Energy* 160: 419–430.

Whitton, J., Brasier, K., Parry, I. M., *et al.* (2017) Shale gas governance in the United Kingdom and the United States: Opportunities for public participation and the implications for social justice. *Energy Research and Social Science* 26: 11–22.

Williams, L., Macnaghten, P. M., Davies, R., *et al.* (2017) Framing 'fracking': Exploring public perceptions of hydraulic fracturing in the United Kingdom. *Public Understanding of Science* 26: 89–104.

Yenneti, K., Day, R. and Golubchikov, O. (2016) Spatial justice and the land politics of renewables: Dispossessing vulnerable communities through solar energy mega-projects. *Geoforum* 76: 90–99.

Part I

Regulatory development and property rights

2 Regulating unconventional shale gas development in the United States

Diverging priorities, overlapping jurisdictions, and asymmetrical data access

Beth Kinne

Introduction

In the United States, shale gas development and its associated activities are regulated by a complex and overlapping network of federal, state, and local laws. Variations in regulation are a product of differing local, state, and national priorities, federal and state constitutional provisions, case law precedent, express or implied pre-emption, and shared or uncertain jurisdiction. Legally-sanctioned barriers to information sharing, lack of in-house technical expertise, or simple budget and staffing constraints also create challenges for timely and effective regulation and hinder informed decision-making by individuals, regulators, and policy-makers.

After providing a brief background on the role that shale gas plays in the US energy landscape and the federalist system of government in the US as it relates to shale gas development, this chapter introduces case studies from several different regulated aspects of shale gas development – water sourcing, water pollution prevention, and natural gas transportation projects – to illustrate the ways that shared, overlapping regulatory frameworks that strive to accommodate various interests can struggle to effectively mitigate the negative impacts of the development of shale gas resources in a way that balances both stakeholder interests and environmental integrity.

The importance of effective shale gas governance

Barring a significant change in trajectory in energy sourcing, shale gas will be a substantial source of energy for the United States for much of the twenty-first century. Natural gas is being promoted as a bridge fuel between "dirtier" fossil fuels like coal and oil and primary reliance on renewables (Calton et al., 2014; Howarth, 2014). However, as of 2017, renewables made up only 10 percent of energy production in the US (U.S. Energy Information Administration, 2017b), and natural gas production increased annually between 2004 and 2014 (U.S. Energy Information Administration, 2016). More than 34,000 miles of pipelines have been added since shale gas development began (U.S. Energy Information Administration, 2015), and given the current contribution of renewables and investment in natural gas infrastructure, continued development and reliance on natural gas resources are likely.

The impacts of natural gas development are widely distributed across the United States and experienced by communities located far from active drilling locations. While five states – Texas, Pennsylvania, Wyoming, Oklahoma, and Louisiana – provide 65 percent of the gas produced in the United States (U.S. Energy Information Administration, 2017a), as of 2015, over 30 states have active drilling or production (Rubright, 2017). A distribution network of pipelines, compressor stations and storage facilities traverse the country, and due to permitting requirements and geological variability, raw materials are sourced and wastes are often disposed of across state lines. As drilling technologies make additional geological formations profitable, the number of locations experiencing the impacts of shale gas development may increase.

Regulation of shale gas in a federalist system: conflicting goals and varied results

The US federalist system creates shared authority between state and federal governments over many areas of mutual interest, including environment, health, and oil and gas development. State property rights and regional regulatory regimes dominate water sourcing. Federal pollution standards, largely implemented by states, attempt to balance local and national interests (Burger, 2013). Regulatory authority over transportation and storage projects depends on the location and nature of the project (Kelly & Neinast, 2013). Municipal governments largely maintain power over land use decisions within their jurisdictions and, when not pre-empted by state oil and gas laws, have asserted their own power over drilling activities.

While federal environmental and health laws govern many aspects of fracking, states, tribes, and industry have opposed comprehensive federal fracking regulations. The Bureau of Land Management's (BLM) final rules standardizing fracking on federal and Indian lands in 2015 (Oil and Gas; Hydraulic Fracturing on Federal and Indian Lands; Final Rule, 2015) were challenged by industry, the Ute Indian tribe, and states with high percentages of drilling on federal lands (WY, CO, UT, ND). A federal judge found the rules to be an overreach of agency authority (*Wyoming* v. *U.S. Dept. of the Interior*, 2016). The BLM argued it had jurisdiction to govern shale gas drilling on federal lands pursuant to the general public resource management authorities created by the Federal Land Management Policy Act, the Indian Minerals Leasing Act and the Minerals Leasing Act and appealed the decision (Bartlett & Lynch, 2016). Pending resolution of this dispute, state mining and oil and gas laws continue to govern the regulation of drilling on federal lands.

River Basin rules further complicate the regulatory landscape, creating differences in regulation even within the same state. The Delaware River Basin Commission (DRBC) (covering New York, Pennsylvania, New Jersey, and

Delaware) tabled proposed rules to govern fracking in the watershed in 2011 due to opposition by member states (Negro, 2012), resulting in a de facto moratorium. This created a stark contrast to those Pennsylvania counties in the Susquehanna River Basin, where thousands of wells have been drilled (Stutz, 2015). In September 2017, the DRBC announced plans to publish a revised set of draft regulations taking into account advances in scientific understanding of impacts of fracking on water resources and existing regulations in basin states (Delaware River Basin Commission, 2017a, 2017b). (See Chapter 7 by Wildermuth et al. in this volume for additional discussion of river basin commissions.)

Finally, while municipalities (counties, cities, and towns) have considerable discretion over land use decisions through zoning laws, authority to regulate oil and gas activities may be limited or precluded by state pre-emption doctrines. Colorado courts, for example, held that state statutes governing oil and gas preempt almost all local efforts to regulate oil and gas drilling, invalidating moratoria on fracking in the cities of Fort Collins (*City of Fort Collins* v. *Colorado Oil and Gas Association*, 2016), and Longmont (*City of Longmont* v. *Colorado Oil and Gas Association*, 2016). In contrast, New York courts held that municipalities could ban hydraulic fracturing from their jurisdictions (*In the Matter of Mark S. Wallach* v. *Town of Dryden*, 2014). New York's Governor subsequently banned fracking statewide, citing uncertainty surrounding environmental and health impacts (Kaplan, 2014). Pennsylvania's high court relied on a clause in the state Constitution that requires the state to "conserve and maintain" public resources for the "benefit of the people" to preclude the state from applying a 2012 law preventing local governments from regulating drilling (*Robinson Township* v. *Commonwealth of Pennsylvania*, 2013).

The differences in content and interpretation of state, regional, and local laws significantly impact if and where oil and gas development is allowed and how citizens participate in the decision-making processes on regulation. While this structure allows for the promotion of state and local goals, compliance and mitigation requirements can vary significantly (Wiseman, 2014), with impacts on citizens and corporations varying from state to state, and even municipality to municipality.

Regulation of water resource use and pipelines

The following examples examine the regulation of water resource use, water pollution, and pipelines to illustrate how inadequate or asymmetrical access to information, differences in legal frameworks, and conflicting priorities can result in less than predictable, and potentially inadequate, regulation. New initiatives meant to fill the gaps also have limitations and are influenced by stakeholder priorities.

Regulating water withdrawals

Comprehensive water regulation requires meshing local, state, regional, and sometimes international water use precedents and priorities. Water withdrawals are regulated by individual states, and in some cases by interstate or international basin commissions, e.g., the Susquehanna River Basin Commission and the Ohio River Water Sanitation Commission in the Marcellus Shale region. In addition to state or river basin commission restrictions, water withdrawals may be limited by federal requirements such as those under the Clean Water Act (33 U.S.C. 1251 et seq., 1972, as amended) and the Endangered Species Act (16 U.S.C. 1531 et seq.), or international commitments such as those in the Great Lakes-St. Lawrence River Basin Sustainable Water Resources Agreement (2005).

The combination of variance in legal regimes coupled with variation in water resource availability results in water resource regulation that is predictably inconsistent over time and space. In western states with highly-developed, quantity-driven legal regimes for allocating water, shale gas-related withdrawals are subject to the same scrutiny as other water withdrawals: new users must prove their use does not threaten more senior water rights, and may be curtailed if and when they do. Eastern states' riparian rights doctrines historically allowed owners of land abutting a waterway to make reasonable use of that water, without significantly altering the flow or quality. As water shortages like those historically seen in the US West emerge in the East (Alder, 2010; Government Accountability Office, 2014), eastern states are responding to growing demands and the uncertainty of climate change with increasingly regulated forms of riparianism (Kundis Craig, 2010).

New York State updated its Water Resources Law (WRL) in 2012, partly to comply with requirements to register withdrawals in accord with regional and international commitments under the Great Lakes-St. Lawrence River Basin Water Resources Compact (New York State Assembly, 2012). The WRL requires registration and Department of Environmental Conservation (DEC) approval of new and existing withdrawals over 100,000 gallons per day per intake. To date, reviews of existing withdrawals have not led to curtailment, suggesting that with respect to existing uses, the DEC is using the WRL mainly as a registration and monitoring tool, rather than a mechanism for reducing withdrawals (Treichler, 2015). Should New York reverse its 2014 ban on high volume hydraulic fracturing, the WRL would require an environmental review of new withdrawals for fracking, and permit applicants would have to comply with restrictions and rules consistent with New York State law, the Great Lakes Compact, and in some areas, the Susquehanna and Delaware River Basin Commissions' rules.

Federal laws also influence water withdrawals. Under the Clean Water Act, states assume regulatory and enforcement authority over water quality within their boundaries once state regulatory plans meet federal requirements. States establish water quality criteria (e.g., turbidity, chemical and biological oxygen demand, minimum flows) sufficient to support designated uses (drinking water, fish propagation, recreation, navigation, etc.) assigned to each surface water body in their jurisdiction. An anti-degradation requirement proscribes permitting uses that allow decline in water quality including reducing flows in some circumstances (Antidegradation policy and implementation methods, 2015; Clean Water Act, 1972). The Endangered Species Act (ESA, 16 USC 1531, 1973) can prevent withdrawal or disturbance of waters in a delineated critical habitat for listed species. In these ways, federal law can modify the rights granted under state water rights laws, and can limit or prohibit withdrawals for fracking in ecologically sensitive areas or headwaters.

Regulating water pollution from fracking: collaborations and initiatives

Much of the water pollution from fracking is regulated by existing federal environmental laws. The Clean Water Act regulates discharges of pollutants into surface waters. The Safe Drinking Water Act (SDWA, 42 U.S.C. 300f et seq.) protects groundwater sources of drinking water by governing in-ground injection of wastes. The CWA requires a National Pollutant Discharge Elimination System (NPDES) permit for any discharge of a pollutant into a surface water body, including discharges of erosion and sediment from pad site construction, or of produced water from drilling operations. State versions of the NPDES may be more stringent, some covering discharges into groundwater in addition to surface water, for example. However, the benefit of NPDES permits requires data collection and enforcement, which is largely dependent on agency budgets and priorities. Decisions not to enforce are largely beyond judicial review (Coplan, 2014). In addition, fluids introduced to wells for the purpose of fracking are largely exempt from regulation until they become wastewater. The Energy Policy Act of 2005 confirmed the exemption from regulation for hydraulic fracturing fluid under the Safe Drinking Water Act, except where diesel fuels are used (Energy Policy Act, 2005; Safe Drinking Water Act, 1974, as amended; Tiemann & Vann, 2015). A 2016 study by the EPA on the impacts of fracking on drinking water supplies concluded that significant data gaps precluded a full understanding of the threats to water resources (U.S. Environmental Protection Agency, 2016a).

Federal legislators, state regulators, and industry have attempted to standardize regulation of reporting of fracking chemicals, with limited success. In 2009, the Fracturing Responsibility and Awareness of Chemicals Act (the "FRAC Act," HB 1085, S. 58) was introduced in the House and Senate by representatives from states where fracking was occurring (Pennsylvania and Colorado) or seemed imminent (New York).[1] The FRAC Act would have required drillers to report to the state all chemicals *intended* to be used (before drilling) and *actually* used (after drilling) and make this data available to the public. However, the Act failed to become law, leaving regulation of fracking chemical reporting up to each state.

States are refining methods of record-keeping and water quality testing, but reporting requirements vary widely with little consensus on their efficacy. Minimum chemical disclosure rules follow Occupational Safety and Health Administration (OSHA) requirements, which use Material Safety Data Sheets to warn workers of exposure risks (Groves, 2012). However, OSHA regulations focus on chemicals and exposures that are hazardous in a workplace setting, and therefore are of limited utility for assessing threats caused via environmental pathways (McFeeley, 2012). Efforts to establish more comprehensive chemical use and water quality data collection run up against limitations on funding, expertise, and the willingness of industry to take additional, and sometimes costly, steps. For comparison, water testing requirements in Canadian provinces range from minimal, e.g., British Columbia where testing is only required when the landowner requests it, to required pre- and post-drill testing of water wells within a certain distance from a gas well, e.g., Quebec (Gagnon et al., 2016).

In 2011, state water regulators in the Ground Water Protection Council (GWPC) collaborated with the Interstate Oil and Gas Compact Commission to initiate FracFocus, an online database of voluntary disclosures of chemicals used in hydraulic fracturing. The GWPC promotes best management practices and "effective but fair" regulation (Groundwater Protection Council, n.d.). At the time of writing, 23 states use FracFocus as the official reporting repository for fracturing fluid constituent disclosures, and over 1,000 companies are participating members (www.fracfocus.org). Widespread use of the FracFocus site has centralized data reporting for many states and increased public access to reported data. However, some states require disclosure of all chemicals used while others require only disclosure of chemicals classified as "hazardous" under the Occupational Safety and Health Act (Hall, 2013). Data are not audited for accuracy or searchable, and terms of use preclude data reproduction. These realities reduce the value of data for analysis of risks or development of regulatory responses (Coplan, 2014).

Canadian Provinces and Territories, like US states, have varying reporting and compliance requirements for operators, and information reported to FracFocus.ca reflects the variance in provincial and territorial laws. The Canadian BC Oil and Gas Commission has adopted a Canadian version of FracFocus, described as "a collaboration between Provinces, Territories, regulators and industry to provide Canadians with objective information on hydraulic fracturing ..." (FracFocus.ca, 2017). Many drillers are members of the Canadian Association of Petroleum Producers (CAPP), which has its own standards for well water testing near drilling rigs and requirements to collaborate with local authorities to develop groundwater monitoring programs.

Disposal of returned water from fracking also threatens water resources. While the qualities of the rock formation under development govern volumes of returned water, in general, hundreds of thousands of gallons per well must be treated or disposed of. Treatment of returned water has evolved significantly since the early 2000s (Schmidt, 2013). High salinity levels, heavy metals, and naturally occurring radioactive materials ("NORMs") in returned water prompted states to prohibit or limit treatment of fracking water by municipal wastewater treatment plants that were incapable of removing salts and radionucleotides (Hurdle, 2016; Schmidt, 2013). In 2016, the EPA followed suit, limiting treatment of fracking water to industrial wastewater treatment plants nationwide (U.S. Environmental Protection Agency, 2016b). When recycling of wastewater is no longer economical, disposal via deep well injection is necessary. Deep well injection of wastewater for disposal is regulated by the EPA under the SDWA Class II injection well requirements (SDWA, 1974). There has been significant support for centralized treatment of fracking wastewater dilution and re-use processes minimizing total freshwater use per well and reducing the environmental impact (Easton, 2013). In Pennsylvania between 2008 and 2011, treatment and reuse of wastewater increased, disposal in public wastewater treatment plants decreased, and the overall distance traveled by wastewater decreased 30 percent, but researchers still recommended systematic tracking to better manage wastewater (Rahm et al., 2013). Disposal of wastes across state lines increases the geographic scope of the footprint of shale gas development.

Limits on development of comprehensive data to support regulation

In spite of increased reporting requirements and common repositories, privity of contract, non-disclosure agreements, and trade secret laws still limit data disclosure. When oil and gas companies order groundwater tests, they control what is tested for and who can access the results. Where private drinking wells are contaminated, drilling companies may truck in water or connect the household to the public system. The price for this solution, however, is often a non-disclosure agreement signed by the owner of the contaminated well, by which the signer is precluded from disclosing the type or extent of contamination, and that any water quality complaints to the state regulatory body be voluntarily dismissed (Smith, 2016). Under state trade secret laws, which largely follow the federal Uniform Trade Secrets Act, companies self-determine which constituents are exempt from reporting, and few states require submission or review evidence of the need for trade secret protection (Coplan, 2014). Even reported data may be exempt from open records laws (Murrill & Vann, 2012). Finally, since May 2016, the federal Defend Trade Secrets Act (18 U.S.C. §1836.b) offers a federal cause of action for violation of trade secret protection (Fernandez, Hanlon Leh, & Donaldson, 2016). Canadian companies also self-determine which chemicals are worthy of secret protections, although protection of materials deemed hazardous are reviewed by the Hazardous Material Information Review Commission, now administered by Health Canada. Reporting exemptions are designed to protect industry privacy and competitiveness, but data that are not searchable or sortable and include notable gaps frustrate tracking of risks and identification of exposure pathways.

A simple lack of pre-drilling baseline water quality data further frustrates identification of contamination, determination of liability, and the development of effective regulations. Some states, like Colorado, Wyoming, North Carolina, and Illinois, require mandatory pre- and post-drilling water quality tests, while others, such as West Virginia and Pennsylvania, presume causation when water within a certain number of feet from a vertical well bore is found to be contaminated within a certain number of months from active drilling (Bosquez et al., 2015). The presumption is rebuttable, creating an incentive for drilling companies to conduct pre-drilling testing where they otherwise might not. A 2016 Pennsylvania court case applying the state law presumption of contamination based on geographic proximity resulted in large damages for plaintiffs suffering from water well contamination, a precedent that provides further incentives for precaution and testing on the part of oil and gas companies (*Ely* v. *Cabot Oil & Gas*, 2016). Increased data collection will support improved understanding, promote resolution of legal disputes, and help regulators develop sound legal norms to govern fracking.

Regulation of natural gas pipelines

Recovered shale gas must be moved to populations of users of natural gas through an extensive network of interstate and intrastate pipelines, compressor stations, and storage facilities, also known as midstream infrastructure. In 2015, there were just under 1,586,000 miles of natural gas pipeline in the US (Bureau of Transportation Statistics, 2016). Approximately 300 companies own and operate interstate transmission pipelines, and another 1,100 own and operate local distribution lines (ibid.).

Regulators have a large number of parties to monitor in a variety of jurisdictions and environments. There is little or no regulation of many smaller pipelines that do not cross interstate boundaries, while regulation increases with pipeline diameter and interstate status (Kelly & Neinast, 2013). Generally, production lines (those coming out of a well), gathering lines (those collecting gas from multiple wells) and local distribution mains (those that distribute gas to consumers at the other end) are regulated by individual states (ibid.). In contrast, the construction and operation of interstate transmission pipelines fall under the jurisdiction of the Federal Energy Regulatory Commission (FERC), in accordance with the 1938 Natural Gas Act (NGA). The NGA gives FERC jurisdiction over gas transported or sold for purposes of resale in interstate commerce as well as import or export.

FERC classifies a pipeline as jurisdictional or non-jurisdictional via application of a complex, multi-factored, and somewhat subjective test, largely exempting from FERC jurisdiction those pipelines used for production, gathering and distribution, but the NGA does not specifically define these terms (ibid.). The industry has developed its own standards for gathering infrastructure, which are published in the *American Petroleum Institute's Recommended Practices 80* (ibid.). FERC approvals for pipeline construction provide for public input and usually require the applicant to comply with state and local regulations, thereby incorporating locally relevant impacts, such as noise and environmental pollution. However, in practice, local governments and citizens are seldom well equipped to participate in the permitting or monitoring processes. The general public is largely unaware of the energy infrastructure unless an accident occurs (Klass & Meinhardt, 2015), and local governments often lack in-house expertise and funds to hire that expertise.

Two recent projects, The Constitution Pipeline and the Northeast Energy Direct Project, illustrate the interface between federal, state, and local government priorities with respect to shale gas transmission pipelines and storage. Both pipeline projects were conditionally approved by the Federal Energy Regulatory Commission but have run into hurdles at the state and local levels. One failed to comply with environmental impact mitigation requirements; the other failed to comply with state rate regulation laws and prohibitions on rate-payer financing.

The Constitution Pipeline Project

The Constitution pipeline runs from northern Pennsylvania to Schoharie County, New York, where, via the Wright Interconnection Project, it transfers natural gas to the Iroquois Gas transmission system supplying gas to New York and New England. In December 2014, FERC issued a Certificate of Public Convenience and Necessity for the Constitution Pipeline Project and the Wright Interconnection Project after reviewing an environmental impact statement and with input from agencies such as the US EPA, the Army Corps of Engineers, the Federal Highway Administration and the New York State Department of Agriculture and Markets (Federal Energy Regulatory Commission, 2014, p. 22).

FERC concluded that the project would have significant environmental impacts (crossing 289 surface water bodies, impacting 95 acres of wetlands and 36 square miles of interior forest habitat), and required that Constitution's developers obtain all other necessary approvals, including state water and air pollution permits (Federal Energy Regulatory Commission, 2014, p. 25). The New York State Department of Environmental Conservation denied Constitution's application for a section 401 Water Quality Certification under the Clean Water Act, citing "loss of water body habitat, thermal impacts, increased erosion and creation of stream erosion and turbidity" (NY Department of Environmental Conservation, 2016, p. 3). On appeal, the court affirmed the state's denial of the CWA permits (*Constitution Pipeline Company* v. *New York State Dept. of Cons.*, 2017a; Lowther, 2017). Constitution also sued the NYDEC in federal court for failure to act on the other state permits. The judge ruled that failure to issue the other permits did not injure Constitution, as the water pollution permit was still not granted, and dismissed the case for lack of standing (*Constitution Pipeline Company* v. *New York State Dept. of Env. Cons.*, 2017b).

This project illustrates how shared jurisdiction among agencies and differing rules among states complicate pipeline siting. FERC's approval pending state permits and coupled with New York's conclusion that the project was in violation of Clean Water Act standards resulted in delay and uncertainty. Projects subject to multiple jurisdictions can also result in waste and social unrest. In this case, the pipeline company completed deforestation of private property taken by eminent domain for the segment of the pipeline that runs through Pennsylvania before the New York segment had been approved, in one particular instance, while armed federal marshals kept protestors at bay (Hurdle, 2017).

Most gas carriers fall under the public use allowance and can take private land through eminent domain powers (Evers, 2015). The scope of eminent domain power for private parties, including oil and gas companies, has been a contested landscape since a 2005 Supreme Court Decision, *Kelo* v. *City of New London* (2005). In *Kelo*, the Supreme Court found that the city's transfer of blighted land taken via eminent domain to a private developer in the interests of economic development fell within the scope of public purpose, thereby broadening the scope from traditional uses of eminent domain. The pushback against the *Kelo* ruling has increased opposition to pipelines, which, although designated "common carriers" do not necessarily benefit the public, and may cause significant environmental and economic harm (Somin, 2016). Forty-five states passed legislation limiting the scope of eminent domain to projects which are actually public use – such as parks and roadways (Kinder Morgan), with notable impacts on pipeline projects in some states such as Georgia (Kinder Morgan, 2016) and South Carolina (Public Utilities, Services and Carriers, 2016).

The Northeast Energy Direct Project

Attempts to construct pipelines can also run afoul of state rate regulation laws. Kinder Morgan's Northeast Energy Direct (NED) pipeline would have run from a point west of Albany, New York, to Dracut, Massachusetts. Public input from residents and environmentalists concerned about impacts to communities and valuable habitat along the pipeline's route resulted in significant re-routing of the line. The project was eventually abandoned due to a combination of state regulations, court decisions, and a lack of commitment by customers.

In 2014, the Massachusetts Department of Public Utilities (DPU) initiated a rule allowing rate payers to be charged to fund pipeline construction, which would have enabled construction of the NED pipeline. Proponents argued that this rule would bring cheaper natural gas to New England and reduce overall electricity rates. The Conservation Law Foundation challenged the DPU rule (Conservation Law Foundation, 2016b) and the Massachusetts high court invalidated it on the grounds that requiring rate payers to subsidize infrastructure would expose them to the very type of risks from which a 1997 state law restructuring the electric industry sought to protect them (Conservation Law Foundation, 2016a, 2016b). FERC's order issuing a certificate and conditional approval of the project stated: "The pipeline must be prepared to financially support the project without relying on subsidization from existing customers" (FERC, 2014). In May 2016, Kinder Morgan withdrew its application to FERC for the pipeline (Moffat, 2016).

Conclusion

The regulation of shale gas in the United States is carried out via overlapping and intersecting powers of federal, state, and local governments, each promoting various political, economic, environmental, and social values. While increasing the consistency of regulation across the country may seem desirable, the high value placed on states' rights, and the longstanding precedent for local municipal control over land use decisions make standardization of regulation of unconventional oil and gas development improbable. Existing environmental and natural resource regulation regimes allow for environmental impact assessments accompanying permitting processes at both state and federal levels, helping to balance multiple interests. However, data availability, political will, and government capacity at various jurisdictional levels influence the outcomes of these laws. Interpretations of constitutional law also impact oil and gas infrastructure projects. Balancing strong property rights regimes seen in water law, local land use law, trade secret law, and eminent domain law against common interests in environmental protection and public health and the requirements of efficient shale gas development and transmission will continue to be a challenge. Increased collection of and access to data will support better regulation, but variation in state, local, and federal goals and priorities is unavoidable given the nature of shale gas development, current energy dependencies, and asymmetrical distribution of benefits and costs of this industry.

Note

1 The FRAC Act was introduced in 2009 by Representatives Diana DeGette (CO), Jared Polis (CO), and Maurice Hinchey (NY), and by Senators Bob Casey (PA) and Charles Schumer) (NY).

References

Alder, R. W. (2010). Climate Change and the Hegemony of State Water Law. *Stanford Environmental Law Journal, 29*, 1–61.

Antidegradation policy and implementation methods, 40 C.F.R. §131.12 (2015).

Bartlett, B., & Lynch, K. (2016). *Brief of Interested Public Lands, Natural Resources, Energy and Administrative Law Professors as Amici Curiae in Support of Respondent-Appellants*. Retrieved from www.eenews.net/assets/2016/08/18/document_ew_02.pdf

Bosquez, T., IV, Carmeli, D., Esterkin, J., et al. (2015). Fracking Debate: The Importance of Pre-drill Water Quality Testing. *American Bar Association Section of Litigation*.

Bureau of Transportation Statistics. (2016). *National Transporation Statistics: Table 10–1: U.S. Oil and Gas Pipeline Mileage*. Retrieved from www.rita.dot.gov/bts/sites/rita.dot.gov.bts/files/publications/national_transportation_statistics/html/table_01_10.html

Burger, M. (2013). The (Re)Federalization of Fracking Regulation (Roger Williams Univ. Legal Studies Paper No. 141). *Michigan State Law Review, 2013*(5), 1483–1545.

Calton, D. R., Shepson, P. B., Santoro, R. L., et al. (2014). Toward a Better Understanding and Quantification of Methane Emissions from Shale Gas Development. *Proceedings of the National Academy of Sciences of the United States of America, 111*(17), 6237–6242. doi:10.1073/pnas.1316546111.

City of Fort Collins v. Colorado Oil and Gas Association, No. 2016 CO 28 (2016).

City of Longmont v. Colorado Oil and Gas Association, No. 2016 CO 29 (2016).

Clean Water Act, 33 USC 1251 et seq. (1972).

Conservation Law Foundation. (2016a). Massachusetts' Highest Court Rejects Public Subsidies for Fossil Fuels. Retrieved from www.clf.org/newsroom/massachusetts-highest-court-rejects-public-subsidies-fossil-fuels/

Conservation Law Foundation. (2016b). *SJC-12052: Conservation Law Foundation vs. Department of Public Utilities. Slip Opinion.* Retrieved from www.clf.org/wp-content/uploads/2016/08/12051.pdf

Constitution Pipeline Company v. *New York State Dept. of Env. Cons.*, No. 16–1568 (2d. Cir. 2017).

Constitution Pipeline Company v. *New York State Dept. of Env. Cons.*, No. 1:16-cv-00568, F. Supp. 3d – (N.D.N.Y. 2017).

Coplan, K. S. (2014). Citizen Litigants, Citizen Regulators: Four Cases where Citizen Suits Drove Development of Clean Water Law. *Colorado Natural Resources, Energy, and Environmental Law Review*, 25(1).

Delaware River Basin Commission. (2017a). DRBC to Consider Resolution to Publish Revised Draft Rules Addressing Natural Gas Development Activities within the Delaware River Basin. Press release. Retrieved from www.nj.gov/drbc/home/newsroom/news/approved/20170911_newsrel_natgas.html

Delaware River Basin Commission. (2017b). A Resolution Directing the Executive Director to Publish for Public Comment Revised Draft Regulations Regarding Certain Natural Gas Development Activities in the Delaware River Basin. Retrieved from www.nj.gov/drbc/library/documents/ResforMinutes091317_natgas-initiate-rulemkg.pdf

Easton, J. (2013). Fracking Wastewater Management: Is Centralized Treatment the Way Forward? *Water and Wastewater International*, 28(5).

Ely v. *Cabot Oil & Gas*, No. 3:09-CV-2284 (M.D. PA 2016).

Energy Policy Act, 42 U.S.C. § 13201 et. seq. (2005).

Evers, P. S. (2015). Constitutional Law and Fracking. *International Journal of Business and Public Administration*, 12(2).

Federal Energy Regulatory Commission. (2014). *149 FERC 61,199: Order Issuing Certificates and Approving Abandonment.* Retrieved from www.ferc.gov/CalendarFiles/20141202171918-CP13-499-000.pdf

Federal Energy Regulatory Commission. (2016). FERC Order Issuing Certificate: Tennessee Gas Pipeline, LLC, 154 FERC ¶ 61,191 C.F.R.

Fernandez, B., Hanlon Leh, N., & Donaldson, K. (2016, November 16). How Energy Firms Can Use the Defend Trade Secrets Act. *Law360*. Retrieved from www/law360.com/articles/863414/how-energy-firms-can-use-the-defned-trade-secrets-act

Gagnon, G. A., Krkosek, W., Anderson, L., et al. (2016). Impacts of Hydraulic Fracturing on Water Quality: A Review of Literature, Regulatory Frameworks and an Analysis of Information Gaps. *Environmental Reviews*, 24(2), 122–131.

Government Accountability Office. (2014). Freshwater: Supply Concerns Continue and Uncertainties Complicate Planning (GAO-14-430). Retrieved from www.gao.gov/assets/670/663343.pdf

Groundwater Protection Council. (n.d.). Retrieved from www.gwpc.org

Groves, J. (2012). Rule 29 or: How the Texas Railroad Commission Stopped Worrying and Learned to Love Hydraulic Fracturing. *Texas Tech Administrative Law Journal*, 14.

Hall, K. (2013). Hydraulic Fracturing: Trade Secrets and the Mandatory Disclosure of Fracturing Water Composition. *Idaho Law Review*, 49.

Howarth, R. W. (2014). A Bridge to Nowhere: Methane Emissions and the Greenhouse Gas Footprint of Natural Gas. *Energy Science and Engineering*, 2(2), 47–60. doi:10.1002/ese3.35.

Hurdle, J. (2016, June 14). EPA Bans Disposal of Fracking Wastewater at Public Treatment Plants. *State Impact PA*. Retrieved from https://stateimpact.npr.org/pennsylvania/2016/06/14/epa-bans-disposal-of-fracking-waste-water-at-public-treatment-plants/

Hurdle, J. (2017, January 2). Friends and Foes of the Constitution Pipeline Await Appeals Court Ruling. *State Impact Pennsylvania*, online. Retrieved from https://stateimpact.npr.org/pennsylvania/2017/01/02/friends-and-foes-of-constitution-pipeline-await-appeals-court-ruling/

In the Matter of Mark S. Wallach v. Town of Dryden, 23 728 (New York Court of Appeals 2014).

Kaplan, T. (2014, December 17). Citing Health Risks, Cuomo Bans Fracking in New York State. *New York Times*. Retrieved from www.nytimes.com/2014/12/18/nyregion/cuomo-to-ban-fracking-in-new-york-state-citing-health-risks.html

Kelly, S., & Neinast, V. (2013). Getting Gas to the People. In E. L. Powers & B. Kinne (Eds.), *Beyond the Fracking Wars: A Guide for Lawyers, Public Officials, Planners, and Citizens*. Chicago: American Bar Association, Section of State and Local Government Law.

Kinder Morgan. (2016). White Paper: Eminent Domain. Retrieved from www.kinder-morgan.com/content/docs/White_Eminent_Domain.pdf

Klass, A., & Meinhardt, D. (2015). Transporting Oil and Gas: U.S. Infrastructure Challenges. *Iowan Law Review*, 100, 947–1053.

Kundis Craig, R. (2010). Adapting Water Law to Public Necessity: Reframing Climate Change Adaptation as Emergency Response and Preparedness. *Vermont Journal of Environmental Law*, 11.

Lowther, F. M. (2017). Constitution Pipeline: The 2d Circuit Reaffirms a State's Right to Veto a FERC-approved Interstate Pipeline Project. Retrieved from https://energytrendswatch.com/2017/08/22/constitution-pipeline-the-2d-circuit-reaffirms-a-states-right-to-veto-a-ferc-approved-interstate-pipeline-project/

McFeeley, M. (2012). *State Hydraulic Fracturing Disclosure Rules and Enforcement: A Comparison*. Natural Resources Defense Council, NRDC Issue Brief, July 22, 2012, B; 12-06-A. Retrieved from www.nrdc.org//sites/default/files/Fracking-Disclosure-IB.pdf

Moffat, C. J. (2016, May 23). Notice of Withdrawal of Certificate Application. Tennessee Gas Pipeline Company, L.L.C., Docket No. CP16-21-000.

Murrill, B. J., & Vann, A. (2012). *Hydraulic Fracturing: Chemical Disclosure Requirements*. Congressional Research Service Report R42461. Retrieved from https://fas.org/sgp/crs/misc/R42461.pdf.

Negro, S. E. (2012). Fracking Wars: Federal, State and Local Conflicts over the Regulation of Natural Gas Activities. *Zoning and Planning Law Report*, 35(2).

New York State Assembly. (2012). *Memorandum in Support of Legislation, Bill No. A05318A*. Retrieved from http://assembly.state.ny.us/leg/?default_fld=&bn=A05318&term=2011&Summary=Y&Memo=Y

NY Department of Environmental Conservation. (2016). Letter to Lynda Schubring, PMP Re: Joint Application: DEC Permit# 0-9999-00181/00024 Water Quality Certification/ Notice of Denial. Retrieved from www.dec.ny.gov/docs/administration_pdf/constitutionwc42016.pdf

Oil and Gas; Hydraulic Fracturing on Federal and Indian Lands; Final Rule, (2015).

Public Utilities, Services and Carriers, South Carolina Code of Laws 58-7-10 (2016).

Rahm, B. G., Bates, J. T., Bertoia, L. R., et al. (2013). Wastewater Management and Marcellus Shale Development: Trends, Drivers and Planning Implications. *Journal of Environmental Management*, 120, 105–113.

Robinson Township v. *Commonwealth of Pennsylvania*, 83 901 (Supreme Court of Pennsylvania Middle District 2013).

Rubright, S. (2017). 34 States Have Active Oil and Gas Drilling in U.S., Based on 2016 Data. FrackTracker Alliance. Retrieved from www.fractracker.org/2017/03/34-states-active-drilling-2016/

Safe Drinking Water Act, 42 U.S.C. 300(f) et seq. (1974, as amended).

Schmidt, C. (2013). Estimating Wastewater Impacts from Fracking. *Environmental Health Perspectives (Online)*, *121*(4).

Smith, J. (2016). Government Failure to Protect Water Resources. Paper presented at the 16th National Conference on Science, Policy and the Environment: Food-Water-Energy Nexus, Washington, DC.

Somin, I. (2016). The Growing Battle Over the Use of Eminent Domain to Take Property for Pipelines. *Washington Post*. Retrieved from www.washingtonpost.com/news/volokh-conspiracy/wp/2016/06/07/the-growing-battle-over-the-use-of-eminent-domain-to-take-property-for-pipelines/?utm_term=.6ea00254bda5

Stutz, B. (2015, October 20). As the Fracking Boom Spreads, One Watershed Draws the Line. *Yale Environment*, *360*. Retrieved from https://yale.edu/features/as_the_fracking_boom_spreads_one_watershed_draws_the_line

Tiemann, M., & Vann, A. (2015). *Hydraulic Fracturing and Safe Drinking Water Act Regulatory Issues*. *Congressional Research Service Report R41760*. Retrieved from https://fas.org/sgp/crs/misc/R41760.pdf

Treichler, R. (2015, April 2). DEC Speeds Up Water Permit Giveaway. Retrieved from http://nywaterlaw.com/blog/2015/04/0402permits.html

U.S. Energy Information Administration. (2015). *Natural Gas Explained: Natural Gas Pipelines*. Retrieved from www.eia.gov/energyexplained/index.cfm?page=natural_gas_pipelines

U.S. Energy Information Administration. (2016). *U.S. Crude Oil and Natural Gas Proved Reserves, Year-end 2015*. Retrieved from www.eia.gov/naturalgas/crudeoilreserves/index.cfm

U.S. Energy Information Administration. (2017a, January 10). Natural Gas Explained. Retrieved from www.eia.gov/energyexplained/index.cfm?page=natural_gas_where

U.S. Energy Information Administration. (2017b). *Short-term Energy Outlook: Renewables and Carbon Dioxide Emissions*. Retrieved from www.eia.gov/outlooks/steo/report/renew_co2.cfm

U.S. Environmental Protection Agency. (2016a). *EPA's Study on Hydraulic Fracturing and its Potential Impact on Drinking Water*. Retrieved from www.epa.gov/sites/production/files/2016-12/documents/hfdwa_executive_summary.pdf

U.S. Environmental Protection Agency. (2016b). *Pretreatment Standards for the Oil and Gas Extraction Point Source Category*. Retrieved from www.epa.gov/sites/production/files/2016-06/documents/uog-final-rule_fact-sheet_06-14-2016.pdf

Wiseman, H. J. (2014). Regulatory Islands. *New York University Law Review*, *89*(5), 1661–1742.

Wyoming v. *U.S. Dept. of the Interior*, 46 20114 (District of Wyoming 2016).

3 A complex adaptive system or just a tangled mess?

Property rights and shale gas governance in Australia and the US

Jeffrey B. Jacquet, Katherine Witt, William Rifkin, and Julia H. Haggerty

Introduction

Australia and the United States (US) have many similarities in the regulation of unconventional oil and gas (UOG) development.[1] In both countries, federal governance is largely absent, and oil and gas regulation is instead formed at the nexus of state policy, industry actors, and private property owners. Thus, regulations and practices can vary from state to state, region to region, and even town to town as differences in legal jurisdiction, the capacity of individual actors, and cultural discourse all influence facets of development. This lack of an overarching regulatory environment can be viewed both as a complex adaptive system nimble enough to adapt to local changes or, alternatively, as a tangled mess of regulations and responsibilities prone to policy failures.

In both Australia and the US, property rights are highly influential in shaping the governance of UOG. Globally, land and resource ownership is embedded in culture and law, and considered in terms of either private, state-based, or communitarian models (Ostrom 1990; Bromley 1991). In both Australia and the US, a settler colonial history led to systems that prioritize private property rights. The right to own property is cherished as a moral right to freedom and opportunity, and strongly associated with other cultural ideals of democracy, meritocracy and a free market.

While cultural expectations of private land ownership and limited federal oversight are similar in the two countries, the institutional arrangements, and regulatory environment have evolved differently. Here we provide a comparative glimpse into these property rights institutions and how they influence public participation and government responses to shale development. We draw on existing historical and contemporary literature to examine and compare the rise of property rights and energy regulatory regimes in both countries, as well as examining major political and cultural discourses occurring in both nations. We attempt to make sense of these unique regulatory structures with the "complex system" and "tangled mess" descriptors. We conclude by describing some fertile areas of inquiry as oil and gas regulations continue to evolve in these countries.

Energy governance

Energy governance intersects property rights through geographic issues of jurisdiction and scale. In both the US and Australia, remoteness from decision-making centers and limited capacity in local government have long contributed to an institutional void in rural regions (Cheshire 2010; Burton et al. 2013). In regard to regional governance, Morrison (2014: 101) cites a policy literature challenged by changing conditions, shifting demographics in the US and Australia as well as "devolved planning responsibilities, privatised resource rights, and networked management approaches." Everingham et al. (2013: 585) similarly refer to rural resource governance in Australia as "characterized by (1) variety of institutions, (2) attention to mining-specific impacts, and (3) dispersal of resources, responsibilities, and authority."

As a result, in both Australia and the US, the most local scales of governance – individual property owners and residents, municipalities, townships, and counties – negotiate directly with industrial capital about oil and gas development; yet, rarely yield any real leverage in these negotiations. In both countries, the circumstances stem from (1) the complex legal evolution of the ownership of subsurface minerals toward a system favoring private interests and the resulting split interest in land and subsurface estates; and (2) the devolution of national regulation found in relation to many other industries.

Mineral ownership and property rights

Land and mineral rights in both Australia and the US are based on the thirteenth-century common law principle of "*cuius est solum, eius est usque ad coelum et ad infernos*," which means whoever owns the land surface, owns to the skies above and to the depths below. While surface owners' rights have been limited to various degrees in both countries, this maxim largely remains the starting point to define the scope of owners' rights over and below the surface (Hepburn 2013).

Private property in the United States

Private property ownership represents a core component of what is called "The American Dream" of upward economic mobility based in large part on home ownership (Megbolugbe & Linneman, 1993). The US is also one of very few countries (along with Canada, for example) that allows individuals to own subsurface minerals, a practice that predates the US government; in colonial North America, the British Crown relinquished these rights as few precious metals were available to claim and fossil fuel resources were largely unrecognized (Harrison 1989).

After federation in 1776, the United States emerged with a clear focus on the protection of various individual rights, including the protection of privately held property, as the US Constitution notably outlaws "private property to be taken for public use, without just compensation" (Matthews 2014). Meanwhile, the more mundane laws and regulations were left up to the state governments, a development with implications for contemporary UOG governance.

Leasing and the split estate

By the 1880s, the federal government began to withhold mineral interests from the bundle of ownership rights when it transferred land to private parties; by 1915, the US Supreme Court upheld the legality of these actions. The result is the ability for private mineral ownership to trade hands independently of surface rights, giving rise to what is now known as "split" or "severed estate" (Gates 1968). Court cases later established that in the case of disputes between surface owners and mineral owners, the mineral owner enjoy a "primacy" of ownership in that surface owners must allow mineral owners to ability to develop their assets (Jones, Wellborn, & Russell 2013).

In order to develop energy resources, companies must sign legally binding contracts with the mineral owners called leases, that dictate the amount of payment for development rights, the percentage royalties to be paid to the mineral owner from the sale of the energy, the terms by which the energy will be extracted, and the amount of time the company has to develop the resource (Jacquet 2015; Bugden et al. 2016). In areas of high potential for energy development, these contracts can provide private mineral owners with considerable wealth (ranging in the tens of thousands to millions of dollars per year depending on the number of wells drilled and other market factors); conversely, landowners who do not own the mineral rights beneath their property typically receive no monetary windfall beyond modest payments to offset surface impacts.

Private property in Australia

In Australian land law, the rights of surface landowners have been significantly diminished from the original common law principle. Following Australia's essentially egalitarian approach to land ownership and public policy (Collins 1985), private rights to minerals below the surface (including petroleum and gas resources) have been abrogated to a public ownership model, and ownership is held by the State (or in Australia, as a constitutional monarchy, held by the Crown). Under the Australian Constitution, these Crown rights are vested in the six individual states.

States allocate these rights to miners, subject to conditions, including a land access agreement with the landholder. The resource company must pay a fee for the use of the rights and a royalty to the State based on revenue from the resource (Ryan 1974). Increasingly, more conditions are being placed on extractive industries, including addressing environmental and social impacts, rehabilitation when resource extraction ends, and observing rights to surface and subsurface water, and the rights of current landowners, and the rights of aboriginal or native peoples.

Landowners can be compensated for disruption to the surface and for loss of rights to exclusive access and use, but they have no claims to royalties or revenue from the resources. Additionally, surface landholders cannot exclude those with rights to develop mineral resources. These aspects are fundamental and profound distinctions from the US model, where private interests often stand to gain from mineral lease revenues. Despite the lack of private mineral ownership in Australia, private land rights loom large over public discourse and the governance of the UOG industry.

Rights of possession and property discourses in Australia

In Australia, economic rights and political expediency appear paramount in discourses on possession and property rights, though other concerns also play into the debate and the imposition of moratoria on onshore gas.

The expectation of exclusive use of land is an interesting phenomenon in Australia as all of the land (like all of the minerals) is retained in public ownership and held by the Crown. Rights to occupy, access, and use the land are distributed by the State as either private freehold or other forms of leasehold title. A freehold title in land confers a secure bundle of property rights to the individual (or corporation) but, as is often overlooked, the Crown remains the ultimate owner of the land and can resume it (with compensation) "in the public interest." One of these rights is possession, which confers rights to control access to and use of resources on the property. Consistent with that, those who have rights to the surface of the land are often referred to as "landholders" rather than "landowners." Expectations of landholders surrounding the right of possession in both freehold and leasehold tenures have been challenged over the last three decades as Indigenous Australians seek to reclaim traditional ownership (Trigger et al. 2014). The legal framework has been amended in response.

Within their mineral and petroleum rights, each Australian state has an associated framework to regulate land access. State policies differ regarding the extent of landholders' rights to refuse access to a resource company. The land access provisions were largely created in response to small-scale mining and mineral exploration, which has occurred in Australia for more than 100 years. They were later adapted to attempt to address much more complex extraction scenarios, such as UOG.

Australian discourse around property rights has grown prominent, especially in relation to expanding environmental regulation and the protection of landholders' rights to control their land (Reeve 2002). The entrance of the UOG industry in Queensland followed a decade of contention between farmers, environmental groups, and governments over a series of environmentally focused legislation, such as around the clearing of native vegetation by farmers. Such legislation was thought by many to erode the rights of private property (Thomson 2005). Since farmers—the majority landholders in the gasfield region of Queensland—do not own the mineral rights under their lands, they do not stand to benefit financially from resource development. Thus, it is not surprising that farmers can perceive the government's approval of gas development as yet another encroachment on their rights.

Although often simplistically represented as a purely environmentalist anti-fracking initiative (Makki 2015), Lock the Gate played a role in reigniting a debate weighing the landholders' surface rights against a resource company's rights to develop the underground resource (Hutton 2012: 15), while questioning the distribution of benefits from public gas resources. Lock the Gate and similar campaigns have attempted to assert a landholder's right to veto resource development on private land, and it challenges the legitimacy of governments to enforce access against the landholder's will (Fahey 2015).

Lock the Gate represented an unusual alliance between right-leaning landholders and left-leaning media-savvy environmental activists—the same ones who had been farmers' antagonists in previous environmental issues. While polarizing, it has resonated with an impetus for policy change (Makki 2014). A Land Access Review Panel was convened (LARP 2012), and Land Access regulations in Queensland were amended in favor of landholders' rights.

New South Wales and the Santos/AGL declaration

In New South Wales, the anti-UOG discourse united the concerns of landholders about water and property rights with environmental groups' concerns. The latter would point to incidents, such as a spill of saline water from a coal seam, which killed vegetation on several acres of the forest floor (Crikey 2012). Perceived threats to groundwater and to the farmland that has remained after suburban expansion (Sherval & Hardiman 2014) are behind the resistance to recent plans to expand an early UOG development in the western Sydney suburb of Camden (Cronshaw & Grafton 2016).

In these contexts, as in Queensland, UOG development brought some left-leaning environmentally-focused residents into alignment with traditionally right-leaning residents concerned about tourism and other business interests in addition to concerns about the groundwater that farmers rely on. An election year meant that issues of onshore gas governance played out in terms of which political party gained traction or retained its majority, with the mechanisms of gas resource governance appearing to be subservient to that.

Within this partisan political context, the NSW Chief Scientist and Engineer was asked to report on the promise and perils of UOG development. Her report (NSWCSE 2014) concurred with reviews in other jurisdictions (e.g., EASA 2014 and Government of New Zealand 2012), that UOG development could occur if leading industry practices (including those recently developed by the Council of Australian Governments) were followed. Nonetheless, the Liberal (conservative) government did not back the UOG industry publicly; instead it issued a setback requirement of 2 km from a racehorse stud farm or a winery (NSW DIRE 2016).

With an alignment of political forces on the left and the right against them, the two leading firms in the UOG industry in NSW—Santos and AGL—sought to instill measures that would enable a "social license to operate." In March 2014, they agreed with peak agricultural bodies to respect landholders' rights of possession, specifically the right to say "yes" or "no" to UOG operations on their land (NSW Farmers Federation 2016). The agreement also means that the companies will not seek to enforce their rights of access granted by the state, as part of their petroleum resource rights, through legal action against a landholder.

Queensland and the CCA

Queensland's land access code, published in 2010 and amended in 2016, provides best practice guidelines and specifies mandatory (i.e., minimum) conditions for the conduct of petroleum lease holders (i.e., gas company personnel) on private property (Queensland Government 2004/2010/2016). The Code aims to establish compensation arrangements and support effective communication and working relationships. It specifies entry notices provided to the landholder by the gas company, the need for conduct and compensation agreements (CCAs) or an agreed alternative, the right of the landholder to restrict access to certain areas, a dispute resolution process, and compensation for costs incurred in negotiation of a CCA (Maurin, Trenorden, & Rifkin, 2016).

The CCAs typically entitle the landholder to thousands and perhaps tens of thousands of dollars in up-front compensation to address disruptions caused by the laying of pipes and other infrastructure. Then, for the 20–30-year life of the well, there are yearly payments averaging from $2,500 per well (D. Phipps, AgForce, pers. comm.) to $10,000 per well (R. Wilkinson, Australian Petroleum Producers and Explorers Association, pers. comm., December 2015). These payments are meant to compensate for land taken up by UOG infrastructure (generally a small percentage of farm or grazing land) and other long-term disruptions.

Even with the advent of the CCA, landholders remain skeptical about the extent to which whether gas companies will act in accordance with the contract. Landholders express a belief that "coexisting" with gas company operations will still be a significant burden on their time. They report investing time in checking for weeds, closing or opening gates, and reassembling the fencing around a well pad (Cavaye et al. forthcoming). Additionally, farmers address concerns to a contractor or company staff member, but they are not handled quickly or effectively (ibid.), which then eats up further time in correspondence and communication with the UOG company (ibid.). The effects of such challenges for landholders can be seen in the low level of trust accorded to UOG companies, with over 80 percent of landholders surveyed reporting low trust in the UOG industry (Gillespie et al. 2016). Trust is divided in the rest of these agriculturally focused communities, with 40–45 percent trusting the industry and 40–45 percent not trusting the industry (ibid.).

Despite the government owning the resource, the discourse in agricultural Queensland can be framed as centering around business-to-business relationships—between the resource industry and the agricultural operators and landholders.

Different regimes across Australia

The gas industry has been received differently in each of the Australian states. In Queensland, where 64 percent of land remains as Crown land under lease arrangement, rapid resource development has been experienced. In Victoria and New South Wales, with more area held in private freehold tenure, the governments have placed a moratorium on gas development.

In one state with extensive unconventional gas development and a neighboring state with potential development that has been delayed (Cronshaw & Grafton 2016), regulations specifically address procedures for negotiating agreements between companies and landholders and for resolving disagreements. The focus is on agricultural landholders and compensation for impositions on their businesses, whether that is mainly cropping or grazing. Thus, the legislation appears to emphasize economic production rather than land valued as an amenity, as a symbol of place-based identity, or as a focus for environmental preservation. So, ownership is addressed as being about economic value rather than about other sorts of rights.

Regulation and property discourses in the US

In the US, the footprint of shale development has emerged across many states for more than 20 years. While summative narratives of US shale development are more difficult, property rights conflicts remain a core driver of UOG discourse and shifts in shale governance.

At the national level, the US has had a federalist and deregulated approach to mining regulations. The oil and gas industry is exempt from many of the 1970s-era regulations that constitute the backbone of US environmental policy (Warner & Shapiro 2013). Consequently, each state has differing regulations and policies for permitting a well, public planning, and siting processes, types of chemicals or substances that may be used, chemical disclosure, wastewater disposal, and virtually every other facet of developing a well. While there are important differences in regulation between states, overall variation is small enough to allow UOG development across dozens of states, often with shared companies and workforces. As of 2017, three states—with varying degrees of resource development potential—have used their regulatory authority to effectively ban UOG: New York, Maryland, and Vermont (Hurdle 2017).

Local governance and the ability to ban

Among the most contentious issue is the ability of local municipalities to regulate drilling activity. The US has a long tradition of regulatory devolution ("home rule"), whereby local governments can regulate their own land uses (through zoning), provided that they do not conflict with state or federal regulations (Vanlandingham 1968). Local officials design zoning regulations with the aim of protecting or increasing the property values of the majority of residents in the jurisdiction (Fischel 1987, 2001).

This tradition of home rule and local zoning regulation sits in stark contrast to state-level oil and gas regulations that exempt local control over the industry (Nolon & Gavin 2013). Cities and towns from several states have attempted to control oil and gas development locations through zoning regulations (Fry, Briggle, & Kincaid 2015) or otherwise restrict the nature of development through specific ordinances with respect to distances of drilling from residential and other land uses (Kroepsch 2016).

The result is a tapestry of municipal zoning authorities that varies widely across states and regions depending on state laws and local culture. This jurisdictional unevenness has led to unresolved legal disputes, state-level Supreme Court rulings, and public referendums over the authority of local entities in dictating local resource development policy (Nolon & Gavin 2013; Fisk 2016). Courts in New York and Pennsylvania have recently ruled that municipalities do have the power to zone drilling locations, while most other states do not allow municipalities to zone drilling locations (Andrews & McCarthy 2014; Fisk 2016). A recent review finds that fewer than 30 percent of local governments in regions experiencing UOG development in the US have pursued formal efforts to regulate fracking (Loh & Osland 2016).

The importance of private property owners

Shale development requires large contiguous acreages, and many UOG deposits in the US occur in areas composed of small-acre parcels owned by private landowners. Contractual negotiations between mineral owners, surface owners, and oil and gas developers have particular importance in the US context, and property rights and ownership remain a dominant narrative in the American discourse on shale energy.

Tideman (1972) notes that a lack of overlap between the *legal* and *moral* rights associated with owning property can cause strife. These tensions are clearly present in the development of shale resources: Proponents see shale development as exercising both the legal and moral rights of the resource owner. Opponents view shale development as potentially causing harm to neighboring communities and as infringing on the moral rights of those communities, if not the legal rights (Vasi et al. 2015).

Landowner coalitions, regulations, and "private participation"

Jacquet (2015) and Jacquet and Stedman (2011) have examined the ability of mineral owners to act collectively to influence development and/or regulation. Groups of mineral owners have organized large areas of largely contiguous property into so-called Landowner Coalitions with the ability to collectively bargain during the leasing process with energy companies. The large, contiguous acreages are desirable to energy companies, and the mineral owners are able to use this leverage to gain advantageous leasing terms, including higher lease payments and royalty rates. In other cases, as shown in Chapter 12 by Smith and Haggerty in this volume, landowner organizations wield political capital associated with private property ideology to advocate for state policy innovation.

Landowners represent some of the only sub-state-level control over development and one of the few ways that local residents can participate in the regulatory process, a phenomenon termed "private participation" (Jacquet 2015). As private participation is largely contractual, conflicts between these parties are primarily a legal matter often settled out of court, obfuscated by non-disclosure agreements (Throupe, Simons, & Mao 2013).

Discussion

Shale governance in both the US and Australia primarily operates at "local" rather than national scales of governance specifically via states, municipalities, and private landowners. In this context, a continued set of negotiations juxtaposes local with state or industry power, whether it be authority to stipulate the terms of drilling on private property or authority to exclude UOG from certain spaces through zoning. Defenders of local authority have successfully harnessed both property rights and environmental discourses in a surprising and often effective alignment of conventionally disparate ideologies.

There are notable differences in the outcomes of such negotiations in the US and Australian circumstances, however. State government and local government have generally been more protective of landowners in Australia than in the US. Similarly, industry actions suggest a greater concern about procuring and maintaining a Social License to Operate in Australia than in most of the US. Exploring these differences suggests two possible narratives: a tangled mess with little rhyme or reason easily captured by industry, or a complex adaptive system still in the process of adjustment.

A tangled mess

In this model, a combination of forces results in policy failings that jeopardize public health and safety and prioritize industry above other interests (Ogneva-Himmelberger Huang 2015). The tangled mess emerges out of the stronghold of property rights ideology, a devolution of authority to actors that lack necessary capacity (Freudenburg 1993), and other challenges inherent to UOG, such as the boom-bust cycle.

Policy at the federal level and in many US and Australian states does little to balance the playing field on which neighbors, landowners, mineral owners, and oil and gas development companies interact. As other chapters in this collection suggest, the ability of property owners and their proxies to influence development varies widely, not only as a function of the local regulatory environment but also due to cultural, social, and political idiosyncrasies of individuals and communities. Taken together, these factors reflect a regulatory vacuum, one that has been filled with contentious and often inconclusive debates about the rights and responsibilities of mineral and property owners, industry, and government.

Wealthier communities with more restrictive zoning laws may avoid long-term "legacy issues" associated with environmental costs of fossil fuel development and receive better concessions from energy firms that are able to drill wells. Poorer communities with less restrictive regulatory environments may enjoy greater fiscal revenues and economic stimulus in the short term, although they may face a greater chance of long-term problems. Such stratification resulting from energy extraction naturally draws comparisons with "the resource curse" literature (a phenomenon whereby locales with higher natural resource extraction tend to have lower indicators of social and economic well-being) (Ross 1999), but it remains to be seen if long-term socio-economic outcomes of contemporary US and Australian energy host communities will exemplify the resource curse phenomenon.

Thus, decentralized regulation of the UOG carries major risks to landowners and local governments left to enforce the terms of leases and other agreements. During industry downturns, when companies restructure or disappear into bankruptcy, legal liability becomes a complicated chain of custody. Absent robust state regulation and enforcement, landowners and the public can inherit substantial burdens, as in the case of the coalbed methane industry that has left thousands of orphaned wells in the American West (Frosch & Gold 2015; see Chapter 4 by Walsh and Haggerty, in this volume).

Or a complex adaptive system?

On the other hand, what at first resembles a tangled mess may upon closer examination demonstrate a legible complex system. In this model, UOG industry and governance evolve over time through the interactions among a number of logics about the appropriate balance between individual, industry, local, state, and federal responsibility. Viewing these multiple dimensions of gas development as a complex system helps structure assessments of UOG governance in the US and Australia.

Regulation in both nations is relatively uncoordinated and demonstrates the absence of nationally coherent policy approaches to unconventional development. An overlay of different logics at different scales, in different locations, and for different physical domains—water, land, financial, socio-economic—influences multiple diverse development trajectories. Continuous eruptions of localized disputes about oil and gas development are the logical products of such a system as the system adapts in response to local cultural and political forces.

This model suggests an explanation for the apparent stronger leanings in favor of industry constraint and landowner protections in Australia. From a complex systems perspective, Australia's UOG industry is simpler: it is younger, in fewer places, involves fewer players, and features less variability among property regimes. This relative simplicity may encourage an emergent property where local geographies have greater leverage in determining industry's social license than in the US.

Conclusion

In this chapter, we have briefly traced the histories of oil and gas regulation in Australia and the US, noting the important roles that property rights and a lack of federal oversight play in these regulatory systems. These systems entangle and obscure the traditional debates over individual rights and collective goods, especially as landowner rights vary widely and public goods become abstract, involving climate change and energy security.

The result is complex and decentralized systems that are both adaptive and also deeply limited. It is too early to identify definitive emergent properties of this complex system, as legislative and legal proceedings continue to shape the nature of shale governance in both Australia and the US. As these systems continue to adapt and mature, important questions emerge, especially regarding the equity of the system among landowners and industry, wealthy and poor communities, and mineral owners and landowners. An intriguing perspective emphasized in an adaptive system framework is the way time and experience will create feedbacks among temporal and spatial scales of development and regulatory and governance approaches. Future research should prioritize the dynamic interactions among key system properties, such as property regimes, property ideologies, local politics, and market patterns as they play out, especially in development downturns.

Note

1 Coal seam gas (CSG) is the primary unconventional resource being developed in Australia and shale oil and gas are the primary resources in the United States. In this chapter, we treat the "above-ground" aspects of these energy sources as largely analogous and refer to both as unconventional oil and gas (UOG); however, we recognize differences in geology and specifics of the extractive technologies.

References

Andrews, E., & McCarthy, J. (2014). Scale, shale, and the state: Political ecologies and legal geographies of shale gas development in Pennsylvania. *Journal of Environmental Studies and Sciences*, 4(1), 7–16.

Bugden, D., Kay, D., Glynn, R., & Stedman, R. (2016). The bundle below: Understanding unconventional oil and gas development through analysis of lease agreements. *Energy Policy*, 92, 214–219.

Burton, L. M., Lichter, D. T., Baker, R. S., & Eason, J. M. (2013). Inequality, family processes, and health in the "new" rural America. *American Behavioral Scientist*, 57(8), 1128–1151.

Bromley, D. W. (1991). *Environment and Economy: Property Rights and Public Policy.* Oxford: Blackwell.

Cavaye, J., Kelly, L., Rillorta-Goloran, T., Martin, M., Cameron, D., Muriuki, G., & Baldwin, S. (forthcoming). CSG & Agriculture: Two Industries on One Landscape. Brisbane, Queensland: Centre for Coal Seam Gas, University of Queensland.

Cheshire, L. (2010). A corporate responsibility? The constitution of fly-in, fly-out mining companies as governance partners in remote, mine-affected localities. *Journal of Rural Studies*, 26(1), 12–20.

Collins, H. (1985). Political ideology in Australia: the distinctiveness of a Benthamite society, in S. Graubard (ed.) *Daedalus*, Winter 1985: Australia: Terra Incognita? American Academy of Arts and Sciences, Richmond, Virginia, vol. 114, pp. 147–170.

Crikey (2012, March 8). Behind the seams: who's asking questions about coal seam gas and health? Available at: www.crikey.com.au/2012/03/08/behind-the-seams-whos-asking-questions-about-coal-seam-gas-and-health/ (accessed November 30, 2016).

Cronshaw, I., & Grafton, R. (2016). A tale of two states: Development and regulation of coal bed methane extraction in Queensland and New South Wales, Australia. *Resources Policy*, 50, 253–263.

European Academies' Science Advisory Council (EASA). (2014). *Statement: Shale Gas Extraction: Issues of Particular Relevance to the European Union*. Brussels: EASAC.

Everingham, J. A., Pattenden, C., Klimenko, V., & Parmenter, J. (2013). Regulation of resource-based development: Governance challenges and responses in mining regions of Australia. *Environment and Planning C: Government and Policy*, 31, 585–602.

Fahey, L. (2015). "Lock the Gate": Accessing private land for energy. *Australian Resources and Energy Law Journal*, 34(3), 226–250.

Fischel, W. A. (1987). *The economics of zoning laws: A property rights approach to American land use controls*. Baltimore, MD: Johns Hopkins University Press.

Fischel, W. A. (2001). *The homevoter hypothesis: How home values influence local government taxation, school finance, and land-use policies*. Boston: Harvard University Press.

Fisk, J. M. (2016). Fractured relationships: Exploring municipal defiance in Colorado, Texas, and Ohio. *State and Local Government Review*, 48(2), 75–86.

Freudenburg, W. F. (1993). Risk and recreancy: Weber, the division of labor, and the rationality of risk perceptions. *Social Forces*, June 1993 v71 n4 p909(24).

Frosch, D., & Gold, R. (2015, February 25,). How 'orphan' wells leave states holding the cleanup bag. *Wall Street Journal*. Available at: www.wsj.com/articles/how-orphan-wells-leave-states-holding-the-cleanup-bag-1424921403 (accessed 30 November 2016).

Fry, M., Briggle, A., & Kincaid, J. (2015). Fracking and environmental (in)justice in a Texas city. *Ecological Economics*, 117, 97–107.

Gates, P. W. (1968). *History of Public Land Law Development*. Washington, DC: Public Land Law Review Commission, US GPO.

Gillespie, N., Bond, C., Downs, V., & Staggs, J. (2016) Stakeholder trust in the Queensland CSG industry. *APPEA Journal*, 56, 239–245.

Government of New Zealand, Parliamentary Commissioner for the Environment. (2012). *Evaluating the Environmental Impacts of Fracking in New Zealand: An Interim Report*, 43. Available at: www.pce.parliament.nz/publications/evaluating-the-environmental-impacts-of-fracking-in-new-zealand-an-interim-report (accessed November 14, 2016).

Harrison, S. L. (1989). Disposition of the mineral estate on United States public lands. *Public Land and Resources Law Review*, 10, 131–156.

Hepburn, S. (2013). Does unconventional gas require unconventional ownership? An analysis of the functionality of ownership frameworks for unconventional gas development. *Journal of Environmental and Public Health Law*, 8(1), 1–54.

Hurdle, J. (2017) National Public Radio State Impact Webpage. Published April 4, 2017. Available at: Retrieved from: https://stateimpact.npr.org/pennsylvania/2017/04/04/with-governors-signature-maryland-becomes-third-state-to-ban-fracking/ (accessed July 1, 2017).

Hutton, D. (2012). Lessons from the Lock the Gate Movement. *Social Alternatives 31*(1), 15–19.

Jacquet, J. B. (2015). The rise of "private participation" in the planning of energy projects in the rural United States. *Society and Natural Resources, 28*(3).

Jacquet, J. B. & Stedman, R. C. (2011). Natural gas landowner coalitions in New York State: emerging benefits of collective natural resource management. *Journal of Rural Social Sciences, 26*(1), 62.

Jones, K. P., Wellbord, J. F., & Russell, C. J. (2013). Split estates and surface access issues. In *Landmen's Legal Handbook* (5th ed., pp. 181–196): Boulder, CO: Rocky Mountain Mineral Law Foundation.

Kroepsch, A. (2016). New rig on the block: Spatial policy discourse and the new suburban geography of energy production on Colorado's Front Range. *Environmental Communication, 10*(3), 337–351.

Land Access Review Panel (LARP). (2012). *Land Access Framework: 12-Month Review. Report of the Land Access Review Panel.* Queensland Department of Natural Resources and Mines. Available at: https://mines.industry.qld.gov.au/assets/native-title-pdf/Land_Access_Review_Panel_report.pdf (accessed February 15, 2015).

Loh, C. G., & Osland, A. C. (2016). Local land use planning responses to hydraulic fracturing. *Journal of the American Planning Association, 82*(3), 222–235.

Makki, M. (2015). Coal seam gas development and community conflict: A comparative study of community responses to coal seam gas development in Chinchilla and Tara, Queensland. PhD thesis, the University of Queensland.

Matthews, M. (2014, July 31). Anti-fracking laws vs. property rights: Banning drilling also stops landowners from selling their mineral rights. Cue the lawyers. *Wall Street Journal.*

Maurin, C., Trenorden, C., & Rifkin, W. (2016). *Regulatory Approaches in the Unconventional Gas Sector: Scoping Study.* Brisbane, Queensland: University of Queensland, Centre for Coal Seam Gas.

Megbolugbe, I. F., & Linneman, P. D. (1993) Home ownership. *Urban Studies, 30*(4–5), 659–682.

Morrison, T. J. (2014). Developing a regional governance index: The institutional potential of rural regions, *Journal of Rural Studies, 35*, 101–111.

New South Wales Chief Scientist and Engineer (NSWCSE). (2014). *Final Report of the Independent Review of Coal Seam Gas Activities in NSW*, September. Sydney: Government of New South Wales.

New South Wales Department of Industry, Resources and Energy (DIRE). (2016). Landholders & community, Coal seam gas, The facts on CSG, Protections and controls. Available at: www.resourcesandenergy.nsw.gov.au/landholders-and-community/coal-seam-gas/the-facts/protections-and-controls (accessed November 30, 2016).

New South Wales Farmers Federation. (2016). Available at: www.nswfarmers.org.au/news/global-news/farmer-groups-secure-csg-land-access-principles (accessed November 2, 2016).

Nolon, J. R., & Gavin, S. E. (2013). Hydrofracking: State preemption, local power, and cooperative governance. *Case Western Reserve Law Review, 63*(4), 995–1039.

Ostrom, E. (1990). *Governing the Commons: The Evolution of Institutions for Collective Action.* New York: Cambridge University Press.

Ogneva-Himmelberger, Y., & Huang, L. (2015). Spatial distribution of unconventional gas wells and human populations in the Marcellus Shale in the United States: Vulnerability analysis. *Applied Geography, 60,* 165–174.

Queensland Government. (2004/2010/2016). *Petroleum and Gas (Production and Safety) Act 2004.* Brisbane: Department of Natural Resources and Mines.

Reeve, I. (2002). Tiptoeing round the slumbering dragon: Property rights and environmental discourse in rural Australia. In L. Bourke & S. Lockie (Eds.), *Rurality Bites: The Social and Rural Transformation of Rural Australia.* Sydney: Pluto Press.

Ross, M. (1999). The political economy of the resource curse. *World Politics, 51*(2), 297–322.

Ryan, B. (1974). The law surrounding "miner's right": Origin of the mining law of Queensland. *Journal of the Royal Historical Society of Queensland, 9*(5), 101–114.

Sherval, M., & Hardiman, K. (2014). Competing perceptions of the rural idyll: Responses to threats from coal seam gas development in Gloucester, NSW, Australia. *Australian Geographer, 45*(2), 185–203.

Thomson, M. (2005). The lost battle of Queensland farming. *Review – Institute of Public Affairs, 57*(1), 14–15.

Throupe, R., Simons, R., & Mao, X. (2013). A review of hydro "fracking" and its potential effects on real estate. *Journal of Real Estate Literature, 21*(2), 205–232.

Tideman, T. N. (1972). Property as a moral concept. In G. Wunderlich, & W. L. Gibson, Jr. (Eds.), *Perspectives of Property* (pp. 202–205). Pennsylvania, PA: Institute for Research on Land and Water Resources, State College.

Trigger, D., Keenan, J., de Rijke, K., & Rifkin, W. (2014). Aboriginal engagement and agreement-making with a rapidly developing resource industry: Coal seam gas development in Australia. *The Extractive Industries and Society, 1*(2), 176–188.

Vanlandingham, K. E. (1968). Municipal home rule in the United States. *William & Mary Law Review, 10,* 269.

Vasi, I. B., Walker, E. T., Johnson, J. S., & Tan, H. F. (2015). "No Fracking Way!" Documentary Film, Discursive Opportunity, and Local Opposition against Hydraulic Fracturing in the United States, 2010 to 2013. *American Sociological Review, 80*(5), 934–959.

Warner, B., & Shapiro, J. (2013). Fractured, fragmented federalism: A study in fracking regulatory policy. *Publius: The Journal of Federalism, 43*(3), 474–496.

4 Governing unconventional legacies

Lessons from the coalbed methane boom in Wyoming

Kathryn Bills Walsh and Julia H. Haggerty

Introduction

This chapter brings attention to the complexities of governing post-production oil and gas activities or, in industry terms, the "legacy issues" associated with unconventional oil and gas development in the US context. Legacy issues comprise the safe and thorough decommissioning of wells and pipelines and effective mitigation of environmental and social disruption including reclamation of land and water resources disturbed during production.

Although most shale development has not yet entered a post-production phase, coalbed methane development provides an instructive case study in legacy issues. Coalbed methane does not meet standard geologic criteria for unconventional resources, but the pace and scale of development and the extensive infrastructure necessary for development are consistent. This chapter presents a case study of land reclamation following a coalbed methane gas boom in the Powder River Basin of Wyoming. Between 1998 and 2008, at least 16,000 wells were developed in the Powder River Basin (WYOGCC, 2016a)—an arid, sparsely populated region characterized by extensive grasslands, livestock production, and coal mining. Because coalbed methane development has already gone through the boom-bust cycle and is eight years into the legacy period, this case study offers a series of relevant considerations for shale development landscapes in the United States and Europe.

Specifically, this chapter explains factors that have interfered with the effective definition, regulation, and implementation of the reclamation of land and coalbed methane infrastructure in the post-development period in the Powder River Basin. We argue that defining and implementing effective reclamation present a highly complex governance challenge due to three major factors: (1) the absence of clear guidance from the scientific literature about what constitutes successful reclamation; (2) the complexity of both the jurisdictional environment and the oil and gas sector in the coalbed methane space; and, finally, (3) a lack of political will in the state of Wyoming to engage in preemptive environmental regulation. The chapter draws on an extensive review of scientific studies that address the definition and measurement of success in reclamation and policy analysis of developing regulatory and governance issues in Wyoming. The chapter is organized as follows. First, we provide an overview of coalbed methane development in the Powder River Basin and its current legacy challenges. Next, we address the issues of reclamation science, jurisdictional and structural complexity, and the Wyoming policy environment to illustrate that, together, they create a policy environment unlikely to achieve timely and effective reclamation. We then conclude with a discussion relating governance issues identified in the coalbed methane example to the broader scholarly considerations regarding shale governance.

Background: coalbed methane development in the Powder River Basin

The state of Wyoming ranks as one of the most important energy producers in the United States. Second only to Texas in total energy production, the state has a long history of discovering, drilling, and shipping energy resources from its position on the border of the Rocky Mountains and the Central Great Plains to energy hubs and markets. Remote and sparsely populated, Wyoming is one of the last states in the US that remains significantly dependent on natural resource development, at least relative to the overall US economy, which has shifted heavily to tertiary and higher industries. As an outcome of this, and an indicator of Wyoming's dependence on natural resources is the tight coupling of the state's revenue stream to commodity prices. For example, in 2016, in response to the coal industry downturn, the Wyoming legislature cut funds provided to school districts by $36 million and reduced the budget of the University of Wyoming by $34 million, along with making other reductions ("Budget Cuts," 2016).

This boom-bust context is important when considering the dilemmas and complexities surrounding legacy issues in the Powder River Basin. Straddling some 20,000 sq miles of semi-arid grasslands used primarily for livestock production in south-east Montana and north-east Wyoming, the Powder River Basin refers both to a hydrological drainage region and a geologic structural formation. The area's huge coal reserves – some 40 percent of U.S. coal production occurs on strip mines in the region – constitute the source of shallow coalbed methane reserves. In the 1990s, after decades of experimentation, the process to extract coalbed methane advanced with the discovery that underground source formations could be de-watered through pumping to facilitate the escape of gas. By the late 1990s, the boom was on (Ayers, 2002). Operations quickly intensified and up to 3,655 wells were drilled in the Basin in 2001 alone (Ayers, 2002).

As in some shale regions of the United States, the Powder River Basin features a mosaic of different surface, subsurface, and water ownership regimes and a correspondingly diverse group of stakeholders when it comes to regulation and oversight of coalbed methane development. In Wyoming, approximately 11.6 million acres of private land feature a split estate, in which the federal government owns the subsurface minerals ("Split Estate," 2012). Specifically, the Bureau of Land Management (BLM) manages and provides oversight of the federally owned minerals which requires coordination among BLM officials, the surface landowner, and industry.

Ten years after the initial boom in the Powder River Basin, the collapse of the dry gas market in 2008 resulted in a lasting bust, with steep declines in production. In response, many companies that had been active in the region suspended or reduced production, shifting coalbed methane into a post-production phase. However, the failure or restructuring of many companies involved in coalbed methane development has left the state of Wyoming and other stakeholders "holding the bag" when it comes to long-term reclamation of disturbed land and the safe and prudent abandonment of wells and other infrastructure.[1] Four thousand orphaned wells remain on farms and ranches in Wyoming in 2016 ("Orphan Well Program," 2016). Surface reclamation of these wells is especially problematic given the region's semi-arid grassland land cover. Nasen et al. (2011) found that in the grasslands of Saskatchewan, natural gas lease sites established in the 1950s show "no significant improvements in terms of ground cover, species diversity and range health" (p. 203). The authors attribute this to poor impact mitigation strategies and reclamation practices in the study area. They find that "lease sites left abandoned and/or suspended are not returning to a vegetation composition reflective of a healthy, native prairie" (p. 203). This is troubling in light of the extensive scale of surface disturbance by oil and gas activity in the period since 2000 (Allred et al., 2015) and emphasizes the need for a deliberate plan for surface reclamation, as unassisted recovery is unlikely. In Wyoming, neither the state nor federal regulators has inventoried the status of land reclamation efforts, and it stands to reason that where wells are orphaned, so too are reclamation efforts.

Surface reclamation after natural gas development as a multi-dimensional governance challenge

In the following discussion, we outline the key factors contributing to the failure of surface reclamation of natural gas production sites in Wyoming, the ambiguity of reclamation science, and jurisdictional complexity and Wyoming's political context. Our exploration of the consensus – or lack thereof – about what constitutes effective surface reclamation draws from an in-depth review of the literature in ecological and environmental science journals.

Reclamation success in the scientific literature

Post-production reclamation of the Powder River Basin's coalbed methane legacies is an enormous undertaking due to the scale of the development and the harsh physical environment characterizing the region. Coalbed methane production in this remote, arid region involved the construction not only of thousands of wells, but also of thousands of miles of roads, power lines, and pipelines and hundreds of water impoundments. Along the way, thousands of acres of surface vegetation and soil were disturbed. Successful reclamation would remove or permanently ensure the safety and integrity of the pipelines, wells, roadways, and other industrial infrastructure on the landscape and at the same time would attempt to repair the effects of development on soils and surface vegetation. Regulation would in theory focus on documented success in achieving these goals.

However, measuring and documenting reclamation success turn out to be less than straightforward in scientific practice. Indeed, the very concept of defining reclamation "success" has been criticized by reclamation scientists as problematic (Zedler, 2007). Suding (2011) argues that the term "success" has come under fire due to the general ambiguity about the criteria used to measure success, inadequate project monitoring, and limited data availability. Common methods and standards to assess success have not been established. Without explicit criteria to measure success, the language, project outcomes, and implications for policy remain unclear.

Measuring success in studies of restoration science largely consists of assessing technical measures (Ruiz-Jaén & Aide, 2005a; Wortley et al., 2013). Wortley et al. (2013) conducted a comprehensive review of 301 articles on land-based restoration published from 2008–2012 across 71 journals to determine how restoration success is being measured. The authors found that ecological attributes (diversity and abundance, vegetation structure, and ecological functioning) were most often used (94 percent) as opposed to economic and social attributes (3.5 percent). The Society for Ecological Restoration (SER), an international scientific society, suggests six metrics of restoration success (Table 4.1), where the metric is an ecological attribute that can be measured directly or indirectly. SER asserts that "success" involves continued progress toward target goals as demonstrated by some combination of the six attributes. Although the metrics of successful reclamation used by the SER are comprehensive, they are not easily adaptable to policy and accompanying regulations, which often require measurements followed by a determination of project success. Moreover, ecosystem restoration is a time-intensive process. It is not within the scope of most restoration projects to extend their timeframe to allow for full ecosystem recovery, especially considering that unforeseen weather events and pest outbreaks, for example, can delay rehabilitation (Holl & Howarth, 2000). Therefore, measures of success that are promoted by the scientific community may not easily translate into policy.

Moreover, while restoration science has made progress in making its findings relevant to practitioners, the field struggles to provide clear guidance to policy

Table 4.1 SER's six attributes of a successfully restored ecosystem

1	Absence of threats
2	Physical conditions
3	Species composition
4	Structural diversity
5	Ecosystem functionality
6	External exchanges/connectivity

Source: SER (2016).

processes. While there has been a growing body of knowledge that links the work of restoration theory to the practice of reclamation practitioners in the field, the same cannot be said for decision-makers. When Aronson et al. (2010) reviewed the literature published from 2000–2008 in *Restoration Ecology* and 12 scientific journals, they found that 80 percent of the 1,582 peer-reviewed papers analyzed did not address policy impacts or implications of the restoration effort. Without clear language directed at a policy audience, knowledge originating in the scientific community will not translate to decision-makers.

To increase the likelihood of project success and make restoration science more legible for policy-makers, Suding (2011) recommends implementation of evidence-based assessments in restoration science to evaluate the effectiveness of particular restoration techniques. In addition, other studies suggest using reference sites, or sites of comparison, to add rigor to evaluations of restoration success (Choi, 2004; Ruiz-Jaén & Aide, 2005a, 2005b; Wortley et al., 2013). According to the SER (2004), "the reference represents a point of advanced development that lies somewhere along the intended trajectory of the restoration" (p. 5). In addition, historic baselines as a reclamation end goal have been critiqued since ecosystems can shift rapidly based on local conditions and changing climate, making historic targets unrealistic and reclamation success unlikely (Choi, 2004; Hobbs, 2007; Suding, 2011; Zedler et al., 2012). Instead, Choi (2004) champions the acceptance of a futuristic, as opposed to historic, paradigm in restoration (Figure 4.1, where the futuristic approach rejects evaluation based on historic conditions.

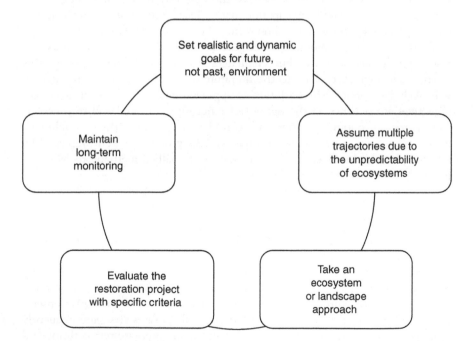

Figure 4.1 Choi's (2004) futuristic restoration.

Similarly, Zedler et al. (2012) argue for the implementation of long-term adaptive restoration acknowledging that restoring lands to their pre-disturbed state may not be achievable. In this framework, restoration practitioners can begin their efforts as long-term experiments, "aiming for historical targets and gradually ruling out those that can no longer be achieved ... as assessments indicate the objectives that are unachievable, more realistic targets would be adopted and new experiments might begin" (p. 38). By doing so, time and money can be saved by allowing restoration practitioners to adjust efforts, based on precise objectives, to more suitable areas. This framework is especially relevant to unconventional oil and gas restoration since this body of knowledge is just emerging and adaptive restoration facilitates a "learn-as-you-go" mentality.

To mitigate common barriers to restoration project success, Geist and Galatowitsch (1999) champion a reciprocal, participatory model predicated on understanding how humans and nature can mutually benefit from restoration. The authors suggest that

> [their] model shows human contributions aimed at addressing the needs of a given restoration area. As the restoration process progresses, the area itself may provide contributions to the needs of humans. As human needs are met, more contributions to the restoration area are possible.
>
> (p. 974)

Geist and Galatowitsch (1999) believe the best way of accomplishing this is through engagement and participation among local community members in the planning, implementation, and monitoring of ecological restoration.

Restoration science provides ample guidelines for increasing the likelihood of restoration project success, but challenges emerge regarding the ways this science is shared. According to the literature, a positive reclamation outcome will likely be reached when a futuristic approach guides projects, clear project objectives are outlined at the outset, reference sites are used and technical as well as socio-economic measures are considered. However, these conclusions have largely failed to translate into policy. This problem is well illustrated by the complexities involved in the governance of coalbed methane reclamation in the Powder River Basin of Wyoming.

Jurisdictional and structural complexity

Two primary sources of complexity exist in the regulatory space around surface reclamation of unconventional oil and gas development: (1) the complicated jurisdictional and ownership regimes of land and minerals; and (2) the structure of the upstream oil and gas industry. Both sources complicate the reclamation of wells and infrastructure by necessitating the involvement of a complex ensemble of stakeholders (Figure 4.2), with industry stakeholders changing frequently as employees cycle through the landscape and with corporate restructuring and ownership change.

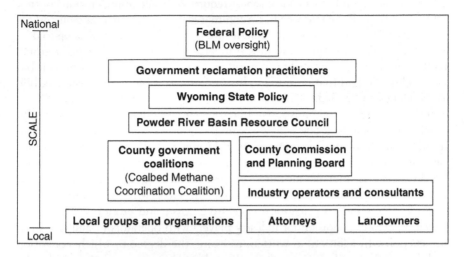

Figure 4.2 Actors contributing to reclamation outcomes in the Powder River Basin, Wyoming.

As an example of this complexity, in Wyoming, the regulatory environment for reclamation differs based on who owns the land (or minerals) that requires reclamation. Reclamation of public, federally-owned land (or minerals) is carried out by the BLM. Conversely, the states are responsible for reclamation on privately-owned land within their boundaries. The criteria for what constitutes reclamation success varies between the federal government and states and also from state to state. According to the BLM (n.d.) *Surface Operating Standards and Guidelines for Oil and Gas Exploration and Development*, or the Gold Book:

> Reclamation generally can be judged successful when a self-sustaining, vigorous, diverse, native (or otherwise approved) plant community is established on the site, with a density sufficient to control erosion and non-native plant invasion and to re-establish wildlife habitat or forage production.... The site must be free of State- or county-listed noxious weeds, oil field debris, contaminated soil, and equipment.
>
> (pp. 43–44)

For lands administered by the state, standards for evaluating reclamation success are vague in comparison to the federal guidelines. According to Wyoming Statute 30–5–401:

> Reclamation means the restoring of the surface directly affected by oil and gas operations, as closely as reasonably practicable, to the condition that existed prior to oil and gas operations, or as otherwise agreed to in writing by the oil and gas operator and the surface owner.

Clearly federal standards are most robust requiring revegetation, erosion control, and removal of all noxious weeds, contaminated soils, and remaining oil and gas equipment. Wyoming state requirements are not as stringent and less up to date with the current literature. Wyoming standards require that the land be restored to the condition that existed prior to oil and gas development. However, it has been acknowledged that restoring to historic targets is often not feasible (Choi, 2004; Hobbs, 2007; Suding, 2011).

Exacerbating this administrative heterogeneity are discrepancies among the ten BLM regional field offices in Wyoming. Curran (2014) compared the reclamation criteria of the Wyoming BLM field offices and found that each office operates using different criteria to assess reclamation success. The most comprehensive criteria include measures of percentage vegetative cover, erosion control, weeds, grass, forbs, shrubs, and plant vigor while the least comprehensive only consider percentage vegetative cover and erosion control. This variation creates confusion for industry players with operators in multiple BLM jurisdictions. In addition, as written, assessing the degree to which vegetation stabilizes soils is subjective and misaligned with recommendations from the literature that promote the use of evidence-based assessments when judging reclamation success (Suding, 2011).

Mirroring the jurisdictional challenges that are a byproduct of the BLM's structure in Wyoming, policy approaches to implementing reclamation vary across and even within administrative scales. The backbone of federal and state reclamation policy is environmental assurance bonding.

Bonding theoretically ensures implementation of reclamation through the following process: Prior to drilling, in the permitting phase, operators must pay a bond to be released after development is completed and a checklist of reclamation activities have taken place. Blanket bonding, a practice that allows operators drilling multiple wells within one state to pay a single bond to cover all wells within the state, pays far lower amounts than if each well was bonded individually but, theoretically, adequate to cover the risk of a small number of abandonments. Bonds provide an incentive for companies to complete final reclamation as opposed to walking away leaving an orphaned well and the reclamation to the state (Gerard, 2000). The incentive is not only financial, but, theoretically, involves their desire to manage their reputation to ensure the success of future proposals to work in the state. Table 4.2 displays the bonding structure imposed by the federal government while Table 4.3 shows the environmental bond

Table 4.2 Federal bond requirements for onshore oil and gas production sites

Bond type	Bond amount ($)
Individual lease bond	10,000
Statewide (blanket) bond	25,000
Nationwide (blanket) bond	150,000

Source: U.S. GAO.

Table 4.3 State of Wyoming environmental bonding system, effective February 1, 2016

Bond type	Bond amount ($)
Individual well	10 per foot of depth
Multiple wells (blanket bond)	100,000

Source: Storrow (2015).

requirements for the state of Wyoming. Consider that for multiple wells drilled on private land by one industry company in Wyoming, a bond of $100,000 would be required while the same scenario on public land would only require a bond of $25,000.

Shortcomings of the environmental bonding system are well documented in the literature (Andersen et al., 2009; Holl & Howarth, 2000; Igarashi et al., 2014; Mitchell & Casman, 2011). Bond amounts are commonly critiqued as being far too low (Andersen et al., 2009; Holl & Howarth, 2000; Igarashi et al., 2014; Mitchell & Casman, 2011). Andersen et al. (2009) found that for orphaned natural gas wells in Wyoming between 1997–2007, there was a difference of $22,253 in the bond amount paid per well and the actual cost of reclamation. Furthermore, companies can decide to forfeit the bond if the cost of reclamation is higher than the bond posted, which it often is, and instead walk away (Holl & Howarth, 2000; Igarashi et al., 2014). Conversely, if the bond is too high, industry capital can be tied up, limiting future investment (Gerard, 2000).

Wyoming offers a case study in the problem of setting bond amounts too low in an uncertain market environment. In the Powder River Basin alone, there are at least 3,000 orphaned coalbed methane wells that require reclamation by the state of Wyoming (Bleizeffer, 2015).

Encouragingly, the Wyoming Oil and Gas Conservation Commission (WYOGCC) has plugged and reclaimed 1,018 orphaned wells since 2014 using funds collected from industry operators through taxation and bonding in a systematic well plugging and clean-up program spearheaded by Wyoming Governor Matt Mead in 2013 (WYOGCC, 2016b). From 2004–2013, the state had only cleaned up 183 orphaned wells (Storrow, 2013). However, despite state efforts, the number of orphaned wells continues to outpace the number reclaimed. The circumstances leading to the orphaned well phenomenon reinforce the governance challenges presented by the characteristics of the shale development industry in the United States.

Approximately 130 industry companies operated in the Powder River Basin at the peak of coalbed methane development. Industry operators came from all over the country, including Colorado, Texas, Illinois, Utah, Oklahoma, Michigan, Montana, Alabama, New Mexico and, of course, Wyoming. When coalbed methane development was expanding, large, established companies like Marathon Oil, Fidelity Exploration and Production Co., and Peabody Natural Gas dominated the production landscape. As profitability waned in a poor price environment, the larger industry companies began selling their mineral holdings to smaller operators. The smaller operators lacked adequate capital to conduct reclamation, and worse, to avoid bankruptcy. The result has been a high number of bankrupt companies that left behind thousands of orphaned natural gas wells across the Basin. Landowners are often left out of the loop on the change of title of mineral rights and are later unable to reach companies involved in bankruptcy proceedings. The chain of communication between surface owner and entities responsible for surface reclamation has been completely broken.

Wyoming policy environment

A lack of political will in the state of Wyoming to engage in pre-emptive environmental regulation has contributed to the governance challenge concerning unconventional oil and gas reclamation. In 2007, mineral development in Wyoming produced $14 billion in revenue through the collection of severance taxes from industry, more than any other means of state revenue generation (Cook, 2014). As a result, the Wyoming regulatory environment has long been subject to industry capture: for example, in the 1980s, the oil and gas sector successfully obtained an exemption to the state's relatively progressive Industrial Siting Act (Haggerty & McBride, 2016). The state of Wyoming created regulations ahead of federal regulators, including those that concern pre-fracking disclosure requirements, chemical identification requirements and trade secret exemptions, under the direction of former Democratic Governor Dave Freudenthal. However, this was only done "[to] preempt federal regulators on this [fracking] to maintain state control over this policy area" (Cook, 2014, p. 107). The intentions here were to pre-emptively ensure state control of Wyoming's growing fracking industry.

Despite the legislature's pattern of reluctance to engage in regulation, some issues have turned into crises that require response. Such was the nature of the orphaned well issue. After the discovery that the state was on the hook for some 4,000 orphaned wells to the cost of at least $125 million, the Wyoming Oil and Gas Conservation Commission (WYOGCC) voted unanimously to update the state's bonding structure effective from February 1, 2016 ("Rule Changes," 2015). The former rules required a bond of $10,000 for individual wells less than 2,000 feet, and $20,000 for wells more than 2,000 feet in depth. The updated rules responded to an economic analysis of real reclamation costs to arrive at a new bond rate of $10 per foot for all individual wells which can be adjusted after three years to account for actual plugging costs and inflation. Blanket bonds were increased from $75,000 to $100,000 (Storrow, 2015). This improvement, although a sign of progress, was enacted long after it could have any impact on coalbed methane reclamation activities. Furthermore, some policy analysts doubt that the increased blanket bond amounts will suffice, specifically when considering the scale of extensive horizontal drilling (Storrow, 2015).

Discussion

The legacy challenges present in the Wyoming coalbed methane landscapes – thousands of orphaned wells, permanently degraded surface vegetation, and largely abandoned water management infrastructure – are clearly a scenario to be avoided at future development sites. The political environment in Wyoming created distinct barriers to effective regulation of the coalbed methane infra-structure. All the same, the coalbed methane legacy crisis in Wyoming high-lights some of the inherent features of unconventional oil and gas development that create enormous difficulties from a policy standpoint. These characteristics merit attention as international policy-making forums undertake strategic environmental assessments to inform the development of novel policy.

The greatest challenge from a legacy management standpoint in coalbed methane is a familiar one for shale development in the United States: the sheer intensity of infrastructure and the number of players involved in its installation, maintenance, and ultimate decommissioning. Even the most robust regulatory framework would be hard pressed to accommodate the basic administrative task of managing the huge number of actors and the great number of facilities in this upstream development space. The turnover and cycling in ownership and asso-ciated reclamation obligations after the bust greatly exacerbated the challenges of overseeing and enforcing existing regulations to the point of a major policy failure.

The case of the abandoned coalbed methane infrastructure and failed recla-mation also points to the need for capacity in the form of funding and technolo-gies to accomplish clean-up, and contingency plans for accomplishing that clean-up in the event of major changes in the economic and market environ-ment. It is clear that bond amounts must be adequate to cover the actual cost of reclamation activities (Andersen et al., 2009; Holl & Howarth, 2000). Without this policy-driven protection, the host state and taxpayers can be left to fund the clean-up effort.

A potential solution to the problem of effective oversight of a sprawling infrastructure and enforcement across a diverse field of players and stakeholders is coordination and capacity building. Here the industry has the potential to be a strong ally, as companies typically hold superior technical and institutional capacities for monitoring and inventorying assets than do state or federal agen-cies. However, in the US, the proprietary nature of corporate assets often halts any effort to use the knowledge base of industry for the benefit of effective regu-lation. Whatever the role of private industry, the necessity to build capacity on the part of regulatory agencies cannot be overstated – their technological, administrative, and enforcement capacities have to grow before they are out-paced by rapid development, and have to remain in place after development slows. Here again, smart technology has the potential to provide important capacity through monitoring networks using tools such as remote sensing.

Coordination to provide effective legacy management proves complicated due to jurisdictional fragmentation, a known problem for shale management in the United States and abroad (Cook, 2014; Rabe, 2014; Warner & Shapiro, 2013; Zirogiannis et al., 2016). The vast differences in shale gas regulation from state to state (Rabe, 2014; Warner & Shapiro, 2013; Zirogiannis et al., 2016) as well as tension and competition between state and local governments for autonomy and authority (Davis, 2014) all work as obstacles to coordinated legacy management.

The related lack of consistency and outdated nature of some of the reclamation standards also speak to the fundamental challenge of simply defining reclamation and establishing the metrics necessary to monitor its progress. However, the recent literature offers policy strategies to accommodate the inherent complexities of reclamation (Igarashi et al., 2014; Mitchell & Casman, 2011). For reclamation on federal lands, the US BLM recently shifted to an approach governed by maximum allowable disturbed acreage meaning, "a firm has to do a sufficient amount of reclamation on currently disturbed lands to qualify for developing wells in other areas" (Igarashi et al., 2014, p. 7). In effect, this is a form of adaptive restoration, a framework championed by Zedler et al. (2012) that necessitates strong project management and regular monitoring. By mandating reclamation throughout the course of the project, restoration techniques can be assessed and modified as needed. Igarashi et al. (2014) illustrate through economic modeling that completing interim reclamation throughout the lifespan of the well decreases terminal reclamation costs after production ceases. Moreover, Chenoweth et al. (2010) compare the costs associated with unsuccessful reclamation of oil and gas production sites to instances when reclamation is completed successfully in its first attempt and found that, "reclamation failures can result in a 50% cost increase over initiating proper reclamation techniques from project implementation" (p. 13). Still, all of these strategies hinge on investment in robust monitoring and implementation capacities, ideally in public-private partnerships that leverage existing technologies and knowledge. We recommend that policy-relevant research should focus not only on the biophysical aspects of reclamation, which have a wide scholarly literature, but also on the stakeholder desires about reclamation processes and their outcomes. Research that accurately describes stakeholder perceptions of reclamation targets can help contribute to effective reclamation policy.

Conclusion

In the Powder River Basin of Wyoming, coalbed methane development was rapid and intense, all the while operating without the necessary policy-driven protections for landowners, the community, and the environment. The result is a landscape littered with orphaned wells that state funds must pay to reclaim. Countless landowners face the challenge of ranching and carrying out daily activities on unreclaimed land without any certainty of when restoration will take place.

Landowners have had to turn to other authorities for information and assistance, including the local resource council and county government coalition. While filling an important niche, the state should adopt a more proactive approach by drafting a deliberate and comprehensive reclamation policy and providing the means for adequate enforcement. The findings of this case study are closely related to what can be expected regarding the legacy of shale gas production. To avoid delayed restoration and destructive legacy issues, a revision of state and federal reclamation policy is needed to prevent the proliferation of orphaned wells in shale basins and the resulting financial burden on host communities and taxpayers.

Note

1 Orphaned refers to wells without a responsible operator. Orphaned wells emerge when the companies that drill and/or operate the wells go out of business at the regional or national scale and are therefore unable to continue overseeing the well. Abandoned is a broader term that includes any wells that have ceased to produce and are no longer actively managed.

References

Allred, B. W., Smith, W. K., Twidwell, D., Haggerty, J. H., Running, S. W., Naugle, D. E., & Fuhlendorf, S. D. (2015). Ecosystem services lost to oil and gas in North America. *Science*, 348(6233), 401–402.

Andersen, M., Coupal, R., & White, B. (2009). Reclamation costs and regulation of oil and gas development with application to Wyoming. *Western Economics Forum*, 8(1), 40–48.

Aronson, J., Blignaut, J. N., Milton, S. J., et al. (2010). Are socioeconomic benefits of restoration adequately quantified? A meta-analysis of recent papers (2000–2008) in *Restoration Ecology* and 12 other scientific journals. *Restoration Ecology*, 18(2), 143–154.

Ayers, W. B. (2002). Coalbed gas systems, resources, and production and a review of contrasting cases from the San Juan and Powder River Basins. *The Association of Petroleum Geologists Journal*, 86(11), 1853–1890.

Bleizeffer, D. (2015). Coalbed methane: Boom, bust and hard lessons. Retrieved February 12, 2016, from www.wyohistory.org/essays/coalbed-methane-boom-bust-and-hard-lessons

BLM (Bureau of Land Management). *Surface Operating Standards and Guidelines for Oil and Gas Exploration and Development*. Retrieved March 11, 2016, from www.blm.gov/wo/st/en/prog/energy/oil_and_gas/best_management_practices/gold_book.html

Budget Cuts. (2016). Wyoming Public Media. Retrieved October 7, 2016, from http://wyomingpublicmedia.org/term/budget-cuts

Chenoweth, D., Holland, D., Jacob, G., Kruckenberg, L., Rizza, J., & Whiteley, B. (2010). Economic benefits of completing reclamation successfully for the first time for oil and gas sites. Paper presented at the 41st International Erosion Control Association, Dallas, Texas.

Choi, Y. D. (2004). Theories for ecological restoration in changing environment: Toward "futuristic" restoration. *Ecological Research*, 19(1), 75–81.

Cook, J. J. (2014). Who's regulating who? Analyzing fracking policy in Colorado, Wyoming, and Louisiana. *Environmental Practice*, 16(2), 102–112.

Curran, M. (2014). Using data management to improve oil and gas pad reclamation. Unpublished master's thesis. University of Wyoming.

Davis, C. (2014). Substate federalism and fracking policies: Does state regulatory authority trump local land use autonomy? *Environmental Science & Policy, 48,* 8397–8403.

Geist, C., & Galatowitsch, S. M. (1999). Reciprocal model for meeting ecological and human needs in restoration projects. *Conservation Biology, 13*(5), 970–979.

Gerard, D. (2000). The law and economics of reclamation bonds. *Resources Policy, 26*(4), 189–197.

Haggerty, J. H. & McBride, K. (2016). Does local monitoring empower fracking host communities? A case study from the gas fields of Wyoming. *Journal of Rural Studies, 43,* 234–247.

Hobbs, R. J. (2007). Setting effective and realistic restoration goals: Key directions for research. *Restoration Ecology, 15*(2), 354–357.

Holl, K. D., & Howarth, R. B. (2000). Paying for restoration. *Restoration Ecology, 8*(3), 260–267.

Igarashi, Y., Coupal, R., Finnoff, D., & Andersen, M. (2014). Economics of oil and gas development in the presence of reclamation and bonding requirements. Paper presented at the 2014 Annual Meeting of the Agricultural & Applied Economics Association, Minneapolis, MN.

Mitchell, A. L., & Casman, E. A. (2011). Economic incentives and regulatory framework for shale gas well site reclamation in Pennsylvania. *Environmental Science and Technology, 45,* 9506–9514.

Nasen, L. C., Noble, B. F., & Johnstone, J. F. (2011). Environmental effects of oil and gas lease sites in a grassland ecosystem. *Journal of Environmental Management, 92,* 195–204.

Orphan Well Program. WYOGCC rules and procedures regarding the Orphan Well Program. (2016). Retrieved October 7, 2016, from http://wogcc.state.wy.us/Orpan-Wells.cfm.

Rabe, B. G. (2014). Shale play politics: The intergovernmental odyssey of American shale governance. *Environmental Science and Technology, 48,* 8369–8375.

Ruiz-Jaén, M. C., & Aide T. M. (2005a). Restoration success: How is it being measured? *Restoration Ecology, 13*(3), 569–577.

Ruiz-Jaén, M. C., & Aide T. M. (2005b). Vegetation structure, species diversity, and ecosystem processes as measures of restoration success. *Forest Ecology and Management, 218*(1–3), 159–173.

Rule Changes. (2015). Retrieved October 7, 2016, from http://wogcc.state.wy.us/downloads/proposed_rules_2015/CH3_CLEAN_Adopted151208.pdf

SER (Society for Ecological Restoration). (2004). *SER International Primer on Ecological Restoration.* Retrieved March 23, 2016, from www.ser.org/docs/default-document-library/ser_primer.pdf?sfvrsn=2

SER (Society for Ecological Restoration). (2016). International Standards for the Practice of Ecological Restoration – Including Principles and Key Concepts. Retrieved May 18, 2017, from http://c.ymcdn.com/sites/www.ser.org/resource/resmgr/docs/SER_International_Standards.pdf

Split Estate Mineral Ownership. (2012, April 18). Retrieved October 7, 2016, from www.blm.gov/wy/st/en/programs/mineral_resources/split-estate.html

Storrow, B. (2013, December 11). Wyoming Gov. Matt Mead announces plan to plug 1,200 abandoned oil and gas wells. *Casper Star Tribune.* Retrieved October 7, 2016.

Storrow, B. (2015, December 8). Wyoming raises bonding requirements for oil and gas wells. *Casper Star Tribune.* Retrieved October 7, 2016.

Suding, K. N. (2011). Toward an era of restoration in ecology: Successes, failures, and opportunities ahead. *Annual Review of Ecology, Evolution, and Systematics, 42,* 465–487.

United States Government Accountability Office. *Surface Mining: Cost and Availability of Reclamation Bonds.* Retrieved March 11, 2016, from www.gao.gov/products/PEMD-88-17

Warner, B., & Shapiro, J. (2013). Fractured, fragmented federalism: A study in fracking regulatory policy. *Publius: A Journal of Federalism, 43*(3), 474–496.

Wortley, L., Hero J.-M., & Howes, M. (2013). Evaluating ecological restoration success: A review of the literature. *Restoration Ecology, 21*(5), 537–543.

WYOGCC (Wyoming Oil and Gas Conservation Commission). (2016a). Coalbed methane wells by county. Retrieved October 7, 2016, from http://wogcc.state.wy.us/countapd.cfm

WYOGCC (Wyoming Oil and Gas Conservation Commission). (2016b). Wyoming Oil and Gas Conservation Commission begins 2016 reclamation work on orphaned wells. Retrieved October 7, 2016, from http://wogcc.state.wy.us/pio/OrphanWellNews Release_052616.pdf

Wyoming Statutes. Oil and Gas Definitions. § 30–5–401 (2011).

Zedler, J. B. (2007). Success: An unclear, subjective descriptor of restoration outcomes. *Ecological Restoration, 25*(3), 162–168.

Zedler, J. B., Doherty J. M., & Miller, N. A. (2012). Shifting restoration policy to address landscape change, novel ecosystems, and monitoring. *Ecology and Society, 17*(4), 36–49.

Zirogiannis, N., Alcorn, J., Rupp, J., Carley, S., & Graham, J. D. (2016). State regulation of unconventional gas development in the U.S.: An empirical evaluation. *Energy Research and Social Science, 11,* 142–154.

5   Governing shale gas in Germany

Annette Elisabeth Töller and Michael Böcher

Introduction

When analysing political processes leading to the adoption of environmental regulation, more often than not, strict regulatory measures are proposed in the beginning, and then, under the pressure of powerful business interests and possibly supported by conservative or liberal political parties, they are watered down until no measure or slim regulation is adopted in the end (Dionigi, 2017; Markussen & Svendsen, 2005). The case of regulating shale gas fracking in Germany is interesting because the logic is the reverse. The process started in 2011 with a weak regulation in place and an only slightly stricter regulation proposed in 2013. Since the regulatory package adopted in summer 2016 came into force in early 2017, commercial shale gas fracking has been prohibited. From a theoretical point of view, this case demonstrates that business interests cannot always influence political decisions and party politicians do not always behave as expected. It can be shown that an analytical framework looking at the interaction of problem structure, institutions and actors, is useful for explaining such contingent results of political processes.

In Germany, there are between 0.7 and 2.3 trillion cubic metres of shale gas that could be extracted through fracking (BGR, 2012, p. 48). The largest shale gas deposits are presumed to be in Lower Saxony and North Rhine-Westphalia (Meiners, 2012, p. 58). Starting in 2007, a number of search permits (called *Aufsuchungsgenehmigungen*), which have the character of licences, were issued, but shale gas fracking has so far not been undertaken.

Although fracking has been discussed politically since 2011, fracking-specific regulation was not adopted in Germany until June 2016. Therefore, fracking, like other, conventional, sectors in the mining of underground fossil resources fell under the regulation of the Federal Mining Act (BBergG) adopted in 1980, the aim of which is to secure the supply of raw materials. In this regulation, neither were, from a *procedural* point of view, the relevant participation of residents, local communities, or water authorities provided for, nor, from the perspective of *substantive* law, were environmental interests considered appreciably. Since 2013, two different federal governments have proposed two very different regulations for fracking under increasing public pressure: A regulation package proposed in 2013 contained a relatively moderate regulation of fracking, but it was not admitted into parliamentary procedure. At the end of 2014, a new draft law was proposed by a new federal government and submitted officially in the Spring of 2015, which contained a relatively far-reaching ban of shale gas fracking. Due to different points of conflict within the grand Coalition as well as between the government and the *Länder* (states), and between the *Länder*, the draft was shelved for a year before it was adopted in late June 2016 – in a clearly tightened-up version. Since this regulation came into force in February 2017, commercial fracking of shale gas has been prohibited. In 2021, the German *Bundestag* (parliament) is supposed to review this prohibition. In principle, four test wells for research purposes will be allowed, but only if the corresponding *Land* government approves this. In the beginning, the debate was not so different from that in the UK (Cairney et al., 2016) and could possibly have ended in shale gas fracking being carried out in the not so distant future. Yet today, the ban comes close to the one adopted in France in 2011 (Chailleux & Moyson, 2016, p. 115), but it took some manoeuvring to reach it.

The amount of scholarly literature on the topic is limited. Aside from a number of scientific-technical assessments (particularly BGR, 2012, 2016; Meiners, 2012; UBA, 2012, 2014) and energy industry publications (for example, Rehbock, 2013; ZEW, 2013), as well as a few more recent review volumes and monographs from different specialised perspectives (Habrich-Böcker, Kirchner, & Weißenberg, 2015; Zittel, 2016), there are mostly legal essays and assessments dedicated to different aspects of fracking (for example, Attendorn, 2011; Ludwig, 2012; Böhm, 2013; Eftekharzadeh, 2013; Frenz, 2013; Gaßner & Buchholz, 2013). To date, analyses in political science have dealt mostly with the relevant influence of citizens' initiatives (Burgartz, 2013; Yang, 2015), the role of discourse and discourse coalitions (Schirrmeister, 2014), as well as the dialogue process that Exxon initiated (Bornemann, 2016). Tosun and Lang (2016) analyse the political process in Germany from the perspective of the advocacy coalition framework and they identify discourse coalitions for and against fracking at different periods. Other chapters in the same book investigate other countries, e.g., the UK (Cairney et al. 2016) and France (Chailleux & Moyson, 2016). The newer developments in Germany (the political process, from the draft in early 2015 to the law in 2016) have been analysed recently in a detailed case study by Töller and Böcher (2016).

This chapter presents a qualitative case study on the process of governing shale gas in Germany. In a first step, it analyses and compares the above-mentioned four different alternatives of governing shale gas and in particular addresses the philosophy of the regulation and the role of different stakeholders (citizens, local communities, water authorities, environmental groups) in it. Comparing the four alternatives across time, we observe an increasing stringency in shale gas regulation, which is opposed to what we would expect in environmental policy. In a second step, the chapter presents an analytical framework and discusses possible driving forces of this somewhat surprising result. Whereas neither the possible role of shale gas for national energy policy development nor partisan politics or energy industry's power had a relevant impact on the decision-making, we identified three major driving forces that caused the strict regulation that was adopted in the end: First, the regionally disparate occurrence of shale gas, which produces, locally and among the *Länder*, different concerns regarding fracking, and so eliminates the party differences, especially at the federal level. Second, the complex distribution of power within German federalism, due to which the *Land* government – even though they have no authority to legislate in this field – had a substantial influence on the regulation of fracking. Third, citizens' initiatives have played a major role in influencing the public debate. The chapter ends with a conclusion that summarises the relevant results and addresses the remaining open questions.

Comparing four alternatives of governing shale gas in Germany

The Federal Mining Act

As long as there was no other regulation, the authorisation for fracking fell under the Federal Mining Act, enacted in 1980, which came into force on 1 January 1982. The primary goal of this law was to secure the supply of raw materials (§1 Nr. 1 BBergG; Böhm, 2013, p. 49). The law sets out the concession and operations plan procedures for the exploration and extraction of mineral resources that are available for mining. The project sponsor attains a legal position with the exploration permit in accordance with Article 7 of the Federal Mining Act, through which he or she is protected from competing applications for the exploration and production fields in question (a concession, Böhm, 2013, p. I). For the actual exploration, other permits are required: operation plans according to the Federal Mining Act and permits according to specialised legislation, e.g. the Water Resources Act (*Wasserhaushaltsgesetz*, WHG) (Böhm, 2013, p. II). According to Article 11 No. 10 of the Federal Mining Act, an exploration permit will be denied when "preponderant public interests preclude the exploration in the entire field", among other reasons. Also, in this category fall environmental issues that are not mentioned explicitly as possible grounds for denial and that are only considered tenuously, due to, among other things, the requirement specifying "the entire field to be allocated" (Eftekharzadeh, 2013, p. 704). Businesses wishing to obtain an exploration permit apply to the appropriate mining authority (at the *Land* level). According to Article 15 of the Federal Mining Act, the mining authority must then give the opportunity to those authorities representing the public interest (water authorities in particular) to express their opinion in accordance with Article 11 No. 10 of the Federal Mining Act (Attendorn, 2011, p. 567). However, their opinion *need not* be taken into consideration. As opposed to the situation in the United Kingdom, municipalities have no guaranteed influence over this decision. Whether municipalities are to be included among these authorities representing public interests is a matter of dispute among lawyers (Böhm, 2013, p. 49f.). In the past, local communities in which exploration was supposed to be carried out were not involved (Attendorn, 2011, p. 567; Eftekharzadeh, 2013, p. 705), so that mayors as well as citizens often found out only through the press that an exploration permit had been issued in the realm of their municipality (Ausschuss für Umweltschutz, Naturschutz und Reaktorsicherheit, 2011, p. 14). At first glance, the mining authority has no discretion, meaning that when there is no reason for denial, the applicant has a legal claim to the issuance of a permit (Böhm, 2013, p. 50). However, legal experts debate whether this could be challenged, insofar as the stipulations derived from water law might redefine the "preponderant public interests" (Frenz, 2016). Environmental impact assessments (EIAs) for fracking projects were required for wells starting at a daily extraction volume of more than $500,000 \, m^3$, according to Article 1 No. 2 of the EIA Mining Ordinance, a level which would usually not be reached in fracking sites.

The regulation proposed in 2013

In February 2013, the former Minister of the Environment, Altmaier from the Conservative Party (CDU) and former Minister of Economics, Rösler from the liberals (FDP), agreed to an initial proposal for a specific regulation for shale gas fracking (BMU & BMWi, 2013), which was sharpened up on a few points in the consultations that followed. The philosophy of the regulation was "that the procedure can be applied under the condition that the protection of drinking water is ensured, and that no adverse impact on the environment occurs" (BMU & BMWi, 2013). Accordingly, the Federal Mining Act, the EIA Mining Ordinance and the Water Resources Act were to be strengthened with regard to the authorisation of fracking. In particular, shale gas fracking in drinking water protection areas was to be prohibited; the mining authorities, moreover, were to be allowed to issue permits only in agreement with the water authorities. Furthermore, a general EIA (Environmental Impact Assessment) requirement was to be introduced for fracking projects. EIA would mean that within the licensing procedure environmental impacts would have to be identified, reported and systematically evaluated and the resulting information would have to be presented to the public. Moreover, participation procedure for the general public, representatives of public interests (local communities, environmental groups, etc.) and a variety of public authorities would be included (Staeck, Malek, & Heinelt, 2001). However, the draft was not introduced to parliamentary proceedings in the summer, because support in the government coalition appeared not to be secured.

The regulation proposed in 2015

At the end of 2014, the grand coalition then in power agreed on a new regulatory package that included major changes to the Water Resources Act, the Federal Nature Conservation Act, as well as to the Federal Mining Act and the EIA Mining Ordinance, and that was officially submitted in April 2015 (BMUB,

2015; BMWi, 2015; BT Drs. 18/4713).[1] By means of a permit requirement for water usage in the Water Resources Act, fracking for natural gas in shale and coal beds was supposed to be categorically prohibited above 3,000 m. Exploration drillings for scientific purposes were supposed to be possible in depths at or beyond 3,000 m, as long as the fracking fluid did not jeopardise water quality. Starting in 2018, an independent expert commission[2] was meant to examine and decide, in annual reports, whether the environmental impacts were innocuous and the risks controllable (Boehme-Neßler, 2015). In this case, the mining and water authorities could issue permits for commercial purposes from 2019 onwards.

Any kind of fracking (shale gas or tight gas ore coalbed gas) in sensitive areas (water protection areas and mineral spring protected areas serving the public water supply) would be banned. This ban was supposed to be able to be extended, by means of state law, to the catchment area of mineral water deposits. Moreover, there was to be no fracking in nature conservation areas or in national parks.[3] If fracking was not prohibited, there should be a general EIA requirement, as well as requirements of publication and reporting of all substances and mixtures used. Finally, in the case of mining damage, the burden of proof should be reversed (BMUB, 2015; BMWi, 2015, BT-Drs. 18/4713). The legal package was enacted at the beginning of April 2015 in the Cabinet and in May 2015 it was debated in the German *Bundestag* and in the *Bundesrat* (Federal Council), but then it was not approved until summer 2016 (see below).

The regulation adopted in 2016

The regulatory package that was finally approved in the German *Bundestag* shortly before the summer recess of 2016 is based essentially on the draft outlined above, but it contains five central changes with regard to shale gas fracking:

1. Commercial fracking in shale, argillaceous rock and marl, as well as coal seams is not permitted, according to the Water Resources Act and is therefore prohibited – no longer with the scientifically controversial restriction, "to 3,000 m".
2. This ban applies indefinitely (as previously intended), but it must be reviewed in 2021 (as opposed to 2019, as stated previously).
3. The number of possible scientific test drillings is limited to four.
4. Although the expert commission may submit a recommendation on whether the environmental impact of the test drilling appears harmless, and therefore the risks for fracking appear controllable, in the end, the Parliament, the German *Bundestag*, will decide whether fracking will be allowed in future.
5. Test drilling can only take place if the competent *Land* government agrees to it (BT Umwelt-Ausschuss, Drs. 18(16)401 and BT-Drs. 18/4713). Fracking for tight gas in sandstone remains permissible, but

only under the conditions described above, however, which have been strengthened in a few points.

(see Töller & Böcher, 2016)

If we compare the four alternatives of governing shale gas in Germany across time (see Table 5.1), it becomes quite clear that they display, both procedurally and substantively, an increasing consideration of environmental issues, starting from the Federal Mining Act, the proposal of 2013 and the regulation package from the end of 2014 to the regulation package finally approved in 2016. This development is opposed to what we usually experience in environmental policy and requires an explanation.

Explaining the result

In Table 5.2, we summarise the most important events during the German fracking debate between 2007 and 2017 (for more details, see Töller & Böcher, 2016).

Our study is based on the theoretical and methodological roots of (comparative) policy analysis (for overviews, see e.g. Brans et al., 2017 or Cairney, 2011). Policy analysis is the sub-discipline of political science that explains the emergence of public policies (policy output). In this field there are two main ways to connect theories with empirical studies (see Wenzelburger & Wolf, 2015). One strand of studies strictly focuses on policy results and – mostly working with large numbers of cases and quantitative methods – tests theories as alternative explanations. For example, they analyse whether it is institutions, partisan politics or the power of organised interests that explain why some countries adopt more or stricter environmental regulations than others (e.g. Scruggs, 1999; Knill et al., 2010). The other strand aims at explaining policy results by applying analytical frameworks. Analytical frameworks combine several explanatory factors, such as actors, institutions, etc. and – mostly working with single cases or small numbers of comparative cases – focus on political processes. Our work belongs to the second strand and in this chapter we apply the Politically Inherent Dynamics Approach (PIDA) (Böcher & Töller, 2016).

The approach is partly based on the Institutional Analysis and Development (IAD) framework developed by Ostrom (2007). It defines a number of factors that potentially have an impact on the political process and its results, among others, problem structures, institutions and actors. Yet different from Ostrom's IAD framework, we see the political process not as a rational, stepwise problem-solving process. Instead, our concept is influenced by the garbage-can model of political processes in which actors pursue other goals than just problem-solving, the influence of power is central, ideas begin an independent life and solutions look for problems (instead of the reverse) (Cohen et al., 1972), which we describe as dynamic political processes. For the aims of this chapter, we focus on three explanatory factors: (1) actors (individual, collective and corporate); (2) institutions (as rule systems); and (3) the problem structure. We will use

Table 5.1 Comparing four alternatives of governing shale gas

Title of regulation	Philosophy	Core of regulation	Participation	Test drillings	Revision
Federal Mining Act (1980)	Extraction of all natural resources must be secured, no special focus on shale gas or environmental impacts	Shale gas extraction should be possible	No participation for citizens, municipalities, or environmental groups. Water authority position can be over-ruled	No limit	Regular parliamentary legislation
Proposal I (2013)	Specific focus on shale gas fracking to be allowed if no adverse impact on the environment occurs	No shale gas fracking in water protection areas, obligatory say of water authorities, duty to perform an EIA	Participation of citizens, local community and authorities according to EIA law	No limit	Regular parliamentary legislation
Proposal II (2015)	As long as there is a lack of knowledge about environmental impacts of shale gas fracking, it should not be allowed	Water use for shale gas extraction above 3000 m is not permitted. Reversal of burden of proof	If shale gas fracking is ever allowed, participation of stakeholders according to EIA law required	No limit	2019 Expert commission
Regulation package adopted (2016)	As long as there is a lack of knowledge about environmental impacts of shale gas fracking, it should not be allowed. Länder have a relevant say if they want to allow fracking in their jurisdiction	Water use for shale gas extraction is not permitted; Reversal of burden of proof	If shale gas fracking is ever allowed, participation of stakeholders according to EIA law required	Maximum four test drillings, only where Land government approves	2021 Parliamentary legislation

Table 5.2 Most important events in the political process on governing shale gas in Germany, 2007–2017

Date	Event
2007–2011	In North Rhine-Westphalia (NRW), licences for shale gas fracking were granted for up to 60 per cent of the *Land*'s surface
2011	Local political debates start in NRW, citizens' initiatives established
2011	Newly elected NRW government stops enforcement of federal mining law in NRW: No more licences for shale gas fracking ("moratorium")
2012	A number of scientific reports on shale gas fracking are published (BGR, 2012; Meiners, 2012; UBA, 2012) which evaluate environmental impacts quite differently
2012	NRW prolongs the moratorium
Late 2012	In Hamburg, a major shale-gas field is licensed in the major agricultural area of Hamburg ("*Vierlände*")
Early 2013	Increasing politicisation at local level, local communities start adopting resolutions against shale gas fracking
February 2013	*Promised Land* is shown at the Berlinale
February 2013	Federal government (conservative-liberal coalition) presents first proposal for new regulation
February 2013	*Bundesrat* (Second Chamber) adopts resolution that fracking should not be allowed as long as its effect on water quality is unclear ("moratorium")
May 2013	26 citizens' initiatives demand that shale gas fracking should be banned ("declaration of Korbach")
June 2013	Federal government withdraws proposal because it would not have a majority in Parliament
Summer 2013	In Hesse, first time in Germany that a licence application for shale gas fracking is rejected
Spring 2015	New regulation proposal is presented by the new government (grand coalition), debated in parliament but adoption is delayed
Early June 2016	The confederation of gas industry (BVEG) announces that it would now insist on the existing law being enforced if a new law is not adopted. It is supported by the government in Lower Saxony.
Late June 2016	A significantly tightened version of the 2015 proposal is finally adopted
February 2017	Regulation comes into force

these categories to structure our analysis which will first present those factors which, in the end, did *not* influence the political process and its results in a significant way and then, second, show which factors indeed did influence the political process and brought about the result sketched above.

Factors that did not influence the policy result

First, the energy policy development in Germany seems to be a relevant context only at first sight: supporters of shale gas fracking cite the security of the supply into the field (*Süddeutsche Zeitung*, July 4, 2014). This is because, in connection with the German CO_2 reduction targets and the German "*Energiewende*" (which includes the political aim to end nuclear energy by 2022 and to strongly increase the share of renewable energy sources, while so far there is no explicit policy on the termination of coal-fired energy production), natural gas, more than 80 percent of which has to be imported now, plays an important role as an intermediary energy source (BT-Drs. 17/7612, p. 2; Töpfer & Kreutz, 2013; cf. Schirrmeister, 2014, p. 1). In the UK, shale gas was generally considered important to fill the gap that came with the decision to end the use of coal for energy production by 2025 (Schneider & Kuhs, 2016, p. 25). While this overall situation was not so different in Germany, there was much more controversy on the relevance of shale gas to energy security. On the one hand, the Federal Institute for Geosciences and Natural Resources argued that shale gas from domestic reserves could "contribute significantly to Germany's natural gas supply" and increase the security of supply in this way (BGR, 2012, p. 48). Furthermore, it added that shale gas would help the German economy to assert its competitiveness (*Die Welt*, 17 September 2013; European Commission, 2014, p. 5; Schirrmeister, 2014, p. 4). On the other hand, relevant opponents consider that fracking is not necessary for energy policy, that it does not contribute relevantly to the energy revolution (SRU, 2013, p. 45), and that it could be even detrimental to the development of energy efficiency (Rehbock, 2013, p. 3; ZEW, 2013). Thus, the role of shale gas in German energy policy remained highly controversial. As opposed to the UK there was no overall feeling that shale gas was needed which could have put environmental and health concerns into perspective.

Second, it is generally held that business interest groups[4] are powerful actors and influential in watering down environmental standards (for the theoretical argument, see Olson, 1965, and for environmental policy case studies, see Dionigi, 2017; Markussen & Svendsen, 2005; Töller & Böcher, 2017). In our case, enterprises and federations of the extraction industry were quite active and used various means of carrot and stick to shape public opinion on shale gas fracking and to build trust, but overall, they were not very influential. For example, Exxon Mobil initiated an independent expert dialogue in 2011 (Bornemann, 2016). The industry also lobbied the Federal government and by doing so was successful in having the government introduce an expert commission into the proposal in 2014 that was meant to evaluate test drillings and de facto decide on the abolition of the ban. However, this was heavily disputed and, in the end, the expert commission was restricted to giving recommendations while the Parliament had the final decision on whether the ban on shale gas fracking should be abandoned. The only real industry success was that the regulation was adopted at all in 2016. While in early June 2016, few people would have bet that the law would be passed in this election period since there remained major points of disagreement, it was the threat by the industry federation (BEVG) to now insist on the enforcement of the valid law (which would mean suing the *Länder* governments) that finally made the majority fractions in the Bundestag find a compromise on matters of disagreement.[5]

Third, it is a relevant theoretical assumption that political actors in parliament and government are strongly driven by partisan politics and that there is systematic variation in policy outputs depending on the parties in government. It is generally held that the green parties in government do in fact follow a more stringent environmental policy; this can also be the case with Social Democrats, under certain conditions (Carter, 2013; Knill, Debus, & Heichel, 2010). In the case of fracking, the picture is highly inconsistent in this regard. The Conservative Party (CDU/CSU), at the federal level, has been split over shale gas frakking since 2013, which was the reason for the failure of the first proposal and for the grand coalition's (elected in late 2013) aim at a relatively strict regulation from the beginning (which was in line with certain sections of the Conservatives and with the Social Democrats). At the same time, at the *Länder* level, a Conservative environmental minister in Hesse demanded the competent authority to reject an application for shale gas licences, while one red-green government (Nordrhein Westfalen, NRW) was strongly against all sorts of fracking while the other red-green government (Lower Saxony) was keen on "saving" tight gas fracking.

Now, why did issues of energy security play such a limited role in the debate?, why did industry have so little influence?, and why were there opponents and supporters of fracking across the parties? We will address these questions next.

Factors that influenced the policy result

The first factor that had a major impact on the policy process and its results is part of what we call the problem structure. It is the fact that shale gas deposits are located in a *regionally disparate pattern*. First, the shale gas deposits in Germany that could possibly be exploited through fracking are unevenly distributed among regions, so that the concern regarding possible environmental effects, which would occur primarily locally, would also be different in different regions. In Germany, major deposits are presumed to be found in Lower Saxony and North Rhine-Westphalia, as are smaller deposits in Baden-Württemberg, Hesse, Thuringia and Saxony-Anhalt (Meiners, 2012, p. 4). While shale gas has been increasingly politicised at the local level since 2011 and more so since early 2013, this did not remain without impact on the locally elected Members of Parliament. On the one hand, they are expected to vote with their party members but they are generally considered more powerful than, for example, their British colleagues and have the possibility of defecting. On the other hand, due to the modalities of the German voting system, they would be held responsible by the voters if they voted for a regulation basically allowing fracking under only soft regulation. One could observe in early 2013 how the Conservative majority fraction in the *Bundestag* was split into the major part with a business-friendly preference for slim regulation (as proposed in 2013). CDU/ CSU Parliamentarians with shale gas deposits in their constituencies started to push for a more stringent regulation of fracking because they feared that their voters (especially in the 2013 elections) would otherwise punish them. They were even called the "natural gas group". When after the election, the grand coalition came to build the government in late 2013, it was this natural gas group among the Conservatives that together with Social Democrats went for strict regulation, and, in fact, a ban on shale gas extraction. Thus, the regionally disparate distribution of shale gas annulled the partisan differences, both at the federal and at the *Länder* level. Yet, there is, unlike the UK, no clear north-south divide with shale gas deposits especially in the areas where economically little else is going on.

The second factor that had a major impact relates to institutions, more precisely, the constellation of German federalism.[6] The federal division of powers produces, with the *Land* governments – beyond the purely legal competences – wilful and at the same time politically influential actors. In accordance with the division of powers of the Constitution, the field of mining (as a subcategory of business law, Article 74, Para. 1, No. 11 of the Constitution) falls under the concurrent legislation (Article 72 of the Constitution), by which the *Länder* have the authority to legislate only as long as the federation has not made use of its legislative authority. Thus, in the field of mining law, the *Länder* no longer have the authority to legislate, since the federal government had already enacted federal legislation in 1980.[7] However, the *Länder* in administrative federalism are responsible for the execution of federal law. The government of North Rhine-Westphalia took this as an opportunity to simply stop the execution of the Federal Mining Act with regard to shale gas extraction applications by declaring a moratorium in 2011. This was, however, legally seen as a highly instable situation, since enterprises applying for a licence – theoretically – had the right to be granted the licence if no "preponderant public interests preclude the exploration in the entire field" (§11 No. 10 Federal Mining Act). Supported by other *Länder*, the North Rhine-Westphalia government took the initiative in the *Bundesrat* in 2012, where they achieved a moratorium for all Federal States to be approved in early 2013, which was of course legally as unstable as the North Rhine-Westphalia moratorium. Furthermore, they asked the federal government to introduce a duty of EIA for all kinds of fracking. In 2014, again the *Länder* in the *Bundesrat* insisted that the federal government should ban shale gas fracking. At the same time, Lower Saxony took extensive action to have any federal law adopted that would – besides banning shale gas fracking – regulate tight gas fracking more strictly and thus allow tight gas fracking in Lower Saxony to resume.[8]

Finally (and contrary to conventional wisdom), when looking at actors, the citizens' initiatives against shale gas fracking were very influential. They started being established in the North of NRW already in late 2010 and then spread across the Republic to places with shale gas (and tight gas, in fact) in 2011 and 2012. While, in the UK, for example, the positions of political actors pro and against fracking were in fact not very distant from each other (Cairney et al., 2016), this was quite different in Germany. Local groups as a relevant part of the anti-fracking movement were strongly opposed to fracking. In the political process on governing shale gas in Germany we can (perhaps for the first time) observe a serious transformation of the forms of organisation and action of environment-related citizens' initiatives and protest groups. Research has shown how such initiatives operate and convey their protest today, where the Internet plays a central role. Anti-fracking initiatives initially indeed did have a mostly local bearing. However, they networked profusely and interregionally, via the Internet, specifically through the website against gas drilling (www.gegen-gasbohren.de), which presents a central platform for some 30 citizens' initiatives against fracking that in their own right have close to no organisational structures (Yang, 2015, p. 290). In addition, these groups act supralocally by reaching a broader public in that they distribute press articles, reports, opinions, and backgrounds via the Internet (blogs, homepages, Twitter, Facebook, etc.). In doing this, visualisation (particularly with help of the film, *GasLand*) and the emotionalisation of their concerns represent important new elements of strategy (p. 284). The collection of signatures against fracking is also made easier by the Internet, for example, through the Open-Petition platform (p. 292). Online petitions, like those using the campaign platform, Compact, play a major role at the federal level (p. 294). Furthermore, web applications are used in order to make transparent the rejection or support of fracking by political parties and individual politicians, and to apply political pressure (p. 295). Different studies show that citizens' initiatives against fracking gained support in the first half of 2013, that the public discussion suddenly increased, and that a discourse coalition against fracking, supported substantially by the most important environmental NGO, BUND, and local citizens' initiatives, was able to influence public opinion decisively (Burgartz, 2013; Schirrmeister, 2014; Yang, 2015, p. 295). Tosun and Lang determined, with the aid of a network analysis, that after the parliamentary elections of September 2013, the discourse coalition critical of fracking had grown and taken up a dominant position in relation to the fracking supporters (Tosun & Lang, 2016: 188), which was never the case in the UK (Cairney et al. 2016). This was the fertile soil for putting pressure on local members of Parliament of any political colour and for most of the *Länder* governments to act as they did.

Conclusion

This chapter compared four alternatives of regulating fracking in Germany (see Table 5.1). The regulation of fracking in the Federal Mining Act, the regulatory packages presented in 2013 and in spring 2015, as well as the regulations adopted in the summer of 2016. The comparison determined that the regulations in the Federal Mining Act contain only the slightest environmental protection, both procedurally and substantively, especially neither the participation of citizens or municipalities nor of environmental groups was provided for. The water authorities' position could be overruled. The 2013 proposal included a "light" regulation including a ban on shale gas fracking in water protection areas, obligatory involvement of water authorities and the duty to perform an EIA with any sort of fracking. In contrast, the regulatory package that the grand coalition envisaged in 2015 and which was adopted in 2016 even in a tightened version, contains comparatively extensive regulations that result in an indefinite ban on commercial unconventional fracking. Of central importance is that it is the democratically elected German *Bundestag* that takes the decisions on a further continuation of the ban and not (as initially intended) the expert commission. The restriction of the test drillings for scientific purposes to four will probably not have any practical relevance, because due to the approval requirements of the respective *Land* government, it is questionable whether test drilling will be conducted anywhere at all. Tight gas fracking, which in Lower Saxony plays an important role, remains permitted, even if under clearly more stringent requirements. We found the increasing stringency of shale gas regulation across time surprising since in environmental policy we usually see the opposite: strict regulation is proposed and is then watered down in the course of the political process.

The analysis of the political process, based on the PIDA-framework presented above, allowed us to determine, in a second step, that neither the issue of energy security or of achieving CO_2-reduction targets nor various attempts to wield influence by the natural gas industry and its associations nor partisan politics had a *decisive* influence on the political process and its results. Rather, it was primarily the regionally disparate distribution of shale gas deposits (i.e. the problem structure), which raised local concern over the topic of fracking, and so led to an annulment of the party differences also on the federal level. Second, federalism worked as an institutional factor that, with the *Länder*, produced an array of wilful political actors operating at different levels. Third, the role of citizens' initiatives as actors is important, as they were able to organise themselves beyond their local sphere in this political process and to influence the process significantly.

Whether there will be any reliable findings of the environmental effects of fracking by 2021, if no scientific test drillings are carried out until then, is an open question. Another open question is whether, considering the possibly long-term development of oil and gas prices, fracking can be carried out profitably at all under stringent environmental requirements. Possibly in some years the necessity for this procedure in terms of energy management will have to be evaluated anew.

Notes

1 The regulation of fracking for tight gas, which has been applied in Lower Saxony for more than 30 years, was also an issue in this proposal and has also been tightened in the finally adopted regulation. This is, however, beyond the scope of this chapter, but see Töller and Böcher (2016).

2 Members of the commission were to come from the Federal Environmental Agency, the Federal Institute for Geosciences and Natural Resources (*Bundesanstalt für Geowissenschaften und Rohstoffe*, BGR), the Helmholtz Centre for Environmental Research in Leipzig, a state office for geology and a state water authority (BMWi, 2015, p. 2).

3 In contrast, in Natura 2000 areas, there should be no ban on conventional fracking.

4 For the role of other organised interests, e.g. the nutrition and beverage industry, see Töller and Böcher (2016).

5 The industry's wish to have the strict regulation adopted better than no regulation can only be understood when looking at Lower Saxony. While the entire issue of shale gas fracking was about potential gains and risks, Lower Saxony had – until 2011 – extracted tight gas with the help of so-called "conventional fracking" (as opposed to shale gas fracking which is labelled "unconventional") for almost 30 years. When the debate on possible risks of shale gas fracking intensified in 2011, in Lower Saxony also tight gas fracking started being challenged, and after two applications for tight gas fracking were delayed, the industry did not apply for it further. Thus, by having shale gas fracking banned and at the same time tight gas fracking regulated more strictly, the industry could expect to at least continue with tight gas fracking in Lower Saxony.

6 Germany is a Federal State with a symmetrical structure (as opposed to the UK). The 16 states (*Länder*) and the federal level (*Bund*) have their own legislative rights. Details are laid down in the Constitution (*Grundgesetz*, Articles 70–75) and are also subject to changes, e.g. in the major reform of federalism in 2006. At the federal level, the main legislator is the Parliament (*Bundestag*). Bills that entail an effect on the organisational and administrative procedures of *Land* authorities (Art. 84 Par. 1, Art. 85, Art. 108 of the Constitution) can be vetoed by the second chamber (*Bundesrat*), in which the *Land* Governments are represented. The *Bundesrat* can also propose federal legislation (Art. 76). In fields in which only the *Bund* (i.e. the Federal parliament, the *Bundestag*, in the first place) is entitled to legislate (as is the case with fracking as such), it is the task of the *Länder* to execute federal law. However, the *Länder* have some rights in the field of water management law.

7 The *Länder* governments participate in the federal legislation through the *Bundesrat*. Whether the consent of the *Bundesrat* was required for the new laws regulating shale gas was a matter of dispute between the federal government and the *Länder* but finally the consent of the *Länder* was not required (Töller & Böcher, 2016).

8 What we say about the gas industry in Lower Saxony in note 5 holds true for the Government of Lower Saxony as well.

References

Attendorn, T. (2011). Fracking – zur Erteilung von Gewinnungsberechtigungen und zur Zulassung von Probebohrungen zur Gewinnung von Erdgas aus unkonventionellen Lagerstätten. *Zeitschrift für Umweltrecht, 12*, 565–570.

Ausschuss für Umweltschutz, Naturschutz und Reaktorsicherheit. (2011). *Korrigiertes Wortprotokoll, 58. Sitzung, Öffentliche Anhörung zum Thema „Trinkwasserschutz und Bürgerbeteiligung bei der Förderung von unkonventionellem Erdgas"*. Berlin: Deutscher Bundestag.

BGR (Bundesanstalt für Geowissenschaften und Rohstoffe). (2012). *Abschätzung des Erdgaspotentials aus dichten Tongesteinen (Schiefergas) in Deutschland*. Retrieved from www.bgr.bund.de/DE/Themen/Energie/Downloads/BGR_Schiefergaspotenzial_in_Deutschland_2012.pdf;jsessionid=1513B40EFBCA6B4081C267D1AE860058.1_cid289?__blob=publicationFile&v=7 (accessed 28 September 2016).

BGR (Bundesanstalt für Geowissenschaften und Rohstoffe). (2016). *Schieferöl und Schiefergas in Deutschland. Potenziale und Umweltaspekte*. Retrieved from www.bgr.bund.de/

DE/Themen/Energie/Downloads/Abschlussbericht_13MB_Schieferoelgaspotenzial_
Deutschland_2016.pdf;jsessionid=256DBD58B9A88BCF1AE88CE0D3FF6ED6.1_
cid331?__blob=publicationFile&v=5 (accessed 28 September 2016).

BMU/BMWi (Bundesministerium für Umwelt, Naturschutz, Bau und Reaktorsicherheit/
Bundesministerium für Wirtschaft und Energie). (2013). *Formulierungshilfe für die Frak-*
tionen der CDU/CSU und FDP. Entwurf eines Gesetzes zur Änderung des Wasserhaush-
altsgesetzes. Berlin: Deutscher Bundestag.

BMUB (Bundesinnenministerium für Umwelt, Naturschutz, Bau und Reaktorsicherheit).
(2015.) *Kabinett beschließt weitgehende Einschränkung für Fracking. Gemeinsame*
Pressemitteilung mit dem Bundesministerium für Wirtschaft und Energie. Retrieved from
www.bmwi.de/DE/Presse/pressemitteilungen,did=699322.html (accessed 28 September
2016).

BMWi (Bundesministerium für Wirtschaft und Energie). (2015). *Stellungnahmen zu den*
Gesetzesentwürfen zum Regelungspaket Fracking. Retrieved from www.bmwi.de/DE/
Themen/Industrie/Rohstoffe-und Ressourcen/Fracking/stellungnahmen.html (accessed
28 September 2016).

Böcher, M. & Töller, A. E. (2016). Inherent dynamics and chance as drivers in environmental policy? An approach to explaining environmental policy decisions. Paper presented at the International Conference on Public Policy, Panel T01P08 – Theories
and conceptions of the political process beyond 'Policy Circle' and 'Multiple Streams',
Milan, 2015.

Boehme-Neßler, V. (2015). Fracking-Entscheidungen durch Experten-Kommissionen?
Verfassungsrechtliche Überlegungen zum Entscheidungsdesign im aktuellen Fracking-
Regelungspaket. *Neue Zeitschrift für Verwaltungsrecht, 18,* 1249–1253.

Böhm, M. (2013). *Voraussetzungen einer bergrechtlichen Erlaubnis nach §7BBerG unter*
besonderer Berücksichtigung der Versagungsgründe des §11 Nr. 10 BBerG. Rechts-
gutachten im Auftrag des Hessischen Ministeriums für Umwelt, Energie, Landwirt-
schaft und Verbraucherschutz. Marburg: Philipps-Universität.

Bornemann, B. (2016). Private participation going public? Interpreting the nexus between
design, frames, roles and context of the fracking "infodialog" in Germany. *Journal of*
Environmental Policy & Planning, 1–20. doi: 10.1080/1523908X.2016.1138401.

Brans, M., Geva-May, I., & Howlett, M. (eds). (2017). *Routledge Handbook of Com-*
parative Policy Analysis. New York: Routledge.

Burgartz, J. (2013). Fracking in Nordhessen. Der Widerstand gegen das Fördern von
unkonventionellem Erdgas. In D. Gawora, & K. Bayer (Eds.), *Energie und Demokratie,*
Entwicklungsperspektiven Nr. 103. Retrieved from www.uni-kassel.de/upress/online/
frei/978-3-86219-612-8.volltext.frei.pdf (accessed 28 September 2016).

BVEG (Bundesverband Erdgas, Erdöl und Geothermie). (2016). Branche fürchtet um
Standorte und Arbeitsplätze. Retrieved from www.bveg.de/Der-BVEG/News/Branche-
fuerchtet-um-Standorte-und-Arbeitsplaetze (accessed 28 September 2016).

Cairney, P. (2011). *Understanding Public Policy: Theories and Issues.* Basingstoke: Palgrave
Macmillan.

Cairney, P., Fischer, M., & Ingold, K. (2016). Hydraulic fracturing policy in the United
Kingdom: coalition, cooperation and opposition in the face of uncertainty. In C.
Weible, T. Heikkila, K. Ingold, & M. Fischer (eds), *Policy Debates on Hydraulic Frac-*
turing: Comparing Coalition Politics in North America and Europe (pp. 81–113). New
York: Palgrave.

Carter, N. (2013). Greening the mainstream: party politics and the environment.
Environmental Politics, 22(1), 73–94.

Chailleux, S., & Moyson, S. (2016). The French ban on hydraulic fracturing and the attempts to reverse it: social mobilization, professional forums, and coalition strategies. In C. Weible, T. Heikkila, K. Ingold, & M. Fischer (eds), *Policy Debates on Hydraulic Fracturing: Comparing Coalition Politics in North America and Europe* (pp. 115–145). New York: Palgrave.

Cohen, M. D., March, J. G. & Olsen, J. P. (1972). A garbage can model of organizational choice. *Administrative Science Quarterly, 17*(1), 1–25.

Dionigi, M. K. (2017). *Lobbying in the European Parliament: The Battle for Influence.* Cham, Switzerland: Springer International Publishing.

Eftekhardazeh, P. (2013). Was spricht gegen Fracking? – Eine Stellungnahme. *Natur und Recht, 35*(10), 704–708.

European Commission. (2014). Communication from the Commission to the European Parliament, the Council, the European Economic and Social Committee, andn the Commitee of the Regions on the exploration and production of hydrcarbon (such as shale gas) using high volume hydraulic fracturing in the EUCOM (2014) 23 final/2, Brussels.

Frenz, W. (2013). Moratorium für Fracking? *Zeitschrift für Neues Energierecht, 17*(4), 344–348.

Frenz, W. (2016). Überwiegende öffentliche Interessen gegen Fracking-Berechtigungen. *Die öffentliche Verwaltung, 8*, 322–329.

Gaßner, H., & Buchholz, G. (2013). Rechtsfragen des Erdgas-Fracking – Grundwasserschutz und UVP. *Zeitschrift für Umweltrecht, 21*(3), 143–150.

Habrich-Böcker, C., Kirchner, B. C., & Weißenberg, P. (2015). *Fracking: Die neue Produktionsgeografie* (2nd edn.). Wiesbaden: Springer Gabler.

Knill, C., Debus, M., & Heichel, S. (2010). Do parties matter in internationalised policy areas? The impact of political parties on environmental policy outputs in 18 OECD countries, 1970–2000. *European Journal of Political Research, 49*, 301–336.

Ludwig, G. (2012). Umweltaspekte in Verfahren nach dem BbergG. *Zeitschrift für Umweltrecht, 3*, 150–157.

Markussen, P., & Svendsen, G. T. (2005). Industry lobbying and the political economy of GHG trade in the European Union. *Energy Policy, 33*(2), 245–255.

Meiners, H.-G. (2012). *Fracking in unkonventionellen Erdgas-Lagerstätten in NRW. Gutachten mit Risikostudie zur Exploration und Gewinnung von Erdgas aus unkonventionellen Lagerstätten in Nordrhein-Westfalen (NRW) und deren Auswirkungen auf den Naturhaushalt insbesondere die öffentliche Trinkwasserversorgung.* Retrieved from www.mweimh.nrw.de/presse/pressemitteilungen/Archiv_2012/2012_09_07_4/NRW-Gutachten-Fracking.pdf (accessed 28 September 2016).

Olson, M. (1965). *The Logic of Collective Action. Public Goods and the Theory of Groups.* Cambridge, MA: Harvard University Press.

Ostrom, E. (2007). Institutional rational choice: an assessment of the institutional analysis and development framework. In P. A. Sabatier (ed.), *Theories of the Policy Process,* 2nd edn. (pp. 21–64). Boulder, CO: Westview Press.

Rehbock, T. (2013). Fracking: Wer nicht „frackt", verliert? *KFW Economic Research, 19.* Retrieved from www.kfw.de/Download-Center/Konzernthemen/Research/PDF-Dokumente-Fokus-Volkswirtschaft/Fokus-Nr.-19-April-2013 Rohstoffe_Wettbewerb.pdf (accessed 28 September 2016).

Schirrmeister, M. (2014). Controversial futures – discourse analysis on utilizing the "fracking" technology in Germany. *European Journal of Futures Research, 2*, 38–46.

Schneider, J., & Kuhs, G. (2016). Kraftwerke im Vereinigten Königreich und in Irland. Ein aktueller Überblick. *BWK, 68*(6), 25–28.

Scruggs, L. A. (1999). Institutions and environmental performance in seventeen western democracies. *British Journal of Political Science, 29*, 1–31.

SRU (Sachverständigenrat für Umweltfragen). (2013). *Fracking zur Schiefergasgewinnung. Ein Beitrag zur energie- und umweltpolitischen Bewertung*. Stellungnahme, No. 18. Retrieved from www.umweltrat.de/SharedDocs/Downloads/DE/04_Stellungnahmen/2012_2016/2013_05_AS_18_Fracking.pdf?__blob=publicationFile (accessed 28 September 2016).

Staeck, N., Malek, T., & Heinelt, H. (2001). The environmental impact assessment Directive. In H. Heinelt, T. Malek, R. Smith, & A. E. Töller (eds.), *European Union Environment Policy and New Forms of Governance: A Study of the Implementation of the Environmental Impact Assessment Directive and the Eco-Management and Audit Regulation in Three Member States* (pp. 33–42). Aldershot: Ashgate.

Töller, A. E., & Böcher, M. (2016). Varianten der Fracking-Regulierung in Deutschland und ihre Erklärung. *Zeitschrift für Umweltpolitik und Umweltrecht (ZfU), 3*, 208–234.

Töller, A. E., & Böcher, M. (2017). Wirtschaftsverbände in der Umweltpolitik. In W. Schroeder & B. Weßels (Eds.), *Handbuch Arbeitgeber- und Wirtschaftsverbände in Deutschland*, 2nd rev. edn. (pp. 531–563). Wiesbaden: Springer VS.

Töpfer, F.-R., & Kreutz, G. (2013). Förderung von unkonventionellem Erdgas – Risiken und Chancen des Fracking. *Energiewirtschaftliche Tagesfragen, 63*, 11–16.

Tosun, J., & Lang, A. (2016). The politics of hydraulic fracturing in Germany. In C. Weible, T. Heikkila, K. Ingold, & M. Fischer (eds.), *Policy Debates on Hydraulic Fracturing: Comparing Coalition Politics in North America and Europe* (pp. 177–200). New York: Palgrave.

UBA (Umweltbundesamt). (2012). *Umweltauswirkungen von Fracking bei der Aufsuchung und Gewinnung von Erdgas aus unkonventionellen Lagerstätten, Teil 1*. Retrieved from www.umweltbundesamt.de/publikationen/umweltauswirkungen-von-fracking-bei-aufsuchung (accessed 28 September 2016).

UBA (Umweltbundesamt). (2014). *Umweltauswirkungen von Fracking bei der Aufsuchung und Gewinnung von Erdgas insbesondere aus Schiefergaslagerstätten, Teil 2*. Retrieved from www.umweltbundesamt.de/publikationen/gutachten-2014-umweltauswirkungen-von-fracking-bei (accessed 28 September 2016).

Wenzelburger, G., & Wolf, F. (2015). Policy theories in the crisis? Comparing the explanatory power of policy theories in the context of crisis. Paper presented at the 2nd International Conference for Public Policy, Milan, Available at: www.icpublicpolicy.org/conference/file/reponse/1433840658.pdf (accessed 19 March 2017).

Yang, M. (2015). Anti-Fracking Kampagnen und ihre Mediennutzung. In R. Speth & A. Zimmer (eds.), *Interessenvertretung als Politikgestaltung* (pp. 283–299). Wiesbaden: VS Verlag.

ZEW (Zentrum für Europäische Wirtschaftsordnung). (2013). *Traum oder Albtraum? – Aussichten für die Förderung unkonventioneller Gase in Europa*. Sonderteil ZEWnews, Januar/Februar 2013. Retrieved from http://ftp.zew.de/pub/zew-docs/zn/schwerpunkte/energiemarkt/Energiemarkt0213.pdf (accessed 28 September 2016).

Zittel, W. (2016). *Fracking. Energiewunder oder Umweltsünde?* München: oekom-Verlag.

6 Experimental regulatory approaches for unconventional gas

The case of urban drilling and local government authority in Texas

Matthew Fry and Christian Brannstrom

Introduction

Governors, legislators, oil and gas commissions, and other state-level (i.e., sub-national) agencies and actors exert significant regulatory authority over oil and gas extraction, production, and transport in the United States (Davis, 2014). The rapid growth in shale and unconventional hydrocarbon production in the 2000s and the expansion of drilling and hydraulic fracturing (fracking) into urbanized areas tested the ability of state-level regulations to protect the health, safety, and welfare of urban residents who normally turn to municipal officials to resolve land-use conflicts (Richardson et al., 2013). The response of municipal governments to unconventional oil and gas production was pronounced in Dallas-Fort Worth, Texas (DFW), the fourth most populous metropolitan area in the country (U.S. Census Bureau, 2015), which lies over portions of the Barnett Shale, the first productive U.S. shale gas deposit. Between 2001 and 2015, 58 cities in DFW enacted drilling ordinances that regulate several aspects of hydrocarbon production. Setback distances, the linear distances between gas wells and residences, schools, and other protected uses, are the most contested regulations because they determine drilling intensity and land area consumed by hydrocarbon production activities. Setback distance policies in DFW municipalities vary because of differences in political culture, socio-economic status, and land use (Fry and Brannstrom, 2017). However, in May 2015, the Texas state government enacted House Bill 40 (HB40), which preempted municipal oil and gas ordinances and introduced the "commercially reasonable" standard against which ordinances will be tested.

A growing body of scholarship focuses on relations between unconventional hydrocarbons and agenda change, legal acts, narratives and governance, and the locus of jurisdictional authority (e.g., Davis, 2014; Hudgins and Poole, 2014; Konschnik and Boling, 2014; Rabe, 2014; Warner and Shapiro, 2013). Determining the polity that regulates unconventional oil and gas is a major debate, with arguments for federal regulation conflicting with arguments for state-level regulation (Davis, 2014), while the presence of municipal-level regulations has introduced a new policy dimension. The passage of HB40 in Texas is but one example of municipal-state tensions in the US regarding hydraulic fracturing, offering parallels to North Carolina and Oklahoma, which passed preemption legislation in 2015, Pennsylvania (2012), and Ohio (2013). Courts later ruled that Pennsylvania's Act 13 did not preempt municipal powers to regulate the location of drilling rigs (*Robinson Twp.* v. *Commonwealth of Pennsylvania*, 2012). Neither New Mexico nor West Virginia expressly prohibited counties or municipalities from regulating oil and gas activities until courts ruled that that authority rests solely with the state (Goho, 2012; Ritchie, 2014). In 2016, the Colorado Supreme Court also struck down city regulations and upheld the state government's authority over oil and gas development (Finley, 2016).

In this chapter, we analyze key moments, events, and actors in the rapid shift from municipal-based urban shale gas governance to state-dominated governance. When, and why, do oil and gas interests initiate their efforts to shift regulatory oversight from municipal to state governments? And what are the origins, intent, and consequences of legislation that shifts governance from municipal to state level? To answer these questions, we focus on constituent components of HB40, the Texas state-level hydrocarbon statute. We also draw attention to the local-scale regulatory and drilling context in Texas, where the preemption of municipal-level authority was notable because of the complexity and historical development of municipal ordinances in the state (Davis, 2014). For example, more than 300 municipalities throughout Texas had some form of oil and gas regulation when HB40 was adopted (Malewitz and Murphy, 2015). On several occasions in the twentieth century, state courts have upheld the constitutionality of municipal authority over surface oil and gas activities within their territory (Riley, 2007). Moreover, HB40 is significant because Texas is the largest oil and natural gas producer in the US and has long served as the bellwether for US state-level legal standards for oil and gas (Godfrey, 2005).

Data were collected over the course of three years (2013–2015) of research on municipal drilling ordinances in Texas. We base our analysis on interviews with 28 key stakeholders in DFW and a unique dataset on municipal oil and gas revenues. To create a rigorous sample frame for semi-structured interviews we used geospatial data from the Railroad Commission of Texas (RRC) to identify gas well locations and compute drilling density within municipalities with drilling ordinances. We used a sample frame, organized in a 9-cell grid according to setback distances (ranging from 200–1,500 feet (61–457.2 m)) and well density within a 15 km buffer of the city territory (ranging from 1.35–8.24 wells/km^2), to randomly select nine cities and purposively sample three cities among the strata. We identified and contacted key actors involved in the development of those 12 municipal setback distances. Semi-structured interviews were conducted with municipal attorneys, municipal staff, elected officials, residents, and industry stakeholders. In 2014, we also obtained annual gas well revenue information, including royalties, signing bonuses, and fees from 80 municipalities in the Barnett that have oil and gas drilling ordinances. We also draw information from first-hand knowledge of debates in the City of Denton gathered during multiple undergraduate field trips that involved discussions with Denton stakeholders and observations of local politics and municipal council meetings leading up to and following the November 2014 popular vote on hydraulic fracturing.

The chapter begins with a review of shale gas governance, municipal policies, and setback distances in Texas. We then outline HB40's key provisions. This is followed by a discussion of the bill's origins and intent. We show that HB40's authors intended to bind municipal ordinances to oil and gas legal standards, which are based on industry technical knowledge and practices rather than zoning or planning guidelines. The ambiguity of the HB40 standards, in turn, create unclear municipal health, safety, and environmental guidelines, which result in greater burdens placed on city residents, who now must contend with the oil and gas industry without recourse to their local government.

Fragmented shale gas governance in Texas

Texas state law maximizes hydrocarbon extraction with minimal regulations (Rahm, 2011). The RRC is responsible for regulating oil and gas activities including exploration, extraction, production, and transport, although the Texas Commission on Environmental Quality (TCEQ) regulates air quality. Until the passage of HB40, no statewide policy regulated oil and gas drilling within populated areas. Significant home-rule powers conferred by the state to municipalities provided legal cover for cities and towns to create drilling ordinances. A further complication in hydrocarbon governance is the separation of subsurface oil and gas ownership (the mineral estate) from surface ownership common in the US. Owners of minerals benefit from hydrocarbon production but may reside far from gas wells; however, surface owners or tenants experience the negative effects of hydrocarbon production and seek relief from municipal and state governments. In Denton, for example, absentee mineral owners, who account for ~70 per cent of the direct financial benefits from drilling in the city, have decision-making power over activities that expose surface owners and renters to potential environmental and health risks (Fry et al., 2015b). Denton's city government serves as the lone voice of the non-mineral owners in shale gas drilling decision-making.

Municipal governments use setback distances to regulate the proximity of oil and natural gas wells to residences and public gathering facilities. Normally, setback distances are determined as linear distance from the borehole. Setbacks are important because they encapsulate many of the debates surrounding the costs and benefits of urban drilling and fracking, such as noise, light, emissions, aesthetics, health, and property rights (Fry, 2013). However, setback distances are politically contentious because city officials have obligations to their citizens including protecting health, safety and welfare, while oil and gas firms complain that long setbacks reduce well density and limit their output in city territories (Fry et al., 2015a). For this reason, there is no single setback distance that all Texas cities use. Instead, municipal ordinances have setback distances that range from 200–1,500 feet (60.9–457.2 m). Variability in distances results from ordinance language copied from nearby municipalities, the work of task forces, and idiosyncratic experiences with controversial gas wells (Fry and Brannstrom, 2017).

Allegations of regulatory takings (instances in which the state's regulations impede access to property by firms or individuals) may develop to resolve contradictions between surface owners who live near wells and mineral owners who seek returns on investment. A long municipal setback distance could make drilling impossible, given certain technologies and hydrocarbon prices. A mineral owner or lessee could challenge a municipal ordinance in a court of law as a regulatory taking of their mineral property if the distance prevented them from exploiting their oil and gas minerals (Welch, 2012). However, to date, there is no legal designation of a setback distance that would constitute grounds for a regulatory takings decision (ibid.). Nor is there an empirically derived safe setback distance (Fry, 2013), although data from McKenzie et al. (2012) suggest 2,640 feet (800 m) between gas well and nearest protected use.

Few DFW municipalities had oil and gas regulations in 2001 when Barnett Shale operators first applied for drilling permits in city territories. A first response, therefore, was to implement drilling moratoria and then to enact new oil and gas regulations. As drilling expanded in the region, other municipalities proactively adopted ordinances. Most municipalities copied provisions, language, and standards from other DFW municipal drilling ordinances (Fry et al., 2015a).

Fort Worth and Denton were the first DFW cities to enact shale gas drilling ordinances and setback distances. Fort Worth's ordinance and its 600 feet (182.8 m) setback distance are particularly influential, as evidenced by the fact that many other DFW cities copied it (ibid.). In 2010, Flower Mound adopted a 1,500 feet (457.2 m) setback distance, the longest in the state, after a real estate consultancy found that home property values declined within 1,500 feet of shale gas wells (Fry, 2013). In 2013, Dallas also adopted the 1,500 feet (457.2 m) setback, prompting some observers to claim that Dallas had effectively "banned" fracking (Fry et al., 2015a).

A key event inspiring the drafting and passage of HB40 was the popular vote in the City of Denton (population: ~120,000) to ban hydraulic fracturing within city limits in November 2014 (Briggle, 2015). In 2001, Denton established its first gas well drilling and production ordinance; a few years later, the city mandated a 500 feet (152.4 m) setback distance. The number of gas wells inside Denton's territory increased from seven in 2001 to ~280 in 2014. Until 2009, there was little controversy about drilling in the city. However, this changed when permits were issued for three gas wells to be drilled near homes, a public park, and a hospital. Fierce citizen backlash in 2010 forced the city council to impose a moratorium on drilling and organize a task force to determine how best to manage drilling and hydraulic fracturing. After citizen and other stakeholder participation, Denton adopted a new ordinance in January 2013 with a 1,200 feet setback distance and other stricter health and safety provisions.

Approximately nine months after approving the new ordinance, EagleRidge Operating LLC drilled three gas wells on previously approved drilling pad sites located within 250 feet of homes in a Denton housing development. Because the pad sites pre-dated the homes, Eagle Ridge's right to drill was grandfathered or "vested" to an earlier gas well ordinance, which provided legal basis for new drilling but did not prevent home construction nearby (Figure 6.1). Some homeowners complained about insufficient notification about the possibility of new gas wells and fracking. Other Denton residents became alarmed at the inadequacies in the city's newest, updated ordinance, which could not prevent the situation from occurring. Ultimately, the controversy reignited debates about the safety of hydraulic fracturing and contributed to a citizen campaign to prohibit fracking within the city (Figure 6.2; Briggle, 2015).

The citizen-driven initiative to prohibit fracking, seen as a last resort by many Denton residents, passed with 59 percent of the popular vote on November 4, 2014. Twelve hours after Denton voters banned fracking, both the Texas General Land Office, a state agency, and Texas Oil and Gas Association (TxOGA), a private organization, sued the city and challenged the constitutionality of such a ban (the lawsuits were later dropped). According to TxOGA, the outcome of the popular vote was "an impermissible intrusion" on the powers of the RRC, the state's oil and gas regulatory agency. Soon after Denton's vote, state officials and industry spokesmen lamented the state's "patchwork" of municipal oil and gas regulations. For example, newly-elected Governor Greg Abbott bemoaned "a patchwork quilt of bans and rules and regulations that is eroding the Texas model" (Tilove, 2015). In a video, TxOGA (2015) critiqued the "patchwork of city drilling rules [that] hinder Texas energy producers and threaten the Texas miracle." Similarly, the Texas Independent Producers & Royalty Owners Association denounced "a growing patchwork effect of local ordinances creating inconsistent regulations across the state" (TIPPRO, 2015). The "patchwork" narrative framed the debate for several legislative bills, introduced in January 2015, aiming to preempt municipalities from regulating oil and gas drilling activities. HB40, dubbed the "Denton Fracking Bill," received the most support from legislators and lobbyists (Malewitz, 2015).

Figure 6.1 A shale gas well site (left) in the vintage neighborhood in Denton, Texas, November 9, 2017.

Source: Photograph by M. Fry.

Figure 6.2 Political signs outside a voting facility in Denton, Texas, on November 4, 2014.

Source: Photograph by M. Fry.

A new statutory approach to urban unconventional gas

HB40 is comprised of two substantive sections and a third indicating when the bill takes effect (Texas Legislature Online, 2015). The first section affirms that the development of oil and gas in Texas has been key to "the growth of healthy and economically vibrant communities for over 100 years" and that state policies and agencies, referring to the RRC and TCEQ, already

> provide effective and environmentally sound regulation of oil and gas oper-ations that is so comprehensive and pervasive that the regulation occupies the field, while facilitating the overriding policy objective of this state of fully and effectively exploiting oil and gas resources while protecting the environment and the public's health and safety.

For this reason, "[t]he legislature intends that this Act expressly preempt the regulation of oil and gas operations by municipalities and other political sub-divisions, which is impliedly preempted by the statutes already in effect."

Section two provides the language that HB40 adds to the State of Texas Natural Resources Code, Sec. 81.0523 (State of Texas, 2015). The statute defines "commercially reasonable" as "a condition that would allow a reasonably prudent operator" to exploit hydrocarbons and preempts municipal authority in hydrocarbon governance unless the measure targets surface issues and is "commercially reasonable" to the "reasonably prudent operator." Finally, the statute defines ordinances as "commercially reasonable" under a *prima facie* criterion if they have been in effect for five years during hydrocarbon operations.

Industry influence over unconventional regulations

The political origin of HB40 was the City of Denton's November 2014 voter-approved ban on hydraulic fracturing. Journalists traced the technical origin of HB40 to two attorneys from Exxon Mobil and TxOGA (Heinkel-Wolfe, 2015a). This origin was suggested at the March 23, 2015 Texas House Energy Resources Committee hearings, where dozens of people including Denton's mayor and many residents testified against the bill, when one of the bill's authors said that the bill's objective was to bind municipal regulations to "a well-established principle in oil and gas law ... the reasonable and prudent operator rule" (Heinkel-Wolfe, 2015b). In addition to the "prudent operator" standard, the "commercially reasonable" standard and the "five-year" clause offer insight into HB40s intent.

The "prudent operator" standard is an outgrowth of the oil and gas mineral lease agreement, a contract between lessors (mineral owners) and lessees (operators). Because of inevitable uncertainties associated with working an oil and gas well, the lease agreement is an incomplete document that leaves many aspects of drilling and production to the operator's discretion. In cases of disagreement, courts use the "prudent operator" standard to protect the mineral owner from the substantial discretionary authority wielded by the operator (Conine, 2001). "Prudent operator" is a standard of performance, which sets an expectation of "whatever would be reasonably expected of operators of ordinary prudence under the circumstances, having regard for ... the mutual advantage of both parties" (ibid., p. 32). The standard obliges operators to utilize specialized knowledge and skills expected in the industry, but only as they pertain to the specific mineral lease in question and not to any circumstances, financial or otherwise, that the individual operator may be dealing with at the time (ibid.). To Ritchie (2016), HB40's authors "incorporated the prudent operator standard to deter operators' claims against local governments that they could not comply with local regulations because of their own atypical technical, financial, or other limitations" (p. 822). In this interpretation, municipal regulations are allowed as long as a hypothetical reasonable operator can produce oil and gas.

The "commercially reasonable" standard sparked significant debate among municipal authorities and city residents. To some legal experts and one of HB40's authors, the courts will define what constitutes "commercially reasonable" (Heinkel-Wolfe, 2015b). To date, there is no direct statement from Texas courts on the meaning of "commercially reasonable," which is most often used in the context of contract obligations (Taylor et al., 2015) and has never been used in the context of municipal drilling regulations. In contract disputes outside Texas, some courts have viewed "commercially reasonable" standards as allowing parties to consider their own economic interests (ibid.). Ritchie (2016) notes that "[a]n ordinance might allow drilling and still be invalid under this commercially reasonable test if compliance costs make operations uneconomical or restrictions impede the production of all recoverable hydrocarbons" (p. 822).

Municipal standards also could be deemed commercially reasonable if established prior to May 2010 ("five years prior") with active oil or gas production subsequently occurring. This *prima facie* clause makes it clear that HB40 not only aimed to overturn Denton's fracking ban, but also targeted municipal setback distances that might be deemed too long by operators. The longest acceptable setback distance seems to be 600 feet (182.8 m), the distance Fort Worth adopted in 2006 as a compromise between citizens, city council, city staff, and the hydrocarbon industry.

Many observers and industry personnel consider that Fort Worth's oil and gas ordinance is the standard for best practices in urban drilling. Other municipalities not only adopted the city's setback distance (39 out of 58 DFW municipalities also have 600 feet setbacks), but also copied provisions and language *verbatim* from Fort Worth's ordinance. As more cities adopted the Fort Worth ordinance, the more it became regarded as the most "tested" model, according to multiple interview respondents, because its regulations had not been challenged in a court of law for a regulatory taking of private mineral property, therefore passing the "regulatory takings" test.

Fort Worth's ordinance was referenced in hearings on HB40 in March 2015 before the Texas House Natural Resources Committee. Few of the nearly 100 speakers received the level of praise by state legislators as did the Fort Worth delegation, who were called "our heroes" by one representative. Another said Fort Worth "has done this right" and that "a lot of people say we should adopt [Fort Worth's] ordinance and say that is the best practice" (Baker, 2015). From the industry's perspective, what Fort Worth did "right" was to allow more than 1,990 producing wells in city territory, which generated more than $200 million in revenues from city-owned mineral properties (City of Fort Worth, 2014).

Although other DFW cities copied Fort Worth's ordinance to cope with legal uncertainties surrounding mineral property rights and fears of regulatory takings lawsuits (Fry et al. 2015a), they were persuaded by industry spokesmen who served as policy entrepreneurs (see Peck, 2011). For example, the director of the Barnett Shale Energy Education Council (BSEEC), which was founded by a consortium of Barnett Shale gas operators in 2007, often described Fort Worth's ordinance as one that "works." The BSEEC director further suggested that adopting 600 feet setbacks would allow other cities and their residents to "enjoy the economic benefits of their mineral rights without having to give up regarding health and safety" (City of Dallas, 2014).

However, as Figure 6.3 demonstrates, Fort Worth is not a typical Barnett Shale municipality. Few cities, if any, could expect similar revenue streams from leasing mineral properties for at least three reasons. First, Fort Worth is almost entirely built over rich deposits of the Barnett. Second, it has a larger territory (~894 km²) than most Barnett municipalities, which allows a greater area for drilling. The large area also decreases the instances of hydraulic fracturing in densely populated areas where citizen backlash is most pronounced. Third, most of the city's bonus revenues from drilling came after 2005 when gas prices and bonus payments were at historic highs. By 2008, bonuses topped $30,000 per acre (~$11,800 per hectare) in the Barnett Shale, but they have plunged since then. Finally, the widespread use of Fort Worth's ordinance and regulations calls into question the idea that a patchwork of dissimilar municipal drilling policies ever existed, and whether these needed to be replaced by a one-size-fits-all state-level policy.

Outcomes and implications of a regulatory shift

As shown above, the technical origin of HB40 was oil and gas industry attorneys, and the bill's intent was to allow operators to more directly determine the parameters of the regulatory powers that formerly resided with municipal governments. Operators can use the "prudent operator" standard, the "commercially

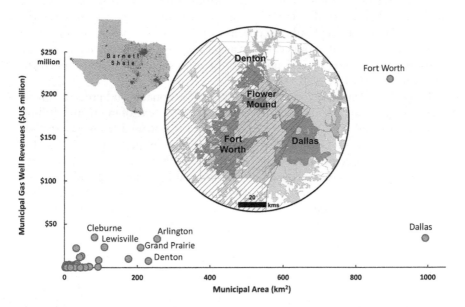

Figure 6.3 Barnett Shale, municipalities, gas well revenues (from royalties, interest, and bonuses) and municipal area. The Barnett shale is located beneath portions of Dallas-Fort Worth Metroplex in Texas (inset). Above the Barnett, 80 municipalities enacted setback distance regulations, 55 received revenues from 2001–2012 (from $645 to $218,434,000); 35 cities receive no revenues.

reasonable" standard, and the "five-year" clause to remove municipal regulations they deem onerous or, conversely, to encourage municipalities to adopt regulations, like Fort Worth's setback distance, that they find acceptable. The ambiguity of HB40's provisions means that city governments and city residents face many uncertainties regarding urban drilling in the future. Although courts could play an important role, threats of lawsuits may be enough to force cities to scale back municipal regulations.

As drilling expanded into DFW cities in the early 2000s, hydrocarbon firms increasingly turned to threats of regulatory takings lawsuits, which represent an expensive legal burden to cash-strapped municipal governments, as a way to minimize municipal regulations and setback distances (Fry et al., 2015a). With HB40, oil and gas operators and the RRC, not city authorities, define what constitutes "commercially reasonable." But the ambiguity of "commercially reasonable" also means that setback distances could vary from one gas well to another, even within the same city territory, depending on market spot prices, topography, and available infrastructure. More likely, the intent of the "commercially reasonable" provision is to persuade cities to implement setback distances that are acceptable to the industry or else face costly lawsuits. In this way, HB40 provides a similar type of power to the industry as did threats of regulatory takings. Although HB40 nominally leaves some powers to cities, that power is ultimately beholden to the industry via threats of lawsuits. The 600 feet (182.8 m) setback facilitated widespread drilling in Fort Worth; therefore, this distance is likely to be what industry will consider "reasonable." Notably, adopting a similar or identical ordinance from a municipality that has been in effect for five years also would not necessarily make a regulation "commercially reasonable" because of variations in population densities, land uses, and topography between cities (BSEEC, 2015).

It also is unclear how courts will interpret a "reasonable and prudent" operator's discretionary decision-making powers in the context of municipal drilling. Despite wide industry acceptance, the standard is not used for most other oil and gas issues because it was "designed to govern a unique relationship within the scope of a specific transaction" (Conine, 2001, p. 24). HB40 places the "prudent operator" standard outside of the mineral lease agreement context and into urban drilling, a novel context, where no contract exists between the operator and city governments, local surface owners, renters, and other residents.

Moreover, one might assume that "reasonable and prudent" would involve operating an urban gas well according to some social license or corporate social responsibility, such as community well-being or a good neighbor policy (see Kotler and Lee, 2008). But thus far the prudent operator standard only has been used to resolve oil and gas drainage, development, exploration, and marketing conflicts between mineral lessors and lessees (Conine, 2001). Instead of contemporary urban land-use zoning and planning considerations of the protection of public health, safety, and welfare, "reasonably prudent operator" standards would seem to dictate that operators should only make decisions based on the technical knowledge and skills required in the industry.

HB40 also will likely force many DFW cities to "choose between enforcing their ordinance below optimum potential or make changes to the language" (Groth, pers. comm., May 11, 2016), according to a former Denton Gas Well Inspector (2010–2015). For example, the designation of an activity such as site clean-up after a well blowout as above ground or below ground will need to be rethought by city governments. Currently, several city ordinances regard well blowouts as above-ground activities, but operators could argue that these are in fact below-ground activities subject to the exclusive jurisdiction of the state government. In this example, cities could enforce emergency response regulations associated with the blowout (per HB40), but their authority to enforce clean-up regulations after the blowout could be challenged as an intrusion on the powers of the RRC. These situations place new burdens on city governments to make changes to their ordinance language; they also limit or even remove municipal power to hold operators responsible for the externalities associated with drilling activities. The onus now seems to reside with operators to determine the level of local regulations they are willing to tolerate, leading activists to allege that democratic processes are the ultimate victim of HB40 (Figure 6.4).

It is possible that courts in Texas could rule in favor of cities and restore their oil and gas regulatory authority if lawsuits challenge HB40. In Pennsylvania, the

Figure 6.4 Citizen protest outside Denton City Hall after the passage of HB40, June 1, 2015.

Source: Photograph by M. Fry.

court argued that "[b]y prohibiting local governments from enacting restrictions on fracking, the state had effectively forced local governments to breach their public trust duties to their citizens" (*Robinson Twp.* v. *Commonwealth of Pennsylvania*, 2012, p. 205). According to van de Biezenbos (2016), Texas cities also could get around HB40 by incorporating existing state environmental laws into their ordinances and thereby force operators to comply with state environmental regulations.

For now, the only certainty with HB40 is that it simultaneously expanded the power of the state government and reduced the power of municipal governments by removing the decision-making power from local government officials. In the words of one municipal official, citizens with complaints about oil and gas drilling activities are now advised to "call Austin," the Texas state capital, rather than their local city council members. In this way, the Texas state government used HB40 to rescale, redistribute, and remove municipal regulatory authority over oil and gas activities, creating an ongoing experiment in regulating urban drilling and hydraulic fracturing.

Conclusion

Analysis of HB40 shows that the legislative bill was written by industry lawyers in response to the November 2014 voter-approved fracking ban in Denton. A five-year *prima facie* clause demonstrates that the bill sought to undermine municipal regulations that the oil and gas industry found unacceptable. Fort Worth's ordinance and setback distance were widely copied by other cities, were supported by industry, and gained status as best practice; therefore, it is the most likely to be deemed "commercially reasonable" by the industry. The ambiguity of the "commercially reasonable" and "prudent operator" standards allows the hydrocarbon industry to continue to use the threat of legal action as an indirect means to influence municipal regulations. Moreover, unlike other industrial regulations that have empirically-derived thresholds, "commercially reasonable" standards respond to legal, political, social, and economic criteria that are not specified in statute and are not based on scientifically-defined risk thresholds. As a result, new burdens are placed on city residents who now must contend with a powerful industry, without recourse to local government.

These findings offer comparative value to other US regions and international sites with hydraulic fracturing. Specifically, the fragmentation of regulatory authority in Texas demonstrates how the hydrocarbon industry and its allies targeted their response to local-scale contestations. Detailed analysis of abrupt shifts in hydrocarbon governance reveals that hydrocarbon firms and their political allies can react rapidly to municipal-scale policy-making that threatens to disrupt industry activities and identifies unintended consequences of anti-fracking electoral success. The passage of HB40 also reflects the broader trend of revising US state-level legal and regulatory statutes, which has been instrumental in enabling shale gas production and commodification (Andrews and McCarthy, 2014). Examining the components, intent, and origins of legislation like HB40 reveals how power, contestation, and geography affect shale gas governance. It also shows that laws are not single, coherent enactments, but more often comprise mosaics of contradictory components (Benson, 2012) and regulatory experiments.

Acknowledgment

The authors acknowledge financial support from National Science Foundation Grants #1262521 and #1262526.

References

Andrews, E. and McCarthy, J. (2014). Scale, shale, and the state: Political ecologies and legal geographies of shale gas development in Pennsylvania. *Journal of Environmental Studies and Sciences*, 4(1), 7–16.

Baker, M. (2015). Fort Worth officials are asked to help rewrite drilling bill. *Fort Worth Star-Telegram*, 24 March, 2015. Available at: www.star-telegram.com/news/business/barnett-shale/article16215755.html

Benson, M. H. (2012). Mining sacred space: law's enactment of competing ontologies in the American West. *Environment and Planning A* 44(6), 1443–1458.

Briggle, A. (2015). *A Field Philosopher's Guide to Fracking: How One Texas Town Stood Up to Big Oil and Gas*. New York: W. W. Norton & Company.

BSEEC (Barnett Shale Energy Education Council). (2015). Fact Sheet: HB 40, Setbacks, and 'Commercially Reasonable.' Available at: www.dropbox.com/s/05qeq3lj2odknw3/FACT_SHEET_HB_40_Setbacks_Commercially_Reasonable_v2.pdf?dl=0 (accessed May 13, 2016).

City of Dallas. (2014). City Secretary's Office: Agendas, Minutes, & Digital Audio Recordings (Current). Available at: www.ci.dallas.tx.us/cso/cMeetings.html

City of Fort Worth. (2014). Gas Well Drilling. Available at: http://fortworthtexas.gov/gaswells/

Conine, G. (2001). Prudent operator standard: Applications beyond the oil and gas lease. *Natural Resources Journal*, 41, 23.

Davis, C. (2014). Substate federalism and fracking policies: Does state regulatory authority trump local and land use autonomy? *Environmental Science and Technology*, 48, 8397–8403.

Finley, B. (2016). Colorado Supreme Court rules state law trumps local bans on fracking. *Denver Post*. Available at: www.denverpost.com/news/ci_29839543/colorado-high-court-rule-state-vs-local-power

Fry, M. (2013). Urban gas drilling and distance ordinances in the Texas Barnett Shale. *Energy Policy* 62, 79–89.

Fry, M., and Brannstrom, C. (2017). Emergent patterns and processes in urban hydrocarbon governance. *Energy Policy*, 111, 383–393.

Fry, M., Brannstrom, C., and Murphy, T. (2015a). How Dallas became frack free: hydrocarbon governance under neoliberalism. *Environment and Planning A*, 47(12), 2591–2608.

Fry, M., Briggle, A., and Kincaid, J. (2015b). Fracking and environmental (in)justice in a Texas city. *Ecological Economics*, 117, 97–107.

Godfrey, C.M. (2005). A brief history of the oil and gas practice in Texas. *Texas Bar Journal*, 68, 812.

Goho, S.A. (2012). Municipalities and hydraulic fracturing: Trends in state preemption. *Journal of Planning and Environmental Law*, 64(7), 3–9.

Heinkel-Wolfe, P. (2015a). City's lobbyists confirm that Exxon attorney Shannon Ratliff and TxOGA's attorney Tom Phillips wrote #HB40 for industry. *The Denton Record Chronicle* Twitter feed, Available at: https://twitter.com/dentonrc/status/613433209104134144

Heinkel-Wolfe, P. (2015b). Did he or didn't he? *The Denton Record Chronicle*, May 1, 2015. Available at: http://newsgatheringblog.dentonrc.com/2015/05/did-he-or-didnt-he.html/

Hudgins, A., and Poole, A. (2014). Framing fracking: Private property, common resources, and regimes of governance. *Political Ecology*, 21, 222–348.

Konschnik, K. E., and Boling, M. K. (2014). Shale gas development: A smart regulation framework. *Environmental Science & Technology*, 48(15), 8404–8416.

Kotler, P., and Lee, N. (2008). *Corporate Social Responsibility: Doing the Most Good for Your Company and Your Cause*. New York: John Wiley & Sons.

Malewitz, J. (2015). Senate Committee Advances "Denton Fracking Bill." *Texas Tribune*. Available at: www.texastribune.org/2015/03/24/senate-committee-advances-denton-fracking-bill/

Malewitz, J., and Murphy, R. (2015). See how local drilling rules vary across Texas. *Texas Tribune*. Available at: www.texastribune.org/2015/03/27/see-how-local-drilling-rules-vary-across-texas/

McKenzie, L. M., Witter, R. Z., Newman, L. S., and Adgate, J. L. (2012). Human health risk assessment of air emissions from development of unconventional natural gas resources. *Science of the Total Environment*, 424, 79–87.

Peck, J. (2011). Geographies of policy: From transfer-diffusion to mobility-mutation. *Progress in Human Geography*, 35(6), 773–797.

Rabe, B. G. (2014). Shale play politics: The intergovernmental odyssey of American shale governance. *Environmental Science & Technology*, 48(15), 8369–8375.

Rahm, D. (2011). Regulating hydraulic fracturing in shale gas plays: The case of Texas. *Energy Policy*, 39, 2974–2981.

Richardson, N., Gottlieb, M., Krupnick, A., and Wiseman, H. (2013). *The State of State Shale Gas Regulation; Resources for the Future*: Washington, DC. Available at: www.rff.org/shalegasrisks

Riley, T. (2007). Wrangling with urban wildcatters: Defending Texas municipal oil and gas development ordinances against regulatory takings challenges. *Vermont Law Review*, 32, 349.

Ritchie, A. (2014). On local fracking bans: Policy and preemption in New Mexico. *Natural Resources Journal*, 54(2).

Ritchie, A. (2016). Fracking in Louisiana: The missing process/land use distinction in state preemption and opportunities for local participation. *Louisiana Law Review*, 76(3), 810–862.

Robinson TWP. v. *Commonwealth of Pennsylvania*. (2012). 52 A.3d 463 (July 26), Available at: www.pacourts.us/assets/opinions/Supreme/out/J-127A-D-2012oajc.pdf

State of Texas. (2015). Natural Resource Code. Sec. 81.0523. Available at: www.statutes.legis.state.tx.us/Docs/NR/htm/NR.81.htm

Taylor, W., Wilkes, L., Fuchs, J., Ghorayeb, B., and Powell, R. (2015). Contracts requiring "Best Efforts" and "Commercially Reasonable Efforts." American Bar Association. Available at http://apps.Americanbar.org/litigation/committees/energy/articles/spring2015-0515-contracts-requiring-best-efforts-commercially-reasonable-efforts.html (accessed May 13, 2016).

Texas Legislature Online. (2015). HB40. Available at: www.legis.state.tx.us/BillLookup/History.aspx?LegSess=84R&Bill=HB40

Tilove, J. (2015). Gov.-elect Abbott: End local bans on bags, fracking, tree-cutting. *Austin American-Statesman*. Available at: www.statesman.com/news/news/state-regional/gov-elect-abbott-end-local-bans-on-bags-fracking-t/njjQg/ (accessed January 9, 2015).

TIPPRO (Texas Independent Producers & Royalty Owners Association). (2015). Senate Natural Resources & Economic Development Committee passes House Bill 40. Available at: www.tipro.org/UserFiles/04.30.15_TIPRO_Statement.pdf (accessed May 3, 2015).

TxOGA. (Texas Oil & Gas Association). (2015). The facts on overreaching bans and predatory ordinances. Available at: www.youtube.com/watch?v=mRvkkB_FwRg

U.S. Census Bureau. (2015). National, state, and Puerto Rico commonwealth totals datasets: Population, population change, and estimated components of population change: April 1, 2010 to July 1, 2014.

van de Biezenbos, K. (2016). Where oil is king. *Fordham Law Review*, Forthcoming. Available at SSRN: http://ssrn.com/abstract=2739172 or http://dx.doi.org/10.2139/ssrn.2739172

Warner, P., and Shapiro, J. (2013). Fractured, fragmented federalism: A study in fracking regulatory policy. *Publius: The Journal of Federalism*, 43(3), 474–496.

Welch, T. (2012). Municipal regulation of natural gas drilling in Texas. Paper presented at the University of Texas at Austin Land Use Planning Law Conference, Austin, Texas, 23 March.

7 The role of multi-state River Basin Commissions in shale gas governance systems

A comparative analysis of the Susquehanna and Delaware River Basin Commissions in the Marcellus Shale region

Grace Wildermuth, John Dzwonczyk and Kathryn Brasier

Introduction

Recent technological advances have allowed for the development of "tight" shale formations through high volume hydraulic fracturing and horizontal drilling. These unconventional methods present challenges to governance institutions created to regulate conventional oil and gas extraction. In the Appalachian Basin, two governing bodies, the Delaware River Basin Commission (DRBC) and the Susquehanna River Basin Commission (SRBC), create an additional layer of regulation with jurisdiction over water resources.

Despite nearly identical founding compacts and a shared border, these commissions have taken radically different approaches to unconventional oil and gas (UOG) development. The SRBC "monitors" water quality issues related to hydraulic fracturing, but intentionally only impacts the process through issuing water withdrawal and consumptive use permits. The DRBC, in contrast, has created a de facto ban on hydraulic fracturing within its boundaries by indefinitely delaying rule-making procedures. This chapter documents the history and actions of the two commissions and describes how differing political, social, and physical contexts led to differing approaches.

River Basin Commissions (RBCs), long uncontroversial, have suddenly become critical institutions because of their role governing the most essential resource in UOG extraction: water. The commissions have become flashpoints for stakeholder engagement, rule-making, and monitoring procedures. However, we know little about their decision-making processes and the scope of their jurisdiction, and how these affect UOG development management. This leads to larger questions about public engagement and equity within natural resource governance systems.

Our research shows that, despite superficial similarity, bureaucracies with nearly identical founding compacts are subject to different stresses, both from internal cultures and external contexts. Depending on their institutional capability and organizational structure, each may be subject to differing extents of bureaucratic capture or co-optation. This chapter examines two RBCs and their approaches to UOG regulation through documentary and interview research. These data are interpreted within the framework of two literatures: political ecology and environmental sociology. This chapter will describe the creation and role of RBCs, highlight the relevant literature, and describe the data collection and analysis methods used for this research. Next, it will consider the factors that have led to divergent regulatory actions, and finally assess the evidence presented to raise questions about domination, informal cooptation, and bureaucratic slippage in relation to these two organizations.

River Basin Commissions in the context of unconventional energy governance

The federal government has historically played a limited role in regulating oil and gas operations, leaving states to take on the primary role (Wiseman 2014). This has resulted in multilevel, fragmented, and decentralized governance structures unique to each state (Rabe 2014; Warner and Shapiro 2013). Oil and gas basins cross state boundaries, yielding differing regulations within one formation. Similarly, most regulation of water resources is at the state level, though it is loosely guided by the federal government, in part, through the Safe Drinking Water Act (Wiseman 2009), which includes regulations on the use of water for oil and gas production. However, water is highly mobile, confounding most regulation attempts at pre-existing administrative scales. The result is an incomplete understanding of the complexity of water system governance. Administrative boundaries are largely unable to account for the complexity of river basins. Such mismatches are not unique to research on hydraulic fracturing (Hussey and Pittock 2012), but they are germane: the EPA has recently identified that impacts of water use at smaller spatial and temporal scales can result in substantially different local impacts than existing research has indicated (EPA 2015).

Recognizing this mismatch and the conflicts thus created, the federal government created seven[1] river basin commissions. These regional bodies focus on managing and monitoring the health of a river system, though each charter is slightly different. RBCs attempt to account for the mismatch between hydrological scales and administrative scales – by sizing the administrative to fit the hydrological, existing regulatory gaps should be closed, resulting in uniform governance within the river basin.

The DRBC and SRBC were founded by Congress with very similar compacts signed by the member states in 1961 and 1972 respectively. Each board consists of one commissioner from each state in the river basin (see Figure 7.1), as well as a representative from the federal government, filled by a representative from

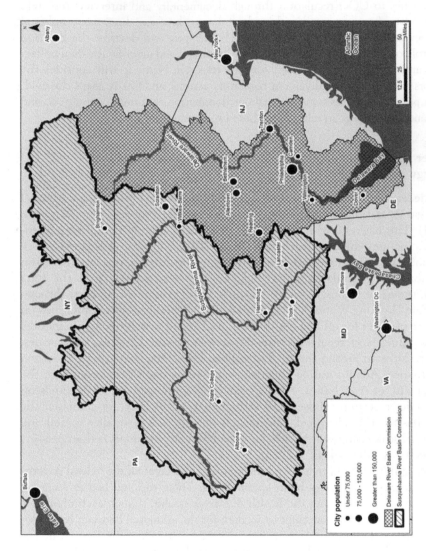

Figure 7.1 Map of the Delaware and Susquehanna River Basin Commissions.

Source: Created by Travis Young.

the US Army Corps of Engineers, the federal body responsible for the care of the nation's waterways (DRBC 1961; SRBC 1972).

These RBCs responded to the introduction of UOG development in markedly different manners. In May 2009, the DRBC announced that natural gas companies could not operate within the basin without applying for and obtaining DRBC approval, and that approvals would not be granted until new rules were adopted by the Commission. In 2010, the DRBC released draft regulations for public comment that applied to "all natural gas development projects ... in the Basin ... and to water withdrawals, well pad and related activities and wastewater disposal activities comprising part of, associated with, or serving such projects" (DRBC 2010: 3).

In response to these draft regulations, the DRBC received thousands of public comments in writing and at meetings throughout the basin. The DRBC published their 2011 Revised Draft Regulations (DRBC 2011), and intended to hold a vote soon after. The DRBC took no additional action on the matter until a resolution was passed at their September 2017 meeting for a revised set of regulations that would permanently ban hydraulic fracturing within the basin (DRBC 2017). Those draft regulations will be open to public comment and reconsidered by the Commission. Currently no UOG development is taking place within the Delaware River Basin. This de facto moratorium continues, despite ongoing legal challenges,[2] with the potential for a permanent ban.

The SRBC has taken a very different approach. After reviewing Pennsylvania Department of Environmental Protection (PADEP) drilling permits issued within their jurisdiction, the SRBC concluded that there was significant potential for the industry to "create adverse impacts to the water resources of the Basin," especially considering the likely quantity, widely distributed extraction locations, and timing of water withdrawals. They began issuing water withdrawal and consumptive use approvals for UOG development using their existing authorities and rules in June 2008 (SRBC 2016). They updated their regulations and permitting procedures, and invited public comment through meetings and written feedback from an engaged and divided public.

While the DRBC released one complete set of regulations specific to hydraulic fracturing, the SRBC made changes to existing regulations as necessary. The SRBC was concerned that existing water withdrawal and consumptive use thresholds did not account for projects in headwater areas and the "unusual nature of water withdrawals and use by the industry" (SRBC 2016). They initially lowered regulatory thresholds in 2008, but modified regulations in 2009 to fit the UOG industry specifically. These included measures to issue approvals for each drilling pad rather than each well, incentives for the industry to use lesser quality water, and encouragement for the reuse of flowback and production fluids (SRBC 2016). Minor modifications were made again in 2010 and 2011, and the Commission continues to make adjustments as necessary to "protect the Basin's water resources and simultaneously allow for the utilization of water by this new industry" (ibid.). The SRBC issued approvals throughout these regulation changes and continues to do so.

River Basin Commissions as natural resource bureaucracies

To understand the RBCs' roles in UOG extraction, we understand them as natural resource bureaucracies existing in a political-ecological context. The following literatures give a foundation for assessing how internal and external characteristics impact decisions the RBCs made, and trace the impacts of those decisions on the development of shale gas resources.

Max Weber attributed the creation of bureaucracy to the need to oversee land, waterways, and other natural resources in a public and collective manner (Weber 1978). Ideally, a rational, scientific bureaucracy would serve everyone equally. However, because of its impersonal character, a bureaucracy is "easily made to work for anybody who knows how to gain control over it" (Weber 1946: 229).

Weber's description of an ideal-type of bureaucracy has been criticized as an unrealistic portrait of how bureaucracies function. Shwom suggests that bureaucracy "conceptualized as an island," independent of outside forces is unjustified, highlighting "employee's personal motivations, external resource dependencies, and external cultural pressures" (Shwom 2009: 273). Shwom advocates for research that places bureaucratic actions "within their proper social, political, and economic relations" (ibid.: 286). In addition, Gilbert and Howe (1991) argue that to understand policy outcomes, it is essential to understand the history and institutional capacity of the bureaucracy, the broader social, economic, and political context in which it exists, and the interests engaged in influencing that organization.

We draw on several interconnected theories of bureaucratic domination, cooperation, cooptation, and capture, which represent specific ways external interests influence bureaucracies. Patrick West's research (1982, 1994) highlights how natural resource bureaucracies in particular are not only susceptible to, but contingent upon, local power structures, and are dependent on a particular set of stakeholders and their relative power.

West's multiple forms of domination (domination through external sanctions, informal cooptation, and domination) acknowledge the interplay between the internal organization and external forces. Domination through external sanctions involves "the exertion of external power sources by a constituency" (West 1994: 418), often via legal or political threats. Recurring or potential threats often result in "a stable form of domination in which threats are unneeded and domination flows evenly and automatically" (ibid.). Informal cooptation draws on Phillip Selznick's ([1949] 2012) concept and refers to "unacknowledged authority within the authority structure of the agency" (ibid.). External interests are informally welcomed into the structure of an organization and granted influence, in effect, granting real power without formal recognition. West (1982) describes two sub-types of informal cooptation. Internal informal cooptation is distinguished by admittance of a group into the internal structure of an organization, while external informal cooptation, on the other hand, occurs when power and control are handed to groups that remain external to the structure of the organization.

Freudenburg and Gramling (1994) add the concept of "capture" to explain how bureaucracies can be influenced by the organizations they regulate. They also introduce "bureaucratic slippage": "the tendency for broad policies to be altered through successive reinterpretation, such that the ultimate implementation may bear little resemblance" to intent (ibid.: 214). Slippage may be seen as the aggregate outcome of multiple mechanisms, and provides evidence of the degree of capture of bureaucracies.

The concepts of cooptation, domination, and slippage concern the ability of external interests to gain influence over a bureaucracy. As a result, other stakeholders lose influence, and may receive inequitable outcomes. Selznick notes that "power in a community is distributed among those who can mobilize resources," that may be used to shape bureaucratic decisions ([1949] 2012: 265). This is West's ultimate argument: "Since the poor have little power, bureaucracies tend to channel resource allocation in ways that perpetuate inequality and poverty" (1994: 1–2).

We also draw on political ecology to demonstrate how geographic and ecological context shape bureaucratic action. Political ecology traditions pay special attention to unequal power structures that shape changes in natural resource allocation and management (Budds 2004), resulting in a description of the ways political and environmental outcomes are shaped by sociopolitical factors (Cousins and Newell 2015).

Political ecology also stresses the need to understand how space and scale shape relationships between nature and society. Natural resources such as water and UOG are created, valued, and used differently at different scales and in different regions. Often, local resource management decisions are the visible expression of complex factors at state, national, and international scales (Bassett 1988). The relative lack of powerful regional institutions means that these links in the chain of explanation are often neglected. RBCs provide an opportunity to explore this intermediate level.

Together these theories inform our research by highlighting the importance of the ecological, social, economic, and political context of natural resource bureaucracies, and how those contexts influence bureaucracies' policy outcomes. Here we trace the decision-making processes of two bureaucracies, the SRBC and DRBC, and attempt to explain their divergent regulatory paths.

Methods and data collection

Data for this project include analysis of public documents and interviews with officials familiar with both agencies. Initially, staff, committee members, and commissioners of both RBCs were contacted for interviews. However, at the time of data collection, pending legal action meant that DRBC staff members declined to participate (*Wayne Land and Mineral Group, LLC* v. *DRBC* 2016). To compensate, we rely on secondary data to understand the DRBC: public documents, meeting notes, and reports. In addition, interviews were purposively conducted with individuals familiar with both RBCs and included questions probing for explicit comparisons. Key informants were identified through public websites, committee reports, and snowball sampling.

Overall, six semi-structured interviews were conducted in July 2016 in person or by phone. Informants were current and former staff members at the SRBC, members of state government agencies that work closely with both commissions, and individuals familiar with both commissions. Interviews ranged from 32–60 minutes, with an average duration of 46 minutes. All interviews were audio-recorded and transcribed verbatim. Major themes were identified and a coding scheme was developed by the authors. To ensure validity, one transcript was coded by two authors and compared for consistency and agreement. Inconsistent codes were discussed and revised. Data were managed using QSR International's NVivo 11 qualitative data analysis software (2015).

Documents, including the websites of the two commissions, the commission compacts, proposed and current regulations, and commission reports were summarized. This evidence was combined with interview data to verify claims and minimize bias.

Findings and discussion

Statutes, interpretations, and organizations

The two RBCs have nearly identical statutory responsibilities: the DRBC is to provide "comprehensive, multi-purpose planning [that] will enable the greatest benefit" from the river's resources; the SRBC is "to provide for cooperative and coordinated planning and action by the signatories with respect to water resources" (DRBC 1961; SRBC 1972). This is intentional: the DRBC's compact was used as the model for the SRBC's (Respondent 4). However, one major difference exists: the DRBC has an explicit mandate to manage *water quality* in the basin. The influence of this slight statutory difference cannot be overstated: it is the core principle that divides the SRBC and DRBC's approaches to UOG development. The SRBC compact has no such explicit requirement and as a result is "water quality shy" (Respondent 6).

The DRBC compact also states that "no project having a substantial effect on the water resources of the basin shall hereafter be undertaken by any person, corporation or governmental authority unless it shall have been first submitted to and approved by the commission" (DRBC 1961: 11). The concern expressed by landowners in the litigation filed is that the DRBC's authority could theoretically be extended to all land use within its basin if a "substantial effect" is determined. At least one respondent considers this a strong possibility:

> I think DRBC's regulations made an attempt to look at overall land use …
> of the impact of the industry on the land in the basin. And SRBC's were
> more focused on … individual locations of withdrawals. Cumulative
> impact, yes. But not the landscape per se or…. We [SRBC] took a very
> focused approach that we don't do traffic, we don't do roads, we don't do
> those kinds of impacts, that that was beyond our scope.
>
> (Respondent 3)

Geophysical and demographic context

The two river basins are similar, but with small differences critical to understanding the paths they have taken. The SRBC covers more than twice the land area, yet has just slightly more than half of the DRBC's population. Their landscapes and primary water uses, however, are quite similar, with roughly equal percentages dedicated to forest, agriculture, and urban landscapes. This combination creates very different cultural and political contexts and a very different set of stakeholders related to oil and gas development (see Table 7.1).

Various types of resource extraction and manufacturing have long histories in the Delaware River Basin, but oil and gas extraction is not one. The opposite is true in the Susquehanna River basin, which has had oil and gas extraction for decades. "… there was never a thought that they [the SRBC] weren't going to allow it at all because this was just a continuation of an industry that had been going on for 50 years" (Respondent 1). This history meant there was an existing regulatory pathway and set of stakeholders engaged in the issue in the SRBC, but not the DRBC.

Looming over the decision processes in the DRBC (but not the SRBC) is the "big gorilla in the room": New York City (Respondent 1). Although it does not fall within the jurisdiction of the DRBC, with a population of over eight million people in the city and over 20 million in the metro area, New York City extends its influence into the Delaware River basin through a vast aqueduct system (Cutcliffe 2014) that provides approximately half a billion gallons of water to the New York City metro area each day. The DRBC commissioners from New York and New Jersey must consider the needs of 20 million people outside their jurisdiction who might be substantially affected by their actions. Although there

Table 7.1 Comparisons of geophysical and demographic attributes of the SRBC and the DRBC

	Susquehanna River Basin (PA DCNR, 2003)	Delaware River Basin (USFS 1997)
Square miles	27,510	13,539
River miles	444	330
Population	3.9 m	7.3 m*
Primary use (% daily withdrawal)	Thermoelectric (79)	Thermoelectric (67)
	Forest (64), Agriculture (26), Development (7), Other (3)	Forest (60), Agriculture (24), Development (9), Other (7)

Note
* The population of the DRB does not include New York City (estimated population: 8.2 million in 2010), which receives half its water each day from the DRB. "Other" land uses include wetlands, bare land, above-ground mining, and surface water.

is disagreement around whether or not proposed gas development in the region could potentially impact New York City's water infrastructure, perceived potential impacts have played a prominent role in the discourse surrounding the issue. In contrast, the SRBC does not have a stakeholder with a large, concentrated, urban population and a unique water supply system.

Reactions to unconventional oil and gas

The two commissions seem to have different views of their authority regarding UOG development. The SRBC sees itself as complementing state regulations. One respondent from the SRBC described its role as to "fill gaps in [member states'] programs but certainly not constrain their programs" (Respondent 3). Another said:

> Based on SRBC's regulations … really our focus is limited to withdrawals and consumptive use of water…. All the other potential impacts, again even if it was possibly related to water, are firmly under the jurisdiction of existing state agencies…. Certainly we are concerned about it, but in consultation with our members, determined early on that that was going to be their jurisdiction and we would focus strictly on quantity: the acquisition and movement of water.
>
> (Respondent 4)

Regardless of the extent to which the commission's authority supersedes the sovereignty of its member states, the SRBC "only chose to exercise the authority needed" and tried to "complement the activity that the states regulated in a way that wouldn't duplicate our actions" (Respondent 6). Consequently, the SRBC chose to approach UOG development using the same methods used for oil and gas industry regulation in the past, with modifications as necessary. One example is its approach to consumptive and non-consumptive use.[3] The SRBC's regulations prior to shale development stipulated that any project proposing to consumptively use 20,000 gallons of water per day or greater, over a 30-day average, would require their approval. That includes the deep-well injection of water (as used in hydraulic fracturing) and so water used by the industry was determined "consumptive use" and subject to SRBC authority (Respondent 3). The SRBC intentionally did not identify UOG development as different from other industries:

> The commission did not put a value judgment and say "Um, the use of water for this purpose is good, bad, or indifferent." … From the commission's perspective, we looked at this type of withdrawal as having the same potential effect as any other withdrawal would have.
>
> (Respondent 2)

However, key informants suggested that the DRBC has treated the UOG industry differently than other industries they regulate. One respondent made this comparison:

[DRBC] never regulated consumptive use…. And then all of a sudden they decided they would start regulating consumptive use with Marcellus … it was like, "How can you say that consumptive use by one industry is any more detrimental than consumptive use by another industry? If you're going to regulate consumptive use, regulate it."

(Respondent 6)

The SRBC did recognize that there were certain industry characteristics that necessitated updates to their regulatory practices. An SRBC informant explained:

We needed to do some things to adapt to really what was a completely different industry to anything we'd seen before. And that's been the next five years: modifying our regulations and putting new practices and policies into place so that we were certain we had the most appropriate oversight.

(Respondent 4)

Using their existing regulatory program as a starting point, the SRBC made three main changes. First, they lowered the existing water withdrawal thresholds: 100,000 gallons per day over a 30-day average for withdrawal, and 20,000 gallons per day over a 30-day average for consumption. The commission decided these thresholds were not adequate to address the threat to water quantity produced by the industry because it is not a "brick and mortar facility situated on an established structure," and can withdraw water from many distributed locations simultaneously (Respondent 4).

We recognized that cumulatively as a project that it was important that all of their water withdrawals came from approved sources. We accomplished this by saying gallon one. Any water you take must come from a source approved by the SRBC.

(Respondent 4)

Second, SRBC increased their scientific and technical staff to manage the increased volume of permit applications:

SRBC did not have the staff at the time, in 2008, to keep up with the onslaught of applications that came in for water withdrawals, consumptive water uses, nor did SRBC have much of a compliance staff to be able to ensure that the requirements that were imposed upon the natural gas industry … were being adhered to.

(Respondent 2)

Third, they increased permit fees in order to hire additional technical, administrative, information technology, and compliance staff, and to open a field office to meet the needs of the rapid increase in UOG development within the basin, which was accounting for about 80 percent of their permitting operations.

In contrast, the DRBC approached UOG development as a unique industry that required new regulations. Defining each well pad as a "project" that could have "substantial effect" on water quality meant the commission needed to develop regulations that would effectively create an additional layer of permitting and regulatory structure. The DRBC first published draft regulations in 2010, which were open to public comment for approximately four months, during which time the commission received nearly 69,000 comments. They published revised regulations in 2011, but they were never voted on or adopted, and new draft regulations are currently forthcoming (DRBC 2017).

The 2011 regulations covered nearly all aspects of well development: approval was required from the DRBC for water withdrawals and diversions, and the transfer or treatment of discharge or wastewater. In addition, all natural gas companies that held leases on more than 3,200 acres of land in the DRBC or with more than five developed well pads had to obtain from the DRBC a development plan which dictates where infrastructure may be sited based on land and water resources (DRBC 2011).

Decision-making procedures

Both RBCs provided opportunities for public comment on their draft regulations. In response to their 2010 draft regulations, the DRBC received nearly 69,000 comment submissions. The commenters included private citizens, government agencies, elected officials, environmental groups, industry, and various other organizations (DRBC 2010). Following the public comment process, the commission published their 2011 revised regulations, which "were guided by the public's comments and commissioners' discussions with their respective staff, advisors, and one another" (ibid.).

The SRBC published their draft regulations in 2008 and subsequently hosted public comment meetings and accepted written comments. Direct comparisons between the DRBC and SRBC are difficult because the DRBC attempted one massive regulatory overhaul while the SRBC made many small rule changes. However, SRBC records indicate two public hearings in relation to a September 2008 consumptive use regulation resulted in 28 comments from individuals, gas companies, and NGOs (Respondent 3, pers. comm., December 2016). Though the magnitude of public comment was smaller than in the DRBC, feedback to the SRBC indicated an engaged and divided public.

SRBC representatives stated that while any and all feedback was welcomed, only scientific and factual input was considered when the commission was making decisions. One respondent explained:

> We were not all that interested in whether people stood up and said "We think natural gas development is a wonderful thing" or "We think it's a terrible thing." The decisions that the commission made were based on science.... If the public had facts, by way of information and input, you

know, that would be useful to the commission in making its decision, that's great. That's welcome. But opinions, that's a different matter.

(Respondent 2)

The emphasis on science was a repeated theme in SRBC interviews, and something about which the commission's members expressed pride. In stark contrast, the DRBC's indecision on hydraulic fracturing is viewed by outside sources as politically-motivated rather than scientifically-motivated:

I can see where they can come up with a scenario where it's not acceptable to do it here, or here. But not everywhere. I mean, they are making it flat out that you can't do it at all. As a matter of fact, they haven't even said that because ... they're saying they're still deciding.... But best I can determine, that's pure politics. It isn't the science behind it.

(Respondent 1)

The two RBCs operate within very different political environments. As one respondent offered, "So how could two commissions with similar authority come down differently? Well, the political dynamics in the Delaware were different than they were in the Susquehanna. I mean, it's that simple" (Respondent 6). The Delaware River Basin is "much more intense and much more political" than its Susquehanna counterpart, explained one respondent (Respondent 1).

The DRBC's public comment process may have increased access for interest groups to influence regulatory decisions. People on both sides of the issue began to see the RBCs as a tool for allowing or preventing UOG development in the region. One SRBC representative described sitting down with major environmental organizations: "You know, they were basically saying, 'You're the one who has the authority. Be our champion. Shut this industry down. Impose a moratorium. Where's your backbone?'" (Respondent 6). As regional regulatory bodies, RBCs were seen as an opportunity to create a multi-state policy on natural gas development. The SRBC's commitment to their perceived regulatory scope, their reception of only factual and scientific input, and their operation in a less politically-charged context precluded them from playing this role. The DRBC, on the other hand, has arguably functioned in this way and continues to do so, currently through their de facto moratorium.

Assessing the evidence for domination, cooptation, and capture

Here we assess the processes and evidence described above to raise questions about domination, informal cooptation, and bureaucratic slippage in relation to these two organizations. Our research shows how the presence and capacities of different interest groups interacted with internal structures and procedures to lead to divergent outcomes. This may also reflect potential differences in susceptibility to "capture" by entrenched interests. We highlight three ways in which these RBCs have been a locus of conflict, and how interests involved in these conflicts have attempted to influence the outcomes of the RBCs.

- *Domination through external sanctions*: A number of groups have sued the DRBC, including a recently filed complaint by a group of landowners alleging the DRBC lacked the authority to regulate (*Wayne Land and Mineral Group, LLC* v. *DRBC* 2016). Previously, an environmental organization sued the DRBC for their authorization of a water withdrawal request from an energy corporation in March 2009 (*Delaware Riverkeeper Network et al.* v. *DRBC et al.* 2011). In addition, the New York Attorney General's Office sued the DRBC and its supporting federal agencies, alleging that they had not completed a proper environmental review of the impacts of natural gas activity on the watershed prior to their 2010 draft regulations (*New York* v. *U.S. Army Corps of Engineers* 2012). DRBC's stalled regulations may indicate a desire to avoid these lawsuits and confrontations, resulting in the de facto outcome of disallowing shale developing in the region. With the exception of the more recent Wayne Land and Mineral Group, LLC lawsuit, the early litigious environment surrounding shale development may have influenced the DRBC's policy direction such that environmental interests and the interests of those concerned with New York City's water supply achieved their goals. A corresponding search for litigation on the topic of shale gas development facing the SRBC returned no results.
- *External informal cooptation*: The active political environment in the DRBC, particularly the issue of protecting New York City's water supply, might have influenced the commission's indecision on hydraulic fracturing regulations. The potential for environmental activism, the extensive public comment period, and the subsequent decision of New York Governor Cuomo to enact a moratorium on shale gas development, created a political environment that could have pushed the DRBC to avoid enacting final rules and permitting the activity in the basin.
- *Bureaucratic slippage*: Both RBCs have a dual mandate, requiring balancing of water resource protection and economic impacts on the population in the basin. While SRBC representatives explicitly noted giving due consideration to both, there is disagreement among respondents about whether the DRBC equally honored both prongs of their mandate, raising questions of bureaucratic slippage through prioritizing, and therefore reinterpreting, one part of its mandate. In addition, the interpretation of specific wording ("substantial effect" and "project") in their compact has led the DRBC into legal proceedings that threatened their fundamental mandate over water quality. The interpretation of the DRBC's mandate as it relates to shale development suggests the UOG industry uniquely affects water quality, and implies a potential expansion of the commission's authority. In comparison, the SRBC sought to fill regulatory gaps and only exercises the authority necessary, interpreting their mandate narrowly.

Conclusion

Because of their roles in governing water resources, RBCs have become flash-points for stakeholder engagement, rule-making, and monitoring procedures for the UOG industry. They are nested within a system of overlapping regulatory structures, leading to ambiguity of authority and role. In the case of the DRBC and SRBC, both commissions began with similar compacts, with the exception of the DRBC's water quality provisions. They have evolved to perceive their regulatory and governance roles differently as those nearly identical compacts have been re-interpreted over time and the cultures within the agencies evolved and diverged. While the DRBC sees itself as a public and semi-political govern-ing body, the SRBC considers itself a semi-public technocracy meant to fill a regulatory gap. The ongoing litigation surrounding the decisions of the DRBC is testing the limits of regulatory jurisdiction and authority as they relate to state and federal entities and regional river basin commissions.

We highlight three ways in which external interests have attempted to influ-ence the outcomes of the RBCs: (1) domination through external sanctions; (2) external informal cooptation; and (3) bureaucratic slippage. Together with differing perceptions of regulatory roles and unique regulatory, demographic, and physical landscapes, these differences have led the DRBC to impose a polit-ically contentious de facto moratorium while the SRBC quietly but scientifically regulates some aspects of UOG development, extensively monitors others, and explicitly recuses itself from still more. Therefore, this research ultimately serves to highlight the threat of powerful interests gaining control over natural resource bureaucracies, potentially leading to inequitable and unjust outcomes for marginalized populations.

At the conclusion of his study, Patrick West says, "Powerful economic inter-ests have exerted considerable influence and domination over public natural resource agencies with respect to distributive equity in access to natural resource use" and that this has "contributed to the maintenance of social stratification and poverty in rural areas" (1982: 110). Though he was discussing the US Forest Service, West could have easily been talking about the role of RBCs in the Mar-cellus Shale region. The powerful economic and political interests of New York City and other urban and industrial centers in the Delaware River basin have coopted the DRBC to satisfy their need for fresh water. In doing so, they have relocated ecological and economic risk from themselves to Delaware River basin residents. The DRBC's de facto ban on hydraulic fracturing removes one natural resource (water) from landowner management, prevents landowners from devel-oping another (UOG), and may have further impacts on unrelated land uses if it is not clarified.

Thus, does a governing bureaucracy, clearly delineated by its physical geo-graphy and ostensibly apolitical, become "captured" by the politics of its member states. This research adds a new dimension to West's theories – he ulti-mately concludes that industry can co-opt bureaucracy, but this research sug-gests that environmental interests can as well. These findings introduce additional applications for West's theories of the cooptation and domination of natural resource bureaucracies that warrant future research.

Notes

1 The US Fish and Wildlife Service (www.fws.gov) lists 40 interstate river compacts, most of which are focused on specific resources (such as fish). The SRBC and DRBC are two of seven identified that have a focus on "Water Resources and Flood Control."
2 In May 2016, a landowner group filed a complaint against the DRBC in which the landowners asked the court to declare that the DRBC lacks the authority under its compact to "review and approve a natural gas well pad, a gas well and related facilities and associated activities" (*Wayne Land and Mineral Group, LLC* v. *Delaware River Basin Commission* 2016). The lawsuit was dismissed in May 2017. WLMG filed a Notice of Appeal in April 2017. Litigation is ongoing.
3 *Consumptive water use*: water evaporated, lost underground, or embodied in a product; it results in a net loss of water in the watershed where the water originates and reduces the water availability of that region. *Non-consumptive water use*: denotes the water that is returned after use to the watershed where it originates; it may generate wastewater and result in degradation of water quality of the region and/or increased costs to treat wastewater. Often referred to as a "withdrawal" when consumption is not specified.

References

Bassett, T. J. (1988). The Political Ecology of Peasant-Herder Conflicts in the Northern Ivory Coast. *Annals of the Association of American Geographers*, 78(3), 453–472.

Budds, J. (2004). Power, Nature and Neoliberalism: The Political Ecology of Water in Chile. *Singapore Journal of Tropical Geography*, 25(3), 322–342.

Cousins, J. J., and Newell, J. P. (2015). A Political–Industrial Ecology of Water Supply Infrastructure for Los Angeles. *Geoforum*, 58(January), 38–50. doi:10.1016/j.geoforum.2014.10.011.

Cutcliffe, S. H. (2014). Systematizing the Flow: Urban Water Supply in America. *Reviews in American History*, 42(4), 697–704. doi: 10.1353/rah.20140097.

Delaware Riverkeeper Network et al. v. *Delaware River Basin Commission et al.*, Case 3:20-cv-05639-AET (NJ District Court 2011).

DRBC. (1961). *DRBC Compact*. Retrieved from www.nj.gov/drbc/library/documents/compact.pdf.

DRBC. (2010). *Natural Gas Development Regulations*. Retrieved from www.nj.gov/drbc/library/documents/naturalgas-draftregs.pdf.

DRBC. (2011). *Natural Gas Development Regulations*. Retrieved from www.nj.gov/drbc/library/documents/naturalgas-REVISEDdraftregs110811.pdf.

DRBC. (2017). *Natural Gas Drilling Index Page*. Retrieved from www.state.nj.us/drbc/programs/natural/.

EPA (Environmental Protection Agency). (2015). Assessment on the Potential Impacts of Hydraulic Fracturing for Oil and Gas on Drinking Water Resources. June 2015. Available at: http://cfpub.epa.gov/ncea/hfstudy/recordisplay.cfm?deid=244651

Freudenburg, W. R., and Gramling, R. (1994). Bureaucratic Slippage and Failures of Agency Vigilance: The Case of the Environmental Studies Program. *Social Problems*, 41(2), 214–239.

Gilbert, J., and Howe, C. (1991). Beyond "State vs. Society": Theories of the State and New Deal Agricultural Policies. *American Sociological Review*, 56, 204–220.

Hussey, K., and Pittock, J. (2012). "The Energy & Water Nexus: Managing the Links between Energy and Water for a Sustainable Future." *Ecology and Society*, 17(1). doi:10.5751/ES-04641-170131.

New York v. U.S. Army Corps of Engineers et al., Case 1:11-cv-03780-CLP (NY Eastern District Court 2012).

Pennsylvania Department of Conservation and Natural Resources (2003). Watershed Education: Susquehanna River Basin Facts. http://dcnr.pa.gov/cs/groups/public/documents/document/dcnr_20031260.pdf.

Rabe, B. G. (2014). Shale Play Politics: The Intergovernmental Odyssey of American Shale Governance. *Environmental Science & Technology* 48(15), 8369–8375.

Selznick, P. ([1949] 2012). *TVA and the Grass Roots: A Study in the Sociology of Formal Organization*. Berkeley, CA: University of California Press.

Shwom, R. (2009). Strengthening Sociological Perspectives on Organizations and the Environment. *Organization & Environment*, 22(3), 271–292.

SRBC. (1972). *SRBC Compact*. Retrieved from www.srbc.net/about/srbc_compact.pdf.

SRBC. (2016). *Water Use Associated with Natural Gas Shale Development: An Assessment of Activities Managed by the Susquehanna River Basin Commission July 2008 through December 2013* (SRBC Publication No. 299).

United States Forest Service (1997). Delaware River Basin Collaborative Environmental Monitoring and Research Initiative: Basin Facts. Available at: www.fs.fed.us/ne/global/research/drb/basin.html.

Warner, B., and Shapiro, J. (2013). Fractured, Fragmented Federalism: A Study in Fracking Regulatory Policy. *The Journal of Federalism* 43(3), 474–496.

Wayne Land and Mineral Group, LLC v. Delaware River Basin Commission, Case 3:16-cv-00897-RDM (PA Middle District Court 2016).

Weber, M. (1946). Bureaucracy. In H. H. Gerth and C. W. Mills, (Eds.) *Essays in Sociology* (pp. 194–244). New York: Oxford University Press.

Weber, M. (1978). *Economy and Society: An Outline of Interpretive Sociology*. Berkeley, CA: University of California Press.

West, P. C. (1982). *Natural Resource Bureaucracy and Rural Poverty: A Study in the Political Sociology of Natural Resources*. Ann Arbor, MI: University of Michigan School of Natural Resources.

West, P. C. (1994). Natural Resources and the Persistence of Rural Poverty in America: A Weberian Perspective on the Role of Power, Domination, and Natural Resource Bureaucracy. *Society & Natural Resources*, 7, 415–427.

Wiseman, H. J. (2009) Untested Waters: The Rise of Hydraulic Fracturing in Oil and Gas Production and the Need to Revisit Regulation. *Fordham Environmental Law Review*, 20: 115.

Wiseman, H. J. (2014). The Capacity of States to Govern Shale Gas Development Risks. *Environmental Science & Technology*, 48(15), 8376–8387. doi:10.1021/es4052582.

Part II

Information, communication, scientific assessment and public participation

8 Unlikely allies against fracking

Networks of resistance against shale gas development in Poland

Aleksandra Lis and Agata Stasik

Introduction: shale gas in the neighborhood and outside of it

In June 2014, after more than a year of persistent occupational anti-fracking protest in a small village in the East of Poland, the global oil and gas corporation Chevron decided to withdraw from the area. It is complicated to assess to what extent the evident lack of a "social licence to operate" (Boutilier 2014; Joyce and Thomson 2000; Nelsen 2006) was the main reason for this decision. This lack of clarity in similar cases is the rule rather than the exception, which leads us to the question: what do local protest movements mean for non-local actors? In the face of this puzzle, we propose to reflect on processes of knowledge-production and mobilization on and between different scales: the local, the global and the European. We inquire into the nature of relations between local mobilization and shale gas politics in the anti-fracking movement and in the EU policy arena.

To shed some light on the issue, we focus mainly on interactions between local actors, representatives of the anti-fracking movement internationally and national NGOs' representatives who mediated these connections; as well as on interactions between local actors and actors from the European Union policy arena. We examine the occupational protest against Chevron's exploration activities in Żurawlów, in the south-east of Poland by drawing on research interviews with activists, rich online documentation posted on the Web by different engaged sides, press materials and a documentary. In order to understand the meaning of local-Brussels relations, we carried out interviews with officials, politicians and activists operating in this arena and we analyzed official reports on shale gas exploration.

Through our analysis, we follow the creation of relations between various actors, usually conceived of as coming from different scales and doing different kinds of politics (local protests, social movements, bureaucracies). At the same time, we study how Żurawlów was created and established as part of shale gas politics in various contexts and at various scales and what it meant there. In our analysis, we draw attention to the fact that during these interactions we can observe interrelated processes of constructing: (1) knowledge claims about the environment and technology (Fischer 2000; Pellizzoni 2011; Wynne 1998);

(2) the social and political identities of actors engaged in interactions around Żurawlów (Callon and Rabeharisoa 2003; Callon et al. 2009; Davies 2013); as well as (3) the construction of various kinds and scales of shale gas politics as global social movements, EU shale gas politics and local shale gas protests (see Jasanoff 2004; Fox et al. 2011).

In this chapter, after discussing our theoretical position, we briefly describe the context of shale gas exploration in Poland, the actions undertaken by the local activists and their allies in Żurawlów their connections with representatives and objects connected to the global anti-fracking movement and the political and non-governmental actors from Brussels. Finally, we offer conclusions.

Shale gas in Poland and in the EU: the rise and fall of a dream about power

Despite the fact that Polish geologists and professionals from the oil and gas sector had been aware of the existence of natural gas in shale formation for decades, by the time the "shale gas revolution" started in the US around the beginning of the 2000s, the Polish deposits had not been considered to be technically accessible. In fact, licenses for shale gas exploration have been granted in Poland since the late 1990s but the shale gas issue only began to be publicly debated in April 2011. The main trigger for that was the EIA (U.S. Energy Information Agency) report with a preliminary assessment of shale gas deposits around the world (EIA 2011). The assessment for Poland was very optimistic. Poland was supposed to possess the richest deposit in Europe estimated at 187 tcm (5.3 bn cubic meters) of technically accessible natural gas. However, the authors of the report emphasized the preliminary character of their assessment and the analysis that followed from other institutes (based on the same set of archival data) showed lower estimates (Gautier et al. 2012; PIG-PIB 2012). An assessment based on the recent drilling has not been issued as yet, as more geological data is needed.

Shale gas was welcomed by Polish politicians for many reasons. It promised independence from the foreign (mainly Russian) gas supplies (Lis and Stankiewicz 2016; Upham et al. 2017), as well as a solution to the climate change conundrum. Since Polish electricity production is mainly based on coal combustion, domestic shale gas could serve as a reliable transition fuel and a back-up source for renewable energy. Therefore, in the discussion on shale gas, the political, economic and geo-political gains were highlighted over potential environmental risks (Lis and Stankiewicz 2017). Political support came from the whole spectrum of the political arena in Poland. While adopting geopolitical and economic framing in the central government and in the mainstream media, issues important from other perspectives – such as environmental concerns and discussions about the possible impacts of production on local communities – were not addressed in detail by Polish policy-makers (ibid.). Working on the assumption that technology presents no danger to the environment, the possibilities of enforcing tighter environmental regulations by EU institutions were presented as one of the main risks to shale gas development in Poland. The lack of such regulations coming from the EU was interpreted as a success for Polish diplomacy (interview, Warsaw, January 2015).

Seventy-eight exploratory drillings have been carried out in Poland in the past five years. In 2014, 93 licenses for shale gas prospecting were issued by the Ministry of Environment, while in August 2016 companies were active only on 28 licenses. Most of the operating companies decided to leave Poland without giving many public details about the reasons for their withdrawal. Low prices of oil on the global markets and unfavorable geological conditions for shale gas extraction have often been considered to be behind these decisions. It is, however, still believed that future changes in the global oil and gas markets and the progress of extracting technologies may bring the issue of Polish shale gas back onto the table.

While the Polish government was working on legislative frameworks for the future shale gas production in Poland, the need to regulate shale gas at the European level came from various actors and for various reasons. First, the environmental and health impacts of shale gas exploration have been seen as controversial by some governments and publics mainly due to the use of the technology of hydraulic fracturing (fracking) (Gene et al. 2014; Hopke and Simis 2015; Vasi et al. 2015; Williams et al. 2015). Despite the fact that the method is widely used (and thus considered to be "safe enough") in the United States, fracking is banned in France and Bulgaria. For a while, Great Britain and Germany also put moratoria on the use of hydraulic fracturing for commercial purposes. In some of these countries, organized publics expressed concerns through a vast range of protest actions, both local and national (Control Risk Group 2012; Vasi et al. 2015; Szolucha 2016). At the same time, governments of other states tried to encourage oil and gas companies to invest in shale gas production, implicitly assessing the benefits as outweighing the risks. This is, for example, the position of the Polish government, which in fact has been supported by the general public (as measured by public opinion polls) (Stasik and Stankiewicz 2014). However, despite the enthusiasm shared by political elites and the public, inhabitants of some regions where exploration was planned opposed these projects on the grounds of uncertain environmental and socio-economic impacts. Against this background, the question about relations between communities, policy-makers and civil society organizations from different scales: local, European, and global, and the meaning that local protests have for shale gas politics at different scales are particularly interesting.

This is even more so as many EU-level actors, Members of the European Parliament and lobbyists from green organizations have actively supported local and national activists in their opposition against shale gas development. They have visited protest sites and invited local protesters to visit other protest sites and EU-level institutions. The way these relations unfolded, and the meaning they acquired for various actors are of interest for this analysis. How much – and through which channels – has the voice of "ordinary citizens" been amplified by alliances with specialized organization through production of papers, reports or public hearings and conferences?

Problem: relational politics and the creation of Żurawlów

At the EU level, where a myriad of actors compete over access to policy-makers, it is difficult to pin down events, actors and arguments which influence the framing of policy proposals (Greenwood 2003). Moreover, there is an ongoing discussion about the relative strength of different interest groups in the legislative process in the EU, as a number of studies show, civil society actors are relatively weaker in terms of their influence on EU policy processes than corporate actors (Eising 2001; Greenwood 2003). However, some of the more recent studies show that they may be more successful than business lobbyists (Dür et al. 2015). Less is known about the meaning of local communities for the EU-level policy processes. In addition, the European process of shale gas regulation is far from over: one cannot say what factors may shape the outcome of debates on shale gas regulations.

In this study, we attempt to reconstruct the relations into which Żurawlów was inscribed and which gave it the meaning of "an issue" and "a case of an anti-fracking protest" also outside of its locally bounded space. We try to reconstruct how these relations were established, what kinds of knowledge and meaning were produced as a result of these relations. We draw on concepts, perspectives and sensibilities from the material-relational approach (see Blok 2010; Lippert 2016; Simons et al. 2014), in order to examine what kinds of relational politics produced Żurawlów as a case of anti-fracking protests and how its meaning transformed depending on the relations that it has been constructing.

At the same time, the material-relational approach helps us to reflect on the problem of scale and scale-making (Demeritt 2001; Blok 2010; Simons et al. 2014), namely, to answer the question about how different scales of politics are produced through relations between various actors. In this approach, the scales which we use to operate are not seen as objectively given realities but rather as constructs of actors' interactions, of their practices of relating things, people and concepts to each other. Scales are thus actors' own achievements, they are negotiated in political processes whereby actors struggle to reify some relations into more real and durable scales and claims about the world (for example, the global, the local, the European). The material-relational approach draws attention to the role of objects and their material qualities in stabilizing relations and building the scalar infrastructure for actors' operations (Demeritt 2001; Blok 2010; Simons et al. 2014).

Through our analysis, we also aim to contribute to the literature about the role and status of local knowledge in policy and governance processes (Martello 2001; Jasanoff and Martello 2004; Beerkens 2008). The adopted relational approach not only allows us to "trace" the flow and the meaning of locally produced knowledge throughout the network, but also to critically examine relations within which "local knowledge" is produced. In other words, we ask: how "local" is local knowledge if we go beyond conceptualizing the local as bounded within geographically limited spaces (Rozema et al. 2015)? And what does this local knowledge mean when it is moved to the site of policy-making by actors who conceive of themselves as "international," "EU-level," or "global"?

But how can this whole process be understood in the framework of production and circulation knowledge for decision-making? In our reading, from the point of view of the residents living in the nearby area, usually the first question to ask after hearing about the prospect of shale gas production is: "How will the new industry affect our life?" We understand the process of searching for locally acceptable, reliable answers to this question as the process of "local knowledge production," even if the activists themselves often talk just about "learning" (as in the interviews). However, even if the residents usually did not carry out their own physical investigations (so did not produce knowledge that was understood as the results of physical measurements, etc.), but relied on knowledge claims supported and published by different actors, we do not perceive them as passive "recipients": they collected, compared and discussed different issues and assessed them in the light of their own, unique situation and conditions. It means that to construct relevant knowledge, two types of questions had to be asked at the same time: questions about local conditions, needs, interests and values, and questions about what is known about shale gas production from different contexts (see Latour 2004). As a part of a symmetrical process, "the story of Żurawlow protest" may become one of the building blocks of local knowledge concerning possible interactions between the shale gas industry and local community members somewhere else: in EU institutions or different sites of the oil and gas industry operations. But to make this process of knowledge flow possible, the networks through which "facts travel" had to be built and maintained (Latour 2005).

In the following sections, we present a theoretically-oriented reconstruction of the local protest in Żurawlów. Applying case study strategy (Stake 1995; Yin 2003), we used a number of techniques to gather information: from collecting rich primary data in the form of blog entries, photos, official documentation, a documentary movie, or shorter video materials posted by engaged actors, through interviews conducted with four of the key actors by the members of the research team in the spring and autumn of 2015, to the short research stays in Żurawlów after the end of the protest, during the locally organized annual celebrations of the victory of the community over the unwanted giant. Additionally, interviews were conducted with representatives of the nongovernmental lobbying organization operating on the level of European Union as well as with European politicians active in the issue, focused on their assessment of the impact of local protest on the European policy (six interviews). Interviews were transcribed, and materials were analyzed using CAQDAS.

Żurawlów and the global anti-fracking movement

Protest in Żurawlów lasted for 399 days and attracted considerable media attention in Poland and abroad. Faced with the prospect of extractive industry development in a traditionally agricultural area, local residents, mainly farmers, started to develop their own attitude toward this future. During the process, they acquired considerable knowledge about shale gas and fracking using

different existing sources, from materials available on the Internet, through official consultation meetings, to face-to-face contact with experts they trusted in
their own network created alongside the protest (Lis and Stasik 2017; Lis 2017).
In March 2013, residents started an occupational protest, blocking the area so as
not to allow the company to start the work. They were persistent in their resistance and gained support from numerous anti-fracking communities in Europe
and in the EU. The site of the protest was visited by many supporters from
Poland and from abroad: MEPs, anti-fracking activists (including representatives of the organizations engaged in European policy-making, such as No Fracking France) and informal groups of supporters. The "Occupy Chevron" slogan,
chosen by protesters following advice from foreign activists, made it easier for
the international public to associate the local protest with a "global cause," connecting with both anti-capitalist and environmentalist agendas: bottom-up
popular protests against the big corporation in defense of local autonomy and
lifestyle. As a result, thanks to successful alliances with actors who had better
access to international networks of solidarity, support was transmitted to people
from Żurawlów through the Internet from around the world. In September
2013, a delegation of activists went on a trip to Brussels to express their concern
to the MEPs. In September 2014, Chevron decided to withdraw from the area
(and from other areas in Poland, also those where protests did not take place).

The mode of existence of the "global anti-fracking" movement is not easy to
capture as its shape, content and boundaries are uncertain; one may argue that
what exist is, first, the series of local protests; second, diverse materials on the
shale gas industry and on protests produced by its participants and supporters,
circulating through different channels, first of all through the Internet (Hopke
2015; Mazur 2016; Vasi et al. 2015); and third, materials produced by certified
centers of knowledge production, as academic and expert institutions on this
global movement (see e.g., Control Risks Group 2012).

According to the leaders of the Żurawlów protest,[1] after they had learnt
about the planned mining activities in the neighborhood, their first reaction
was to try to figure out the possible consequences. They searched for facts and
opinions on the Internet. By this simple means, people living in the Żurawlów
village gained access to the materials produced and distributed globally by
different actors, including activists. But as many of these materials were not
available in Polish, resources (mainly videos) published by activists from
environmental organizations from Poland were very important to them,
"opening their eyes" to the risks they were facing. Arguments presented by
Polish activists are very similar to the ones raised by anti-fracking activists
around the world: water safety, waste disposal and corporate privileges. Leaders
of the Żurawlów protest stressed that it helped them to make up their minds
about the planned investment and they started to focus on these risks to the
local community. We can thus state that without this initial contribution from
external activists, which draws on the international experience of the anti-
fracking resistance, it would have been very hard for the locals to formulate
their doubts and adopt an effective strategy.

As the next step, leaders of the Żurawlów protest contacted activists from Polish organizations with similar agendas and invited them to take part in the meeting held in Żurawlów, to serve as providers of "counter-expertise" against experts from gas and oil companies and from mainstream organizations, such as the Polish Geological Institute (PIG) or technical universities. In different stages of the long protest, people from Żurawlów received support from nationalistic groups (opposing the expansion of foreign capital), anarchistic groups (opposing capitalist expansion and the worldwide process of "landgrabbing," the large corporations taking land from the hands of farmers and communities), and environmental groups (stressing the potential harm to the environment). They were also supported, and their actions were documented and described in the reports published by a Polish group of activists, who launched a program of citizens monitoring *Obywatele Kontroluj* (*Citizens Control*) and supported by funds for NGOs from new European member states. At the same time, protesters were supported by representatives of EU institutions: European MPs (from Greens/European Free Alliance, left-wing faction which is not represented in the Polish parliament or by Polish European MPs), European pro-environmental lobbying institutions (Food and Water Watch), and global pro-environmental organizations (Greenpeace). These allies contributed simultaneously to two interconnected processes: of shaping and straightening activists' identities and essential skills and constructing knowledge about the planned industrial operations, or the legal context of the business operation, etc.

In the course of the protest, leaders became familiar with different arguments, facts and opinions; they served in their community as "transmitters" of these knowledge claims during community meetings organized bottom-up and in occupational protest: this form of protest creates a space to meet and interact face-to-face, to share knowledge, discuss its implication and possible strategies. During these discussions, "global knowledge" become melted and filtered through knowledge about local needs and conditions.

This process of using "global resources" to mobilize local resistance also has an interesting reverse side: activists not only used the output of the "global anti-fracking movement," but also contributed to its creation and proliferation. As a result of their actions and networking with supporters from different countries from around the world (e.g., the Czech Republic, Lithuania, France, the UK), Żurawlów become one of the landmarks of "the global anti-fracking movement" and a part that constitutes and strengthens it. Knowledge about the protest spread through different networks and was "packed" into packages supporting different causes, such as: (1) a documentary film directed by an American director of Polish origins, Lech Kowalski *Drill, Baby, Drill*, who presented the resistance of the Polish farmers as a way of avoiding the gruesome fate of the Pennsylvanian residents; (2) a blog written from the point of view of protesters, translated into several languages, to mobilize support and extend national and international networks; (3) the exhibitions of photos taken during the protest, presented in the European arena; (4) an international collection of signatures to support the struggle of protesters from Żurawlów; (5) visits paid by representative of protesters to other communities abroad in order to inspire them and teach effective "technologies of resistance." This way, activists from Żurawlów are not "in debt" to the "global anti-fracking movement," but "paid it back," contributing to the story of global resistance against the extraction of fossil fuels (see Klein 2014).

Inscribing Żurawlów into the Brussels arena

Apart from the social movement actors, the Żurawlów protest also attracted the attention of actors from the European Union policy arena. Lech Kowalski, the American film maker, together with his wife, contacted the French MEP, José Bové, who had given his support to various anti-fracking protest actions. In June 2013, José Bové sent a letter of support to the Żurawlów protesters, in which he promised to intervene in the Polish government to stop drilling in that area. In the same month, the French newspaper, *Libération*, published an article on Żurawlów. At the end of June, five MEPs, Keith Taylor (England), Reinhard Bütikofer (Germany), Sandrine Bélier (France), Michele Rivasi (France), and Pavel Poc (Czech Republic), sent a joint letter to the Polish Prime Minister Donald Tusk and to the Polish Minister of Environment, in which they supported the protest action in Żurawlów and demanded the withdrawal of Chevron.

Contact with actors from the EU arena resulted in the visit of several activists from Żurawlów to a conference organized by the European Greens in Brussels in September 2013. They were invited by three MEPs – José Bové, Carla Schlyter and Sandrine Bélier. Representatives from Żurawlów were given ten minutes to speak. One of them, in a research interview (Żurawlów, April 7, 2015) said that, in his view, their presence was beneficial for the MEPs who were able to draw more attention to their anti-fracking activities at the EU level. Żurawlów representatives did not see any immediate influence of their presence in Brussels on the EU-level policy process.

In November, José Bové (MEP), Rebecca Harms (MEP) and Lech Kowalski paid a reciprocal visit to the protest site. Circumstances were favorable because it was the time when the UNFCCC conference of the parties was taking place in Warsaw in November 2013. Bové and Harms sent another letter to the Polish Minister of Environment asking to stop drilling in Żurawlów. Żurawlów also sent its representation to the COP meeting in Warsaw, which took part in the climate march organized in Warsaw on this occasion.

There are two interesting aspects of the Żurawlów-Brussels relations. First, as the account above has shown, this relation was initiated and mediated by foreign actors and not by the Polish ones. Lech Kowalski, who lives outside of Poland, mobilized José Bové. José Bové, in turn, mobilized the European Greens from other countries. Literature on interest representation at the European level suggests that a domestic path of interest representation is more likely to be taken by the CEE interest groups than a foreign path (Beyers 2004). The Żurawlów case shows an opposite situation: access to the EU political arena was enabled by foreign actors from France, the Czech Republic and Germany. Foreign MEPs used Żurawlów as an argument in the shale gas debates at the EU arena but they also tried to influence the Polish government by sending letters and petitions. The choice of these unlikely allies should be explored and explained more thoroughly. At the moment we pose a hypothesis that support for shale gas among Polish political actors was so overwhelming and universal across all the political parties and factions that it was impossible to mobilize any domestic support for the anti-fracking cause.

The second interesting aspect of the Żurawlów-Brussels relations is the meaning of this relation for the two sides. Based on our interviews, activists from Żurawlów saw some benefits in having support from the EU-level politicians for their impact on the national political arena. Even though no specific policy changes occurred, they hoped that future regulations of fracking might be stricter because of the knowledge that spread about their protest in Żurawlów. Simultaneously, according to our interviewees from Brussels (representatives of green lobbying organizations., Food & Water Watch Europe and EEB), who actively supported anti-fracking protests in Poland, a local protest such as the one in Żurawlów gives legitimacy to their activities in Brussels. However, even though the case was known because of them, they were of the opinion that it did not take a prominent place in the EU-level debates. Thus, as far as protests give NGOs a sense of legitimacy to represent communities all around Europe, they are not used as arguments when they do their lobbying in the EU institutions.

Another informant, an assistant of the Polish MEP, admitted that he knew little about Żurawlów. His activities between Brussels and Warsaw focused mainly on mobilizing support in favor of fracking in the EU. According to him, the Polish pro-fracking political front was strong and united across different parties and organizations. He recalled a visit of a delegation of Polish activists to the European Parliament. The testimony was registered in a form of a protocol, but it did not provoke any further debates or political action in the Parliament.

While Żurawlów became one of the iconic sites for the anti-fracking movement and is still a living symbol today (at the end of June 2015 a big international festival to commemorate the protest will be organized in Żurawlów), it seems that in Brussels it became inscribed into bureaucratic reports of the European Parliament and it stayed there in a reified form. The knowledge about Żurawlów can be mobilized at the EU level in the future but for the time being it has not given traction to any political activities, debates or policy decisions.

Conclusion

The chapter has presented an interpretation of the dynamics of the Żurawlów anti-fracking protest with regard to establishing relations between local and international actors and their role in the circulation of knowledge about fracking and about the protest itself. We have shown that the local framing of the anti-fracking protest and the framing of specific risks were not an "organic product," in the sense that it was constructed with the active assistance of Polish and international anti-fracking activists. This conclusion may be a good starting point for future analysis, in particular with regard to the production of stabilized and transferable knowledge claims and facts about fracking which are accepted and shared by various anti-fracking groups all around Europe. This stabilized knowledge, in Latour's words, "the immutable mobiles," are a crucial factor in the construction of an international anti-fracking movement, which, when analyzed from an organizational perspective, is still a rather fragmented, spread-out conglomerate of locally embedded actors. But even if it still looks like that, the movement already has its "scale" – a global scale – which has been built through the weaving of relations and through relating local protests to international actors and other sites of protest. The use of Internet technologies, social media and movies is crucial for the constitution of this movement and its scale. The analysis has also shown the crucial role of non-governmental actors in mediating between these different protest sites and in circulating and stabilizing facts about the risks of fracking.

Another important conclusion pertains to the political role of community protests, such as the one in Żurawlów. Protests give traction to the social movements like politics. They fuel movements and are fueled by the actors who actively construct international movements by connecting various sites. Żurawlów is still important for the anti-fracking movement and the Żurawlów activists know how to sustain its role for other anti-fracking communities. According to our interviews, they keep in touch with activists from all over Europe and the US, they support them with advice and information. However, while protests attract the attention of actors from the policy field – in our case, MEPs – they do not translate into arguments used in the policy-relevant debates. Activists' visits to Brussels are demonstrations of the connection to the people and in this sense, they serve to overcome the alleged "democratic deficit" of the European Union, rather than contribute with local knowledge and local arguments (problematizations and solutions) to the policy-protest. Today, Żurawlów is "dead" in Brussels. At the same time, "local" issues indirectly constitute the European scales of politics through different practices that demarcate the local from the trans-border, from the European. As one of the officials whom we interviewed admitted: "We are not that much interested in local issues. There is local administration to deal with it. We always act where a given issue has a trans-border effect" (interview, Brussels, June 2015).

Note

1 The following account is based on the research interviews.

References

Beerkens, E. 2008. University policies for the knowledge society: global standardization, local reinvention. *Perspectives on Global Development and Technology*, 7, 15–36.

Beyers, J. 2004. Voice and access political practices of European interest associations. *European Union Politics*, 5(2), 211–240.

Blok, A., 2010. Topologies of climate change: actor–network theory, relational-scalar analytics, and carbon-market overflows. *Environment and Planning D: Society and Space*, 28, 896–912. doi:10.1068/d0309.

Boutilier, R. G. 2014. *Frequently asked questions about the social licence to operate.* Impact Assessment and Project Appraisal, 32(4), 263–272. doi:10.1080/14615517.2014.941141.

Bulkeley, H., 2005. Reconfiguring environmental governance: towards a politics of scales and networks. *Political Geography*, 24(8), 875–902. doi:10.1016/j.polgeo.2005.07.002.

Callon, M., Lascoumes, P. and Barthe, Y. 2009. *Acting in an Uncertain World: An Essay on Technical Democracy.* Cambridge, MA: MIT Press.

Callon, M. and Rabeharisoa, V. 2003. Research "in the Wild" and the shaping of new social identities. *Technology in Society*, 25, 193–204.

Control Risk Group. 2012. *The Global Anti-Fracking Movement. What It Wants, How It Operates and What's Next.* See www.marcellusprotest.org/sites/marcellusprotest.org/files/shale_gas_white_paper.pdf

Davies, A. 2013. Identity and the assemblages of protest: The spatial politics of the Royal Indian Navy Mutiny, 1946. *Geoforum*, 48, 24–32.

Demeritt, D., 2001. The construction of global warming and the politics of science. *Annals of the Association of American Geographers*, 91(2), 307–337. doi:10.1111/0004-5608.00245.

Dür, A., Bernhagen, P. and Marshall, D. 2015. Interest group success in the European Union: When (and why) does business lose ? *Comparative Political Studies*, 48(8), 951–983.

EIA. 2011. *World Shale Gas Resources: An Initial Assessment of 14 Regions Outside of the United States.* Washington, DC: U.S. Energy Information Administration.

Eising, R. 2001. Interessenvermittlung in der Europäischen Union. In W. Reutter, and P. Rütters (Eds.) *Verbände und Verbandssysteme in Westeuropa.* Opladen: Leske+Budrich, pp. 453–476.

Fischer, F. 2000. *Citizens, Experts, and the Environment.* Durham, NC: Duke University Press.

Fox, T., Versluis, E, and Van Asselt, M.B.A. 2011. Regulating the use of bisphenol A in baby and children's products in the European Union: Current developments and scenarios for the regulatory future. *European Journal of Risk Regulation*, 2(1), 21–35.

Gautier, D. L., Pitman, J. K., Charpentier, R. R. et al. 2012. *Potential for Unconventional Gas and Oil Resources in the Polish-Ukrainian Foredeep.* Available at: pubs.usgs.gov/fs/2012/3102

Greenwood, J. 2003. *Interest Representation in the European Union.* New York: Palgrave Macmillan.

Hopke, J. E. 2015. Hashtagging Politics: Transnational Anti-Fracking Movement Twitter Practices. *Social Media + Society*, 1–2: 1–12. http://doi.org/10.1177/2056305115605521

Hopke, J. E., and Simis, M. 2015. Discourse over a contested technology on Twitter: A case study of hydraulic fracturing. *Public Understanding of Science*, 1–16. doi:10.1177/0963662515607725.

Jasanoff, S. (Ed.). 2004. *States of Knowledge: The Co-Production of Science and Social Order.* New York: Routledge.

Jasanoff, S. and Martello, M. L. 2004. *Earthly Politics: Local and Global in Environmental Governance.* Cambridge, MA: The MIT Press.

Joyce, S. & Thomson, I. 2000. Earning a social license to operate: Social acceptability and resource development in Latin America. *CIM (Canadian Mining and Metallurgical) Bulletin*, 93(1037), 49–53.

Klein, N. 2014. *This Changes Everything. Capitalism vs. the Climate.* New York: Simon & Schuster.

Latour, B. 2004. *Politics of Nature: How to Bring the Sciences into Democracy.* Cambridge, MA: Harvard University Press.

Latour, B. 2005. *Reassembling the Social: An Introduction to Actor-Network-Theory.* New York: Oxford University Press.

Law, J., 2009. Actor network theory and material semiotics. In B. S. Turner (Ed.) *The New Blackwell Companion to Social Theory.* Oxford: Blackwell, pp. 141–158.

Lis, A. and Stankiewicz, P. 2016. Framing shale gas for policy-making in Poland, *Journal of Environmental Policy & Planning*, doi: 10.1080/1523908X.2016.1143355.

Lis, A., and Stasik, A. 2017. Hybrid forums, knowledge deficits and the multiple uncertainties of resource extraction: Negotiating the local governance of shale gas in Poland. *Energy Research and Social Science*, 28: 29–36. http://doi.org/10.1016/j.erss.2017.04.003

Martello, M. L. 2001. A paradox of virtue?: "Other" knowledges and environment-development politics. *Global Environmental Politics*, 1(3), 114–141.

Mazur, A. 2016. How did the fracking controversy emerge in the period 2010–2012? *Public Understanding of Science*, 25(2), 207–222. http://doi.org/10.1177/09636625 14545311

Nelsen, J. L. 2009. Social license to operate. *International Journal of Mining, Reclamation and Environment*, 20(3), 161–162. doi:10.1080/17480930600804182

Pellizzoni, L. 2011. The politics of facts: Local environmental conflicts and expertise, *Environmental Politics*, 20(6).

PIG-PIB. 2012. *Ocena zasobów wydobywalnych gazu ziemnego i ropy naftowej w formacjach łupkowych dolnego paleozoiku w Polsce (basen bałtycko-podlasko-lubelski*. Polish Geological Institute.

Rozema, J. G., Cashmore, M., Bond, A. J. and Chilvers. J. 2015. Respatialization and local protest strategy formation: Investigating high-speed rail megaproject development in the UK. *Geoforum*, 59, 98–108.

Simons, A., Lis A. and Lippert I. 2014. The political duality of scale-making in environmental markets. *Environmental Politics*, doi:10.1080/09644016.2014.893120.

Stake, R. (1995). *The Art of Case Study Research.* Thousand Oaks, CA: Sage.

Stasik, A. 2017. Global controversies in local settings: anti-fracking activism in the era of Web 2.0. *Journal of Risk Research.* http://doi.org/10.1080/13669877.2017.1313759

Stasik, A., and Stankiewicz, P. 2014. *Raport: poszukiwanie i wydobycie gazu łupkowego w Polsce – wiedza, opinie, oceny.* Warsaw: Pa stwowy Instytut Geologiczny. Available at: http://infolupki.pgi.gov.pl/sites/default/files/czytelnia_pliki/1/sondaz_pig_raport_gaz_lupkowy.pdf (accessed October 2016).

Szolucha, A. 2016. The human dimension of shale gas development in Lancashire, UK: Towards a social impact assessment. Unpublished report.

Taylor, B., and de Loë, R. C. 2012. Conceptualizations of local knowledge in collaborative environmental governance. *Geoforum*, 43, 1207–1217.

Upham, P., Lis, A., Riesch. H., & Stankiewicz, P. 2015. Addressing social representation in socio-technical transitions with the case of shale gas. *Environmental Innovation and Societal Transitions*, 16, 120–141. doi:10.1016/j.eist.2015.01.004

Vasi, I. B., Walker, E. T., Johnson, J. S. and Fen, H. 2015. "No Fracking Way!" documentary film, discursive opportunity, and local opposition against hydraulic fracturing in the United States, 2010 to 2013. *American Sociological Review* 80(5), 934–59. doi:10.1177/0003122415598534.

Williams, L., Macnaghten, P., Davis, R. and Curtis, S. 2015. Framing "fracking": Exploring public perceptions of hydraulic fracturing in the United Kingdom. *Public Understanding of Science*, 1–7. doi:10.1177/0963662515595159.

Wynne, B. 1998. May the sheep safely graze? A reflexive view of the expert–lay knowledge divide. In S. Lash, B. Szerszynski, and B. Wynne (Eds.), *Risk, Environment and Modernity: Towards a New Ecology*. London: Sage, pp. 44–84.

Yin, R. (2003). *Case Study Research: Design and Methods* (3rd ed.). Thousand Oaks, CA: Sage.

9 Community representations of unconventional gas development in Australia, Canada and the United States, and their effect on social licence

Hanabeth Luke and Darrick Evensen

Introduction

Unconventional gas development provides a fascinating opportunity for a better understanding of how the intersection of local social structure and external industrial pressures shape rural landscapes. Previous research on social responses to unconventional gas development (UGD) explores motivations for supporting or opposing industry development. Research has revealed differing perceptions in areas where the UGD industry emerged early versus later on (or not at all). We take up the question of why systematic differences may exist between regions at different stages of development, integrating social representations theory with the concept of social licence to operate to explain differences in attitudes to UGD.

Born in social psychology, social representations theory describes how communities characterise concepts, ideas, or objects. Social representations underpin the development of community views, opinions, attitudes and behaviours, and are useful for understanding how communities respond to novel industrial developments (Deaux & Philogène, 2001; Evensen and Stedman, 2016; Moscovici, 2001). Social representations are collectively generated characterisations of an issue that are then internalised to various extents by individuals. A 'social licence to operate' is also a community-level attribute that has a mix of societal-level and individual-level antecedents. The concept of a social licence to operate provides a frame for understanding community responses to industrial developments, upon which a spectrum of community views, opinions, attitudes and behaviours can be placed (Dare, Schirmer, & Vanclay, 2014; Luke, Lloyd, Boyd, & den Exter, 2014b; Thomson & Boutilier, 2011). Social representations could include portrayals of both the effects of UGD and of the UGD industry, each potentially shaping the assessment of the extent to which social licence may exist or not.

Social representations theory

Social representations are built on shared knowledge and understandings of a common social reality (Billig, 1993; Deaux & Philogène, 2001), influencing our thoughts, opinions, attitudes, behaviour and language, giving meaning to objects, concepts, processes, and our relationships (Moscovici, 2001). Public conversation integrates novel and complex ideas, processes, and objects into everyday life via two processes: 'anchoring' and 'objectification' (Deaux & Philogène, 2001; Moscovici, 2001). Anchoring occurs by linking the novel idea to similar concepts, objects or processes that have been discussed previously or are already well understood in the community – often shared cultural, social, and historical experiences (Deaux & Philogène, 2001). Objectification concretises the novel concept/object by associating it with certain terms, images and descriptive language.

Social licence

Social licence is a term broadly used to describe the level of support a community has for an existing or proposed industrial development (Boutilier, 2011; Boutilier & Thompson, 2014). The concept is often described as 'fundamentally intangible', and subject to change over time. Levels of support for developments have been described as acceptance, approval, or, at the highest level, 'psychological identification' with an industry (Boutilier, 2011). Beyond rejection of industry or withdrawal of social licence, non-support can be characterised by processes of resistance, with relationships being developed with resistance movements (Luke, 2017).

Dare et al. (2014) describe multiple social licences that may exist within a community, with diverse and sometimes opposing views held by different groups and individuals. Understanding the distribution of social licence within communities has been achieved through polling and quantitative survey questions (e.g. Luke et al., 2014b; Walton, McCrea, & Leonard, 2014); however, qualitative research, such as individual and focus group interviews, can be used to understand *how* social licence is enacted and represented in a community (e.g. Luke, Lloyd, Boyd, & den Exter, 2014a). We assert that one way in which social licence is enacted is through social representations.

Public attitudes to UGD

Commonly cited individual-level factors leading to favourable perceptions of UGD include potential for new jobs and an improved economy; negative perceptions stem from concerns over environmental and water impacts, and impacts on social well-being, including roads, traffic, community character, and public health (Thomas et al., 2017). In their extensive review of the research on public perceptions of unconventional gas development in North America, Thomas et al. found that regions already experiencing UGD viewed development more positively, when compared with regions without extensive development. Comparisons between New York and Pennsylvania residents consistently found survey respondents in New York (no UGD) believed risks outweighed benefits; the opposite was true for Pennsylvania (much UGD) residents (Borick, Rabe, & Lachapelle, 2014; Stedman et al., 2012). Other research has found that public views may become more polarised in areas of extensive development due to individual positive/negative experiences with industry (Schafft & Biddle, 2014; Theodori, Willits, & Luloff, 2012).

We use social representations theory to explore why systematic differences exist in social licence between regions with and without development, presenting research from multiple regional contexts across three nations.

Methods

This research uses interview and survey data collected from a series of case studies in regions of Australia, Canada and the United States subject to UGD. Case studies are useful for examining complex phenomena occurring in a regional or localised context. Yin (2013) defines case study as 'an empirical enquiry that investigates a contemporary phenomenon within its real-life context, especially when the boundaries between phenomenon and context are not clearly evident'. Case studies can illuminate a set of decisions, why they were taken, how they were implemented, and with what results.

In the Northern Rivers in Australia, the first author conducted ethnographic research, from 2011–2016, including: focus group research, observations of protest groups, gas industry consultations, and interviews with 30 individuals reflecting a range of views. In 2012 and 2013, election surveys took place in the Northern Rivers that included open, qualitative questions relating to the motivations for support of or opposition to developments. An additional 38 interviews took place in the Western Downs in Australia; six individuals were interviewed twice between 2011 and 2013. These interviews took place with farmers, business leaders and other local residents, representing a range of perspectives on UGD. A simple, open question was posed to all respondents initially: 'What does the CSG [coal seam gas – the term used in Australia] industry bring to your region?' Interviews were identified through a snowball approach that followed initial interviews in 2011.

The second author conducted interviews in the US states of New York (NY) and Pennsylvania (PA) in March–April 2013. Because social representations are dependent on and shaped by local discourse, often including agenda-setting mass media sources (Breakwell & Canter, 1993), we used content analysis of local newspapers in the Marcellus Shale region of the northeast US as a point of departure for identifying local representations and communities in which to further explore social representations (see Ashmoore et al., 2016 and Evensen et al., 2014, for a review of that research). Twenty-one key informant interviews were conducted with individuals heavily involved in shaping or facilitating local discourse on UGD. These key informants represented a range of perspectives on

UGD, from those in favour to those opposed, to those simply seeking to facilitate informed decision-making on the issue. The interviewees were distributed across three communities in southern NY (where there was discussion of UGD, but a moratorium at the time of the research) and three communities in northern PA (where heavy development was underway).

With an output of 18.5 million cubic feet of natural gas per day as of February 2017, the Marcellus Shale is the largest natural gas-producing region in the US (US EIA 2017). Ninety-two per cent of gas reserves in the basin are estimated to lie under PA and NY (US EIA 2012). Unlike in Australia or Canada (and most other nations), mineral rights are not necessarily owned by the government in the US; a number of mineral governance regimes exist in the US. In NY and PA, however, most mineral rights are privately owned, often by the same individual who owns the surface rights on that land.

The second author also conducted 26 interviews with a similar range of key informants in the province of New Brunswick in Canada in May 2013 – including activists on all sides of the issue, municipal officials, journalists, NGO leaders, members of industry, government officials and academics. The key question that framed the discussion in each interview in the US and Canada was: 'What is the first thing that comes to mind when I mention "shale gas development via hydraulic fracturing"?' This question was designed to elicit social representations of development; the researcher then followed up to explore the ways in which these representations were embedded in local history, culture, and discourse.

Our comparative analysis arising from the case studies in three nations applies social representations theory to understand how emergent communal discourse shaped social licence to operate in similar ways across national, political, cultural, and regulatory contexts.

Case study areas

In each country, some of our study communities have experienced UGD development for more than a decade, while other areas have not (yet) experienced UGD.

Australia

Australian land use planning, where significant assets are not impacted, is regulated by State governments; governance and community tolerance of extractive industries varies across the states. The State of Victoria was the first to legislate a state-wide ban in 2016 (ABC, 2016). In contrast, the State of Queensland in Eastern Australia has facilitated rapid coal seam gas (CSG) industry expansion, including extensive drilling, pipelines and export facilities that produce 90 per cent of the state's gas supply (Baer, 2014; Freij-Ayoub, 2012; Luke et al., 2014b; Measham & Fleming, 2014). The Queensland coal-seam gas industry has grown exponentially over the last few decades, with a record of 1,634 wells drilled in 2013–2014 (DNRM, 2016). The Western Downs region in Queensland has traditionally been a broad-acre cotton and beef farming region, with low population density of 0.87 persons per km² (ABS, 2015).

In contrast, CSG exploration in the neighbouring state of New South Wales (NSW) is at a much more preliminary stage, with substantial protest activities in several regions leading to the development of new regulatory frameworks, slowing down industrial development (Brown, 2012; Hazzard, Hodgkinson, & Hartcher, 2013; O'Kane, 2013). The Northern Rivers in NSW is just over half the size of the Western Downs, but with almost ten times the population (density of 12.6 persons per km²). Known for its 'extraordinary natural beauty', with rich soils and a subtropical climate, it is a popular tourist destination, with thriving creative industries, festivals and community activism. The Northern Rivers is often referred to as the 'Rainbow Region', an identity which dates back to the Aquarius Festival of 1973, when the existing population was 'transformed' by the presence of a new generation keen to embrace sustainability and communal ways of living (Lismore City Council, 2015).

The United States

Under Democratic and Republican governors from 2006–2014, expansion of the UGD industry in Pennsylvania was encouraged, resulting in 4,935 unconventional wells being drilled in the three years prior to our research (2010–2012). In NY, the Governor had imposed a moratorium on high-volume hydraulic fracturing in 2008, effectively prohibiting unconventional gas development. This moratorium was still in effect during our research in 2013, and later became a ban in December 2014.

Our study communities in the USA lie in six municipalities in the northern portion of the Marcellus Shale region. The three NY towns all historically heavily relied on farming and had little experience with extractive development. Forestry and outdoor recreation were important in Cummings, PA, while the other two PA communities were invested in farming. None of the PA communities had a history with coal development themselves, but neither were they far away from regions of PA that historically had experienced extensive coal extraction. We highlight the key characteristics of each municipality in Table 9.1.

Canada

Our three study communities in Canada were all proximate to the one million hectares of mineral rights that the New Brunswick provincial government leased for unconventional gas exploration and extraction in 2010; additionally, one community, Sussex, had seen previous UGD (32 wells in total) since 2004. Very little unconventional development had occurred in the province by the time of our research, but the then provincial government was strongly advocating for the industry. Canada, like the US and Australia, uses a federal system in which governance of mineral resources is devolved primarily to the state/provincial level.

Table 9.1 Characteristics of the US study communities for interviews

Town/township/ borough	Population density (persons/ sq. mi.)[1]	Unemployment rate (%)[1]	Median household income ($)[1]	Individuals below poverty level (%)[1]	Residents with at least a Bachelor's degree (%)[1]	% of county voted for Obama (2008)[2]	% of county voted for Obama (2012)[2]
Dryden, NY	153	4.5	75295	10.0	43.1	70.2	68.2
Sanford, NY	28	10.5	41563	13.1	16.9	53.2	50.9
Spencer, NY	63	5.8	53269	6.0	18.8	44.1	41.4
Cummings, PA	4	8.9	40125	2.8	15.8	37.3	32.7
Damascus, PA	45	7.8	51522	7.5	16.6	43.3	38.8
Towanda, PA	2655	5.5	39671	21.7	22.3	40.0	36.9

Notes
1 2008–2012 American Community Survey 5-year estimates, US Census Bureau.
2 The Washington Post (www.washingtonpost.com/wp-srv/special/politics/election-map-2012/president/).

Unlike the US, but akin to Australia, mineral ownership in Canada is vested to the Crown, meaning that the province controls leasing and that any royalties accrue to the government, as opposed to accruing directly to private landowners – as is often the case in the US.

Our study sites for interviews in New Brunswick were the towns of Richibucto and Sussex, and the village of Doaktown. All three had a strong focus on using and interacting with the local environment. Doaktown was heavily reliant on forestry and timber industry and benefited from a major river running through the village used for recreation and tourism. Sussex had a notable potash mine, which had caused local environmental contamination; farming and forestry also occurred locally. Richibucto is on the Atlantic Ocean, just south of a large national park, and has many residents involved in the tourism and fisheries industries. We highlight key characteristics of each town/village in Table 9.2.

Results and discussion

We organise the sub-sections within these results according to leading themes that emerged via the social representations our interviewees shared. While we offer data across three different nations, it is evident that the emergent representations align much more closely between those areas in each nation accepting social licence (and then across the regions rejecting/challenging social licence) than do representations within individual nations. For this reason, we cluster emergent themes into two broad categories reflecting whether the region accepted or challenged social licence.

Social representations in areas accepting social licence

In the Western Downs in Queensland, Australia, in the communities of northern Pennsylvania in the US, and in one community in New Brunswick, Canada (Sussex), social licence to operate was widely accepted. Our research quickly revealed that the (level of) acceptance of social licence was not uniform within

Table 9.2 Characteristics of the final Canadian study communities for interviews

Town/ village	Population density (persons/ sq. mi.)[1]	Unemployment rate (%)[2]	Residents with at least a Bachelor's degree (%)[2]	Native English speaker (%)[1]	Native French speaker (%)[1]	Population change (2006–2011) (%)[1]
Doaktown	71	35.0	6.3	97	3	−10.7
Richibucto	280	20.5	4.7	28	71	−0.3
Sussex	1232	7.4	12.6	97	2	+1.7

Notes
1 2011 Census, Statistics Canada.
2 2011 National Household Survey, Statistics Canada.

these communities, but on whole, broad support for the industry was manifest. Below, we identify some of the social representations that allowed such licence to develop.

Social identity: 'not an activist'

In the Western Downs region of Queensland our interviews began in 2011, prior to the production and construction phase of the Queensland gas boom, with further interviews during, and following the boom. It became immediately apparent that social identity (Turner, 1975) played a key role in isolating stronger-anti-UGD representations to a small subset of the community. Identities, an indicator of shared culture, constrained which representations could emerge. Representations of UGD were anchored in various identities, most generally objectified along the lines of 'us/locals' and 'the out-group'. Historically negative perceptions of social protest and activism maintained an important role for farmers in the Western Downs, stemming from associations anchored in a lengthy political history where activism was frowned upon by 'respectable' citizens (Lloyd, Luke, & Boyd, 2013). The stereotyping of 'the out-group' was also because the first residents to complain about UGD had settled in the region during recent decades on cheap, poor quality land, known as 'lifestyle blocks', lending them the stigmatised title of 'blockies' (ibid.).

An activist leader opposed to UGD stated in 2013 that the locals are 'too scared to come out and complain, so we look like a group of radicals from outside the area'. This view was supported by a local pub-owner (male, ~50 years): 'Most protesters aren't locals ... pub-wise, it's a dream for us!' A cotton farmer, who was also the chairman in 2013 of a local group taking a measured, cautious approach to UGD – the Basin Sustainability Alliance – made it clear that they were keen to disassociate from the objectified out-group category of 'activists', and saw activism to be insignificant in the Western Downs: 'There's nothing around here that's a huge lobby group against CSG.' When asked about their perceptions of 'Lock the Gate' (a major activist group opposed to UGD in Australia), one farmer responded (female, ~45): 'To me, the Lock the Gate Alliance thing is a heap of "blockies".' Another farmer responded to this comment with: 'They're just activists' (female, ~40).

Halfway across the world, similar themes emerged in the United States and Canada. Pro-development interviewees in two PA communities and Sussex, NB, were quick to chide anti-development leaders with the objectification of being 'professional activists' – meaing that their views on UGD were not valid in the local community due to not being part of the local social representation. Whatever produced the activism was not, ostensibly, shared history and culture. In Damascus, PA, an interviewee explained that much of the opposition to development actually comes from New York State, which is just on the other side of the river that forms the township's eastern border. The key activist group there, Damascus Citizens for Sustainability, is actually based in NY, a point that pro-development interviewees were quick to critique. Few major opposition groups formed in PA communities, whereas many existed throughout nearby southern NY.

Whether accurate or not, 'activists' were viewed as non-locals, either due to actually not living locally or having lived there for less time than families who had been grounded regionally for generations. Because of the strong sentiments against 'activists' in these communities, local residents opposed to development either objectified themselves as 'accidental activists' (see Wilber, 2012, for a discussion of this phrase) or worked diligently to disavow the moniker altogether, substituting alternate objectifications without stigma. A Dryden, NY, resident explained, 'I am not an activist; I am a hermit. I like it that way.' After she attended a few meetings and heard from other locals about development and its potential effects, however, she become 'terrified', which 'forced' her to become involved. A Richibucto, NB, resident objectified the French-speaking Acadians in her community as 'like Hobbits; we try to stay away from the big people', but she felt the issue of UGD was simply too important for her to remain quiet. A Sussex, NB, resident noted that many of the people who have fought UGD there since it began almost a decade ago are farmers; yet, farmers are 'not normally civically active' in that area, so those speaking out are frequently stigmatised for deviating from the accepted representation of that identity.

Reluctant acceptance

In locations where development began early, before much discourse on UGD had occurred and before time allowed for emergence of social representations, people represented UGD as much more acceptable for their communities. Importantly, the representation of UGD as acceptable came years after development began, but we contend this acceptance is linked to whether the representations of UGD formed before development occurred or not. After experience with development, some residents still viewed UGD as very positive (approval), whereas others described the need to take the good with the bad (acceptance); yet others expressed resignation to their fate, defeat, and/or an inability to effect change (reluctant acceptance).

A farmer (female, ~50) from the Western Downs, Australia, who had embraced the industry, anchored her positive representation of UGD in the area's economic past: 'Town's booming – lots of good changes.... This way's better than the old way.' A 2011 interviewee based her representation of UGD on an objectification (shared widely) that the water produced by the UGD industry could 'turn the area into a salad bowl' (meaning it would increase capacity for growing crops), however, her husband (~55) indicated a more complicated representation of UGD; he perceived threats, but saw development as inevitable:

> The businesses in town are doing well, I hold no grudges, but landholders have the most at stake, we are ... fighting to retain what we have, to keep water safe and maintain our lifestyle. We can't say no, companies follow the path of least resistance and will come back.

Early interviews in the Western Downs in 2011 found residents to be open to developments, objectifying UGD as an inevitable form of progress: 'We just go with the flow' (male businessman in construction, ~50); others reflected how social representations are not static but continue to evolve (Moscovici, 2001), stating, 'it's a constant source of re-evaluation'. When interviews took place with farmers, business owners, and other local residents in 2013, the general mood was that the gas, whether liked or not, was an inevitable part of people's lives, and was anchored in regional narratives of subsistence and livelihood. Several business owners in Chinchilla and Miles, servicing the gas industry, anchored changes to positive economic representations, as an 'opportunity to make money. You can't stop progress, I wouldn't want to' (business owner in construction, ~50); 'everything is booming' (politician, male, ~45). Yet, by 2016, interviews indicated that there had been a rapid industry downturn: 'It built up expectations to dizzying heights, and a lot of people have fallen on the sword' (female farmer, ~35). A businessman who in 2011 said, 'we just go with the flow', and in 2013, 'you can't stop progress', reported much more cynicism after the bust: 'There was no loyalty from the [CSG] companies ... I think they've got a lot to answer for, as do the Council for letting it all happen.' Yet, he still remained optimistic and not opposed to development: 'A little bit more industry might be coming soon, I've heard on the grapevine ...'.

The general acceptance of social licence arising from the qualitative data is supported by surveys that took place in the Western Downs in early 2014 (Walton et al., 2014). Questions on community attitudes indicated that overall, only 9 per cent of the population reported 'rejecting' the industry, with 91 per cent of respondents indicating varying levels of support. One third of respondents were 'tolerating' the presence of the UGD industry. Of all respondents, 14 per cent 'approved'; 8 per cent 'embraced' the UGD industry, and 37 per cent 'accepted' it. When asked about their well-being, 6 per cent viewed changes to be improving the region and 47 per cent reported to be 'adapting'. The rest were 'only just coping' (34 per cent); 'not coping' (9 per cent), with just 6 per cent reporting to be 'resisting' UGD developments (Walton et al., 2014). A third of those 'only just coping' elected that they were indeed 'tolerating' it, which is still a measure of acceptance. These findings further support the idea that social licence, in communities with a longer history of UGD, may stem from reluctant acceptance and/or unwillingness to fight the current state of affairs.

The reluctant acceptance of UGD in areas with early development – where there was little communal discourse about development before UGD started and thus no opportunity for social representations to emerge in advance of UGD occurring – was also manifest in North America. A township supervisor near Cummings, PA, where hundreds of wells had been drilled with a few miles, offered nuance on concerns related to water. He recognised that small spills of chemicals do occur, but observed that all spills in his area had been quickly cleaned up and had left no residual contamination. He also reflected that truck traffic has degraded roads substantially in PA, but that the gas companies have paid for repairs. Another local resident commended the repairs, but noted that the main road construction season is also the main tourism season locally, frustrating tourists. These interviewees represented UGD as welcome economic expansion but with the caveat that ignoring the costs is naïve.

A second township supervisor near Cummings, PA, explained that local businesses (e.g. restaurants, machine shops, supply stores) have benefited from the gas industry, but that housing (availability and price) has fortunately not been affected in his municipality much because gas workers do not want to live in his township due to poor mobile phone coverage. Nevertheless, he acknowledged serious problems with rent increases elsewhere – akin to the problems in the Western Downs, Australia, where one local expressed: 'If you don't own your own house, you're buggered' (female Chinchilla resident, ~40), and another (female ~70) lamented: 'I'm a pensioner – I have to leave town 'cause the rates are too high.' The PA supervisor also explained that the PA state impact fee created a windfall for his township's budget; the township collected $500,000 from the impact fee in one year, when their annual tax base is less than $50,000. He noted, however, that the amounts communities receive and the impacts that they need to fund out of this largesse vary substantially across the landscape – the funds can be a 'windfall or a small check' that does not cover related expenses.

In the Western Downs and in PA, the social representations fostering general acceptance became nuanced and conditional on various facets of local context as experience with the industry increased; for many interviewees, it was not wholly positive or negative, black or white. Direct experience with goods and bads of UGD allowed for gradations of social licence acceptance. This sentiment was also reflected in Sussex, NB, where the president of the local chamber of commerce stated that the chamber and he personally were neither entirely supportive of nor opposed to UGD. He saw the retention of local jobs associated with the incipient (and potentially growing) gas industry as a way to sustain local services that required a critical population mass, such as a small local hospital; yet, concerns of environmental contamination and disruption of rural life associated with UGD and the local potash mine were clearly present in his mind, and those of other interviewees.

Latent opposition

We do not mean to create the impression that in areas generally accepting UGD, that opposition to industry development did not exist – it certainly did in all of the Australian, United States, and Canadian communities we reference above. Nevertheless, we seek to illustrate here some of the social representations and communal discourses about UGD that led to a general acceptance of development in these communities – in contrast to the opposition in the communities detailed below.

In the Western Downs, Australia, some opposition derived from previous negative experience with and representations of related industries: 'our land has been devastated by coal and gas mining' (female farmer, ~30). Many 2013 interviews identified a somewhat uneasy co-existence due to uneven impacts and benefits being felt across the community. Town residents and farmers alike identified a disparity between those who felt the challenges and benefits the UGD industry was bringing to their region: 'Farmers are taking a kick in the guts for the town's prosperity' (female Chinchilla resident, ~40). A cotton farmer (male, ~55) stated, 'It just feels, it's all take, take, take and it's governed by (Queensland) legislation, so you've got to "cop it".'

Previous negative experience with related industries, objectification of UGD's distribution of impacts as 'unfair', and anchoring representations of UGD in negative views of landscape industrialisation likewise motivated some opposition in the North American communities with overall acceptance of social licence to operate. A journalist in northern PA we interviewed (Evensen and Stedman 2017), who reported extensively on UGD and who had interviewed numerous local residents herself, explained that local discourse about previous experience with coal mining had anchored representations of UGD, 'We live in a town and a region that is still very visibly environmentally scarred from a history of coal mining. It comes up here a lot that people are concerned about another environmental legacy like that one.' A resident from Cummings, PA, similarly exclaimed that the timber harvesting in his area during the preceding century left a horrible legacy of environmental destruction. He asked, therefore, why would the community 'want to go through [the destruction] again'?

Opposition to industrialisation was present in the communities accepting social licence, but it was a key representation in the communities challenging social licence (see below). A Sussex resident (Evensen and Stedman 2017) put it clearly, 'The rural beauty feeds our souls. An industrial landscape is a grievous insult to the people who live in the rural areas here – to the community.'

Social representations in areas challenging social licence

As in the previous section, we do not seek to create a strawman contending that everyone in communities challenging UGD was opposed to development. While we do not have the space to fully explore the continuum of degrees to which social licence was accepted or withheld in all of our communities or regions, we acknowledge a broad spectrum of views and degrees of acceptance. Nevertheless, each community could be classified as either accepting or challenging the UGD industry's social licence to operate. We describe social representations that influenced social licence in the latter set of communities below.

Social and place identity: environmentally attuned

Collective social identities, deeply rooted in shared local history and culture, served as strong anchors for representations of UGD in communities challenging social licence to operate, just as social identity did in communities accepting social licence. In distinction to the communities seeking to avoid activism (above), residents in the Northern Rivers region of New South Wales, and in multiple communities in New York and New Brunswick, held environmental sentiments that anchored their opposition to industrialisation and led them to seek to preserve peace, quiet, and natural beauty. In addition to environmentally attuned personal identities, residents in these locations saw a pristine environment as central to the identity of the place itself in which they lived.

In the Northern Rivers, Australia, widespread community opposition was identified by several university surveys and a local government election poll in 2012 (Luke et al., 2013, 2014b). Dialogue was rooted in value systems where financial considerations did not appear to be a primary concern; rather, representations of UGD were anchored in common worries over the sustainability of rural livelihoods, and water impacts. One of the earliest residents to activate on this issue (from 2010) relayed a clear objectification of gas as not essential for life, in a 2011 interview:

> You can't eat gas, it's that simple. They want to put the pipeline right through our most productive country…. This is all about water: our head waters are just up the road here at Lynches Creek, and we depend upon these aquifers for the farms and for the towns.

"You can't eat coal, can't drink gas" later became a common protest call, anchored broadly in the narrative of the UGD resistance movement (Luke, 2016). A second interviewee described his rationale for getting involved in protest activities, linked strongly to long-term sustainability for both humans and nature:

> I'm worried that if we keep digging up, drilling and injecting the earth, everything is going to die. I've got kids, I basically work for the future, that's what I do. I'm working for the animals too, and the trees.

An indigenous Australian, an elder, reinforced how UGD representations were anchored in sustainability: 'The basic thing is that if you look after Country, Country will look after you.'

The environmental identity of people and place was perhaps the strongest anchor for social representation of UGD in the Australian and North American communities stalwartly challenging social licence; it allowed communal discourse to paint UGD as predominantly an environmental issue. The representations were rooted in shared culture and experience. Interviewees frequently offered that people live in their community due to the 'beauty' characterising that place. A Dryden, NY, resident began the conversation by stating, 'I live where I do because I love this life; peace and quiet is the essence of living here … Heavy industry would destroy all that is important in life.'

Many people who cited natural beauty (visual, auditory, olfactory) as reasons for being concerned about or opposed to UGD explained that beauty, peace, and quiet were the essence of those communities. In Doaktown, NB, one resident contended that his community is 'about clean air, water, and peace and quiet'. Another Doaktown resident alleged, 'People come here for the quiet life, the slow pace, and the sense of community.' He viewed all three as threatened by development. These representations come from a shared cultural affinity for the environment.

One of the Doaktown residents anchored his representation of UGD in the identity of the major river passing through the village: 'Clean air and water are the lifeblood of the region ... one spill destroys the heart, soul, and identity of the Miramichi [River]. Without the river, the environment, we are nothing.' A second Doaktown resident supported this view: 'We still have our salmon, but with shale gas, we could lose them.' A Richibucto, NB, resident aptly anchored representations of UGD threatening beauty, peace, and quiet in shared social identity:

> It's about what's important to you.... Here, money's important; everyone likes money. But our lifestyle is really, really important.... I think a lot of people would say no to money because they don't want to lose what they have.

Timing of discourse and development

In the regions where UGD began early, when little discourse on the topic had taken place locally, reluctant acceptance of industry was the norm at the time of our research (see above); in communities where substantial discourse had occurred but widespread development had still not taken place by the time of our research, representations were more polarised and oppositional. In the latter communities, emergent representations were of UGD as something that needed to be supported or opposed. In the former communities, UGD was represented as inevitable, thus opening space for discussion of the good and bad.

In the Northern Rivers, while the local press was initially supportive prior to early 2011, it soon became critical of the UGD industry, which created a feedback-cycle of caution regarding developments. Since 2011, the city of Lismore has become a hot-spot of social action on UGD. In 2012, the Lismore local government instigated an election-poll on UGD, with 87 per cent of the community voting not to support developments (Luke et al., 2014b), ultimately banning the passage of any CSG-related equipment on Lismore City Council roads and funding a baseline study of local water systems (Luke et al., 2013). Casino, a town 20 minutes away that shares much local mass media with Lismore, replicated the exit-poll survey, revealing similar sentiments (Luke et al., 2013); the social representations had spread.

A few pivotal points emerged in the development of social representations of UGD in the Northern Rivers. Anti-UGD representations gained strong traction from early 2011, leading to large-scale action and community protests that attracted up to 7,000 protesters. A lot of information and social capital were shared during these events and the movements that produced them. In contrast, the continual maintenance of activists as an 'out-group' in Western Downs society led to very little social protest.

Having time to organise opposition in advance of UGD also allowed voices against development to become stronger in several North American communities. While some of the residents in the communities with broad social acceptance (above) represented their relationship to UGD as one of resignation, defeat, and/or an inability to affect change, this was not the case in the other communities, because there was still a viable goal (i.e. stopping *all* UGD) for which to fight. Word of mouth, local newspapers, the Internet, and public meetings were cited by our NY and NB interviewees as their most oft consulted information sources on UGD. Irrespective of the validity of information from each respective source, it takes time for discourse to develop via each medium. The Internet and social media took time to generate the monstrous swell of information that now ebbs and flows daily on UGD throughout the world. The communities with early development did not have access to such information; for example, a farmer (female, ~35) from the Western Downs, Australia, who had early exploration wells drilled on her property in 2001, recounted, 'In 2005 when we were approached by (the first gas company), we were desperate, we couldn't get any information.'

Two NY residents (Dryden and Sanford) explained that some of the most fruitful conversations about UGD occurred at the 'kitchen table'. Likewise, a Doaktown, NB, resident contended that 'the best ideas are exchanged in Tim Horton's' [the local coffee shop]. People trying to learn more about the issue gathered together in person and shared bits and pieces, facts and stories they had collected. Word of mouth knowledge that was passed on via local organization meetings also contributed prominently to discourse on development in NY (some of these groups were focused on UGD, but they also included previously extant groups like the local Kiwanis Club).

The mayor of Doaktown, NB, and residents from Richibucto, NB, cited using the Internet to find technical research on UGD. A Richibucto resident mentioned receiving daily e-mail digests from her friends and colleagues with a series of English and French news articles about UGD. Many NB interviewees explained that the Internet was their only option for information because all the English newspapers and some of the French newspapers in the province are owned by a powerful industry family, biasing the newspapers in the minds of virtually all Canadian interviewees. A Richibucto resident expressed, 'If it were not for the Internet, no one would know anything about this [UGD].'

Another Richibucto resident exclaimed, 'We would not be where we are [on this issue] without the Internet. It has collapsed the industry.' The nuanced mayor of Richibucto expounded, 'The people, disenchanted, went on the Web, finding sensational information. Now it is hard for people to obtain objective information.' The mayor highlights that the Internet is highly partisan; some online news articles can provide good coverage, but many interviewees cited using Google searches and Facebook, which could (and do) turn up anything. Even to the extent that Internet information is accurate, the Internet provides an excellent means for selectively identifying information that speaks to a limited range of representations and confirms one's a priori representations of UGD.

None of the Internet information or the social network connections were available to the communities where development occurred early. By the time the information became available, they had already lived with UGD for several years and their local discourse had evolved measurably from the common Internet message of stopping development before it starts.

Conclusion

Our research demonstrates that locations in which UGD extraction occurred before communal discourse proliferated have notably different social representation than communities where extensive debate occurred prior to development (in all of the latter cases in our study, development is banned or on hold). Our investigation into social representations surrounding UGD revealed a strong tendency for communities with early development to accept UGD to some degree, indicating the industry generally held a social licence, while communities where development did not take hold early on experienced heavy discourse on the topic and challenges to the social licence of the unconventional gas industry grew.

The amount of discourse prior to heavy development emerges as a key factor related to community appraisals of social licence. With common themes occurring across all three nations, it could be suggested that representations emerging from these geographical communities are now influencing representations expressed by the 'community of interest' of the global resistance against UGD. This has clear implications for considering how communities in places like Europe will assess social licence; Europe is just starting to move forward with potential UGD, but intense discourse has already permeated many nations.

We do not pretend to have examined comprehensively social representations of UGD or every factor affecting social licence in this chapter; an entire social scientific literature has emerged (and is rapidly growing) in this area. We believe we have, however, introduced a few key representations that strongly shape social licence assessments. Social identity is one such aspect of shared culture that seems to anchor social representations, discussed here in two forms – distaste for activism and being environmentally/aesthetically attuned. While concerns around environmental impacts and long-term sustainability have been cited repeatedly as key factors affecting opposition to UGD, a shared community identity as a place and people that seek to preserve beauty, peace, and quiet to retain local character and a way of life also play a critical role. Considering social identity as a key aspect of shared culture and history that influences social representations could help provide a more detailed understanding of whence social licence derives.

Finally, our international comparison prompts us to note that in many cases, emerging social representations and evaluations of social licence were more common *across* nations than *within* nations. Social identity and timing of development seemed to exert substantial influence on social representations of UGD. These representations lead to acceptance of or challenges to social licence more so than did governance regimes – which certainly do vary between the United States, Canada, and Australia. A major similarity in governance across these three nations, however, is that they all have federal systems in which decision making on UGD has been primarily delegated to the state/provincial level. This approach to governance of mineral resources is uncommon in Europe. Without this devolved approach to regulation, it is unlikely that we would have observed the within-nation differences that emerged. State-level differences in regulation allowed Queensland and Pennsylvania to move ahead full steam with UGD in the early years, while New South Wales and New York put on the brakes and then banned development. The international character of our case studies suggests that our findings should have some transferability, but applications to non-federal systems could be tenuous.

References

ABC. (2016). Victorian unconventional gas exploration ban to end fracking and CSG extraction. *ABC News Online*. Retrieved from www.abc.net.au/news/2016-08-30/victoria-to-ban-csg-fracking-and-unconventional-gas-exploration/7796944

ABS. (2015). Data by region. Retrieved from http://stat.abs.gov.au/itt/r.jsp?databyregion#.

Ashmoore, O., Evensen, D., Clarke, C., Krakower, J., & Simon, J. (2016). Regional newspaper coverage of shale gas development across Ohio, New York, and Pennsylvania: Similarities, differences, and lessons. *Energy Research and Social Science*, 11, 119–132.

Baer, H. A. (2014). Australian coal: Should it be left in the ground? *Monthly Review*, 66(1), 38.

Billig, M. (1993). Studying the thinking society: Social representations, rhetoric, and attitudes. In G. Breakwell & D. Canter (Eds.), *Empirical Approaches to Social Representations* (pp. 39–62). Oxford: Clarendon Press.

Borick, C., Rabe, B. G., & Lachapelle, E. (2014). Public perceptions of shale gas extraction and hydraulic fracturing in New York and Pennsylvania. *Issues in Energy and Environmental Policy*, 14, 1–18.

Breakwell, G., & Canter, D. (1993). *Empirical Approaches to Social Representations*. Oxford: Clarendon Press.

Brown, R. B. (2012). Legislative Council Inquiry into coal seam gas. Retrieved from Sydney: www.parliament.nsw.gov.au/prod/parlment/committee.nsf/0/318a94f2301a0b 2fca2579f1001419e5/$FILE/Report%2035%20-%20Coal%20seam%20gas.pdf

Dare, M., Schirmer, J., & Vanclay, F. (2014). Community engagement and social licence to operate. *Impact Assessment and Project Appraisal*, 32(3), 188–197. doi:10.1080/1461 5517.2014.927108.

Deaux, K., & Philogène, G. (2001). *Representations of the Social: Bridging Theoretical Traditions*. Oxford: Blackwell.

DNRM. (2016). Queensland's petroleum and coal seam gas 2014–2015. Retrieved from Brisbane: www.dnrm.qld.gov.au/__data/assets/pdf_file/0020/238124/petroleum.pdf

Evensen, D., Clarke, C., & Stedman, R. (2014). A New York or Pennsylvania state of mind: Social representations of gas development in the Marcellus Shale. *Journal of Environmental Studies and Sciences, 4*, 65–77.

Evensen, D., & Stedman, R. (2016). Scale matters: Variation in perceptions of shale gas development across national, state, and local levels. *Energy Research and Social Science, 20*, 14–21.

Evensen, D., & Stedman, R. (2017). 'Fracking': Promoter and destroyer of 'the good life'. *Journal of Rural Studies*. doi:10.1016/j.jrurstud.2017.02.020.

Freij-Ayoub, R. (2012). Opportunities and challenges to coal bed methane production in Australia. *Journal of Petroleum Science and Engineering, 88–89*(0), 1–4. doi:http://dx.doi.org/10.1016/j.petrol.2012.05.001.

Hazzard, B., Hodgkinson, K., & Hartcher, C. (2013). NSW government protects key farmland and homes. Media release. Sydney: New South Wales Government.

Lismore City Council. (2015). History of Lismore. Retrieved from www.lismore.nsw.gov.au/cp_themes/default/page.asp?p=DOC-URM-86-70-52.

Lloyd, D. J., Luke, H., & Boyd, W. E. (2013). Community perspectives of natural resource extraction: coal-seam gas mining and social identity in Eastern Australia. *Coolabah, 10*, 144.

Luke, H. (2016). Social license for industrial developments in rural areas. A case study of unconventional gas developments in the Northern Rivers, Australia, PhD thesis. Southern Cross University, Lismore, Australia.

Luke, H. (2017). Social resistance to coal seam gas development in the Northern Rivers region of Eastern Australia: Proposing a diamond model of social license to operate. *Land Use Policy, 69*, 266–280.

Luke, H., den Exter, K., Lloyd, D. J., Boyd, W. E., & Roche, B. (2013). Developing the Lismore CSG Poll: a university/local government collaboration. *Journal of Economic and Social Policy, 15*(3), 6–27.

Luke, H., Lloyd, D. J., Boyd, W. E., & den Exter, K. (2014a). Improving conservation community group effectiveness using mind mapping and action research. *Conservation and Society, 12*, 43.

Luke, H., Lloyd, D. J., Boyd, W. E., & den Exter, K. (2014b). Unconventional gas development: why a regional community said no, a report of findings from the 2012 Lismore City Council election poll and exit-poll survey. *Geographical Research, 52*(3), 263–279. doi:10.1111/1745-5871.12071.

Measham, T. G., & Fleming, D. A. (2014). Impacts of unconventional gas development on rural community decline. *Journal of Rural Studies*. doi:http://dx.doi.org/10.1016/j.jrurstud.2014.04.003.

Moscovici, S. (2001). *Social Representations: Explorations in Social Psychology.* edited by G. Duveen. New York: New York University Press.

O'Kane, M. (2013). *Initial Report on the Independent Review of Coal Seam Gas Activities in NSW by NSW Chief Scientist & Engineer.* Sydney, Australia: NSW Government. Retrieved from: www.chiefscientist.nsw.gov.au/coal-seam-gas-review

Schafft, K. A., & Biddle, C. (2014). School and community impacts of hydraulic fracturing within Pennsylvania's Marcellus Shale Region, and the dilemmas of educational leadership in gasfield boomtowns. *Peabody Journal of Education, 89*(5), 670–682. doi:10.1080/0161956X.2014.956567.

Stedman, R. C., Jacquet, J. B., Filteau, M. R., et al. (2012). Environmental reviews and case studies: Marcellus Shale gas development and new boomtown research: Views of New York and Pennsylvania residents. *Environmental Practice, 14*(4), 382–393. doi:10.1017/S1466046612000403.

Theodori, G. L., Willits, F. K., & Luloff, A. E. (2012). *Pennsylvania Marcellus Shale Region Public Perceptions Survey: A Summary Report*. Retrieved from www.shsu.edu/centers/rural-studies/Publications/PA%20Marcellus%20Summary%20Report%20final%20version.pdf

Thomas, M., Pidgeon, N., Evensen, D., et al. (2017). Public perceptions of hydraulic fracturing for shale gas and oil in the United States and Canada. *WIREs Climate Change, 8*, e450.

Thomson, I., & Boutilier, R. G. (2011). Social license to operate. In P. Darling (Ed.), *SME Mining Engineering Handbook* (vol. 15, pp. 1779–1796). Littleton, CO: Society for Mining, Metallurgy and Exploration.

Turner, J. C. (1975). Social comparison and social identity. *European Journal of Social Psychology, 5*, 5–34.

U.S. Energy Information Administration (EIA) (2012). *Annual Energy Outlook 2012*. Washington, DC: U.S. Department of Energy. Available at: www.eia.gov/forecasts/aeo

U.S. Energy Information Administration (EIA) (2017). *Drilling Productivity Report for Key Tight Oil and Shale Gas Regions, January 2017*. Washington, DC: U.S. Department of Energy. Available at: www.eia.gov/petroleum/drilling/

Walton, A., McCrea, R., & Leonard, R. (2014). CSIRO survey of community wellbeing and responding to change: Western Downs region in Queensland. Retrieved from www.researchgate.net/profile/Rod_Mccrea/publication/312043695_CSIRO_survey_of_Community_Wellbeing_and_responding_to_change_Western_Downs_region_in_Queensland/links/586c769008ae8fce4919e776.pdf

Wilbur, T. (2012). *Under the Surface*. Ithaca, NY: Cornell University Press.

Yin, R. K. (2013). Validity and generalization in future case study evaluations. *Evaluation, 19*(3), 321–332.

10 Evidence-based and participatory processes in support of shale gas policy development in South Africa

Gregory O. Schreiner, Megan J. De Jager,
Luanita Snyman-Van der Walt, Andile Dludla,
Paul A. Lochner, Jarrad G. Wright, Robert J. Scholes,
Doreen Atkinson, Paul Hardcastle, Hendrik Kotze and
Surina Esterhuyse

Introduction

The science-policy interface is an iterative, multi-way engagement process. It entails the generation of knowledge from processes which are shared between researchers, practitioners, policy-makers and stakeholders, the so-called 'co-production' of knowledge (Scholes *et al.*, 2017). Evidence-based and participatory processes are known to be useful for generating knowledge for issues of significant technical complexity, where there exists scientific uncertainty and societal conflict (Ash *et al.*, 2010). In spite of an established understanding of the importance of policy informed by good science, operationalising the science-policy interface has proved challenging and attempts to do so have not necessarily translated into cogent decision-making (Juntti *et al.*, 2009; Raymond *et al.*, 2010; Fernández, 2016).

The scientific assessment of shale gas development[1] in the Central Karoo (see Scholes *et al.*, 2016), requested widely by the stakeholder community in South Africa and commissioned by the government in 2015, offers an example of evidence-based and participatory processes which sought to promote the convergence of societal opinion on a highly divisive national issue (De Wit, 2011). Drawing on the key lessons from the South African experience of running a large, complex and multidisciplinary assessment, it is intended that the process, especially those aspects that relate to project governance and stakeholder participation, will serve as a useful reference point for future assessment processes of high societal contention in the arena of shale gas or other important social questions.

International and local context

By 2010, the shale gas revolution in the United States had sparked worldwide interest in domestic gas development. Global oil prices were around $100 per barrel, and horizontal drilling and gas extraction technologies were rapidly improving (Zuckerman, 2013). Shortly thereafter, the United States Energy Information Administration issued a series of reports providing initial assessments of world shale gas resources, with South Africa's Karoo Basin ranking in the top ten globally in terms of technically recoverable reserves (Kuuskraa et al., 2011). Some excitement about the potential for shale gas in South Africa followed, largely inspired by the shale gas boom in the United States (De Wit, 2011).

The main Karoo geological Basin covers approximately 700,000 km², representing more than half the land surface of South Africa (Raseroka and McLachlan, 2008). Deep drilling during the 1960s and 1970s had shown shale formations of the Karoo Basin to contain natural gas at depths of around 2–3 km, although in the absence of modern exploration data, the magnitude, distribution and economic recoverability of the gas resource are not well understood[2] (Burns et al., 2016). Even though the Karoo Basin is characterised by geological complexity, such as the presence of dolerite intrusions, the region is still considered an attractive target for shale gas, since the target formations have a relatively high organic carbon content and occur over a large area (Department of Mineral Resources, 2012).

The South African energy system is currently based mainly on coal mined in South Africa, complemented by imported oil and petroleum fuels, with small quantities of natural gas. Most energy in South Africa is supplied as electrical power, about 90 per cent of which is generated by burning coal. The integration of natural gas into the energy mix is widely advocated in policy (Department of Minerals and Energy, 1998). The National Development Plan (NPC, 2013), the overarching guiding plan for the country, encourages increasing natural gas use in the energy mix, irrespective of whether that gas is imported or sourced domestically. This policy objective is supported by evidence that including more natural gas in South Africa's energy mix would make the energy system more resilient, efficient, cheaper and reliable (Wright et al., 2016).

In 2010, the national Department of Mineral Resources received five Exploration Right applications to explore for shale gas from three different international companies. Collectively, the scope of the Exploration Right applications cover 124,000 km² of the Central Karoo and include exploration campaigns involving seismic surveys, deep vertical boreholes and horizontal drilling with test hydraulic fracturing (Golder Associates, 2011, 2015; SRK, 2015).

The Exploration Right application processes, ongoing since 2009, have been met with resistance by some organised community groups in South Africa[3] (Glazewski and Esterhuyse, 2016). The 'great shale debate in the Karoo' exploded into South African popular culture around this time and quickly became a polarised argument between those attracted by the opportunity of economic prosperity and energy independence versus those who believed shale gas development would result in unacceptable environmental and social consequences (De Wit, 2011). In response to this concern, the South African

Cabinet imposed a moratorium on decisions relevant to the shale gas Exploration Right applications and ordered a preliminary intergovernmental assessment into the risks associated with hydraulic fracturing (Department of Mineral Resources, 2012).

Following the results of the assessment, the moratorium was lifted in 2013, with the recommendation to 'authorise hydraulic fracturing … under an augmented regulatory framework'. Technical regulations, which prescribe the technological and best practice processes which must be employed during shale gas development processes, were released in 2013 for public comment (RSA, 2013). Voluminous submissions from numerous non-governmental organisations (NGOs) and individuals were received within a mandatory public comment process (Glazewski and Esterhuyse, 2016), after which the regulations were promulgated (RSA, 2015). Shortly thereafter, the regulations were contested in the Courts by a coalition of South African anti-shale gas development organisations, citing a lack of relevant scientific content in the regulations and insufficient public engagement on the intergovernmental assessment and technical regulations gazetting process (TKAG, 2015a). The court challenge is still pending at the time of writing (June 2017) and no decisions on the Exploration Right applications have been made.

An uncertain socio-ecological and regulatory environment

The Central Karoo is a semi-arid environment which assigns a premium value to freshwater resources for sustaining local communities and their livelihoods (Hobbs et al., 2016). Towns and farmers mainly rely on groundwater resources for domestic and livestock supplies and the sustenance of local economic activity, including irrigated agriculture and tourism (Burns et al., 2016). The dry, extensive landscapes of the Central Karoo are experienced by many people as a place of austere but compelling beauty (Toerien et al., 2016). The region includes high levels of biodiversity, distinctive heritage features and scenic resources (Burns et al., 2016) which make it attractive to a growing niche tourism market with 'space, silence and solitude' becoming hallmarks of tourism brand and lifestyles (Toerien et al., 2016).

On the other hand, the Central Karoo is a region with high levels of poverty and limited economic opportunity for local people (Atkinson et al., 2016). The regional gross domestic product is low when compared to towns and cities located outside the region and local government already have a major challenge of dealing with poverty and unemployment. Many municipalities are barely able to cope with current service delivery functions such as water provision, sanitation, electricity and roads management (van Huyssteen et al., 2016). Proponents of shale gas have promoted the industry as a means to enhance energy independence (Wright et al., 2016), reduce the national trade deficit and promote local economic development in a marginalised region of the country desperately in need of new growth and investment opportunities (Atkinson et al., 2016).

This narrative bears similarities to that advanced by the South African government, which has made public commitments to initial shale gas exploration activities to prove or disprove economic recoverability. Such positions have been made at the highest levels of government, for example, through the national Cabinet and in statements made by the President, such as that in State of the Nation Address in 2014 when the President proclaimed that 'we will pursue the shale gas option within the framework of our good environmental laws'.

Anti-shale gas development organisations have highlighted the fact that shale gas operations require relatively large quantities of water, proppant, fracturing fluids, trucks and other infrastructure to support a domestic gas industry, none of which are currently available in the Central Karoo. In addition, the prospect of shale gas development has created fears that municipalities may be overwhelmed by new tasks and challenges (van Huyssteen *et al.*, 2016), and that municipal officials and politicians may succumb to undue influence from large companies (Atkinson *et al.*, 2016).

In South Africa, the environmental management and development planning domains are dynamic and have been characterised by significant recent policy and law reform initiatives (Plit, 2016). In addition, South Africa does not have an unconventional gas industry and the potential for shale gas development has triggered the need to deeply consider an appropriate policy and legislative framework to regulate the industry should it advance (ASSAf, 2016).

The need for a participatory and transparent assessment

Despite the fact that the moratorium had been lifted, the technical regulations promulgated and a continued political commitment to shale gas exploration, no decisions on any of the existing Exploration Right applications have been made. In order to provide a tested evidence-base, designed to promote a convergence of opinion among stakeholders rather than the damaging polarisation, the government commissioned an independent scientific assessment of shale gas development in May 2015 (DEA, 2015), which was grounded in the principles of legitimacy, credibility and saliency (Ash *et al.*, 2010).

Legitimacy means that the process must be mandated by the authorities responsible for decision-making and is enhanced by implementing a process perceived by a wide range of stakeholders as being fair and unbiased. This is usually achieved by considering a broad balanced range of values, concerns and perspectives from different stakeholders in society. Saliency means addressing the questions which society is concerned about in a comprehensive manner and in doing so, producing material which is strategically useful for policy-makers.

Credibility means meeting the standards of scientific and technical rigour, where the sources of knowledge are considered trustworthy and independent. Appointing experts who are widely acknowledged by the stakeholders as having appropriate and leading knowledge and experience for the given topic (which may include 'indigenous' and 'local' knowledge, and expertise in fields not conventionally thought of as 'scientific'), and following a rigorous, transparent and documented peer review process, are considered essential. The extent to which the process achieved the implementation of the legitimacy, saliency and credibility principles will be discussed in the sections which follow.

Large-scale assessments on other topics, characterised by simultaneously having high technical complexity and high societal interest, have been developed and refined over the past three decades through a series of modern scientific assessments, such as those conducted by the Intergovernmental Panel on Climate Change (IPCC, 2013) and the Intergovernmental Platform for Biodiversity and Ecosystems (IPBES, 2016) and tested once in South Africa on the controversial issue of elephant management in conservation areas (Scholes and Mennell, 2008).

Drawing on the principles and learning from previous scientific assessment processes, the mission statement of the shale gas national assessment was drawn from the National Development Plan 2030 (NPC, 2013) and the Constitution of South Africa (RSA, 1996), and framed as a process designed to 'provide an integrated assessment and decision-making framework to enable South Africa to establish effective policy, legislation and sustainability conditions under which shale gas development could occur' (CSIR, 2015).

The mission statement, developed in collaboration with government at the first Executive Committee meeting, was purposefully phrased in the conditional. It did not presume that development *will* occur in the future, since no modern exploration has yet been undertaken, but does assume that it *could* occur if initial exploration results prove promising and the necessary environmental and planning permits are obtained.

Following the launch of the shale gas assessment in the public domain, the main anti-shale gas development organisation published a statement in support of the process:

> We are most encouraged by this development. A strategic environmental assessment is a fundamental step in the appropriate evaluation of shale gas in South Africa, and it is a process for which we have been calling since 2011. TKAG will be involved in the process and it intends to use every opportunity to play a pivotal role – from defining terms of reference, to placing specific data in front of the assessors in an effort to ensure that government policy is informed by science.
>
> (TKAG, 2015b)

Participatory processes for the assessment

Four, generally not mutually exclusive, 'pathways' of participation, appropriate for the various stakeholders, were provided through the South African assessment. This contrasts with the narrow public consultation which characterises most Environmental Impact Assessment (EIA) processes (Audouin and Hattingh, 2008). The four pathways were through: (1) project governance; (2) the generation of salient questions and engagement sessions; (3) content development through authorship; and (4) commentary on and review of content.

Participation through project governance

The Executive Committee and the Custodians Group were the two overarching governance structures commissioned to monitor conformity with the assessment process plan and principles as outlined in the 'process document' drafted by the project co-leaders (Scholes and Lochner, 2015) (Figure 10.1).

The key role of the Executive Committee was to ensure that the scope of the assessment was policy-relevant, salient for government users and that the project co-leaders and management team kept the process within brief and budget, as outlined in the process document. The Executive Committee also helped to satisfy the South African Constitutional requirements for co-operative governance, between departments and between different levels of government (RSA, 1996).

Members of the Custodians Group were nominated by the Executive Committee, the management team and the broader stakeholder community based on their credibility in the sector they represented and on their organisational representativeness. The Custodians Group was tasked with providing feedback to the Executive Committee and their respective constituencies, that the pre-agreed process and principles were followed in accordance with the vetted process document. Their specific mandate was to evaluate the process guided by the following five key questions:

1   Does the assessment cover the material issues that are of concern to people?
2   Has the assessment followed the guidelines in the process document?
3   Do the author teams have the necessary expertise and show balance in their composition?
4   Are the identified expert reviewers independent, qualified and balanced?
5   Have all the review comments received from expert and stakeholder reviewers been addressed and have the responses been adequately documented in a public repository?

Members of the Custodians Group were not appointed as 'representatives' of their organisation in a narrow sense, but were expected to reflect the breadth of opinion from their sectors (Figure 10.2). The Custodians Group was neither 'approving' nor 'disapproving' of shale gas development, nor did it have a say on the detail of the content of the assessment. It was a trustworthy collective nominated by society, tasked with ensuring that the process of evidence collection, evaluation and presentation was comprehensive and unbiased. This distinction remained critical, especially for the NGO members of the Custodians Group, as they and their respective organisations did not necessarily agree with every outcome of the assessment. It was also critical for the individuals involved in the Custodians Group to communicate effectively with their constituencies

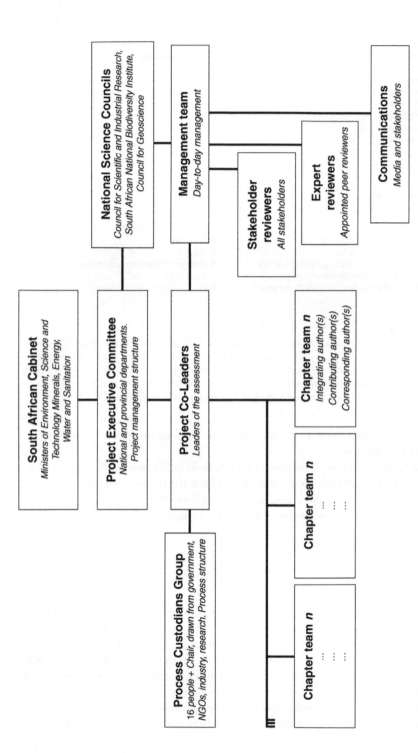

Figure 10.1 Integrated project governance structure. The Executive Committee comprised of the national and provincial government departments which commissioned the assessment. The Custodians Group consisted of 16 eminent people, drawn approximately equally from government, NGOs, the private sector, including the oil and gas sector and the research community.

Source: after Scholes *et al.* (2016).

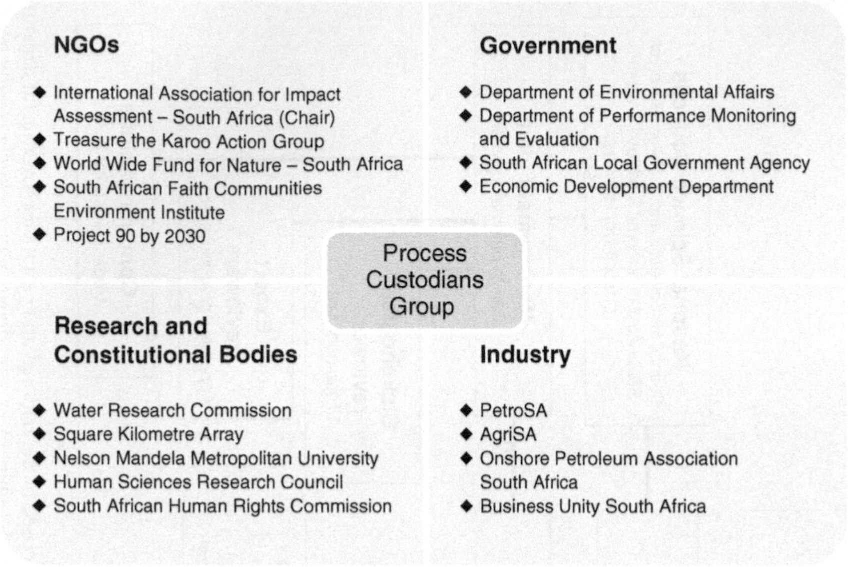

NGOs

♦ International Association for Impact
  Assessment – South Africa (Chair)
♦ Treasure the Karoo Action Group
♦ World Wide Fund for Nature – South Africa
♦ South African Faith Communities
  Environment Institute
♦ Project 90 by 2030

Government

♦ Department of Environmental Affairs
♦ Department of Performance Monitoring
  and Evaluation
♦ South African Local Government Agency
♦ Economic Development Department

Process
Custodians
Group

**Research and
Constitutional Bodies**

♦ Water Research Commission
♦ Square Kilometre Array
♦ Nelson Mandela Metropolitan University
♦ Human Sciences Research Council
♦ South African Human Rights Commission

Industry

♦ PetroSA
♦ AgriSA
♦ Onshore Petroleum Association
  South Africa
♦ Business Unity South Africa

Figure 10.2 The composition of the Custodians Group, representing NGOs, government, research and constitutional bodies; and private sector members. Its
purpose was to monitor the assessment process in terms of five specific
process questions and report back to the Executive Committee and sector
constituencies on the saliency, legitimacy and credibility of the process.

about their involvement with, and role in the assessment, so as to avoid perceptions of co-optation.

The final Custodians Group meeting was held in September 2016 before publication of the final draft assessment, after which the management team received
sign-off from the Custodians Group, via the Chair, that the *process* undertaken
had been comprehensive, balanced and fair in light of the available evidence
and information.

Participation through the generation of salient questions

Seventeen topics were addressed by the assessment and were generated by a
combination of 'top-down' and 'bottom-up' dialogues (do Rosário Partidário,
2012) over the course of many months and engagements. Each topic was
addressed as a specific chapter. Candidate topics were gleaned from peer reviews
of shale gas development experience worldwide in the existing literature, assem-
bled and organised into a large online repository by the assessment co-leads and
management team.

'Top-down' dialogues indicated that experience with shale gas development
elsewhere in the world (mainly the USA, where shale gas development is most

advanced) had revealed some potential negative consequences. This included the presence of gas in surface aquifers from deep sources following hydraulic fracturing (Vengosh *et al.*, 2014) and methane leakage during the extraction and transportation of gas (Bradbury *et al.*, 2013; Field *et al.*, 2014). Surface disturbances associated with development activities, such as road construction and increased traffic (Drohan *et al.*, 2012), water and waste management (Rahm *et al.*, 2013), and associated gas transport and utilisation infrastructures (Ziemkiewicz *et al.*, 2014), were also reported. As were sensory impacts of shale gas development in non-industrial environments and the unintended socio-economic impacts of attracting migrant labour to 'boom towns' in formerly rural economies (Christopherson and Rightor, 2011).

The outcomes of the 'top-down' dialogues were unpacked in summary format and released to the public as a Zero Order Draft (ZOD) for comment. The ZOD was a reasonably detailed 60-page skeletal structure of the entire assessment, including the risk assessment approach (IPCC, 2013), which would guide the assessment of each of the chapters. The ZOD included the structure, content and initial indication of the key issues which would be covered within the scope of each chapter. The ZOD was drafted in collaboration with the Integrating and Contributing Authors of the assessment following the first author meeting and then debated with stakeholders and governance groups to check that the questions most relevant to society were suitably addressed within the scope of the ZOD.

This engagement was undertaken through an early round of three local community meetings in the Central Karoo in November 2015 and a consultative meeting with stakeholders, with the ZOD as the focal point of attention (see Figure 10.3). Initial meetings were important for setting a trustworthy base of engagement and the management team used multiple communication mediums such as face-to-face meetings, the publication of written documents, explanatory video graphics and materials on the project website (http://seasgd.csir.co.za/), interviews with the media, press releases and even alternative communication methods such as art exhibitions. During these processes, stakeholders were asked the following three questions:

1 Does the process as described in the process document seem fair, unbiased and transparent?
2 Does the ZOD of the assessment cover all the material issues of concern?
3 What additional issues or concerns need to be included within the scope of the assessment?

One example of a 'bottom-up' knowledge flow concerned the issue of human health. In the initial ZOD presented to stakeholders and governance groups, the issue of human health was not included as a standalone assessment chapter. Following engagement with the Custodians Group and the meetings held with general stakeholders, it was evident that stakeholders believed that the topic of human health was sufficiently important to warrant standalone investigation.

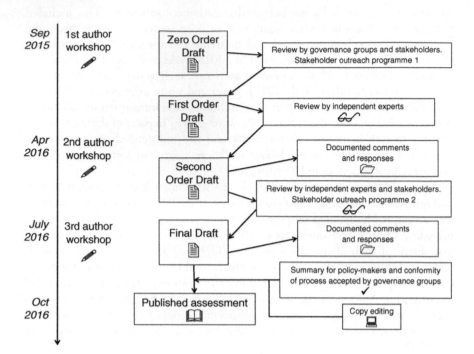

Figure 10.3 Two-loop review system and public outreach programme. The scientific assessment phase began with Author Meeting # 1 and the production of ZOD, followed by the first draft text, including tables and figures in the FOD, which was subsequently sent for national and international peer review. Incorporating the comments from the peer review experts, the multi-author teams developed the Second Order Draft (SOD), which was sent back to the peer review experts and simultaneously released to the general public for comment. Based on the feedback from the peer review experts and the general stakeholder comments, the final scientific assessment was published.

Source: after Scholes *et al.* (2017).

Following this decision, made in collaboration with assessment participants, the co-leads and management team commissioned a separate assessment chapter for human health (Genthe *et al.*, 2016).

This bi-directional approach allowed for the incorporation of different types of knowledge (technical and tacit) to be obtained during the framing of the assessment scope. The engagements with the public at the outset may not have contributed significantly new information regarding the salient questions to be answered by the author teams; however, this was never the main purpose. The engagements served an important role in legitimizing the outcomes of the assessment with the broader stakeholder community by demonstrating a genuine interest in addressing the issues of concern to society (Ash *et al.*, 2010).

The engagements were designed to get to know the relevant stakeholders and initiating or strengthening relationships with them. Through discussion and information sharing about the ZOD and the broader process, stakeholders were able to form a credible vision and understanding of the assessment. It assisted in making the process salient for them, and improved the likelihood that they would use its outcomes as a basis for future decision-making.

Participation through generation of content

The process leading to the development of the evidence base in the 18 chapters of the assessment was highly inclusive. In order to advance the principles of credibility and saliency, the latter demonstrating balance and comprehensiveness, the assessment adopted a multi-author team approach, in contrast to the usual EIA approach of appointing a single consultant per topic. Each of the chapters had an average of 6–8 authors, ranging between three (in the case of the earthquake chapter) and 45 authors (in the case of the biodiversity chapter) (Table 10.1). The multi-author team concept relied on two principles:

1 That each major topic is addressed by a team of authors, each author being a recognised expert.
2 That remuneration is based on covering expenses rather than at a level that could be reasonably construed to constitute an inducement to give a biased finding (Table 10.2).

Authors comprising the multi-author teams within the specific chapters were required to have acknowledged expertise and were drawn from a range of sectors such as research institutions, government, NGOs, universities and across different regions of South Africa to ensure a broad balance of interest was represented through the author structures. Authors were selected according to their formal qualifications, publications and experience, as well as widespread peer-group consensus based on their track record of valuable contributions on the topic.

Some 146 assessment authors were drawn from a broad range of employment backgrounds and from many regions of South Africa, with a range of gender and ethnicities. There was a deliberate attempt to ensure diversity and a balance of interests, disciplinary background, experience and perspectives in the team, a process which was overseen by the Custodian Group.

Participation through review and response

Following approval of the scope of the ZOD by the governance groups and the stakeholders, the multi-author teams initiated drafting the First Order Draft (FOD) of the assessment. The FOD chapters were submitted to 25 local and 46 international independent experts for peer review. These experts were selected by the management team, with the approval of the governance structures, based

Table 10.1 The final scope of topic chapters and the composition of the author teams commissioned to generate the content

Chapter	Title	IAs	CAs	CoAs	PRs	SRs
1	Scenarios and Activities	1	11	4	4	8
2	National Energy Planning and Security	1	3	0	4	6
3	Air Quality and Greenhouse Gas Emissions	1	5	0	4	7
4	Earthquakes	1	2	0	4	9
5	Water Resources	2	10	1	7	9
6	Impacts on Waste Planning and Management	1	1	1	5	9
7	Biodiversity and Ecological Impacts	2	5	38	5	15
8	Impacts on Agriculture	1	3	3	4	6
9	Impacts on Tourism in the Karoo	1	3	0	4	6
10	Impacts on the Economy	1	3	1	4	6
11	Impacts on Social Fabric	1	3	2	4	4
12	Impacts on Human Health	1	5	0	4	8
13	Impacts on Sense of Place	1	2	3	4	2
14	Visual, Aesthetic and Scenic Resources	1	3	2	6	3
15	Impacts on Heritage	1	3	5	6	4
16	Noise Generated by Shale Gas-Related Activities	1	1	1	3	4
17	Electromagnetic Interference	1	2	0	2	2
18	Impacts on Integrated Spatial and Infrastructure Planning	2	3	1	2	6
Total		21	63	62	76	114

Notes
The FOD was reviewed by nominated national and international peer reviewers. The SOD was reviewed by the same peer reviewers along with a number of stakeholder reviewers. IAs = Integrating Authors; CAs = Contributing Authors; CoAs = Corresponding Authors; PRs = Peer Reviewers; SRs = Stakeholder Reviewers.

Table 10.2 Author roles, remuneration structure and assessment responsibilities

Role and remuneration	Responsibility	Custodians Group role
Integrating Author (IA) (1–2 per topic). Expenses plus token stipend for acknowledged time investment.	Chairs the chapter team meetings, allocates writing tasks, ensures they are done on time and to specification, allocates reviewer response tasks and ensures they are done. Experienced expert in own right, part of overall summary/synthesis team.	Approves Integrating Author selection based on expertise, experience, credibility, availability.
Contributing Authors (CA) (3–5 per topic). Expenses only, modest honorarium fee for self-employed.	Collate, evaluate and summarise available information. Lead writer of an allocated section, participates in team discussions on entire topic and takes collective responsibility for it. Responds to reviewer comments in allocated section and revises drafts accordingly.	Approves Contributing Author team based on expertise and balance, can suggest authors.
Corresponding Author (CoA) (No limit, as needed). No fee.	Provides short input text on area of narrow or special expertise. May be asked to respond to reviewer comments on the material provided.	Notified of corresponding authors.
Peer reviewer (PR) (>2 per issue). No fee. Many were international experts.	Reads first and second draft and provides written, specific and evidence-based, referenced comments.	Approves list of expert reviewers, can suggest names, checks that their comments have been taken into account appropriately.
Stakeholder reviewer (SR) (No limit). No fee or entry barrier.	Reads second draft and provides written, specific comments. The degree to which they will be taken into account in the final draft depends on the evidence supplied and its credibility.	Checks that stakeholder comments have been taken into account appropriately.

Note
The nomination of potential authors was open to the general public and the Custodian Group, the latter responsible for vetting the final author composition which was then commissioned by the management team to develop the chapters.

on their experience in relation to shale gas development or specific knowledge of the Central Karoo social and ecological systems. Expert reviewers were drawn from government, NGOs, academia, and the private sector, with many international volunteers coming from the United States of America, Canada, Australia and European countries.

Peer and stakeholder review comments were submitted as structured page-and-line numbered statements which evaluated the accuracy, balance and comprehensiveness of the chapter content. The peer review comments were used in the development of the content for the Second Order Draft (SOD) and the responses to the comments by the multi-author teams were required to be sufficiently descriptive for the stakeholders to be able to trace them in the text or understand the basis upon which they had been accepted or rejected. The primary criterion was to demonstrate that multi-author teams had adequately applied their minds in the consideration of the comments from the peer reviewers.

The same peer review experts reviewed the revised SOD which was also released for broader stakeholder review with a second round of public outreach. Before finalisation of the published scientific assessment, the draft findings were presented to the same local and stakeholder communities to check that the key issues had been addressed. Their feedback was incorporated via the review process and facilitated where necessary for stakeholders without access to the internet, by capturing verbal input at the public meetings.

Lessons learned

It is a common misconception that the decision regarding shale gas development is a binary 'yes' or 'no'. There are a number of decisions to be made, via a number of decision-making processes, across all levels of government and society (including the private sector), over a protracted period of time. Most of these decisions will be conditional rather than absolute, meaning that an action may be permitted in one location and not another, or within a requisite set of management actions to reduce risk.

In South Africa, a democratic country with a strong developmental focus, it is important that public processes are informed by inclusive and deliberative knowledge generation exercises. The success of resource governance in a country which has no experience in domestic onshore oil and gas production is dependent on processes which seek to include broader society in both the generation of knowledge and subsequent decisions made relative to that knowledge.

In the Central Karoo, the biggest challenge is the lack of an existing infrastructure and the requisite skills within the private and public sector to manage the shale gas industry in a manner that does not give rise to unacceptable consequences. Thus, the capacity factors limiting the Central Karoo will have to be considered within future site-specific assessments, with practical alternatives or management actions stipulated by the practitioners and applicants. This must provide decision-makers with a clear indication of the trade-off implications associated with each decision option.

The success of future site-specific assessments, as was the case for the national scientific assessment, will depend on the extent to which stakeholders are included in the information gathering and decision-making processes. Additionally, site-specific assessments for exploration must promote the principle of avoidance. It has been demonstrated that even under a relatively intensive exploration scenario, that there is sufficient physical space in the expanse of the Central Karoo to avoid sensitive social and ecological features (Schreiner and Snyman-Van der Walt, 2018). The relatively small physical footprint associated with shale gas exploration activities means that there is a high degree of flexibility in the positioning of well fields, well pads, roads and other associated infrastructure. This can only be guided by focused site-specific assessments which embrace local knowledge.

Decision-making for site-specific assessments will require a step-wise approach, rooted in the concept of adaptive management. In other words, a focus on the importance of baseline and ongoing information for testing both the management actions employed to mitigate undesired outcomes and the assumptions which underpinned those actions. As a starting point, South Africa is in the advantageous position of being able to accumulate such a baseline dataset and start building the institutions capable of collecting, managing and analysing that data in a responsible and transparent manner.

Due to the continuous evolution of the science-policy interface, ongoing research is also required to ensure that environmental policies and regulations keep pace with shale gas development. This is not to suggest that no development should take place until all risk is mitigated to zero. Rather, if South Africa does choose to proceed with shale gas exploration, and assuming an economically suitable reserve is discovered, then the decision-making processes to arrive at that point must be inclusive of society and based on evidence which is broadly considered trustworthy.

About the authors

Greg Schreiner and Luanita Snyman-Van Der Walt headed up the management team for the national assessment with Megan De Jager and Andile Dludla acting as project interns. The management team was based out of the Stellenbosch office of the Council for Scientific and Industrial Research (CSIR). Bob Scholes of the University of the Witwatersrand and Paul Lochner from the CSIR co-led the assessment. Jarrad Wright was the Integrating Author of the Energy Planning chapter and is also based at the CSIR. Doreen Atkinson works at the Nelson Mandela University and is a resident of the Central Karoo. She is Director of the Heartland and Karoo Institute and acted as the Integrating Author on the Social Fabric chapter. Paul Hardcastle is based at the Western Cape Department of Environmental Affairs and Development Planning and was a member of the Executive Committee overseeing the scientific assessment.

Hendrik Kotze helped to design the public engagement component of the assessment and acted as an independent facilitator during the stakeholder outreach and engagement sessions over the 12 months process. Surina Esterhuyse is a hydrogeologist, based at the University of the Free State; she acted as one of the Contributing Authors on the water resources chapter.

Notes

1 The term 'shale gas development' is used to collectively refer to the full life-cycle of activities associated with shale gas exploration, production, downstream utilisation and eventual decommissioning of gas extraction, transportation and combustion infrastructure.
2 Results from the assessment indicate that technically recoverable reserves of shale gas within the study area of the Central Karoo could range between 71 and 153 trillion cubic feet (tcf). Taking a conservative approach, applying a recovery factor of around 10 per cent, the 'Small Gas' and 'Big Gas' scenarios considered in the assessment were 5 and 20 tcf of economically recoverable gas respectively (Burns *et al.*, 2016).
3 See Treasure the Karoo Action Group (TKAG), www.treasurethekaroo.co.za.

References

Ash, H. 2011. EPA launches hydraulic fracturing study to investigate health and environmental concerns while North Dakota resists regulation: Should citizens be concerned? *North Dakota Law Review*, 87(717), 717–741.

Ash, N., Blanco, H., Brown, C. *et al.* (eds.). 2010. *Ecosystem and Human Well-Being: A Manual for Assessment Practitioners*. Washington, DC: Island Press.

ASSAf (Academy of Science South Africa). 2016. South Africa's technical readiness to support the shale gas industry. doi: http://dx.doi.org/10.17159/assaf.2016/0003.

Atkinson, D., Schenk, R., Matebesi, Z. *et al.* 2016. Impacts on social fabric. In R. Scholes, P. Lochner, G. Schreiner, L. Snyman-Van der Walt and M. de Jager (eds) *Shale Gas Development in the Central Karoo: A Scientific Assessment of the Opportunities and Risks*. CSIR/IU/021MH/EXP/2016/003/A. Pretoria: CSIR. Available at: http://seasgd.csir.co.za/scientific-assessment-chapters/.

Audouin, M. and Hattingh, J. 2008. Moving beyond modernism in environmental assessment and management. In M. Burns and A. Weaver (eds) *Exploring Sustainability Science: A Southern African Perspective*. Stellenbosch, South Africa: Sun Press, pp. 205–242.

Bradbury, J., Obeiter, M., Draucker, L., Wang, W. and Stevens, A. M. 2013. *Clearing the Air: Reducing Upstream Greenhouse Gas Emissions from US Natural Gas Systems*. Washington, DC: World Resources Institute.

Burns, M., Atkinson, D., Barker, O. *et al.* 2016. Scenarios and activities. In R. Scholes, P. Lochner, G. Schreiner, L. Snyman-Van der Walt and M. de Jager (eds) *Shale Gas Development in the Central Karoo: A Scientific Assessment of the Opportunities and Risks*. CSIR/IU/021MH/EXP/2016/003/A. Pretoria: CSIR. Available at: http://seasgd.csir.co.za/scientific-assessment-chapters/

Christopherson, S. and Rightor, N. 2011. How shale gas extraction affects drilling localities: lessons for regional and city policy makers. *Journal of Town & City Management*, 2(4), 350–368.

Council for Scientific and Industrial Research (CSIR). 2015. Strategic environmental assessment for shale gas development. Available at: http://seasgd.csir.co.za/

Department of Environmental Affairs (DEA). 2015. Ministers E. Molewa and N. Pandor and Deputy Minister G. Oliphant: launch of the Strategic Environmental Assessment of shale gas development. Available at: www.environment.gov.za/mediarelease/molewapandor_strategicenvironmental_assessment

Department of Mineral Resources (DMR). 2012. *Report on the Investigation of Hydraulic Fracturing in the Karoo Basin of South Africa.* Sunnyside: Department of Mineral Resources.

Department of Minerals and Energy (DME). 1998. White Paper on the Energy Policy of the Republic of South Africa, Department of Minerals and Energy. Available at: www. energy.gov.za/files/policies/whitepaper_energypolicy_1998.pdf

De Wit, M. J. 2011. The great shale debate in the Karoo. *South African Journal of Science,* 107(7/8). Commentary.

do Rosário Partidário, M. 2012. *Strategic Environmental Assessment Better Practice Guide: Methodological Guidance for Strategic Thinking in SEA.* Lisbon: Portuguese Environmental Agency and Redes Energéticas Nacionais (REN), SA.

Drohan, P. J., Brittingham, M., Bishop, J. and Yoder, K. 2012. Early trends in landcover change and forest fragmentation due to shale-gas development in Pennsylvania: a potential outcome for the Northcentral Appalachians. *Environmental Management,* 49(5), 1061–1075.

Fernández, R. J. 2016. How to be a more effective environmental scientist in management and policy contexts. *Environmental Science & Policy,* 64, 171–176.

Field, R. A., Soltis, J. and Murphy, S., 2014. Air quality concerns of unconventional oil and natural gas production. *Environmental Science: Processes & Impacts,* 16(5), 954–969.

Genthe, B., Maherry, A., Steyn, M. *et al.* 2016. Impacts on human health. In R. Scholes, P. Lochner, G. Schreiner, L. Snyman-Van der Walt and M. de Jager (eds) *Shale Gas Development in the Central Karoo: A Scientific Assessment of the Opportunities and Risks.* CSIR/IU/021MH/EXP/2016/003/A. Pretoria: CSIR. Available at: http://seasgd.csir.co.za/scientific-assessment-chapters/

Glazewski, J. and Esterhuyse, S. 2016. Introduction: setting the scene. In J. Glazewski and S. Esterhuyse (eds) *Hydraulic Fracturing in the Karoo: Critical Legal and Environmental Perspectives.* Cape Town: Juta.

Golder Associates. 2011. Environmental Management Plan, South Western Karoo Basin Gas Exploration Application. Petroleum Agency South Africa (PASA) Reference No. 12/3/219.

Golder Associates. 2015. Updated Environmental Management Programme Report in support of application for Petroleum Exploration Rights within the Magisterial Districts of Somerset East, Graaff-Reinet, Cradock, Pearston and Jansenville, Eastern Cape Province. Prepared for Bundu Gas and Oil Exploration (Pty) Ltd. Report number: 1400417–13204–1.

Hobbs, P., Day, E., Rosewarne, P., Esterhuyse, S. *et al.* 2016. Water resources. In R. Scholes, P. Lochner, G. Schreiner, L. Snyman-Van der Walt and M. de Jager (eds) *Shale Gas Development in the Central Karoo: A Scientific Assessment of the Opportunities and Risks.* CSIR/IU/021MH/EXP/2016/003/A. Pretoria: CSIR. Available at: http://seasgd.csir.co.za/scientific-assessment-chapters/

Intergovernmental Science-Policy Platform on Biodiversity and Ecosystem Services (IPBES). 2016. Summary for policymakers of the assessment report of the Intergovernmental Science-Policy Platform on Biodiversity and Ecosystem Services on pollinators, pollination and food production. Edited by S. G. Potts, V. L. Imperatriz-Fonseca,

H. T. Ngo, *et al.* Bonn, Germany: Secretariat of the Intergovernmental Science-Policy Platform on Biodiversity and Ecosystem Services. Available at: www.ipbes.net/work-programme/pollination

International Panel on Climate Change (IPCC). 2013. *Climate Change 2013: Fifth Assessment Report of the Intergovernmental Panel on Climate Change*, Cambridge: Cambridge University Press. Available at: www.ipcc.ch/report/ar5/wg1/

Juntti, M., Russel, D. and Turnpenny, J., 2009. Evidence, politics and power in public policy for the environment. *Environmental Science & Policy, 12*(3), 207–215.

Kuuskraa, V., Stevens, S., Van Leeuwen, T. and Moodhe, K. 2011. *World Shale Gas Resources: An Initial Assessment of 14 regions Outside the United States.* US Energy Information Administration, pp. 1–365. Prepared by: Advanced Resources International, Inc. Available at: www.eia.gov/analysis/studies/worldshalegas/pdf/fullreport.pdf

NPC (National Planning Commission). 2013. *National Development Plan 2030.* Available at: www.environment.gov.za/sites/default/files/docs/national_development_plan_2030 vision.pdf

Plit, L. 2016. Regulating petroleum extraction: the provisions of the Minerals and Petroleum Resources Development Act 28 of 2002. In J. Glazewski and S. Esterhuyse (eds) *Hydraulic Fracturing in the Karoo: Critical Legal and Environmental Perspectives.* Cape Town: Juta.

Rahm, B. G., Bates, J. T., Bertoia, L. R. *et al.* 2013. Wastewater management and Marcellus Shale gas development: trends, drivers, and planning implications. *Journal of Environmental Management, 120,* 105–113.

Raseroka, L. and McLachlan, I. R. 2008. The petroleum potential of South Africa's onshore Karoo Basins. Adapted from expanded abstract prepared for AAPG International Conference and Exhibition, Cape Town, South Africa, October 26–29.

Raymond, C. M., Fazey, I., Reed, M. S. *et al.* 2010. Integrating local and scientific knowledge for environmental management. *Journal of Environmental Management, 91*(8), 1766–1777.

RSA (Republic of South Africa). 1996. Constitution of the Republic of South Africa. Act No. 108 of 1996.

RSA (Republic of South Africa). 2013. Proposed technical regulations for Petroleum Exploration and Exploitation. *Government Gazette,* No. 36938, Notice 1032, 15 October.

RSA (Republic of South Africa). 2015. Regulations for petroleum exploration and production. *Government Gazette,* No. 38855, Notice 466, 3 June, Pretoria.

Scholes, R. J. and Lochner, P. A. 2015. Strategic Environmental Assessment (SEA) for shale gas development in South Africa: SEA Process Document. Report Number: CSIRIUEMSIR20150001A. Available at: http://seasgd.csir.co.za/library/#anchor1

Scholes, R. J., Lochner, P., Schreiner, G., Snyman-Van der Walt, L. and de Jager, M. (eds). 2016. *Shale Gas Development in the Central Karoo: A Scientific Assessment of the Opportunities and Risks.* CSIR/IU/021MH/EXP/2016/003/A. Pretoria: CSIR. Available at http://seasgd.csir.co.za/scientific-assessment-chapters/

Scholes, R. J. and Mennell, K. G. (eds). 2008. *Elephant Management: A Scientific Assessment for South Africa.* Johannesburg: Wits University Press.

Scholes, R.J., Schreiner, G. O. and Snyman-Van der Walt, L. 2017. Scientific assessments: matching the process to the problem, *Bothalia, 47*(2), a2144. https://doi.org/10.4102/abc.v47i2.2144.

Schreiner, G. O. and Snyman-Van der Walt, L. (2018). Risk modelling of shale gas development scenarios in the Central Karoo. *International Journal of Sustainable Development and Planning, 13*(2), 294–306. doi: 10.2495/SDP-V13-N2-294-306

Seeliger, L., de Jongh, M., Morris, D., *et al.* 2016. Impacts on sense of place. In R. Scholes, P. Lochner, G. Schreiner, L. Snyman-Van der Walt and M. de Jager (eds) *Shale Gas Development in the Central Karoo: A Scientific Assessment of the Opportunities and Risks.* CSIR/IU/021MH/EXP/2016/003/A. Pretoria: CSIR. Available at: http://seasgd.csir.co.za/scientific-assessment-chapters/

SRK. 2015. Petroleum Exploration Right – Environmental Management Programme: Seismic Survey, Southern Karoo Basin. Prepared for Falcon Oil & Gas Limited. Report Number: 424473/04.

Toerien, D., du Rand, G., Gelderblom, C. and Saayman, M. 2016. Impacts on tourism in the Karoo. In R. Scholes, P. Lochner, G. Schreiner, L. Snyman-Van der Walt and M. de Jager (eds) *Shale Gas Development in the Central Karoo: A Scientific Assessment of the Opportunities and Risks.* CSIR/IU/021MH/EXP/2016/003/A. Pretoria: CSIR. Available at: http://seasgd.csir.co.za/scientific-assessment-chapters/

Treasure the Karoo Action Group (TKAG). 2015a. Published fracking regulations inadequate. Available at: www.treasurethekaroo.co.za/news/press-statements

Treasure the Karoo Action Group (TKAG). 2015b. Department of Environmental Affairs launches study on fracking. Available at: www.treasurethekaroo.co.za/news/press-statements

Van Huyssteen, E., Green, C., Paige-Green, P. *et al.* 2016. Impacts on integrated spatial and infrastructure planning. In R. Scholes, P. Lochner, G. Schreiner, L. Snyman-Van der Walt and M. de Jager (eds) *Shale Gas Development in the Central Karoo: A Scientific Assessment of the Opportunities and Risks.* CSIR/IU/021MH/EXP/2016/003/A. Pretoria: CSIR. Available at: http://seasgd.csir.co.za/scientific-assessment-chapters/

Van Zyl, H., Fakir, S., Leiman, T. and Standish, B. 2016. Impacts on the economy. In R. Scholes, P. Lochner, G. Schreiner, L. Snyman-Van der Walt and M. de Jager (eds) *Shale Gas Development in the Central Karoo: A Scientific Assessment of the Opportunities and Risks.* CSIR/IU/021MH/EXP/2016/003/A. Pretoria: CSIR. Available at: http://seasgd.csir.co.za/scientific-assessment-chapters/

Vengosh, A., Jackson, R. B., Warner, N., Darrah T. H. and Kondash, A. 2014. A critical review of the risks to water resources from unconventional shale gas development and hydraulic fracturing in the United States. *Environmental Science & Technology*, 48(15), 8334–8348.

Wright, J., Bischof-Niemz, T., Carter-Brown, C., and Zinaman, O. 2016. Effects on national energy planning and energy security. In R. Scholes, P. Lochner, G. Schreiner, L. Snyman-Van der Walt and M. de Jager (eds). 2016. *Shale Gas Development in the Central Karoo: A Scientific Assessment of the Opportunities and Risks.* CSIR/IU/021MH/EXP/2016/003/A. Pretoria: CSIR. Available at http://seasgd.csir.co.za/scientific-assessment-chapters/

Ziemkiewicz, P.F., Quaranta, J.D., Darnell, A. and Wise, R. 2014. Exposure pathways related to shale gas development and procedures for reducing environmental and public risk. *Journal of Natural Gas Science and Engineering*, 16, 77–84.

Zuckerman, G. 2013. *The Frackers: The Outrageous Inside Story of the New Billionaire Wildcatters.* New York: Penguin.

11 Campus organizing toward the democratization of shale oil and gas governance in higher education

Sarah T. Romano and Wendy Highby

Introduction

Shale gas extraction in the United States began quietly in the 1970s when the Department of Energy started to promote investment in unconventional oil and gas development (USDOE, n.d.; USEIA, 2016). Today, the US is recognized globally for its use and advancement of hydraulic fracturing technologies, producing over 11,000 billion cubic feet of gas in 2013 (USEIA, 2015). Shale oil and gas resources are "technically recoverable" in over a dozen countries worldwide (USEIA, 2015), yet North America's energetic embrace of new shale gas extraction technologies contrasts with other countries' more cautious approach. For example, Germany, France, Bulgaria, and the Czech Republic have opted to ban fracking (see BBC, 2015; "German Government," 2016; Jolly, 2013; see also Neslen, 2015; Schirrmeister, 2014). Shale gas exploration and development are expanding in Latin America, which holds an estimated 25 percent of reserves globally. This expansion dovetails with the region's historical dependence on resource extraction, yet may be constrained by public opposition as well as technological, political, and institutional factors (Hill, 2015; Mares, 2012; Shortell, 2015).

Despite the apparent national consensus on shale gas development in the US, researchers and public officials increasingly recognize that use of fracking technology has outpaced research examining its environmental and socio-economic impacts (e.g., Lave and Lutz, 2014; Navarro, 2012; Werner et al., 2015). Public health impacts have risen to the fore (see e.g., Adgate, Goldstein, and McKenzie, 2014; Colborn et al., 2011; Physicians for Social Responsibility, 2015), as have environmental and socio-economic implications (Fry et al. 2012; Fry, Briggle, and Kincaid, 2015; Malin and DeMaster, 2016). Concerns are also global in scope: environmental scientists warn that the "expansion of shale gas fracking is inconsistent with climate change mitigation" due to the rate of methane leakage from shale gas wells and a carbon footprint that is similar to coal when compared over the long term (Staddon and Depledge, 2015, p. 8270; see also Finkel and Hays, 2013; Marchese et al., 2015; Turner et al., 2016). Oftentimes, political and policy struggles over fracking, ranging from local to global scales, pit health, safety, and environmental concerns against economic ones.

Recently, fracking technology in the US has spread to urban areas, showing up in backyards and near playgrounds. Not surprisingly, this encroachment of fracking and its associated industrial activities has aroused the concern of residents, including parents, students, school administrators, and even some industry workers who are aware of the increasingly documented impacts of living near wells. Conflicts over fracking reveal not only the potential for greater fragmentation of decision-making within states (Rabe, 2014), but also call for increased local citizen participation in governance of this industrial activity. While state-level protection of resource extraction has undermined local efforts to shape fracking operations through democratic initiatives (see e.g., Enockson, 2014; Negro, 2012; Smith and Ferguson, 2013; Toan, 2015; see also Goho, 2012; Finley, 2016; Wines, 2016),[1] city-level bans and moratoria reflect calls for increased citizen engagement. They also demonstrate the promotion of energy development logics that transcend narrow economic considerations.

This chapter examines institutions of higher education as a site of local political contestation over fracking. Universities constitute microcosms of the procedural and substantive justice issues pertaining to energy governance; they also embody the trend of corporatization affecting cities' and states' promotion of fracking as a means of income and economic development. We examine organized responses to the possibility of shale gas operations near or on campus property on the part of faculty, staff, and students at four universities in the US: Allegheny College (Meadville, Pennsylvania), Bethany College (Bethany, West Virginia), Ohio University (Athens, Ohio), and the University of Northern Colorado (Greeley, Colorado). In particular, we examine how organized responses reflect the promotion of "ecological democracy" (Mitchell, 2006) in the context of university corporatization through their degree of: (1) representativeness of campus stakeholders; and (2) comprehensiveness of research and education efforts in terms of transcending the economic logic of corporatization.

Analyzing variance in stakeholder representation and research and education processes, we found a degree of difference in cases where the impetus for organized inquiry into campus fracking came from the university administration: the resulting processes were more representative of stakeholders and engendered more comprehensive education efforts and research products than in cases where administrations did not seek or support organized inquiry and research processes. Our findings thus demonstrate the democratization of energy governance via expanded representation and participation to be *greater* in cases where the administrations' actions promoted organized participation in campus dialogue, education, and decision-making. Across cases, we contend this campus-based organizing has transformative potential in the context of corporatization, even in cases where efforts are not actively supported by the university administration.

Methods

Research for this chapter occurred between 2013–2016. At the University of Northern Colorado (UNCO), where the authors are faculty, extensive participant observation of meetings and campus events related to oil and gas development was conducted from 2013–2015. Data pertaining to UNCO are also drawn from a campus-wide survey (428 respondents, or 3.25 percent of faculty, staff, and students) which the authors implemented in May 2014 to assess knowledge and attitudes about hydraulic fracturing, as well as awareness of the university's mineral lease. The survey was most heavily responded to by staff (57 percent), followed by faculty (37 percent). A small minority of respondents (7 percent) were students.[2] Semi-structured interviews were conducted with seven "Hydrofracturing Task Force" members from January–May 2015; participants were those who responded to an email invitation originally sent to all 19 members of this group (including the authors) in July 2014. Interviews and survey data were coded thematically; some of the results are discussed in the empirical section of this chapter.

Discussion of the remaining three cases is informed by analysis of primary and secondary documents including universities' oil and gas leases, campus websites, Facebook pages, newspaper articles, and documents published on the web by the campus groups under examination.

Organized responses to fracking in the university context

Examining hydraulic fracturing at institutions of higher education requires situating within the broader trend of university corporatization. Corporatization reflects, in practice, a "context of shrinking state budgets for public education and the growing expectation that university presidents function as CEOs more preoccupied with the institution's 'bottom line' than with the quality of its programs" (Schoorman, 2013, p. 511).[3] In the US, the fall 2016 issue of the American Association of University Professors' journal *Academe* was devoted to "The Corporate Reach" in higher education, with articles highlighting "the annexation of academia by the commercial world" (Barlow, 2016, p. 2; see also Silvey, 2002). This trend is not entirely new (see Chile and Black, 2015; Fisher and Koch, 2004), yet is receiving renewed attention at an international scale (e.g., Brulé, 2015; Blum and Ullman, 2012; Christopher, 2012; Healy and Debski, 2017; Morrissey, 2015).

Part of the significance of corporatization lies in the assessment that it compromises universities' commitments to the public good and "the democratic mission of public education" (Schoorman and Acker-Hocevar, 2010, p. 312; see also Schneider, 2015; Schoorman, 2013). The cases discussed herein demonstrate how university corporatization – via the leasing of mineral rights and/or campus land to oil and gas companies – may create perceptions of misguided decision-making and/or undermined "shared governance norms" on US campuses (Pasque and Carducci, 2015, p. 283). Corporatization thus provides a point of departure for understanding campus stakeholders' responses to decisions guided by narrow economic logics which may not align with the missions and/or procedural norms of university governance.

We contend that the fracking-related organizing and activism of faculty, staff, students (and in some cases, alumni) reflect the promotion of "ecological democracy" as an "alternative democratic model" that "strives to incorporate interested citizens into environmental decision-making" (Mitchell, 2006, p. 463). Promotion of ecological democracy may encompass activities such as organized educational forums, panels or debates; it may also take the form of engaged, critical scholarship that sheds light on stakeholders' interests and concerns and promotes environmentally-sound practices. In its pursuit of ecological democracy, the organizing examined in this chapter is similar to contemporary campus activism, primarily student-led, to encourage divestment from fossil fuels (Bratman et al. 2016; Grady-Benson and Sarathy, 2015). The divestment movement is global in scope, with at least 81 university "divestment commitments worldwide" spanning North America, Europe, Australia, and New Zealand (Healy and Debski, 2017, p. 6). As the research on divestment at institutions of higher education grows, that on fracking lags behind; importantly, organizing pertaining to both on college campuses reflects the promotion of ecological democracy through shedding light on the diverse dimensions and implications of energy-related and social justice-related issues.

Embracing the administration's call: Allegheny College and Ohio University

At both Allegheny College and Ohio University (OU), campus advisory groups representing multiple campus stakeholders were created by university administrators as the issue of leasing land and mineral rights arose. At Allegheny, the land in question formed part of the Bousson Environmental Research Reserve, located roughly 2 miles from campus.[4] Allegheny acquired the Reserve in 1935 and its use has primarily been restricted to faculty and student research pertaining to soil, water, and aquatic life. In 2012, three landowner groups and a seismic testing company approached the university, necessitating "a decision [regarding oil and gas development] in a short time-frame" (BAG, 2013, p. 6).

The impetus for the formation of Allegheny's Bousson Advisory Group (BAG) came via the college's President, and reflected a group broadly representative of campus stakeholders, including students, faculty, administrators and alumni. While the President created the group as an explicitly "non-decision-making body," a principal goal was research and education that would "result in the community being better informed on all aspects of the subject of potential gas exploration at Bousson" (ibid., p. 3), in part, through sharing results of the group's research with the university administration. Moreover, the President's charge emphasized that the BAG "[facilitate] a transparent and inclusive process of communication on campus." Roughly a dozen individuals ultimately participated, including two women and representatives from the social, physical, and biological sciences. The group decided that while reaching "consensus" as a group was unlikely, there would be a commitment to submit to the university administration a "qualified mix of opinions" from across the university (BAG Minutes, 11/2/2012). Various means of engaging the campus community – a student government survey, campus discussions, and a student petition calling for the rejection to lease campus property for shale gas development – complemented the BAG's efforts (BAG, 2013; Dunegan et al., 2013).

At OU, located above the Marcellus and Utica Shale formations, the Eastern campus of the six-campus system was targeted for oil and gas extraction by Chesapeake Energy and Exxon Mobil in 2012 (Phillips, 2012).[5] Notably, in late 2011, administration and faculty had been outspoken against proposed hydraulic fracturing in neighboring Wayne National Forest. Board of Trustees (BOT) meeting notes indicate a dovetailing of administration and other campus stakeholder concerns: "after [President McDavis'] consultation with faculty members on the Ecology and Energy Conservation Committee and the President's Advisory Council for Sustainability Planning … he submitted a letter of protest due to [fracking's] proximity to the Hocking River." The meeting minutes indicated the President postponed all potential activity "due to the increased concern that was voiced by the University and others" (OU BOT, 2011).

OU's Ad hoc Mineral Rights Committee (AHMRC) formed in 2012, precipitated by 2011 state legislation that created a commission to administer mineral rights leasing associated with land owned by state agencies. Under the law, OU and all state agencies were required to inventory land holdings and associated mineral rights in preparation for bids from developers. As a result, the BOT Chair requested that a report be prepared, prompting a participatory, multi-campus, and multi-committee process. One group, the AHMRC, composed of nine administrators and two faculty members, was mandated to "prepare a report regarding the implementation of Ohio House Bill 133 and the protection of University mineral rights under that statute," and was to include the examination of the BOT's fiduciary rights and responsibilities. Public education and gathering of community opinion were an intentional, well-organized part of the AHMRC's process: forums were held on all six campuses and participants were invited to complete an online survey. Two pre-existing standing committees, the Ecology and Energy Conservation Committee and the President's Advisory Council for Sustainability Planning, supported and assisted the group in creating the report. In addition to students, faculty, and staff, the latter also had the participation of two municipal employees (OU AHMRC, 2012).

The research and educational processes undertaken by campus groups at Allegheny and OU reflect a high degree of comprehensiveness in transcending the narrow, income-generating logics of corporatization. For example, the BAG's November 2013 Report to Trustees was attentive to "physical, economic, social and philosophical concerns" (p. 10) regarding the impacts of seismic testing, mineral leasing, and drilling on university property. The report detailed potential impacts pertaining to water resources, air quality, land use, earthquakes, the economy, the community, and college reputation resulting from shale gas exploration and extraction. The report's emphasis on the "complexities" of the issue was informed by feedback gathered at "a series of education and discussion sessions" on campus in 2013, and via BAG's webpage. Notably, comments on the website and gathered as part of the Student Government's survey on the topic of drilling elicited concerns about a mismatch between Allegheny's stated environmental principles and the decision to allow seismic testing on university property. As one student stated, "I do not see Allegheny's educational ideals and environmental commitments to be consistent with this type of resource extraction," and in the words of a parent, "Your credibility as a leading environmental institution will certainly be jeopardized." Aligning with these comments, 58 percent of respondents to the student survey on the topic of horizontal drilling indicated that Allegheny's "sustainability reputation" affected their opinion on the issue.[6]

In April 2012 at OU, the AHMRC and two standing committees submitted their 61-page Report to the BOT. The Report embraced the "lens of institutional sustainability and climate neutrality" and referenced the authoring group as "stewards to the environmental, financial and personal health and well-being of the campus." Hence, like Allegheny, OU explicitly introduced dimensions of oil and gas development not visible through the economic lens of corporatization.[7] The Report revealed the OU administration to have an understanding of fiduciary responsibility that included environmental stewardship. The administration took seriously its ACUPCC pledge[7] and viewed southern Ohio as an ecosphere in which the impacts of fracking needed to be considered. The AHMRC's Report was chiefly precautionary in nature, recommending a moratorium "until additional information can be gathered to insure the long-term protection of our campus environments and surrounding communities" (p. 2).

Confronting the administration's decision: UNCO and Bethany College

In contrast to experiences at Allegheny and Ohio University, campus stakeholders at UNCO and Bethany College encountered energy governance contexts in which the administrations did not seek engagement of the campus community. Lying over the Eastern plains above the Niobrara shale formation, UNCO (in Greeley, Colorado) leased its mineral rights through unanimous approval by the BOT in 2011. The lease granted Mineral Resources, Inc., a subsurface easement for the drilling of directional wells underneath the campus. The developer selected two urban drilling sites: one in a densely populated neighborhood, 451 feet from a rental apartment building and two blocks from University family and student housing; the second site was less than 1,000 feet from an elementary school playground. Reflecting the values of corporatization, BOT meeting minutes stated that "UNC[O] has a positive financial opportunity" and referenced a year-long period of "discussions regarding oil and gas on UNC[O]'s property" (UNCO BOT, 2011). The President was quoted in March 2013 that this kind of entrepreneurial partnership was not unusual in an era of rising tuition and falling state support (Cotton, 2013). Though individual students spoke out against fracking through editorials in the independent student newspaper, *The Mirror*, and class projects (Woods, 2013), no student-organized response or protest emerged. The first and last lease-related email communication from the President came in spring 2013, almost two years after the least was signed; it indicated that drilling was predicted to begin within 18 months and that the campus would be kept apprised of changes.

Similar to UNCO, Bethany College is located atop a large shale formation, the Marcellus, on the northern panhandle of West Virginia – a key locale for energy resource extraction according to the U.S. EIA (2016). Bethany's campus property includes the Parkinson Forest, donated to the small, private college in 1914 "under the stipulation that the forest must remain preserved and be an asset in the education of students at Bethany" (Bethany College, 2005–2006). Seemingly in contravention of these land use stipulations, the local newspaper reported in 2011 that the Bethany BOT had leased mineral rights under college property to Chesapeake Energy. Surface operations would be located on forest property, about a third of a mile from student housing (Schackner, 2011). Original press coverage of the lease emphasized the potential economic benefits: "In recognizing the possible job creation and market activity that could result from local drilling, [President] Miller hopes the college can be a catalyst in helping to promote the burgeoning industry" (Junkins, 2011). Although final licensing terms were never publicly disclosed, the BOT unanimously approved the lease, defending the agreement in part on the grounds that the college's $40 million endowment was "too low" and "must grow to ensure the college's long-term stability." It pledged that drilling royalties would supplement the endowment to "provide added resources for more competitive faculty salaries and campus improvements – all of which are extremely important to the long-term health and well-being of the college" (Bethany College BOT, 2011).

Campus stakeholders at both UNCO and Bethany responded to administrative decisions at their universities, albeit each effort had more limited representation and overall less activity than emerged at Allegheny and OU. UNCO's Hydrofracturing Task Force (HFTF) began in 2013 with four faculty who drafted the group's principal goal: "to propose informed and ethical policy, and/or resolution(s), and transmit same to the Faculty Senate and the campus community for its consideration" (Highby et al., 2013). Although the Senate declined a proposal to create an official faculty task force, it agreed to commit two members as representatives. In an attempt to reach students, the HFTF sent an electronic news bulletin to the entire campus community. Ultimately, the group primarily represented the institutional "middle," or faculty and staff (Brinkhurst et al., 2011): 19 faculty and staff from social, physical and biological science departments and campus libraries, and two students (undergraduate and graduate, respectively), participated. The HFTF also extended a direct invitation to the Environmental Health & Safety Office for administrative representation.

The report issued by UNCO's HFTF in May 2014 was based upon the research and writing efforts of primarily a smaller sub-set of members, all women. It came in the wake of several open-to-the-public speaking events about fracking on campus in 2014. In the view of task force members, these were not well attended, particularly by students. More successful in term of campus-wide engagement was a survey the authors conducted as HFTF members in spring 2014 (428 respondents), which revealed student, faculty, and staff health, safety, environmental, and university reputational concerns if drilling were to proceed near campus. As one respondent stated: "Students are already asking faculty and others about how fracking will affect their health and the health of the university. Will we continue to attract students as negative impacts of fracking receive more research and more media attention?"

The HFTF's three-page (in contrast to OU's 61-page) document had educational as well policy aims: it provided basic data regarding the 2011 lease and issued recommendations to administration. These included a moratorium on the proposed drilling until certain research and education criteria were fulfilled, and mitigation of the school's current carbon footprint through joining the international "Go Fossil Free" divestment initiative. Although environmental concerns received significantly more attention in the reports produced by Allegheny and OU, the HFTF emphasized non-economic criteria in its assertion that "Substantial knowledge gaps exist, particularly with regard to cumulative risk estimates [of fracking] pertaining to a number of different health, environmental, socioeconomic, and psychosocial stressors" (p. 1). The administration representative on the HFTF declined to sign his name to the Report and its recommendations. The report was disseminated to the university President, BOT, and broader campus community via email. Unlike Allegheny's BAG, UNCO's HFTF received no response from the administration, although the group sought meetings with the President's office, the second of which the President attended in summer 2014.

Setting Bethany apart from the other three institutions examined in this chapter, no organized response to fracking on campus emerged on the part of faculty, staff, or students.[8] After announcement of the lease, alumni promptly created a Facebook page, "No Bethany Fracking," expressing shock at the decision.[9] The concerned parties demanded more information in a July 2011 post:

> What we do deserve to know are the details surrounding the deal … These should be a matter of college record and those with interest in the college – whether financial, as an alumni or parent, or as a townsperson – deserve to know what the frack is going on here.
>
> (No BethanyFracking, 2011)

Within weeks, the page had developed a following of more than 300 (currently over 400), and through April 2012, continued to convey concerns about long-term environmental health and safety impacts of fracking. In response to Facebook-produced queries, the BOT posted informational documents about the lease on the College website, revealing that the lease agreement had developed behind closed doors over several years (Bethany College BOT, 2011).

Bethany's 2014 State of the College report portended more fracking on college property (Miller, 2014, pp. 5, 14).

In terms of *potential* avenues for campus stakeholder engagement, Bethany's infrastructure of shared governance appeared extremely limited during President Miller's term (2008–2015). The College's news archives from 2010–11 cite the President heralding the economic benefits of fracking to the "college's long-term growth and development" while asserting the school's responsibility as "good stewards of our environment and [to] ensure safety of our community."[10] Reflecting a change in perspective on faculty governance, Miller's replacement in 2015 entailed the creation of 15 new faculty committees, including, among others, Assessment, Budget, Curriculum, Faculty Development, and Interdisciplinary Studies.

While corporatization and minimal space for faculty in governance appear to have created a culture where faculty were reluctant to speak out against fracking at Bethany,[11] a student's project that drew upon interviews painted a picture of fellow students as uninvolved and uninformed. As he wrote:

> Franklin [a student] noted that the environmental presence on campus was largely "apathetic" ... students have not felt any impacts of hydrofracking thus far. This year [2012], a Student Life representative stated that the Environmental Science Club was actually disbanded since to a lack of student interest. Other than the Outing Club, this was the only environmental organization on campus.
>
> (Fenrich, 2012, p. 10)

Fenrich's paper hints at potential intentional minimization of drilling controversy on campus in citing the BOT's 2012 Trustee Statement emphasizing limited effects of resource extraction on Bethany's "campus or in the college's operations" (p. 10).

Contesting corporatization "from within"

This chapter's findings demonstrate some inherent opportunities and limits to organizing internally within higher education institutions. A direct *causal* relationship between level of campus leadership support and faculty, staff, and student organizing to promote ecological democracy on campus would be hard to assert; however, our data do reveal a correlation. While not a representative sample, our four cases demonstrate the democratization of energy governance to be greater where the administrations' actions promoted organized participation in campus dialogue, education, and decision-making.

For Allegheny College and Ohio University, the impetus for an organized investigation into campus health, safety and environmental concerns came from the administration. The resulting campus groups and research and educational processes were broadly representative of campus faculty, staff, and students. Moreover, beyond integrating key campus stakeholders, organizing in each of these cases reflected comprehensiveness in line with the promotion of ecological democracy: not limited to economic considerations, the reports generated reflect social, environmental, procedural, and other issues and concerns, and a promotion of their consideration in current and future decision-making. At both universities, highly supportive leadership contributed to the inclusiveness and efficacy of ad hoc campus stakeholder groups. Perhaps most notably, both campus groups had the "listening ear" of their Presidents and BOTs; in OU's case, the administration was even an active ally of campus stakeholders in resisting hydraulic fracturing.

In contrast, UNCO campus stakeholders organized in the context of an administration that actively promoted fracking near campus. The HFTF did not achieve the desired levels of campus stakeholder engagement as it worked toward its report – which was issued to an administration that did not agree with its findings and recommendations. Organizing at Bethany College was absent, ostensibly constrained by an institutional context pervaded by the logic and values of corporatization.

Across cases, however, the transformative potential of campus organizing in the context of corporatization is found not only in the use and creation of democratic spaces on campus, but also in its tangible impacts on shale oil and gas resource extraction. OU's campus response reflected a democratic institutional governing structure with the administration affording decision-making influence to faculty which, minimally, delayed fracking of the Eastern campus. The opportunity to influence resource extraction outcomes was not limited to cases where university leadership supported campus groups: at UNCO, campus organizing very likely impacted the decision of the company to move the location of wells further from campus shortly following the HFTF's issuing of its report. This is perhaps not surprising when considering that the report placed heavy emphasis on the school's reputation, including potential damage to its public image, if drilling were to proceed near campus. Given the variable influence of broader social and political contexts, more extensive qualitative research could usefully illuminate how multiple factors converge with campus organizing to influence trajectories of local shale oil and gas development.

This research also indicates that universities' mineral leasing strategies justified by corporatist logics can backfire. Alumni and parents at all four institutions expressed concern about their institutions' reputations and potential impacts on employee and student recruitment and retention. The potential negative impact of shale oil and gas development on student enrollment, and hence university income, presents a notable irony given the revenue-boosting justifications for land and mineral rights leases. As a UNCO survey respondent expressed: "I wonder how future enrollment could be affected if it is widely believed from families in Colorado that UNC[O] is not a safe campus do [sic] to beliefs regarding fracking, the oil and gas community, etc." Many of the alumni who left comments on Allegheny's BAG webpage indicated they would withhold donations to the university if the oil and gas development proceeded on college property. At both schools, students in particular raised the question of how royalty money would be spent. These questions call upon administrations to be more forthcoming regarding their economic rationales for mineral rights and/or land leasing. Otherwise, promises and pledges may fall short in the eyes of stakeholders.

Universities' role in the democratization of energy governance

Importantly, the case studies in this chapter reveal that institutions of higher education offer the potential use of existing as well as creation of new democratic channels for organized responses to energy development. With the exception of Bethany, each of the cases examined reflects university stakeholders organizing research and education efforts on campus pertaining to hydraulic fracturing near and/or underneath campus property. Hence, lack of support from the administration does not necessarily impede campus stakeholders from organizing; the divestment movement highlights this same finding as many BOTs do not support student-promoted divestment policies. Contributing to a proclivity to organize internally may be the institutional norm of faculty governance bodies, like Senates and curriculum committees, which provide avenues for faculty engagement in university decision-making. These bodies and related decision-making channels reflect ideas about shared governance characterizing college campuses in the US (Bok, 2013), which may empower faculty to seek to influence campus leadership. This was the case at UNCO, where the administration neither invited nor encouraged engagement in fracking-related decision-making on campus. Yet even though the HFTF was not an administration-sanctioned group, the group sought legitimacy through approaching the Faculty Senate for recognition and did see regular participation of one staff member from an administrative office on campus. Ultimately, the UNCO HFTF reflects increased democratization of campus governance, despite minimal support from the administration.

For the foreseeable future, the national energy governance system in the United States will be highly decentralized, with "much of the responsibility for developing regulations, rules and procedures for striking effective balance between energy development and environmental protection in the hands of individual states and localities" (Rabe, 2014, p. 8370). As a ground level perspective from institutions of higher education makes clear, ongoing struggles over fracking cannot be framed as simplistic debates over the tradeoffs between economic growth and energy development, on the one hand, and health, safety and the environment, on the other. The development of energy resources subsumes a number of concerns that will continue to undergird local, national, and international efforts to shape decisions surrounding hydraulic fracturing. University administrators, policy-makers, and other key decision-makers would best fulfill their commitments to the short- and long-term public good by taking citizens' and residents' concerns and voices seriously – including through embracing commitments to citizen engagement and shared governance.

Notes

1 Despite laws and legal rulings reflecting state preemption of local policy, procedural justice struggles continue to play out in city council meetings and ballot initiative processes.
2 The authors have several ideas about why the student response rate was low. These include that the survey offered no incentives for participation and was administered near the end of the semester, close to finals week.
3 The decline of state funding has been particularly steep in Colorado, dropping some 69.4 percent from 1980 to 2011 (Mortenson, 2012).
4 All data pertaining to Allegheny College in this section have been drawn from the Bousson Advisory Group's website and their Report to Trustees, as well as Allegheny College's website.
5 Eastern OU is located in Belmont County, OH, only 27 miles from Bethany, WV.
6 Approximately 473 students were surveyed.
7 The Report references OU's participation in the American College & University Presidents Climate Commitment (ACUPCC), something Bethany College's President also signed in 2008, three years before that campus leased its mineral rights. OU's Report noted that 303 out of the 383 respondents to the online survey were opposed to the leasing of mineral rights on OU property (p. 3).
8 Although the available documentation is scarce, this does not equate to a lack of concern of employees and students on campus and may be attributable to the chilling effect of corporatization on campus.
9 Notably, the Facebook page's posts lack mention of Bethany faculty and staff.
10 Featured in the book, *The Entrepreneurial President*, President Miller was noted by the Chronicle of Higher Education (2015) to have had salary increases disproportionate to the college budget, although during his tenure the college endowment increased from $41 million to $53 million (Miller, 2014).
11 One faculty member who provided a detailed statement to the authors on the events unfolding in 2011 – which described this culture – retracted it several weeks later, which itself provides possible evidence of continuing fears of a backlash at Bethany.

References

Adgate, J. L., Goldstein, B. D., and McKenzie, L. M. (2014). Potential public health hazards, exposures and health effects from unconventional natural gas development. *Environmental Science & Technology*, 48(15), 8307–8320. doi:10.1021/es404621d.

Barlow, A. (2016, September/October). The annexation of academia, *Academe*, 2.

BBC News. (2015, June 15). Fracking bid should be approved, Lancashire council officers say. *BBC News*. Retrieved from: www.bbc.com/news/uk-england-lancashire-33132569.

Bethany College. (2005–2006). Bethany College trail restoration project completed [Website]. Retrieved from: www.bethanywv.edu/about-bethany/news/2005-06-news/bethany-college-trail-restoration-project-completed/

Bethany College Board of Trustees (2011–16). Trustee Statement: Bethany College and Marcellus Shale: The Board's Perspective [Website]. Retrieved from: www.bethanywv.edu/about-bethany/marcellus-shale-drilling/trustee-statement/

Blum, D. and Ullman, C. (2012). The globalization and corporatization of education: The limits and liminality of the market mantra, *International Journal of Qualitative Studies in Education*, 25(4), 367–373. doi:10.1080/09518398.2012.673031.

Bok, D. (2013). *Higher Education in America*, Princeton, NJ: Princeton University Press.

Bousson Advisory Group. (2013). Report to Trustees: Shale gas development and the Bousson Environmental Research Reserve. Allegheny College. Retrieved from http://sites.allegheny.edu/boussonadvisorygroup/

Bratman, E., Brunette, K., Shelley, D. C., and Nicholson, S. (2016). Justice is the goal: Divestment as climate change resistance. *Journal of Environmental Studies and Science*, 6(4), 677–690. doi:10.1007/s13412-016-0377-6.

Brinkhurst, M., Rose, P., Maurice, G., and Ackerman, J. D. (2011). Achieving campus sustainability: Top-down, bottom-up, or neither? *International Journal of Sustainability in Higher Education* 12(4), 338–354. doi:10.1108/14676371111168269.

Brulé, E. (2015). Voices from the margins: The regulation of student activism in the new corporate university. *Studies in Social Justice*, 9(2), 159–175. Retrieved from: https://brock.scholarsportal.info/journals/SSJ/article/view/1154

Chile, L.M. and Black, X.M. (2015). University-community engagement: Case study of university social responsibility. *Education, Citizenship and Social Justice*, 10(3), 234–253. doi:10.1177/1746197915607278.

Christopher, J. (2012). Governance paradigms of public universities: An international comparative study. *Tertiary Education and Management*, 18(4), 335–351. doi:10.1080/13583883.2012.724705.

Chronicle of Higher Education. (2015, August 21). Chief executives at private colleges who made the most relative to the college budget, 2012. *Almanac*, 61(43), 16. Retrieved from: www.chronicle.com/specialreport/The-Almanac-of-Higher/4

Colborn, T., Kwiatkowski C., Schultz K., and Bachran, M. (2011). Natural gas operations from a public health perspective. *Human and Ecological Risk Assessment*, 17(5), 1039–1056. doi: 10.1080/10807039.2011.605662.

Cotton, A. (2013, March 24). Weld County schools use oil, gas leases to tap into revenue streams. *Denver Post*. Retrieved from: www.denverpost.com/ci_22857558/

Dunegan, A. et al. (2013). Perceptions on deep shale gas exploration at Allegheny College. Advanced Special Topics Course, Political Ecology, April 25. Retrieved from: http://sites.allegheny.edu/boussonadvisorygroup/student-research-action/

Enockson, P. S. (2014). State legislation: Will state authority or local preference regulate Colorado's fracking? *Natural Gas & Electricity*, 30(9), 12–17. doi:10.1002/gas.21753.

Fenrich, H. (2012, November 29). Public perception: The most important issue of all. Retrieved from: http://sitesmedia.s3.amazonaws.com/boussonadvisorygroup/files/2013/07/FS-ES-201-Fenrich.pdf

Finkel, M. L. and Hays, J. (2013). The implications of unconventional drilling for natural gas: A global public health concern. *Public Health*, 127(10), 889–93. doi:10.1016/j.puhe.2013.07.005.

Finley, B. (2016, May 2). Colorado Supreme Court rules state law trumps local bans on fracking. *The Denver Post*, Retrieved from www.denverpost.com/2016/05/02/colorado-supreme-court-rules-state-law-trumps-local-bans-on-fracking/

Fisher J. L. and Koch, J. V. (2004). *The Entrepreneurial College President*. Westport, CT: Praeger.

Fry, M., Briggle, A. and Kincaid, J. (2015). Fracking and environmental (in)justice in a Texas city. *Ecological Economics*, 117, 97–107. doi:10.1016/j.ecolecon.2015.06.012.

Fry, M., Hoeinghaus, D. J., Ponette-Gonzalez, A. G., Thompson, R., and LaPoint, T. W. (2012). Fracking vs faucets: Balancing energy needs and water sustainability at urban frontiers. *Environmental Science & Technology*, 46(14), 7444–7445. doi:10.1021/es302472y.

Goho, S.A. (2012). Municipalities and hydraulic fracturing: trends in state preemption. *Planning & Environmental Law*, 64(7), 3–9. doi:10.1080/15480755.2012.699757.

Grady-Benson, J. and Sarathy, B. (2015). Fossil fuel divestment in US higher education: Student-led organizing for climate justice. *Local Environment: The International Journal of Justice and Sustainability*, 21(6), 661–681. doi:10.1080/13549839.2015.1009825.

Guardian (2016, June 24). German government agrees to ban fracking after years of dispute ... Retrieved from: www.theguardian.com/environment/2016/jun/24/germany-bans-fracking-after-years-of-dispute

Healy, N. and Debski, J. (2017). Fossil fuel divestment: Implications for the future of sustainability discourse and action within higher education. *Local Environment: The International Journal of Justice and Sustainability*, 22(6). doi:10.1080/13549839.2016.125 6382.

Highby, W. et al. (2013). Charge of the hydrofracturing task force and description of the process. Unpublished document. University of Northern Colorado.

Hill, D. (2015, February 23). Is Bolivia going to frack 'Mother Earth'? *Guardian*. Retrieved from: www.theguardian.com/environment/andes-to-the-amazon/2015/feb/23/bolivia-frack-mother-earth.

Jolly, D. (2013, December 10). France upholds ban on hydraulic fracturing. *New York Times*. Retrieved from: www.nytimes.com/2013/10/12/business/international/france-upholds-fracking-ban.html?_r=0.

Junkins, C. (2011, July 1). College dives into drilling pool: Bethany inks deal with Chesapeake Energy. *The Intelligencer/Wheeling News-Register*. Retrieved from: www.the intelligencer.net/page/content.detail/id/556690/College-Dives-Into-Drilling-Pool.html

Lave, R. and Lutz, B. (2014). Hydraulic fracturing: A critical physical geography review. *Geography Compass*, 8(10), 739–754. doi:10.1111/gec3.12162.

Malin, S. A. and DeMaster. K. T. (2016). A devil's bargain: Rural environmental injustices and hydraulic fracturing on Pennsylvania's farms. *Journal of Rural Studies*, 47(A), 278–290. doi:10.1016/j.jrurstud.2015.12.015.

Marchese, A. J., Vaughn, T. L., Zimmerle, D. J. et al. (2015). Methane emissions from United States natural gas gathering and processing. *Environmental Science & Technology*, 49(17), 10718–10727. doi:10.1021/acs.est.5b02275.

Mares, D. R. (2012). The new energy landscape: Shale gas in Latin America. Washington, DC: Inter-American Development Bank, Infrastructure and Environment Department, Discussion Paper No. IDB-DP 253. Retrieved from: http://idbdocs.iadb.org/wsdocs/getdocument.aspx?docnum=37660771

Miller, S. (2014, August 19). State of the College, President Scott D. Miller [Bethany College]. Retrieved from: www.bethanywv.edu/files/1914/2746/8422/StateoftheCollege 2014.pdf

Mitchell, R.E. (2006). Green politics or environmental blues? Analyzing ecological democracy. *Public Understanding of Science*, 15(4), 459–480. Retrieved from: http://pus.sagepub.com/content/15/4/459

Morrissey, J. (2015). Regimes of performance: Practices of the normalized self in the neoliberal university. *British Journal of Sociology of Education*, 36(4), 614–634. doi:10.1080/01425692.2013.838515.

Mortenson, T. G. (2012, Winter). State funding: A race to the bottom. *The Presidency: The American Council on Education's Magazine for Higher Education Leaders*. Retrieved from: www.acenet.edu/the-presidency/columns-and-features/Pages/state-funding-a-race-to-the-bottom.aspx

Navarro, M. (2012). State considering studying health impacts of fracking, *New York Times*, Retrieved from: http://green.blogs.nytimes.com/2012/08/31/state-considering-studying-health-impacts-of-fracking/

Negro, S. (2012). Fracking wars: Federal, state and local conflicts over the regulation of natural gas activities. *Zoning and Planning Law Report*, 35(2), 1–14. Retrieved from: http://legalsolutions.thomsonreuters.com/law-products/Newsletter/Zoning-and-Planning-Law-Report/p/100027537.

Neslen, A. (2015, June 10). Majority of MEPs support fracking moratorium in symbolic vote. *Guardian*. Retrieved from: www.theguardian.com/environment/2015/jun/10/majority-of-meps-support-fracking-moratorium-in-symbolic-vote

No Bethany Fracking (2011). Facebook page. Retrieved from: www.facebook.com/NoBethanyFracking/

OU Ad hoc Mineral Rights Committee (2012). Report to the Board of Trustees: Potential Leasing of Oil and Gas Rights on Ohio University Owned Lands Viewed through a Sustainability Lens. Retrieved from: www.acfan.org/wp-content/uploads/2011/11/Mineral-Rights-Committee.pdf

OU Board of Trustees (2011, November 18). Minutes, 11–18–2011. Retrieved from: www.ohio.edu/trustees/agendas/index.cfm

OU Voinovich School of Leadership and Public Affairs. (2016). Baseline environmental data collection at Ohio University Eastern Campus and Dysart Woods in Belmont County, Ohio. Retrieved from: www.ohio.edu/ce3/resources/upload/Baseline-Data-Study-OU-Eastern-Campus-Dysart-Woods-Final-Report-May-2016.pdf

Pasque, P. A. and Carducci, R. (2015). Critical advocacy perspectives on organization in higher education. In M. B. Paulsen (ed.) *Higher Education: Handbook of Theory and Research* (pp. 275–333). Dordrecht: Springer International.

Phillips, J. (2012, April 22). Trustee board wonders: Will law allow OU to say no to fracking? *The Athens News*. Retrieved from: www.athensnews.com

Physicians for Social Responsibility and Concerned Health Professionals of New York. (2015, October 14). Physicians for Social Responsibility, health and science experts call on Obama, Surgeon General & Governors of Maryland, Pennsylvania to stop fracking, citing national health impacts. Press release. Retrieved from: http://concernedhealthny.org/category/press-releases/

Rabe, B. G. (2014). Shale play politics: The intergovernmental odyssey of American shale governance. *Environmental Science and Technology*, 48, 8369–8375. doi:10.1021/es4051132.

Schackner, B. (2011, November 6). Drilling on campus: Marcellus shale boom puts colleges at crossroads, *Pittsburgh Post Gazette*. Retrieved from: www.post-gazette.com/news/environment/2011/11/06/Drilling-on-Campus-Marcellus-Shale-boom-puts-colleges-at-crossroads/stories/201111060278

Schirrmeister, M. (2014). Controversial futures – discourse analysis on utilizing the "fracking" technology in Germany. *European Journal of Futures Research*, 2(38), 1–9. doi:10.1007/s40309-014-0038-5.

Schneider, J. (2015). Frackademia, divestment, and the limits of academic freedom. Paper presented at the 2015 Conference on Communication and Environment in Boulder: Bridging Divides: Spaces of Scholarship and Practice in Environmental Communication. International Environmental Communication Association, Boulder, Colorado, June 11–14.

Schoorman, D. (2013) Resisting the unholy alliance between a university and a prison company: Implications for faculty governance in a neoliberal context. *Cultural Studies, Critical Methodologies*, 13(6), 510–519. doi:10.1177/1532708613503777.

Schoorman, D. and Acker-Hocevar, M. (2010). Viewing faculty governance within a social justice framework: Struggles and possibilities for democratic decision-making in

higher education. *Equity and Excellence in Education*, 43(3), 310–325. doi:10.1080/106
65684.2010.494493.

Shortell, P. (2015). Latin America weighs risks and rewards of shale revolution. *World Politics Review*. Retrieved from: www.worldpoliticsreview.com/articles/15802/latin-america-weighs-risk-and-rewards-of-shale-revolution

Silvey, R. (2002). Sweatshops and the corporatization of the university. *Gender, Place & Culture*, 9(2), 201–207. doi:10.1080/09663960220139725.

Smith, M. F. and Ferguson, D. P. (2013). 'Fracking democracy': Issue management and locus of policy decision-making in the Marcellus Shale gas drilling debate. *Public Relations Review*, 39(4), 377–386. doi:10.1016/j.pubrev.2013.08.003.

Staddon, P. L. and Depledge, M. H. (2015). Fracking cannot be reconciled with climate change mitigation policies. *Environmental Science & Technology*, 49(14), 8269–8270. doi: 10.1021/acs.est.5b02441.

Toan, K. (2015). Not under my backyard: The battle between Colorado and local governments over hydraulic fracturing. *Colorado Natural Resources, Energy and Environmental Law Review*, 26(1). www.colorado.edu/law/research/journals/colorado-natural-resources-energy-environmental-law-review

Turner, A. J., Jacob, D. J., Benmergui, J. et al. (2016). A large increase in U.S. methane emissions over the past decade inferred from satellite data and surface observations. *Geophysical Research Letters*, 43, 2218–2224. doi:10.1002/2016GL067987.

UNCO BOT (University of Northern Colorado, Board of Trustees), 2011. *Minutes* [online]. Retrieved from https://digarch.unco.edu/islandora/object/cogru%3A3413

USDOE (n.d.). Shale research and development [online]. Retrieved from: http://energy.gov/fe/science-innovation/oil-gas-research/shale-gas-rd.

USEIA. (2015). Natural gas: shale gas production [online]. Retrieved from: www.eia.gov/dnav/ng/ng_prod_shalegas_s1_a.htm

USEIA. (2016). Shale gas in the United States [online]. Retrieved from: www.eia.gov/energy_in_brief/article/shale_in_the_united_states.cfm

Werner, A.K., Vink, S., Watt, K., and Jagals, P. (2015). Environmental health impacts of unconventional natural gas development: A review of the current strength of evidence, *Science of the Total Environment*, 505, 1127–1141. doi:10.1016/j.scitotenv.2014.10.084.

Wines, M. (2016, May 2). Colorado court strikes down local bans on fracking. *New York Times*. Retrieved from: www.nytimes.com/2016/05/03/us/colorado-court-strikes-down-local-bans-on-fracking.html?_r=0

Woods, W. (2013). *The ethics of knowing* [video online]. Retrieved from https://vimeo.com/54580189

12 Devolved governance and alternative dispute resolution programs

An example from the Bakken

Kristin K. Smith and Julia H. Haggerty

Introduction

Shale governance strategies in the United States have been works in progress over the past decade, with policy development often occurring in response to emergent impacts and local concerns. As most shale development in the United States involves non-federal land where the federal government has opted to provide few policy guidelines, management of surface impacts focuses on state, local, and non-governmental domains. This devolution in policy scale creates an opportunity to reflect on the costs and benefits of localized solutions to shale governance – a trend also apparent in non-US contexts such as Australia and Canada. Devolved strategies have the potential to accommodate local context, something of merit, given the wide variety in geographies of shale development in the United States. However, given the power imbalance between local stake-holders and the oil and gas industry, the risk of regulatory capture is a real concern in devolved governance. In addition, governance can create substantial uncompensated burdens for local stakeholders, raising additional questions about equity. This chapter takes up the tradeoffs involved in devolved shale governance through a case study of a landowner association in north-western North Dakota, the location of the Bakken shale oil play, and its associated oil boom from the mid-2000s through 2014.

The character of the Bakken boom as an environmental, social, and political phenomenon is heavily shaped by the rural nature of western North Dakota and eastern Montana, where farmers and tribal nations are the major landowners and high value small grains production and extensive livestock ranching are the dominant land uses. As a result of this agriculture-energy overlay, rural land-owners and farmers are first-order stakeholders in the impacts of a decade of infrastructure expansion involving construction of thousands of new wells, new roads and/or road upgrades, well pads, storage fields, processing facilities, trans-portation hubs, and miles upon miles of gathering lines and transmission pipe-lines. Formed in 2009, the Northwest Landowners Association (NWLA) in North Dakota has emerged as an influential force in the development of govern-ance in response to the surface impacts of shale development, especially though not exclusively in the arena of pipeline construction impacts.

Through detailed profiles of three key members in the Northwest Landowners Association (NWLA) and their work on a specific program to address pipeline impacts, this chapter explores the strategies developed by NWLA and their implications both for leaders of the organization and for the landowners they represent. This approach allows for a discussion of how devolved approaches to surface impact management present opportunities and challenges for landowners that host energy development in rural areas. Specifically, the analysis addresses the tensions in maintaining an accommodating approach toward industry while attempting to advocate effectively for landowner interests, as well as familiar questions about the costs of devolved governance strategies, with respect to their efficacy and high dependence on individuals.

Shale governance and alternative dispute resolution programs

Shale governance

The unique property rights regime and the political and economic context in the United States create a complicated and challenging scenario from the perspective of regulating unconventional fossil fuel (UFF) as a form of industrial development (Jacquet & Kay, 2014; Small et al., 2014; Whitton, Brasier, Charnley-Parry, & Cotton, 2017). Due to a political economy that favors privatization, deregulation, and delegation (Harvey, 2005; Levi-Faur, 2005), the majority of UFF development activities in the US, such as land use planning, waste management, drilling, and so forth, occurs at the state level, where the scope and nature of regulation can vary wildly from one place to the next (Warner & Shapiro, 2013; Zirogiannis, Alcorn, Rupp, Carley, & Graham, 2016). What results is a "halting patchwork of rules" frustrating industry on the one hand (Konschnik & Boling, 2014, p. 1), and a dispersed, uncoordinated assemblage of regulations, regulators, and responsible parties, frustrating landowners and communities on the other (Haggerty & Haggerty, 2015).

Within this challenging regulatory system, landowners often have limited opportunities to impact governance systems (Whitton et al., 2017). (We use the notion of governance as governing through multi-stakeholder/multi-sectoral collaboration and non-statutory strategies (Bridge & Perreault, 2009)). In response, landowners in various energy development contexts have created associations, coalitions, and taskforces that seek to empower landowners through a variety of means. Landowner groups take on various roles, ranging from sharing resources and information to forming bargaining units to negotiate collective leases (Balliet, 2008). Drawing comparisons to forest and agriculture cooperatives, Jacquet and Stedman (2011) argue that landowner associations are often formed to maximize members' individual benefits but can have broader positive effects on the community, such as helping to protect watersheds or fragile ecosystems.

The Northwest Landowners Association (NWLA) is an example of one such landowner association, representing an important exception to a general trend of limited landowner organizing in the Bakken. This is in contrast to other regions, such as the Marcellus Shale Play and the Powder River Basin, where landowner collective advocacy and management are more evident (Brasier et al., 2011; Jacquet & Stedman, 2011; Klassen & Feldpausch-Parker, 2011). NWLA formed in 2009 in response to a proposed wind development, but the organization has continually adapted to address the needs of landowners impacted by the Bakken shale boom. As of 2016, NWLA had 477 due-paying members. A key transition in the group's evolution is its increasing focus on negotiating and lobbying for state policy changes. It gained 501(c)(6) status in 2012, a legal mechanism that allows NGOs in the United States to maintain tax-free status while actively lobbying to influence political processes. Since then, NWLA has effectively advocated for policy changes regulating oil and gas development at the state level. This is perhaps due to NWLA's conscious strategy of collaborating with – rather than antagonizing – the shale industry.

The Pipeline Restoration and Reclamation Oversight Program, known as the pipeline ombudsman program, is an outcome of this focus and strategy. As pipeline construction scaled up alongside UFF production during the Bakken boom, farmers and ranchers increasingly experienced problems with reclamation during and after pipeline construction phases. This led to a perceived wariness among landowners to continue signing easements – e.g., a risk to the industry's social license to operate (SLO). To address this emerging conflict, NWLA partnered with the North Dakota Department of Agriculture and the energy industry to propose the Pipeline Restoration and Reclamation Oversight Pilot Program. NWLA's lobbying resulted in the program being funded in 2015.

The pipeline ombudsman program sits within the state's Department of Agriculture. Landowners with pipeline reclamation issues on their land can request assistance from the Department, who will then assign the landowner a local ombudsman. The ombudsman meets with the landowner and the pipeline company to help facilitate a solution to the problem and avoid litigation. The goal is to develop a collaborative plan, timeline, and monitoring agreement to address the issue(s). From April 2015 to November 2016, the Department received 55 official complaints. Common issues included unsatisfactory reclamation efforts (rough or uneven ground and/or incomplete re-vegetation), loss of topsoil, and introduction of weeds (Junkert & Goehring 2016). Of the 55 complaints filed, all of them but one resulted in successful negotiations, with the negotiation process lasting anywhere from several days to over two years.

Global approaches to alternative dispute resolution

North Dakota's pipeline ombudsman program is an example of a trend emerging globally: alternative dispute resolution programs that seek to foster voluntary solutions to problems between the energy industry and landowners. Both Alberta and Queensland have alternative dispute resolution programs for landowner-energy conflicts. The Alberta Energy Regulator's (AER) Alternative Dispute Regulation was developed, according to its manual, "in response to the desire of AER stakeholders to be more directly involved and have more control in resolving disputes" (Alberta Energy Regulator, 2013, p. 1). Between 2012 and 2016, the AER's successful resolution rate for disputes ranged from 80–95 percent (Alberta Energy Regulator, 2016). Similarly, in Queensland, in response to the coal seam gas (CSG) boom, a bill was introduced in 2017 to form a land access ombudsman. The program was proposed after a review of the Gasfields Commission found that "landholders expressed an overwhelming sense of powerlessness" (Scott, 2016, p. 6). Notably, the Australian Petroleum Production & Exploration Association (APPEA), Australia's top oil and gas industry group, is in favor of the legislation, citing the need for industry and landholders to have a "balanced, timely, transparent, and accessible process to resolve [disputes]" (Murphy, 2017, para. 6).

The emergence of ombudsman programs and alternative dispute resolution mechanisms emphasizes the role of devolved, non-regulatory approaches to addressing surface impacts from shale development. Alternative dispute resolution strategies are classic examples of governance solutions that hinge on a range of stakeholders operating through non-regulatory mechanisms. The success of these approaches may be influential in the maintenance of SLO by industry. Building trust and having high-quality, meaningful engagement with stakeholders are key determinants of SLO (Moffat & Zhang, 2014) – and trust and meaningful engagement are critical to both the development of and implementation of governance solutions, such as these alternative dispute mechanisms. This chapter explores why key NWLA members decided to lobby for the ombudsman program and some of the tensions that arise when landowners use industry's desire and need for SLO to create governance solutions.

Methods

This chapter focuses on the history and evolution of NWLA from the perspective of key members who contributed to the organization's lobbying for the state's pipeline ombudsman program. NWLA was selected as a case study based on consultation with local stakeholders who identified the organization as having a large impact on state policy. To develop the organization's history, we employed a mixed method approach. First, we conducted document analysis using the organization's materials as well as regional news media coverage, which helped inform our interview script. We next conducted in-depth interviews with five key NWLA members. Four of the interviews were conducted in person during May 2016 and the final interview was performed the following month over the phone. Interviews were semi-structured, meaning they followed a script but the interviewer was also given the "freedom to digress" to explore emerging themes (Berg & Lune, 2004, p. 61). Three of the interviewees were farmers or ranchers with energy development on property that they owned, one was a rancher dealing with energy development on leased land, and the final interviewee was instrumental in the organization's operations but was neither a farmer nor a rancher. The organization's leadership identified our interviewees.

We do not claim that the material developed here represents the full suite of NWLA members' experiences but rather a range of opportunities and challenges in mitigating impacts from shale development through landowner organizing from the perspective of the organization's core members.

Interviews were in-depth with the shortest taking 51 minutes and the longest lasting two hours and 52 minutes; the average interview lasted one hour and 40 minutes. After collecting the data, interviews were transcribed verbatim using a professional transcriber. Transcriptions were coded by hand. Through repeated readings of the transcripts, we highlighted and categorized emerging themes, collapsing and expanding codes as needed (Lindlof, 1995). Three of the interviews were crafted into in-depth profiles due to their close involvement with both NWLA and pipeline issues. To provide anonymity, their names have been changed. We used the narratives presented here to build toward an inventory of the diverse ways that landowner coalitions benefit and challenge the needs of individual landowners in energy development contexts.

Profiles of members of the Northwest Landowners Association

Profile 1. Ellen: "I wasn't looking to create chaos in my own personal life, but I just felt like somebody needed to step up ..."

Ellen grew up in north-western North Dakota and returned to the area with her husband and children during the beginning of the shale boom. Instead of finding the quiet, pastoral life she envisioned for her family, she moved to a community undergoing an immense amount of development. Or, as she explained, "I don't even call it development because it wasn't managed at all, just this rapid growth." She was particularly frustrated with how the benefits and costs of shale development were distributed unequally throughout the state and noted that the revenue her county received did not cover the full costs of impacts. She questioned the large tax breaks energy companies received, given her perception of the high costs on local landowners from energy-related impacts: "There's just these trickle-down impacts [so] that the cost of doing business gets pushed on to the agriculture community, who does pay property taxes [sic]." In addition to these broader frustrations, Ellen's neighbors started complaining about interactions with landmen and sharing concerns about leases.

Ellen represents the perspective of landowners dealing with energy development but not receiving the royalties from production – the mineral rights below her ranch had long ago been sold to private parties outside her family. When a landman approached Ellen about a surface use agreement, she refused to sign and felt that she lacked power in negotiations as a non-mineral rights owner. Afterward, Ellen helped to start a local landowner association, which was later subsumed within NWLA. She was also elected to public office. When questioned about why she didn't sign the agreement and why she started to organize landowners, she stated:

I wasn't looking for volunteer work. I wasn't looking to create chaos in my own personal life, but I just felt like somebody needed to step up and start talking about this and just not get distracted by the checks and the promises, and so I did that.

This story simultaneously explains why Ellen became a member of NWLA while also emphasizing the toll her involvement in managing energy impacts has taken on her personal life; the "chaos" that she has experienced.

Before NWLA existed, landowners in Ellen's community had limited options for voicing their concerns related to UFF development. While many landowners were members of larger state associations like the North Dakota Farmers Union or the North Dakota Farm Bureau, these organizations did not directly address energy issues. According to Ellen, NWLA was the first organization in her region that "focus[ed] on surface rights as they intersect[ed] with energy development, the mineral aspect, and that our surface and our minerals are by a majority segregated." When asked about the organization's role with regards to policy, she described how the mission expanded to include regulatory issues:

The mission really is to educate, and through that educational process, I think people are starting to realize that there are some very deficient areas in our state law or in our administrative rules in the different departments that oversee development.

Ellen believes that NWLA became more actively involved with lobbying for governance solutions due to members' perceptions that state regulations were inadequate and/or did not address landowner concerns.

To help mitigate negative impacts from pipeline development, Ellen advocated for a local pipeline ombudsman program. As she explains, "People were just really exhausted [due to problems with pipeline operations] and didn't want to continue to sign easements and allow right of ways." In response, the conservation district for Ellen's region proposed an ombudsman program. At the same time, an alternative plan had evolved to develop a statewide ombudsman program. "There were these two concepts, go very local or go from state down." NWLA, as an organization, supported the statewide plan. Ellen disagreed, convinced that only the local conservation district had the requisite experience with the highly erodible soils and sparse population that posed unique challenges to reclamation for her and her neighbors. Ultimately the statewide plan won the funding, eclipsing the proposal for a conservation district-scale program.

The tensions about the appropriate scale of the ombudsman program highlight several complexities in landowner organizing for policy change and governance solutions. While Ellen felt the conservation district would result in the most effective alternative dispute resolution program, NWLA leadership worried that creating multiple, local pipeline ombudsman programs could result in inconsistent services for their members. Ellen remains involved in NWLA, but regrets the choice to pursue a state rather than a local ombudsman program.

From her perspective, NWLA's statewide approach not only created a tradeoff between administrative efficiency and innovation in reclamation strategies, but also reduced local involvement in the program. Ellen attributed the low program participation among her neighbors to general mistrust of state agencies. Given the consequences of poor enrollment in the program, this is a key observation about the importance of scale in local shale governance strategies. According to Ellen, the statewide approach and its tradeoffs have resulted in unaddressed pipeline impacts in her community.

Profile 2. Jim: "We're not there representing anyone else. We're representing ourselves ... we're living it."

Jim has lived in north-western North Dakota his entire life. Before starting his farm, he worked in the energy sector during the 1970s oil boom to help save money to buy his farmland. While Jim is in favor of UFF extraction, he experienced negative impacts from recent development on his land and, like Ellen, felt mistreated by landmen. After describing how the increases in heavy truck traffic damaged roads near his farm, he said, "We're mad. We're fighting it. We just don't like it, and we're crabby." In another story, Jim voiced his frustration about the energy companies' failure to take local knowledge seriously. When an oil company proposed a well on a neighbor's nearby farm, his friend informed the contractors that the location was frequently flooded in the spring during snow melts. The company continued construction until the pad was flooded in the spring, and they had to move it. Jim noted, "They had no idea what's there ... so when you see things like that you think, 'Oh my God.' It bugs you, but that's the way things are."

Given these frustrations, the Northwest Landowners Association provided Jim an outlet to make changes to a system that he considers flawed:

> We're at the point where we adapted and got used to it, and it ain't going away. I can fight it and be mad forever, or I can try to make it work better. It was sometime in there ... [that] I got involved with Northwest Landowners.

Jim wants to accommodate industry but in ways that work for farmers and ranchers. To do so, he became heavily involved with NWLA's lobbying efforts. In 2015, Jim estimated that he spent over 35 days in the state capitol lobbying during the 64th legislative session. The pipeline ombudsman program was a major policy win for NWLA during this session. When asked how NWLA decided to focus on the ombudsman program, Jim answered, "Whatever our members come with, that's what we're going to fight for. And reclamation is the big one, reclamation of pipelines." As a lobbyist for NWLA, Jim understands his role as being a collective voice for the members.

To help pass the ombudsman bill, Jim described how NWLA strategically cultivated relationships with industry over many years, which, according to Jim, marked a shift from earlier approaches:

So many people are anti-everything else. It's my way or no way.... And, that's the way we started. Northwest Landowners started with that view of you guys are the bad guys. Oil is the bad guy; we're the good guys. We care about the land. That got us nowhere.

Jim described NWLA's current strategy as being more solution-oriented and collaborative. To illustrate this shift in tactics, he compared NWLA to another organization working on shale development issues, the Dakota Resource Council (DRC). In describing the DRC's approach to advocacy, he explained, "[T]hey have a bad reputation of being very negative, very controversial." This strategy, he explained, hinders their ability to create change. "[T]hey do not have a good name. In fact, they're discounted. We've had industry and state people tell us that they're not a factor anymore." In contrast, NWLA is effective because they position themselves as part of a collaborative solution between industry and landowners. Jim reiterated this throughout the interview by explaining that he could call industry representatives or government officials when he needed advice or wanted to report a problem.

After the ombudsman bill passed, Jim felt that NWLA was increasingly seen as important stakeholders on policy issues: "I don't want to sound like I'm bragging, but things just went really good for us last session. We get invited to the table a lot ... so they're asking us what we think!" Later in the interview, however, he described the NWLA as being constrained by the UFF industry's power. When he reflected back on his first session lobbying, he suggested that they only succeeded with their early proposals because the industry representatives allowed them to: "[the UFF industry] threw us some bones so we could say, 'Yeah, we got something.'" Throughout the interview, Jim was proud of NWLA's achievements but also aware of the power dynamics that shaped what the organization was able or unable to accomplish.

Jim's accounts of his involvement with the organization point to the power of NWLA to be both empowering and exhausting for members. Jim is proud of his volunteer efforts to help create the alternative dispute resolution program, as well as his efforts to educate landowners and industry representatives about pipeline reclamation and landowner associations. He also enjoyed having direct access to industry representatives. Despite these benefits, he is at times skeptical of NWLA's impact and often made off-hand comments about getting tired of the process: "That's why I go to [the state capitol], because I have to. Try to get other people, but there's no one else..." During a follow-up interview a year after first talking with Jim, he was no longer involved with NWLA. Jim's empowerment through NWLA and subsequent fatigue with the process speak to larger opportunities and challenges of participating in a landowner association to manage energy impacts.

Profile 3. Garret: "Now these get documented to the state, which is very, very important."

The final profile is of Garret, a farmer who heard about NWLA from Jim. Garret has over 80 miles of pipeline beneath his fields. When we talked with him, he was dealing with three pipeline reclamation problems, and he noted several other minor but unresolved issues. According to Garret, "We could literally hire someone on a full-time basis just to work with oil field issues, a 40-hour week, every week, every month all summer long, most of the winter." Garret attributed his negative experiences with pipelines to his initial lack of knowledge about leasing negotiations and contracts. When asked why he decided to get involved with NWLA, he stated:

> All these pipeline issues have to do with signing leases and how your lease is structured. Here's how the oil field works. They move into a new area. We're all brand new at this, and we think, "100% for it!" I just was thrilled about it because here's our pathway to energy independence. But they move into an area where nobody knows anything and they just run over the top of you. And they did to the point where something has to be done. The only way to stop that is to be affiliated with a group.

In another example, an energy company proposed building a storage and transportation facility next to his farm but failed to identify the project's full range of risks. After it was completed, Garret felt the project did not meet his expectations:

> So now we have this pipeline to take trucks off the road, but guess where the trucks are going to come? Right here! So what's the use? They don't lie. They just don't tell you, and you don't know the right questions to ask. That's why it's important to get a hold of landowner groups that have already been there.

Both statements reveal a belief that landowner organizations are important not only to mitigate impacts, but also in addressing systemic knowledge and power imbalances between individual landowners and energy companies.

Garret cited the state's regulations as reinforcing these imbalances instead of helping to protect landowners, an example of regulatory capture. He explained, "[the] oil field does whatever they want to do. The state of North Dakota has given them tacit approval to do whatever they need to do to get the money because they want money." He attributed this lack of regulation to disconnections between statewide legislatures and the localized impacts experienced in north-western North Dakota. Since energy tax revenues are redistributed statewide, legislators from other regions benefit from new sources of revenue and thus have little incentive to propose regulations to manage growth. Garret argued, "What do you think [the state legislators] think? They think this is a gold mine. They don't want to slow it down." Garret particularly felt disempowered when he went to the statehouse to testify about energy development impacts: "We got told, without saying so, we got told in no uncertain terms that we didn't matter." Again, Garret's comments speak to a form of regulatory capture in which state regulations fail to address entrenched power and knowledge imbalances between industry and the public.

Given the lack of regulation and landowners' limited knowledge about the legal and regulatory system, Garret encouraged landowners to join a group like NWLA to help manage impacts. He noted, "Having a group like [NWLA] that's in touch with other groups gets you up to speed faster." In addition to knowledge sharing, Garret appreciated NWLA's ability to monitor policy proposals and negotiations. Even in years without legislative sessions, he noted, "[NWLA members] are monitoring everything that goes on." While Garret often commented that he would like state legislatures and industry to be more proactive, he relied on NWLA to make his own voice heard and to act as a watchdog at the statehouse by monitoring policies.

Notably, Garret has directly benefited from the statewide pipeline ombudsman program. When Garret's fields developed large holes due to inadequate reclamation and none of the pipeline companies would claim responsibility, he used the ombudsman program to negotiate solutions. Before the ombudsman program, landowners would have had limited options, besides litigation, about how to resolve this problem. With the alternative dispute resolution program, explained Garret, "I can take care of ten pipelines in one morning instead of spending ten days to take care of one pipeline." In addition to creating a better communication system, the program has institutionalized a way for landowners to file complaints. According to Garret:

> Now these get documented to the state, which is very, very important. All these other issues that we deal with here are just between you and the company, and as long as nobody says anything out loud, they can pretty much do what they want. But these get recorded, and that is the effectiveness of it.

While Garret is currently a strong advocate of NWLA, he initially refused to become a member during the organization's early years due to its more oppositional strategy. As mentioned in the previous profile, the organization originally approached industry more antagonistically. Garrett only joined NWLA when the leadership changed, and the organization switched to its current, more collaborative approach. As a landowner who is generally in favor of energy development, he did not want to be seen as oppositional and also acknowledged that the energy industry is not monolithic, stating, "There's some very good companies out there." His more nuanced views of the industry reinforce his openness to working with industry and not against it. However, he has also experienced many challenges on his farm due to impacts from energy development. His involvement with NWLA and his views about energy development suggest tension between a willingness to accommodate industry and a desire to protect landowners' rights.

The benefits and risks of NWLA

The NWLA has taken on a substantial set of challenges: a commitment to pursuing policy solutions to undesired impacts of energy development without antagonizing industry, and doing so on behalf of landowner members with attitudes toward formal government that could be described as ambivalent at best. Aligning with the NWLA approach appears to offer both benefits and risks for members, including the leadership. While our interviewees acknowledged the influence of NWLA in developing mitigation strategies for unwanted impacts, these solutions were not without their costs. In this final section, we explore the tradeoffs in landowner organizing and governance solutions involving industry partnerships.

A key benefit for members is that NWLA helps to equalize power dynamics between individual landowners and energy companies. Each of the members profiled here joined NWLA due to perceived power and knowledge imbalances between the individual landowner and the energy companies. The system, they argued, is built to keep individuals separate from each other. As Ellen noted, "[I]t's really a business philosophy," suggesting that industry is strategically separating community members to maximize their own benefits. The landowners felt the imbalance of knowledge is why an organization like NWLA is important. Each landowner agreed that his or her voice was amplified by NWLA, which was critical, given the individualized system in which contracts, leases, and easements are negotiated. This finding aligns with findings from the Queensland Gasfields Commission's review, which also found that landowners felt powerless in relation to coal seam gas development.

NWLA has worked strategically to present itself as a collaborator with industry and state government agencies. Jim emphasized the need to focus on solutions and not just complaints, suggesting that NWLA's collaborative strategy was superior to a more antagonistic approach. NWLA has focused its efforts on building its relationship with industry and government agencies. Though this process took years to achieve, NWLA members now have access to top Petroleum Council representatives, the Secretary of Agriculture, and other important political figures. The pipeline ombudsman program with its collaborative approach to solving issues between industry and landowners, is a clear outcome of this strategy.

While this strategy helps landowners, industry, and policy-makers to work together, it also exposes NWLA to the risk of being criticized as being too close to industry. An ongoing point of tension is whether or not they are enabling industry interests at the expense of landowners' rights. If, for example, they are becoming "token mascots" of the shale industry's social license to operate. NWLA leaders must constantly balance their partnerships with industry with their ability to uphold landowner rights in order to maintain the relevance of the organization to their members.

Finally, active leadership in the development of governance solutions created a major time burden on a small group of NWLA volunteers. To create the ombudsman program, NWLA members spent countless hours in meetings with state representatives and regulators, in addition to attending hearings and testifying. Developing empathy and trust from industry and legislators took many years to achieve. The key members profiled in this chapter believe that the association's increasing success is largely due to the passion of their current leader and the enormous amount of time invested by several key volunteers. These individuals worked hard to make sure that organization was represented and present at all the "right" meetings. This model of governance has taken a personal toll on members, as shown by Jim's fatigue. In the absence of federal energy policy, NWLA members had to invest large quantities of time to organize, plan, inform, and lobby to create a better regulatory framework for North Dakota. The long-term sustainability of this model, however, is questionable.

NWLA's experiences lobbying for the alternative dispute resolution program suggest important lessons for residents in other shale plays looking to mitigate undesired impacts or create alternative dispute resolution mechanisms. Landowners may be able to achieve positive governance solutions by strategically partnering with industry. As in North Dakota, Alberta, and Queensland, industry may see these governance solutions as a way to increase and/or maintain their social license to operate. However, landowners in other shale plays should be aware of the many hours and even years that this strategy may demand.

Conclusion

The devolved governance system in the United States has resulted in a regulatory vacuum that promotes ad hoc responses to managing socioeconomic and environmental impacts from UFF development. In North Dakota, NWLA members began organizing and lobbying for policy and regulatory change at the state level to address undesired impacts, particularly related to pipeline reclamation. Since 2009, the organization has opened up new pathways for landowners to access industry decision-makers and policy-makers, including the pipeline ombudsman program. The NWLA members profiled in this chapter shared personal stories about feeling disempowered and/or taken advantage of by the shale industry. They relied on NWLA to amplify their voices and to help them better manage impacts from energy infrastructure.

NWLA raises questions about how civic organizations can work collaboratively with industry and government to create managed shale development. The emergence of alternative dispute resolution programs in North Dakota, Alberta, and Queensland suggests a general trend toward more formalized structures for collaboration between government agencies, industry, and landowners. While alternative resolution mechanisms are reactive as opposed to proactive, they can help address power inequities that result from devolvement and deregulation. The experiences of the NWLA members profiled in this chapter point to the efficacy of partnering with industry but also vulnerabilities associated with this model, such as how highly dependent NWLA is on a small number of individuals. For landowners in other shales plays, NWLA offers critical lessons about how devolved governance can simultaneously empower landowners while also creating uncompensated burdens.

References

Alberta Energy Regulator. (2013). *Alternative Dispute Resolution Program and Guidelines for Energy Industry Disputes. Manual* 004. Retrieved from http://aer.ca/documents/manuals/Manual004.pdf

Alberta Energy Regulator. (2016). 2015/2016 Annual Report. Retrieved from www.aer.ca/documents/reports/AER2015-16AnnualReport.pdf

Balliet, K. (2008). Should you join a landowner group? (p. 2). State College, PA: Penn State Extension. Retrieved from http://extension.psu.edu/natural-resources/natural-gas/issues/leases/publications/should-you-join-a-landowner-group

Berg, B. L., & Lune, H. (2004). *Qualitative research methods for the social sciences.* Upper Saddle River, NJ: Pearson Education.

Brasier, K. J., Filteau, M. R., McLaughlin, D. K. et al. (2011). Residents' perceptions of community and environmental impacts form development of natural gas in the Marcellus Shale: A comparison of Pennsylvania and New York Cases. *Journal of Rural Social Sciences,* 26(1), 32.

Bridge, G., & Perreault, T. (2009). Environmental governance. In N. Castree, D. Demeritt, D. Liverman, & B. Rhoads (Eds.), *A companion to environmental geography* (pp. 475–497). Oxford: Blackwell.

Haggerty, M. N., & Haggerty, J. H. (2015). Energy development as opportunity and challenge in the rural west. In D. Danbom (Ed.), *Bridging the distance.* Salt Lake City, UT: University of Utah Press.

Harvey, D. (2005). *A brief history of neoliberalism.* Oxford: Oxford University Press.

Jacquet, J. B., & Kay, D. L. (2014). The unconventional boomtown: Updating the impact model to fit new spatial and temporal scales. *Journal of Rural and Community Development,* 9(1), 1–23.

Jacquet, J., & Stedman, R. C. (2011). Natural gas landowner coalitions in New York State: Emerging benefits of collective natural resource management. *Journal of Rural Social Sciences,* 26(1), 62.

Junkert, K., & Goehring, D. (2016). Pipeline Restoration and Reclamation Oversight Pilot Program. North Dakota Department of Agriculture.

Klassen, J. A., & Feldpausch-Parker, A. M. (2011). Oiling the gears of public participation: the value of organizations in establishing Trinity of Voice for communities impacted by the oil and gas industry. *Local Environment,* 16(9), 903–915.

Konschnik, K. E., & Boling, M. K. (2014). Shale gas development: A smart regulation framework. *Environmental Science & Technology,* 48(15), 8404–8416.

Levi-Faur, D. (2005). The global diffusion of regulatory capitalism. *The Annals of the American Academy of Political and Social Science,* 598(1), 12–32.

Lindlof, T. R. (1995). *Qualitative communication research methods* (Vol. 3). Thousand Oaks, CA: Sage Publications.

Moffat, K., & Zhang, A. (2014). The paths to social license to operate: an integrative model explaining community acceptance of mining. *Resources Policy,* 39, 61–70.

Murphy, K. (2017). Queensland gas industry welcomes moves to establish land access ombudsman. *Australian Petroleum Production & Exploration Association*, May 24, 2017. Retrieved from www.appea.com.au/media_release/queensland-gas-industry-welcomes-moves-to-establish-land-access-ombudsman

Scott, R. P. (2016). Independent review of the Gasfields Commission Queensland and associated matters. State of Queensland, Department of State Development. Retrieved from www.statedevelopment.qld.gov.au/resources/report/gasfields-commission-review-report.pdf

Small, M. J., Stern, P. C., Bomberg, E.,et al. (2014). Risks and risk governance in unconventional shale gas development. *Environmental Science & Technology*, 48(15), 8289–8297.

Warner, B., & Shapiro, J. (2013). Fractured, fragmented federalism: A study in fracking regulatory policy. *Publius: The Journal of Federalism*, 43(3), 474–496.

Whitton, J., Brasier, K. J., Charnley-Parry, I., & Cotton, M. (2017). Shale gas governance in the United Kingdom and the United States: Opportunities for public participation and the implications for social justice. *Energy Research & Social Science*, 26, 11–22.

Zirogiannis, N., Alcorn, J., Rupp, J., Carley, S., & Graham, J. D. (2016). State regulation of unconventional gas development in the US: An empirical evaluation. *Energy Research & Social Science*, 11, 142–154.

13 Fracking communities, fractured communication

Information transfer and transparency of the energy industry

Peggy Petrzelka, Colter Ellis, Douglas Jackson-Smith, and Gene Theodori

Introduction

[Industry] came in and, of course there's no zoning out in the rural areas, they just buy land and … they don't ask or nothing to build a facility, and they put it where they're convenient and they worry about the consequences later. We had no idea this was happening, we never saw any paperwork on it or anything, so one of the communication problems I feel is they need to notify people in that direct area it's gonna be impacted. They [industry] changed their [residents] lives forever, but….

(Community resident)

If they [industry] don't have someone out here in the field every single day representing that company, and answering questions and keeping the open lines of communication … it's just the fact that relationships are, if you want to quote the commercial, they're priceless.

(Industry representative)

Hydraulic fracturing technology is bringing drilling activity to many US rural communities for the first time. This presents challenges and opportunities for both residents and the oil and gas industry. A growing body of industry literature emphasizes the importance of maintaining open and meaningful lines of communication between energy industry actors and residents of affected communities (e.g., Gehman et al., 2016). In particular, discussion has focused on two concepts regarding communication and community engagement: Corporate Social Responsibility (CSR) and Social License to Operate (SLO).

Corporate Social Responsibility (CSR) is defined as the "commitment by business to behave ethically and contribute to economic development while improving the quality of life of its workers … as well as the local community and society at large" (Watts, 2005: 393). Social License to Operate (SLO) is a "means of addressing community relations problems while avoiding regulatory or governmental involvement" (Gehman et al., 2016: 3). Essential to obtaining

SLO within a community is transparency, "based on open dialogue between community members and industry representatives" (ibid.: 5).

While in-depth case studies of how CSR and SLO play out in energy communities in other countries exist (e.g., Gehman et al., 2016; Watts, 2005), case studies of this type of community engagement – in particular, information transfer and transparency by industry – are more limited in US communities experiencing hydraulic fracturing. In this case study, we begin to fill that gap in the literature, by focusing on perspectives of information transfer and transparency from the point of view of industry representatives and residents in two Eagle Ford Shale communities.

Background and methods

The Eagle Ford Shale is located in South Texas, spreading from Laredo, on the Mexican border, up into East Texas just west of Dallas. There are approximately 30 counties that make up this play, "which is roughly 50 miles wide and 400 miles long spanning nearly 20,000 square miles and 12.8 million acres" (http://otacompression.com/blog/the-eagle-ford-shale-play-facts-figues-and-history/).

Substantial oil and gas exploration and development have taken place in this shale play since 2008. Oil production has increased from 352 barrels per day in 2008 to 909,661 earlier in 2017 (http://otacompression.com/blog/the-eagle-ford-shale-play-facts-figues-and-history/). As detailed shortly, this rapid development has had significant consequences for the local population in the Eagle Ford.

The data used in this study come from various sources, including interviews with community leaders and focus groups of residents in two of the most active oil- and gas-producing counties in the Eagle Ford Shale – Karnes and La Salle Counties. Karnes County is considered "ground zero" for the hydraulic fracturing activity in the Eagle Ford. La Salle County, approximately 50 miles west of Karnes, has comparable oil and gas development.

Community leaders in each county were interviewed between May 2013 through January 2014. Interviews were an average length of 75 minutes and most often conducted in the interviewees' workplaces. A snowball sampling method was used and initial contacts were asked to recommend other community leaders in the area. Every effort was made to recruit similar participants from each county. In total, 17 community leaders were interviewed in the two counties. Interviewees consisted of elected leaders such as county judges and city officials (3) and non-elected leaders such as school professionals (3), chamber of commerce members (4), religious leaders (3) and service organization workers (4). There were no refusals, thus providing a 100 percent response rate.

The key informant interviews identified three types of local residents as being adversely affected by the recent energy boom: seniors, service sector employees, and landowners. To better understand their experiences and the nature and degree of communication between industry actors and these residents, focus groups for each subpopulation were organized in our study communities.

Participants were selected and invited by local community leaders in coordination with the researchers. The focus group interviews were conducted in February 2014, with four held in each county (one senior, one landowner, two service sector focus groups). The interviews lasted an average length of 90 minutes and were conducted in restaurants over breakfast, lunch, or dinner. A total of 20 senior residents (age 65 and older), 19 service sector employees, and 15 landowners were interviewed.

Finally, in early 2014, we also interviewed representatives from oil and gas companies who were actively drilling in the Eagle Ford region. Eligible companies were limited to primary operators (i.e., companies from support industries and subcontractors were excluded). Recruitment was done by working with the South Texas Energy and Economic Roundtable (STEER[1]), who provided us their list of representatives who serve on the Stakeholder Relations Committee.

Representatives were contacted at least five times, by both phone and email. Of the 12 identified companies on the list, three refused to participate, and four did not respond to our repeated interview requests. Representatives from six companies agreed to participate in the study, for a 50 percent response rate. Interviews averaged approximately one hour and were primarily phone interviews.

All interviews and focus groups were recorded and transcribed verbatim. Using these transcripts, we coded data into dominant themes for each of the groups represented (community leaders, focus groups, and industry representatives; Aronson, 1994). We reviewed the coding and discussed and resolved any discrepancies among the coding. When changes in coding were made, we reviewed previously coded material to ensure it was coded consistently (Bernard & Ryan, 2010). We compared and contrasted responses across resident groups being represented to ascertain intra-case differences and similarities. The themes presented here are those consistent within the three groups we interviewed.

Fractured communication

Industry perspectives on information transfer and transparency

We begin by discussing what the communication process looks like from the perspective of industry representatives. In our interviews with these representatives, they recognized that they often spend little time on community outreach to provide information to citizens in the Eagle Ford region. Explanations included the view that "the Eagle Ford Shale Play is so large" and therefore it is difficult to get to all the communities, and that until this point with drilling, given it was occurring "in the desert" and in "off-shore drilling," there was no need to engage community residents. But the most common responses from industry representatives when asked about community outreach was to argue that community residents in general are not their stakeholders. Universally, when we asked about information transfer to "community members," the discussion that followed focused solely on "stakeholders" (landowners with mineral rights, local elected leaders, etc.) and how communication occurs with them.

People who own mineral rights are often the first people contacted by industry officials. Company representatives, known as "landmen," work to negotiate mineral leases. The relationship between the landman and leaseholders is often sustained throughout the drilling cycle. As one industry representative detailed: "We have a group of mineral landmen that typically have negotiated the lease with the mineral owners ... and they have, you know, ongoing direct communication with them throughout the life of our contractual relationship." Typically, industry does not initiate meaningful communication with community leaders until after leases are being established with private landowners and significant steps towards drilling have already been taken. At that point, industry representatives typically initiate contact with local emergency responders:

> We have various groups that communicate directly to the community so first we have our HS&E [Health, Safely, and the Environment] people, who immediately when we get in a County, they contact the police department, fire department, those types of emergency responders, talk to them about, you know, what we're doing, what our activities are, what type of response we expect from them, if they have any specific needs....

Communication with emergency responders necessarily requires communication with the County Judge (the highest elected official in Texas counties), but these conversations often do not extend to other community leaders until later stages of development. As development activities increase, industry representatives may begin to engage other elected officials, such as city mayors and managers, and appointed officials such as school superintendents. As one industry representative describes:

> So I start out with the County Officials and then I go down to the community officials and I reach out and, you know, make contact and you develop a relationship with *everybody that has a stake in what we do* and that's all the way from the County Judge, the District Judge, County Commissioners, the local law enforcement people, the volunteer fire departments, the school, school board, school superintendents.
>
> (emphasis added)

Limited community engagement efforts are directed toward the general public despite the fact that they are often the groups (e.g., seniors and service workers) who are most directly affected by energy development activities (Jacquet & Kay, 2014; Taylor, 2014), and despite the fact that both CSR and SLO incorporate the larger community in their definitions.

While our industry informants did appear to be aware of the potential benefits of effective community engagement, few could provide details about specific efforts to reach out to the general public, and even when that was done, those few typically viewed communication as a one-way process of public information. For example, industry representatives reported disseminating fact sheets explaining various drilling processes, contacting local newspapers, establishing informational hotlines, making school presentations, and sponsoring tables at fairs and community events. Often, when asking industry representatives about examples of outreach, they would respond by listing donations made to particular communities, such as donations to purchase new fire trucks or computers given to the local schools. But these activities are designed more to share information about the company and to alleviate perceived "irrational" concerns rather than to solicit information about the experiences and specific concerns of local residents regarding energy development. In addition, and similar to what Loder (2016: 738) found in industry research conducted in North Dakota, these activities are done first and foremost "in order to promote goodwill among local communities," rather than to provide meaningful communication exchange.

Our data also suggest that having a locally-based community engagement representative can be beneficial for industry. Industry informants with stronger and more consistent presence in the communities noted that this made it easier to mitigate potential problems and deal with emergencies before they escalated, and as noted in the epigraph, the local presence of industry representatives to help build relationships in the communities is "priceless."

The confidence felt by locally-based representatives stands in stark contrast to the experiences of community engagement representatives living in San Antonio or Houston. At times, these representatives reported difficulty even trying to understand the basic social context of Eagle Ford communities, as illustrated by this community engagement specialist who only occasionally visited the Eagle Ford:

> [W]e don't have on the ground field people, so unlike a lot of companies, we don't have community relations folks that are bouncing from meeting to meeting and hanging out with County Commissioners and going to Chambers of Commerce, and Agricultural Events, all that sort of stuff. So, it is a bit of an ordeal, you know, ...

Some industry representatives did express a desire to do more, but had few concrete ideas about what that might look like. As one industry representative noted, "That's the area we need to improve upon the most, I think, being able to get that information, distill it into things that are understandable for the community and make certain that we're clearly communicating with them." Added another, "There's pressure on [stakeholder engagement employees] that they need to be out talking to folks in the public realm, [but] they're not entirely sure what the agenda should be, like, why are they going to talk to these people? ..."

The interviews with industry representatives reveal industry has for the most part chosen not to participate in aspects of CSR or SLO, indeed, the terms did not come up in a single interview. The fact that half of the companies' representatives we contacted, despite being involved in the same research project with us, refused to participate in interviews or to share information about their public engagement and communication activities suggests another indicator of low to no community engagement. Nor do industry representatives seem apologetic about this lack of engagement, with most whom we interviewed feeling they are dealing with the members of the community they should be dealing with – their identified stakeholders.

Residents' perspectives on information transfer and transparency

When discussing communication with industry, both community leaders and focus group residents expressed a strong desire for better information and more proactive and timely communication about the detrimental impacts they see occurring with the drilling activity. This is primarily illustrated by concerns expressed about the flaring of hydrogen sulfide (H2S) gas from new pipelines and wells in the area.[2]

> [I'd like to know] exactly what's being burned off, and the impact that has on air quality.
>
> (Seniors Focus Group)

> I don't know enough to even know what I need to be concerned about right now, because when you see all these flares and you drive by a well site and you smell something different, I don't know what it is. I know I smell something different there than I did before … I mean it's just one of those things that you kind of scratch your head and go, "I wonder," but there's no smoking gun *per se* that I can say, this is gonna be an issue, but it's something that I, I wish there would be more information to confirm or deny.
>
> (Community leader)

> I want to know what are they going to do to monitor our air control because if you're here at night you see you all those flames, of course they say, "That doesn't do any, any harm, because it's, you know, flushing out the bad gasses or whatever." Well, I don't care what they say, it's still up in this, in the atmosphere. So, it's still here!
>
> (Seniors Focus Group)

In addition to lack of readily available information, as alluded to in the above quote, residents also report concerns that industry has provided misleading information, illustrated more definitively in this quote from a community leader:

> There's an oil consortium down here … I don't know the name of it … they have hired basically a marketing guy. And so he wrote an article[3] and it was in the *Frío Nueces Current*, and he was trying to basically say that [oil doesn't] use but about a half of the water it takes to grow one crop of peanuts [here]. And that may be true, in fact I did a little research and he's

right. But what they didn't print or what he didn't say was that the water that agriculture uses to grow that one crop of peanuts all goes back into the hydrological cycle. Every bit of it goes back into the hydrological cycle. He did not address the fact that that frack water is now contaminated. And there's only about 5 percent of the disposal companies that are recycling any of that water. So that water that they've used is now contaminated and it's now being disposed of in deep wells that we'll never, ever, ever see again. And people don't realize that. People are not realizing that that water is gone. And we'll never see it again.

When industry information outreach does occur, the attempts are usually seen by community leaders as minimal. For example, when asked about whether industry approached community leaders when they came into the county to initiate communication efforts, business leaders indicated there was: "Not a word. Nobody had a clue. Nobody knew what was happening, it just came in." "Snowballed," noted another. And simply put by a religious leader: "we were hit by a tsunami," implying a lack of warning or advanced preparation for the boom in drilling activity. The absence of outreach and communication efforts in advance of development was a common concern expressed by elected leaders, illustrated here:

> [T]here's not much community outreach with a lot of these companies ... I understand they've got a different business than community outreach but it's something that goes a long ways when they do make that effort.... Community meetings provide the opportunity for locals to put a face with an issue as well as a contact person ... [with] anything face to face I know somebody cares enough to at least make the effort....

The majority of focus group participants also found levels of public communication by industry to be unsatisfactory. Specifically, we inquired if they were ever given an opportunity to talk with industry representatives about what to anticipate with the drilling activity and to address any community concerns. As with community leaders, focus group respondents feel they did not have sufficient opportunities to engage in communication with industry representatives:

> I told my husband, why didn't they have some type of meeting, a town meeting or something and say, "This and this and this is going to happen, how does the community feel about this?"
>
> (Seniors Focus Group)

> There's just been some [public meetings] recently, I know a couple of the oil companies have had these little [public] meetings, but it was already two or three years after the fact.
>
> (Service Sector Focus Group)

Our study findings show what many residents hope for, but clearly are not receiving, is to be adequately and timely informed about the activities by industry in their community, to be told accurate rather than misleading information, and to be provided an opportunity for two-way communication with industry.

Interestingly, while residents expressed a desire to have more information, when asked specifically what they would say to industry regarding their concerns, it was not uncommon for participants in our research to say they most likely would not voice their concerns, as "industry doesn't care."

> I don't think they would care. They [the industry] won't listen to us. They want to do what they're going to do. They're going to do what they're going to do....
>
> (Seniors Focus Group)

> I'm pretty convinced that industry is big enough to where they don't really care ... they've got enough money and enough pull and enough stroke that I don't think they really care ... If something happens, they'll fix it. And put a good spin on it, if it's public.
>
> (Community leader)

> [Industry doesn't care] They don't. They don't because when we met [regarding negative impacts on low-income residents], Anadarko was there, Strike was there, Chesapeake was there, you know, the representatives from those oil field companies, and you know, "We are not here to listen to your problems. ... poor housing, we've got it taken care of. We've got housing for the employees, we've got food for the employees, so really your problems don't really matter to us."
>
> (Community leader)

And several community leaders independently pointed out the proximity of drilling rigs to a high school and noted that promises from oil company representatives to provide H2S air sensors along the fence line had failed to materialize, as yet another example of industry not caring.

There is also a widespread perception among both community leaders and focus group participants that when company efforts to communicate with the public do occur, they are simply a public relations (PR) effort and not a sincere desire to engage in full and transparent dialogue between the communities and industry. According to one community leader:

> [T]ypical [industry] PR guys are all razzle-dazzle deals. And they come into a community such as this and people are just looking at them like, "Hey man, you're the guy from Mars. And you really don't understand how our community works."

And while the donations mentioned earlier by the industry representatives are appreciated, few of our community informants felt that these efforts were substitutes for more direct efforts by industry to be sincerely interested in residents' concerns over the drilling and providing information to address these concerns.

The strongest example of industry-community engagement was found in the case of a locally-based "community engagement" representative, who was hired by a company and worked out of local offices in Eagle Ford communities. This person's central role was community engagement and maintenance of clear and open lines of communication with local leaders. This position was widely cited in our interviews as a success story. For example, one county official noted that this individual's regular attendance at county commission meetings provided opportunities to learn first-hand about emerging issues in the county:

> [One company] has a man, and he's been to our county meetings about 85 percent of the time. He's involved so you know, his contribution outweighs more than ten thousand dollars out of the fire department. The fact that they actually have a fly on the wall here involved.

This quote illustrates how one-time PR efforts such as the $10,000 donation to the local fire department are less effective than efforts to actually be involved *in* the communities. Instead of meaningful engagement with communities, industry falls back on the "Razzle Dazzle," which is not effective. Community leaders felt strongly that companies should have a strong and sustained local presence and that having locally-based representatives improved communication.

As the data from the industry representatives suggest, industry appears to see, or define, "community members" as individual landowners (their primary stakeholders) and sometimes elected officials. They do not often look at the entire community in which their operations are involved, nor do they often view their responsibility to be to the entire community. This is consistent with other studies which have found industry stakeholder management suggests "allegiance to interests that are salient to stakeholders, but may not transcend into the realm of social best interest or the broader social discourse" (Gehman et al., 2016: 5). Yet in our study, *even stakeholders* reported fractured communication with industry, seen in the previous quotes from elected officials, but also in reports by local landowners, who leave their mineral rights to industry;

> My oil field companies are not very timely about getting back to me when I express a concern, and so they probably think I'm the witch from heck, but I just keep calling them, if I have to call them two times, three times a day, two times a week, three times a week. You get a hotline, you get a recording, I hate those recordings. And they still don't have an answer, so I'll just keep bugging them, because that's the only option, you either have to forget it or just keep bugging them.
>
> (Landowner Focus Group)

[INTERVIEWER]: If you ever have concerns with what's going on, on your land, or what's going on with the drilling activity in general, is there someone you can talk to from industry?

[RESPONDENT 1]: The landman usually is the first person to contact and then we start going on up and then there's like a, a disconnect somewhere between here and there.... You get to a point that you go to the landman and he'll say "Oh, you need to talk to the company landman" ... and then it's kind of like, there's nobody else to talk to from that point, you know, you just kind of have to keep hitting that or turn it over to the attorney which is something we'd never thought we'd have to have ... we had to get an attorney. That was obvious....

[RESPONDENT 2]: Well, there's so many things with leases and agreements and stuff that I can look at it and read it and it says one thing but the attorney, "No, that's not what it says," and, it got to the point where there [was], so much paperwork and so we got an oil and gas attorney. Another attorney and an oil and gas attorney.

[RESPONDENT 1]: So a lot of the normal day-to-day business conversations we just go through the attorneys with it now, instead of dealing with it ourselves because it does get to be time-consuming, you know, hours and hours on the phone, just going over and over and over the same thing. It's a whole lot easier to just call and talk to him, let him deal with it and call us back.

Based on our findings, it would seem that communication efforts by unconventional oil and gas development firms have been unsuccessful at engaging some of the most affected residents of communities in the Eagle Ford region. Residents want information they are not getting, the information being put out by industry representatives is perceived as intentionally misleading at times; and there has been little attempt by industry to provide information, outreach, or even a sense that residents' voices matter. Gehman et al. (2016: 4), in their analysis of SLO literature, note that "Maintaining SLO is a continuous practice that requires constant attention in order to maintain rapport with a community." Clearly, this is not occurring in the Eagle Ford, by energy representatives' own admission. And the lack of details in many of our resident interviews on substantive interactions with industry representative indicates the low level at which in-depth communication between industry and even local community leaders generally occurs.

Conclusion

The intense social, economic, and environmental impacts associated with rapid energy booms have both direct and indirect effects on the well-being of local residents. While there are a growing number of examples of a more participatory approach with respect to alternative energy projects (e.g., Anahita & Walsh, 2014; Devine-Wright, 2011), unconventional oil and gas development has a checkered track record of meaningful public communication and engagement (Ziliox & Smith, 2014). Unfortunately, this case study findings add to that checkered track record. Our finding that there is fractured communication between community and industry is consistent with accounts of the oil industry's interactions with extractive community residents in other parts of the world (Valdavia, 2008; Watts, 2005).

In our interactions with industry representatives, we have shared our findings and recommended greater commitment and investments to improve two-way forms of communication and engagement with the public. While our research was generally well received, we have seen little evidence of a change in approach in the years since we began our work. Indeed, an industry-funded community liaison staff position referred to previously (which was one of the bright spots that many community leaders pointed to as an effective approach) has actually been eliminated since we did our fieldwork.

To some extent, the failure to engage the broader public in energy development decisions may be a reflection of larger political-economic forces in which local residents are not seen as having legitimate standing to approve or disapprove of projects (Hudgins & Poole, 2014), and many of their social and economic concerns are treated as issues that fall outside the responsibility of the industry to address (Israel et al., 2015). There are also systemic hurdles that limit the ability or willingness of local governments in rural areas to confront industry leaders about residents' concerns (Ellis et al., 2016). And to some extent the failure may be due to CSR and SLO principles written on paper – yet not carried out in actuality. As Watts (2005) found in his case study of CSR and the oil industry in Nigeria, while, on paper, all oil firms had put CSR in place, what was actually found was "companies ... simply interacted with local elites ... [and] transparency [with communities] remained an issue ..." (p. 399).

The shale gas industry in the Eagle Ford region of Texas gives low priority to communication with local communities, justified by industry representatives when discussing their "stakeholders" and who they are responsible to. The individuals and groups that industry feels it is responsible to are not the same individuals and groups whom the larger community believes industry is responsible to, nor is industry's view of who constitutes "community members" (and who does not) consistent with the definitions of CSR and SLOs offered previously – both forms of community engagement the oil and gas industry has signed on to. And even stakeholders defined by industry specifically – landowners they lease from and elected officials – find the information transfer and transparency inadequate.

Social science research on hydraulic fracturing is expanding daily. This research examines issues such as perceptions of hydraulic fracturing among local residents (e.g., Israel et al., 2015; Schafft, Borlu, & Glenna, 2013; Stedman et al., 2012; Theodori, 2013) and among community leaders (e.g., Anderson & Theodori, 2009; Brasier et al., 2011, Ladd, 2013). The research also examines community impacts (primarily economic and social) of the energy activity (e.g., Jacquet & Kay, 2014; Taylor, 2014). These studies document local residents' concerns about a wide range of social, environmental, and economic issues. Yet, relatively little is known about how local industry actors seek or receive information about these concerns, nor the degree to which industry is making efforts to communicate *with* residents in the communities it is actively drilling in and near. This study begins to fill that gap in the literature, a critical piece to better understanding local community responses to hydraulic fracturing.

Acknowledgments

The authors gratefully acknowledge the voices of all those who shared their thoughts in the Eagle Ford, and the help of Ennea Fairchild in the preparation of this chapter. The research summarized here is a part of the larger Eagle Ford Shale Environmentally Friendly Drilling Technology Integration Program (EFD-TIP), a project coordinated by the Houston Advanced Research Center and funded by the US Department of Energy Research Partnership to Secure Energy for America (RPSEA) Program.

Notes

1 STEER is an industry association, based in San Antonio, working to serve as a bridge between the oil and gas industry and the communities in the Eagle Ford. STEER is also a partner with us in the EFD-TIP detailed in the Acknowledgments.
2 Flaring refers to the burning of gas produced in the drilling activity that is considered a safety problem. In the Eagle Ford, flaring of H2S is commonly done to convert the H2S into less toxic compounds.
3 The article can be found at: www.oilandgaslawyerblog.com/water-rights/

References

Anahita, A. N. J., & Walsh, P. R. (2014). The role of public participation in identifying stakeholder synergies in wind power project development: The case study of Ontario, Canada. *Renewable Energy*, 68, 194–202.

Anderson, B. J., & Theodori, G. L. (2009). Local leaders' perceptions of energy development in the Barnett shale, South. *Rural Sociology*, 24(1), 113–129.

Aronson, J. (1994). A pragmatic view of thematic analysis. *The Qualitative Report*, 2(1). Available at: www.nova.edu/ssss/QR/BackIssues/QR2-1/aronson.html

Bernard, H. R., & Ryan, G. W. (2010). *Analyzing Qualitative Data: Systematic Approaches*. Thousand Oaks, CA: Sage.

Brasier, K. J., Filteau, M. R., McLaughlin, D. K. et al. (2011). Residents' perceptions of community and environmental impacts from development of natural gas in the Marcellus shale: A comparison of Pennsylvania and New York cases. *Journal of Rural Sociology Sciences*, 26(1), 32–61.

Devine-Wright, P. (2011). *Renewable Energy and the Public: From NIMBY to Participation*. New York: Earthscan.

Ellis C., Theodori, G., Petrzelka, P., Jackson-Smith, D., & Luloff, A. (2016). Unconventional risks: Rural communities' response to acute energy development in the Eagle Ford Shale. *Energy Research and Social Science*, 20, 91–98.

Gehman, J., Thomson, D. Y., Alessi, D. S., Allen, D. M., & Goss, G. G. (2016). Comparative analysis of hydraulic fracturing wastewater practices in unconventional shale development: Newspaper coverage of stakeholder concerns and social license to operate. *Sustainability*, 8, 1–23.

Hudgins, A. & Poole, A. (2014). Framing fracking: Private property, common resources, and regimes of governance. *Journal of Political Ecology*, 21: 303–319.

Israel, A. L., Wong-Parodi, G., Webler, T., & Stern, P. C. (2015). Eliciting public concerns about an emerging energy technology: The case of unconventional shale gas development in the United States. *Energy Resource & Social Science*, 8, 139–150.

Jacquet, J. B., & Kay, D. L. (2014). The unconventional boomtown: Updating the impact model to fit new spatial and temporal scales. *Journal of Rural and Community Development*, 9(1), 1–23.

Ladd, A. E. (2013). Stakeholder perceptions of socioenvironmental impacts from unconventional natural gas development and hydraulic fracturing in the Haynesville Shale. *Journal of Rural Sociology Sciences*, 28(2), 56–89.

Loder, T. (2016). Spaces of consent and the making of fracking subjects in North Dakota: A view from two corporate community forums. *The Extractive Industries and Society*, 3, 736–743.

Schafft, K. A., Borlu, Y., & Glenna, L. (2013). The relationship between Marcellus shale gas development in Pennsylvania and local perceptions of risk and opportunity. *Rural Sociology*, 78(2), 143–166.

Stedman, R. C., Jacquet, J. B., Filteau, M. R. et al. (2012). Marcellus shale gas development and new boomtown research: Views of New York and Pennsylvania residents. *Environmental Practice*, 14(4), 382–393.

Taylor, A. (2014). Community impacts from large oil and natural gas ventures in rural and remote areas. *Journal of Rural and Community Development*, 90(1), i–vi.

Theodori, G. L. (2013). Perception of the natural gas industry and engagement in individual civic actions. *Journal of Rural Sociology Sciences*, 28(2), 122–134.

Valdavia, G. (2008). Governing relations between people and things: Citizenship, territory and the political economy of petroleum in Ecuador. *Political Geography*, 27, 456–477.

Watts, M. J. (2005). Righteous oil? Human rights, the oil complex, and corporate social responsibility. *Annual Review of Environment and Resources*, 30, 373–407.

Ziliox, S. & Smith, J. M. (2017). Supraregulatory agreements and unconventional energy development: Learning from citizen concerns, enforceability and participation in Colorado. *The Extractive Industries and Society* 4(1): 69–77.

Part III

Actor networks, participation and social justice

14 Shale gas governance in the United States, the United Kingdom and Europe

Public participation and the role of social justice

John Whitton and Ioan Charnley-Parry

Introduction

The decisions made regarding the development of new energy infrastructure, such as for shale gas exploitation (SGE), are of local, national and international importance. Improved stakeholder-industry dialogue can significantly impact upon the quality of decision-making (Webler, Tuler, & Krueger, 2001), demonstrating a more democratic decision-making process. As Taebi *et al.* (2016) assert, it is not the existence of controversy that causes project failure, but how controversy is dealt with, to which democratic decision-making can contribute. The literature supports democracy, in governance and society, to be a key theme of procedural justice in decision-making (Magis & Shinn, 2009). We have previously embraced the move towards a participatory-based form of dialogue in decisions rather than a technocratic 'top-down', expert-led, 'one-way' form of consultation. In this approach, dialogue is multi-directional and dimensional and incorporative of multiple stakeholders (Innes & Booher, 2004) and stakeholder groups (Whitton, Parry, Akiyoshi, & Lawless, 2015).

This chapter contributes to the growing body of international research on the governance challenges, particularly public participation, surrounding SGE through hydraulic fracturing. In our examination of the current state of shale gas governance (SGG) in the US, the UK, Poland and the Netherlands, we compare the approach to public participation of different countries to what is termed by some scholars as 'one of the most significant innovations in global energy extraction this century' (Bomberg, 2017: 101). These serve as examples of countries that have been enthusiastic in their support of shale gas development and are still pursuing shale gas exploration (the UK, the US), have dramatically reduced exploratory activities during recent years (Poland), or are precautionary and restrictive in their approach to exploiting their shale gas resources (the Netherlands). We then consider the role and importance of social justice within SGG and propose a participatory framework based on the concepts of deliberative dialogue and social sustainability (Whitton *et al.*, 2015).

Public participation in energy systems

Following sustained academic critique, there has been increasing acknowledgement that broad public support for energy technologies cannot be based upon the tacit assumption of public trust in technical expertise and the assurances of developers. We see this in the work of other authors in this volume, such as that carried out by Anna Szolucha in Lancashire and Grabowiec, Poland (Chapter 16) and also Imogen Rattle, James Van Alstine and Tudor Baker in Lancashire and Yorkshire (Chapter 15). These authors highlight the public experience of a system of governance, perceived by residents to favour development over their concerns. Planning and decision-making processes that are technocratic frequently follow the Decide-Announce-Defend (D-A-D) strategy of expert assessment, closed decision-making, and public relations mechanisms of information provision to affected site communities, followed by an increasingly acrimonious battle against the social movements of opposition that inevitably emerge in response. The uncertainty of how local communities and impacted residents will influence the policy-making process surrounding shale gas has been identified as having produced barriers to the 'pro-fracking' government policy in the UK (Cairney, Fischer, & Ingold, 2015). We argue that the existing governance system provides insufficient opportunities for substantive engagement, whereby affected or potentially affected public stakeholders can deliberatively and openly discuss project plans and impacts within a local context, and then inform and influence project-related decision-making processes, thus contributing to a lack of social justice. In the next section, we discuss social justice within SGG, and then consider the opportunities for public participation on shale gas developments in the US, the UK, Poland and the Netherlands.

Incorporating social justice into shale gas governance

Lebel *et al.* (2006) state that the central goal of good governance is social justice, while Fung (2015) describes social justice as a central value of democratic governance. We argue that effective governance requires social justice at its core, and is required to achieve any sense of democratic legitimacy should shale gas exploration occur. We argue that social justice represents the opportunity for and ability of public stakeholders to engage with and influence socially impactful decision-making processes. Due to the early stage of shale gas exploration in the UK, Poland and the Netherlands, whereby the impacts and outcomes of SGE have not yet been experienced, we focus here on public participation in decision-making, and the *procedural* element of justice.

According to Thibaut and Walker (1975), citizens believe that procedures hold importance, because 'fair procedures produce fair outcomes' (MacCoun, 2005: 182). For project developers, meeting procedural justice ideals with transparent decision-making is important to avoid conflict with local residents (Gross, 2007). In this sense, demonstrable justice and fairness during the governance process can influence perceptions locally. Rootes (2006), and Szolucha in Chapter 16 in this volume, expose how an absence of procedural justice reveals an imbalance of power relations between decision-makers and communities, with ethical implications for planning and policy decisions for nationally significant infrastructure projects (NSIPs).

Other researchers (e.g. Cotton, Rattle, & Van Alstine, 2014) have discussed procedural justice in the context of shale gas exploration activities in Lancashire, UK, concerning community benefit practices and community engagement. Here, permitted site licences – obtained prior to exploration activities – do not require Environmental Impact Assessments (EIAs) where sites are declared as being <1 ha in area. In the case of the operator Cuadrilla in the UK, drilling activities have been exploratory as opposed to commercial, thereby complying with the legal regulatory framework (i.e. the Town and Country Planning Regulations 1999 in England and Wales), while being deemed by many not to have acquired social acceptability. Cotton, Rattle and Van Alstine (2014) also observe that by avoiding the EIA, the company's practices avoided generating a social licence to operate (SLO), thus failing to produce any degree of ongoing 'local stakeholder approval' (ibid.: 433), and that gaining SLO requires establishing procedural fairness by engaging communities in decision-making over site licensing (see also Gross, 2007). However, as in the US, Poland and the Netherlands, SLO is not a legal requirement in the UK, and shale gas operators may question the value of or need for such an agreement beyond the potential mitigation of possible conflict. However, as Howard-Grenville, Nash and Coglianese (2008) highlight, gaining SLO is important due to the unintended consequences for industry, such as conflict, opposition and project delays, that may arise by ignoring or acting contrary to the expectations of local publics, and generating perceived social injustice.

Shale gas participation: in the US

Shale gas extraction through hydraulic fracturing has been ongoing in the US since the turn of the millennium and serves as the primary global example of SGE. The US shale energy industry is well established and has largely followed the conventional oil and gas industry with regards to governance procedures and public engagement practices (Whitton, Brasier, Charnley-Parry, & Cotton, 2017). As such, local participation is an area of ongoing controversy and litigation in the US. For example, Pennsylvania's Oil and Gas Act essentially pre-empts the ability of local communities to regulate oil and gas activity. Although some municipalities passed ordinances limiting the location of oil and gas activity, those ordinances are still being adjudicated in the Pennsylvania court system, with their legal standing very much in question (ibid.). Denton, Texas, recently passed a series of ordinances limiting local influence on oil and gas activity. Legislation has since passed and these local ordinances are now pre-empted – see Chapter 6 on Texas by Matthew Fry and Christian Brannstrom in this volume.

The formal mechanisms for participation in the US are public comment periods and hearings for proposed regulatory changes, and directly contacting legislators and regulatory agencies about general issues of concern. Another avenue for public participation is the development and operation of task forces, whose members are appointed by local political bodies (usually county commissioners), serve in an advisory capacity, and enhance communication with industrial representatives working in the area (ibid.). An alternative model is the Eagle Ford Task Force, a multi-county body created by the Railroad Commission of Texas to coordinate activities in the 23-county shale gas plays in South Texas (RCT, 2013). Their goals were to engage with the public and increase communication among stakeholders during early developmental stages to mitigate conflict, a subject discussed in greater detail by Petrzelka and colleagues in Chapter 13 in this volume. However, as previously noted by Whitton *et al.* (2017), the effectiveness of these advisory task forces varies greatly, influenced by the local cultural and political context, and their ability to meaningfully engage with the public remains unevaluated.

Collective behaviour and social movement activities have also become more prevalent in participation approaches, including the involvement of citizens to monitor developmental impacts, sometimes in partnership with local government or research institutes. For example, groups of citizens, such as environmental groups, have begun to collect or enhanced their efforts to collect data used to monitor the health of ecosystems affected by natural gas development (Brasier, Lee, Stedman, & Weigle, 2011; Jalbert, 2016). Organizations in the Marcellus region such as Shale Network have made such databases publicly accessible, enhancing public access to information and monitoring of developmental impacts (Brasier, Jalbert, Kinchy, Brantley, & Unroe, 2017). The development of opposition groups as well as the use of 'fracking bans' or local moratoria on oil and gas activity have also played a role, such as in New York State with the passage of municipal ordinances (Dokshin, 2016). The author finds that bans on hydraulic fracturing for shale gas in New York State occurred primarily on the periphery of development-targeted regions, where 'compelling economic interest in development' (ibid.: 921) was significantly lower, while noting that politically liberal activities in the area reflected patterns of local opposition. In Illinois, Buday (2017) describes the initial collaborations of grassroots anti-fracking activists with statewide environmental coalitions. Activists worked with a professionalized legal advocacy organization named the Community Environmental Legal Defense Fund (CELDF) (see also Whitton *et al.*, 2017), to assert their 'home rule authorities' and thereby 'challenge preemption of oil and gas regulation' (ibid.: 15) by the state of Illinois.

Shale gas participation: in the UK

The UK is beginning to explore the possibilities of how SGE could enhance energy security, create employment opportunities and contribute to local economies. Political interest and support stem from the potential benefits for the UK from large-scale SGE, contributing towards what the IEA describe as a potential 'Golden Age of Gas' (IEA, 2012). The Government's 2013 Spending

Round saw significant incentives being generated for shale gas exploration, including the announcement of industry tax breaks, a new regulatory framework, business rate cuts for local councils and community benefits packages for shale gas host communities (HM Treasury, 2013). The result was a stimulation in the applications for Petroleum Exploration and Development Licences from exploration companies, with associated stakeholder consultation. Some of these exploration efforts, such as Cuadrilla in the West Sussex town of Balcombe in South-east England in July 2013, and iGas in Barton Moss in Manchester, received significant public opposition (i.e. protests) and media attention. This was largely based on a perceived lack of opportunities for community consultation and public involvement on development decisions, in addition to public concerns that regulatory bodies and elected officials were not sufficiently acknowledging and protecting residents' interests (B.P.C., 2012; Cotton *et al.*, 2014).

Conversely, recent rhetorical shifts in the UK appear to demonstrate a move towards greater inclusion and participation of local populations. The recently published Shale Wealth Fund (SWF) consultation document (HM Treasury, 2016) from the UK Government states that local communities should have more control in local decisions, asserting that 'the government believes in empowering local people, and wants to see communities and individuals have greater control of the decisions, assets, and services which affect them' (ibid.: 5). It is one of the few shale-related processes in the UK on which there is published material, relating to local decision-making and public participation proposals. The document briefly presents a number of decision-making-body options for consultation and comment, which include:

1   Using an existing body in the local community (e.g. Parish or District Council), to administer funds.
2   Using an existing body to administer industry community benefits schemes.
3   Establishing an independent decision-making body to administer local-level funding.

The SWF is promoted as a fund which 'could deliver up to £1 billion of funding' (ibid.: 3), a portion of which could be directed towards local communities, thereby sharing 'the benefits of shale developments' (ibid.).

While proposing elements of procedural justice and democratic governance, such as participation, equity and representation, the document also suggests that local community representation should be reflected by those selected as decision-makers, and that local residents should be 'as directly involved in decision-making as possible' (ibid.: 13). It is yet to be seen whether such public participation will be realized should shale gas developments progress beyond exploration.

Shale gas participation: in Poland

Poland still considers fossil fuels to be important for its energy future (LaBelle, 2017). However, shale gas development has been a greater focus in recent years and has attracted growing incentives, primarily in the area of energy security (Johnson & Boersma, 2013) and to reduce carbon emissions (McGowan, 2014). Poland has been described by McGowan as 'the most enthusiastic advocate of shale gas development in the EU' (ibid.: 48), whereby political and public support for shale gas has been broadly positive. In 2014, Polish President Donald Tusk proposed that commercial 'fracking' should commence by 2014 (Neslen, 2015), at which time the shale gas policy regime was robust in Poland. As Goldthau and LaBelle observe, this was based on a 'powerful political narrative', helping to 'establish legitimacy for a political project, ensure institutional and actor support across policy subsystems, and overcome fragmentation among interests and policy levels' (2016: 618–619). However, this is not the case every-where, as Szolucha discusses in Chapter 16 in this volume; from 2012 onwards, there has been sustained opposition in the Graboweic Region.

Despite governmental interest, shale gas activity has not increased consist-ently; there were 115 active exploration concessions in 2012, down from 199 in previous years, and exploration territory has decreased from a total area of 30 per cent to 7.8 per cent recently (P.M.E., 2016). Since 2014, no new wells have been developed through hydraulic fracturing across the country (LaBelle, 2017), and progress has been stymied by recent shifts in energy and innovation policy towards more innovative coal exploitation options (ibid.) and the dearth of identified economically viable sources (Lis & Stankiewicz, 2017).

Despite this, the shale gas industry, like others, is responsive to global shifts in the energy market, whereby the viability of resource exploitation depends on several factors, including fluctuating oil prices (Adamus & Florkowski, 2016). Therefore, SGG will respond to changing economic realities, whereby public and private sector decision-makers will 'monitor developments and re-evaluate the expansion of shale gas extraction in Poland' (ibid.: 177).

However, Polish citizens remain largely absent in decision-making. As Lis and Stankiewicz (2017) observe, communities close to exploration sites often highlight lack of information provision with regards to project investment and local impacts (i.e. public health and natural environmental). Poor communica-tion and limited opportunity to participate in debates or decision-making have led to spontaneous protests by local and regional protest groups. As Anna Szolucha discusses in Chapter 16 in this volume, these groups, led by local farmers, resorted to establishing a long-term (over a year) blockade of Chevron's exploration site in Żurawlów, thus preventing the continuation of exploration activities, in a protest activity termed 'Occupy Chevron'.

Shale gas development is considered a necessary strategic option to maintain energy security (Lis & Stankiewicz, 2017). This has shaped Polish energy policy process significantly, while, as Lis and Stankiewicz propose, political and indus-trial actors have acted to exclude local protest groups and shale gas opponents from the policy process under the framing of 'incompetent actors'. The authors argue that 'dialogue' with local residents is gradually shifting into exercises to 'convince' the public, and that the 'domination of the deficit model' (ibid.: 66) elevates and prioritizes the opinions and knowledge of experts, while de-valuing and excluding public knowledge and preventing public participation in decision-making. The following opinion expressed by a gas company representative during a local meeting (Pomerania region, October 2014) is indicative of this: 'We cannot agree for any form of public participation of local communities in decision-making procedures, because we are simply afraid that incompetent people will have an impact on it' (Lis & Stankiewicz, 2017: 66).

Shale gas participation: in the Netherlands

Since the mid-twentieth century, the Netherlands has been both a major gas producer and consumer (accounting for 40 per cent of its total energy supply) and also an exporter (McGowan, 2014), resulting in the significant depletion of once large gas fields (Cuppen, Pesch, Remmerswaal, & Taanman, 2016). Ligtvoet *et al.* (2016) predict that conventional natural gas resources in the Netherlands will have depleted by 2030, and since 2008, shale gas exploration and production have been a focus of growing interest. In 2009, an exploration licence was applied for by Cuadrilla Resources and the Dutch state-owned EBN BV (ibid.), granted by the Dutch Ministry of Economic Affairs, after which a planning permit for shale gas test drilling was sought (Metze, 2017) for activities in the municipality of Boxtel due for 2011 (Cuppen *et al.*, 2016). This generated public and media interest, and a local network of opposition was formed. Members of parliament, municipalities and local groups became active campaigners against planned shale gas drilling activities (McGowan, 2014). Despite this, the advisory governmental body (the Dutch Energy Council) recommended that shale gas resources in the Netherlands be developed (Energy Council, 2011).

The perception of shale gas in the Netherlands has changed over time. Cuppen *et al.* (2016) observe a discursive shift, from being framed as a local-scale safety and risk issue, towards a broader, national-scale debate on the utility and necessity of shale gas. The government employed a more cautious and consultative approach to shale gas development as public opinion grew more critical, engaging in large-scale consultation exercise that informed a final decision on further exploration and shale gas development (Rijksoverheid, 2012, cited in McGowan, 2014). In the Netherlands, the government acknowledges the potential benefits of shale gas but has adopted a precautionary approach. Initially considered 'business-as-usual', SGG has generated significant national debate, encompassing broader questions about energy transitions in the Netherlands (Cuppen *et al.*, 2016). As Metze (2017) observes, the 'business as usual' narrative of government and experts, with references to conventional gas production and 'a welcome new approach to gas production' (ibid.: 40), aimed to convince the public of 'the benefits of test drilling' (Dodge & Metze, 2017: 8).

This facilitated early progression of exploration activities and the award of drilling permits (Dignum, Correlje, Cuppen, Pesch, & Taebi, 2016), that catalyzed the development of an oppositional movement against Dutch SGE.

Public participation in governance and decision-making in the Netherlands has been influenced by the framing of the issue by government and industrial actors; predominantly as an economic opportunity and national good to address energy security issues. Following a government-implemented moratorium and independent review into the risks of shale gas and coal bed methane in October 2011, a stakeholder advisory board was created and a public consultation commissioned by the EU (December 2012–March 2013), which found low public support for shale gas in the Netherlands. Activists and government officials challenged the results of the independent review, arguing that the concept of 'safety' was too narrowly defined and local impacts were not given sufficient attention (ibid.). Following the results of further commissioned investigations into 'location-specific aspects' (ibid.: 1175), the government then decided to extend the moratorium until 2020.

Discussion

From our review of SGG in this chapter, it would seem that the opportunities for the public to be involved in shale gas decision-making are limited, frustrated by issues surrounding state-level transparency of regulation, fragmentation, and access to information. For example, in the UK, Lancashire County councillors rejected planning consent for Cuadrilla's application to drill and frack a total of eight wells at two sites, on the grounds of unacceptable visual impact and excessive noise. However, the company's appeals against these rulings look to take the decision *away* from local representatives towards national government ministers and the Secretary of State. This has also resulted in pre-emption in areas such as Pennsylvania and Texas in the US. Rasch and Köhne (2016) observe that negotiations about hydraulic fracturing in relation to energy transitions produce new forms of citizenship: 'a process of negotiation between governments ... and citizens ... about who is included and excluded from participation in decision-making processes' (ibid.: 107) – as a result of inclusionary or exclusionary processes, such as decision-making. Such work highlights the importance of exploring how different people experience changes related to energy policy and develop energy-related knowledge and practices.

Stevens (2012) also highlights the differences in governance between the US and Poland, in particular, regulatory aspects such as full disclosure on the composition of fracturing fluids, may inhibit a replication of the US shale gas revolution in Poland, and indeed across Europe. Stevens highlights that regulatory differences with regards to governmental financial support for developers and compensation or financial rewards to individual landowners alter the manner in which shale gas projects are governed and alter their incentives to different stakeholder groups (ibid.).

Metze (2017) argues that the discursive shift in the Netherlands from the early 'business as usual' framing to its recent framing as a potential environmental risk, worthy of significant pre-exploratory research, is born of extensive participation, where shale gas exists as a contested technology and a 'boundary object'. Similar opportunities to influence energy governance have not been available in the UK or Poland, and the cautious approach of the Dutch government, curtailed by the knowledge of a deficit in public support, does contribute to a governance model encompassing, at least on the surface, dimensions of procedural justice and democratic decision-making. Van de Graaf, Haesebrouck and Debaere (2017) propose that the Dutch government are currently employing a 'precautionary' approach, deciding to cease commercial exploration of shale gas resources during the current decade, as have Germany. Thus, SGE is not formally opposed in the Netherlands, but rather has been delayed and restricted since 2013 (ibid.) while further research is conducted.

Comparing the US, the UK, Poland and the Netherlands, it appears that a separation is occurring with regards to the pursuit of SGE. The US continues exploitation activities in supportive states, empowered by the emergence of an export market for US shale gas, however, 'public' opportunities to influence state-level decision-making, even after almost 20 years of exploitation, remain limited. Despite a recent decision in Scotland to ban 'fracking' following a public consultation process, the UK Government in Westminster continues to exhibit a shale-supportive governance approach. However, it has proposed, in conjunction with the SWF, that local communities should be directly involved in shale gas decision-making and associated benefits provision. Conversely, progress on shale gas exploration is stymied in Europe, predominantly for economic reasons in Poland, despite broad public support, and for reasons of risk-based uncertainty and public support in the Netherlands, while an effective moratorium is in place in Germany, as discussed by Töller and Böcher in Chapter 5 in this volume. It appears the greatest opportunity for public participation exists in the UK and the Netherlands. However, recent changes to planning and trespass legislation and continued vocal governmental support in the UK suggest that participation may be limited to influencing how pre-determined shale gas futures are managed as opposed to whether shale gas exploitation will occur, whereas the Dutch government exhibit a greater desire to make more scientifically and democratically-informed decisions. In the US and Poland, it appears market-based governance will continue to steer progress on SGE, supplemented by public participation but in limited forms.

We know that a 'diverse set of publics' (Pidgeon, 2011: 2) exist in energy communities. Cotton echoes this, noting that the 'social and environmental impacts of shale gas exploration are experienced differently by different social groups' (2015: 1945). We respond to research calls such as those of Cairney, Fischer and Ingold, who state that as shale gas policy in the UK moves from the current 'tentative pro-fracking stage at the centre' (i.e. government) towards new local-scale developments, more information is required on 'beliefs, preferences, and strategies of actors in devolved and local areas' (2015: 17). We argue that this is internationally relevant and that an approach is required enabling the exploration of preferences and beliefs in different geographic contexts. We respond to recent calls for researchers to examine the drivers of public opinion on shale gas, and 'the conditions under which contested technologies such as fracking acquire a "social licence"' (Van de Graaf *et al.*, 2017: 15). We argue that deliberative stakeholder dialogue provides opportunities to pursue such research objectives, while revealing stakeholder priorities and knowledge to influence decision-making.

We propose that a systemic, participatory, community-led approach is required to achieve any sense of how participation that is procedurally just and fair can be defined, in a community setting and within the context of energy developments, enhancing governance procedures and achieving social justice. Such an approach incorporates multi-directional dialogue, where local stake-holders are empowered to impact and legitimize decision outcomes, while understanding stakeholder experiences, priorities and opinions. This facilitates a move away from the technocratic D-A-D approach (Decide, Announce, Defend) toward the democratic and collaborative E-D-D approach (Engage, Deliberate, Decide) of governance and decision-making. Scholars have recently called for more public dialogues on hydraulic fracturing which explore topics such as public health, environmental and economic risks and visions of energy futures (Dodge, 2015; Dodge & Metze, 2017), and highlight 'the range of dis-course coalitions' (Dodge & Metze, 2017: 9).

To address this, Whitton *et al.* (2015) have previously proposed an approach with the aim of achieving a form of legitimacy, whereby communities derive social priorities through 'community visioning'. Residents convene to identify and debate community values, highlight current issues and future opportunities, and co-develop plans to achieve an agreed vision (Ames, 2006; Cuthill, 2004). This approach promotes democracy in shale gas decisions and public participa-tion in energy decisions through dialogue between government, industry and local communities, enhancing procedural justice in shale gas decisions that advances a concept of fairness. As such, we argue that it is imperative to ensure social justice is pursued as part of SGG, through dialogue-based stakeholder col-laborations and knowledge generation, and ensuring fairer processes to deliver more just outcomes. In this respect the question asked should be: 'Is the process perceived as fair, and is the outcome equitable?' It is based on the assumption that a diverse range of social priorities is held by stakeholder and social groups within communities, which are relevant to shale gas scenarios. By engaging with different community and stakeholder groups, different values, experiences, atti-tudes and priorities can emerge, reflecting the social heterogeneity of com-munities both internally and internationally, which is then visible to governance actors. We agree with Dodge and Metze: controversial technologies should be studied from an interpretive perspective, whereby the way in which opponents and proponents frame technologies influences 'their social accepta-bility, their future development, and ultimately political decision-making, regu-lation, and application' (2017: 9) and is better understood. As a result, more informed, sustainable and legitimate energy decisions can be made within communities on shale gas development. Also, power imbalances, such as those highlighted in this chapter, can be addressed.

Conclusion

We have discussed the opportunities that systems of energy governance present to the public to participate and become involved in shale gas decisions in the US, the UK, Poland and the Netherlands. SGG in the US has been shown to facilitate and catalyze its development while providing limited opportunities for citizens to formally influence decisions and developments, with hearings being the common forum of public participation. In the UK, the rhetoric of the SWF consultation document and recent court rulings in Northern England highlight the tone of the governmental approach and position on participation, and what opportunities are 'fair' and 'right' for 'shale gas communities' to expect in regard to funding and participation in decision-making.

We also discuss the almost complete absence of public participation in shale gas decision-making in Poland, perhaps in part due to a perceived widespread support for the technology. However, despite government rhetoric on energy security and continued technological support, exploration is now retreating due to the economic realities of oil price fluctuations and the abundance of cheap coal. In the Netherlands, despite early assumptions by government that citizens would perceive SGE as they do conventional gas production, authorities appear to have adopted a more considered, cautious approach to SGG. Upon awareness of widespread public opposition to the technology, a large-scale public consultation was held by the government, resulting in a moratorium. What is interesting here is how the public debate on shale gas has led to wider discussions on the role, utility and necessity of shale gas, so that the future of shale gas in the Netherlands remains uncertain.

It is clear that despite engagement rhetoric and associated processes, public influence on shale gas decisions is broadly perceived to be either minimal or only curtailed in light of public opinion or market-based economics. In response, we propose a conceptualized framework providing an approach to public participation, based on priority exploration through dialogue. The framework highlights notions of transparency, accountability, and social and procedural justice as key components, important to achieving more informed, sustainable and legitimate shale gas governance.

References

Adamus, W., & Florkowski, W. J. (2016). The evolution of shale gas development and energy security in Poland: presenting a hierarchical choice of priorities. *Energy Research & Social Science, 20*, 168–178. doi:10.1016/j.erss.2016.08.010.

Ames, S. (2006). Community Visioning. In F. R. Steiner & K. Butler (Eds.), *Planning and Urban Design Standards* (pp. 39–40). Hoboken, NJ: John Wiley and Sons, Inc.

B.P.C. (2012). *Fracking Poll Results*. Retrieved from Sussex, UK:

Bomberg, E. (2017). Fracking and framing in transatlantic perspective: a comparison of shale politics in the US and European Union. *Journal of Transatlantic Studies*, 15(2), 101–120. doi:10.1080/14794012.2016.1268789.

Brasier, K. J., Jalbert, K., Kinchy, A. J., Brantley, S. L., & Unroe, C. (2017). Barriers to sharing water quality data: experiences from the Shale Network. *Journal of Environmental Planning and Management*, 60(12), 2103–2121. doi:10.1080/09640568.2016.127 6435.

Brasier, K., Lee, B., Stedman, R., & Weigle, J. (2011). Local champions speak out: Pennsylvania's community watershed organizations. In L. W. Morton & S. S. Brown (Eds.), *Pathways for Getting to Better Water Quality: The Citizen Effect* (pp. 133–144). New York: Springer.

Buday, A. (2017). The home rule advantage: motives and outcomes of local anti-fracking mobilization. *Social Currents*, 4(6), 575–593. doi:10.1177/2329496516686614.

Cairney, P., Fischer, M., & Ingold, K. (2015). Hydraulic fracturing policy in the UK: coalition, cooperation and opposition in the face of uncertainty. Paper presented at the Political Studies Association Annual International Conference, Sheffield, UK. Available at: www.psa.ac.uk/sites/default/files/conference/papers/2015/Cairney%20 Fischer%20Ingold%20fracking%20in%20the%20UK%2025%20Feb%202015.pdf.

Cotton, M. (2015). Stakeholder perspectives on shale gas fracking: a Q-method study of environmental discourses. *Environment and Planning A*, 47(9), 1944–1962. doi:10.1177/ 0308518x15597134.

Cotton, M., Rattle, I., & Van Alstine, J. (2014). Shale gas policy in the United Kingdom: an argumentative discourse analysis. *Energy Policy*, 73, 427–438. doi:10.1016/ j.enpol.2014.05.031.

Cuppen, E., Pesch, U., Remmerswaal, S., & Taanman, M. (2016). Normative diversity, conflict and transition: shale gas in the Netherlands. *Technological Forecasting and Social Change*. doi:10.1016/j.techfore.2016.11.004.

Cuthill, M. (2004). Community visioning: facilitating informed citizen participation in local area planning on the Gold Coast. *Urban Policy and Research*, 22(4), 427–445. doi:10.1080/0811114042000296335.

Dignum, M., Correlje, A., Cuppen, E., Pesch, U., & Taebi, B. (2016). Contested technologies and design for values: the case of shale gas. *Science and Engineering Ethics*, 22(4), 1171–1191. doi:10.1007/s11948-015-9685-6.

Dodge, J. (2015). The deliberative potential of civil society organizations: framing hydraulic fracturing in New York. *Policy Studies*, 36(3), 249–266. doi:10.1080/0144287 2.2015.1065967.

Dodge, J., & Metze, T. (2017). Hydraulic fracturing as an interpretive policy problem: lessons on energy controversies in Europe and the U.S.A. *Journal of Environmental Policy & Planning*, 19(1), 1–13. doi:10.1080/1523908x.2016.1277947.

Dokshin, F. A. (2016). Whose backyard and what's at issue? Spatial and ideological dynamics of local opposition to fracking in New York State, 2010 to 2013. *American Sociological Review*, 81(5), 921–948. doi:10.1177/0003122416663929.

Energy Council. (2011). Advisory letter on the emergence of unconventional gas. The Hague: Energy Council.

Fung, A. (2015). Putting the public back into governance: the challenges of citizen participation and its future. *Public Administration Review*, 75(4), 513–522.

Goldthau, A., & LaBelle, M. (2016). The power of policy regimes: explaining shale gas policy divergence in Bulgaria and Poland. *Review of Policy Research*, 33(6), 603–622.

Gross, C. (2007). Community perspectives of wind energy in Australia: the application of a justice and community fairness framework to increase social acceptance. *Energy Policy*, 35(5), 2727–2736. doi:10.1016/j.enpol.2006.12.013.

HM Treasury. (2013). *Harnessing the Potential of the UK's Natural Resources: A Fiscal Regime for Shale Gas*. London: TSO. Retrieved from www.gov.uk/government/consultations/ harnessing-the-potential-of-the-uks-natural-resources-a-fiscal-regime-for-shale-gas

HM Treasury. (2016). *Shale Wealth Fund: Consultation*. London: TSO.

Howard-Grenville, J., Nash, J., & Coglianese, C. (2008). Constructing the license to operate: internal factors and their influence on corporate environmental decisions. *Law & Policy*, 30(1), 73–107.

IEA. (2012). *Golden Rules for a Golden Age of Gas: World Energy Outlook – Special Report on Unconventional Gas*. Retrieved from: www.worldenergyoutlook.org/media/weoweb site/2012/goldenrules/weo2012_goldenrulesreport.pdf

Innes, J. E., & Booher, D. E. (2004). Reframing public participation: strategies for the 21st century. *Planning Theory & Practice*, 5(4), 419–436. doi:10.1080/1464935042000 293170.

Jalbert, K. (2016). Building knowledge infrastructures for empowerment: a study of grass-roots water monitoring networks in the Marcellus Shale. *Science and Technology Studies*, 29(2), 26–43.

Johnson, C., & Boersma, T. (2013). Energy (in)security in Poland: the case of shale gas. *Energy Policy*, 53, 389–399. doi:10.1016/j.enpol.2012.10.068.

LaBelle, M. (2017). A state of fracking: building Poland's national innovation capacity for shale gas. *Energy Research & Social Science*, 23, 26–35. doi:10.1016/j. erss.2016.11.003.

Lebel, L., Anderies, J. M., Campbell, B. *et al.* (2006). Governance and the capacity to manage resilience in regional social-ecological systems. *Ecology and Society*, 11(1), 19.

Ligtvoet, A., Cuppen, E., Di Ruggero, O. *et al.* (2016). New future perspectives through constructive conflict: exploring the future of gas in the Netherlands. *Futures*, 78–79, 19–33. doi:10.1016/j.futures.2016.03.008.

Lis, A., & Stankiewicz, P. (2017). Framing shale gas for policy-making in Poland. *Journal of Environmental Policy & Planning*, 19(1), 53–71. doi:10.1080/1523908x.2016.1143355.

MacCoun, R. J. (2005). Voice, control, and belonging: the double-edged sword of procedural fairness. *Annual Review of Law and Social Science*, 1(1), 171–201. doi:10.1146/ annurev.lawsocsci.1.041604.115958.

Magis, K., & Shinn, C. (2009). Emergent themes of social sustainability. In J. Dillard, V. Dujon, & M. C. King (Eds.), *Understanding the Social Aspects of Sustainability* (pp. 15–44). New York: Routledge.

McGowan, F. (2014). Regulating innovation: European responses to shale gas development. *Environmental Politics*, 23(1), 41–58. doi:10.1080/09644016.2012.740939.

Metze, T. (2017). Fracking the debate: frame shifts and boundary work in Dutch decision making on shale gas. *Journal of Environmental Policy & Planning*, 19(1), 35–52. doi:10. 1080/1523908x.2014.941462.

Neslen, A. (2015). Polish shale industry collapsing as number of licenses nearly halves. *Guardian*, 9 October 2015. Retrieved from: www.theguardian.com/environment/2015/ oct/09/polish-shale-industry-collapsing-as-number-of-licenses-nearly-halves

Pidgeon, N. (2011). *Memorandum on Public Attitudes and Nuclear Power Submitted to the House of Lords Science and Technology Committee Inquiry on 'Nuclear R&D Capabilities'*. 28 June 2011. Retrieved from: file://lha-003/pers-F/0007A1E0/Downloads/Memoran dum%20on%20Public%20Attitudes%20and%20Nuclear%20Power%20.pdf

P.M.E. (2016). Shale gas exploration status in Poland as of April 2016. *Info Shale: Shale Gas & Oil from Shale*. Retrieved from: http://infolupki.pgi.gov.pl/en/exploration-status/news/shale-gas-exploration-status-poland-april-2016

Rasch, E. D., & Köhne, M. (2016). Hydraulic fracturing, energy transition and political engagement in the Netherlands: the energetics of citizenship. *Energy Research & Social Science*, *13*, 106–115. doi:10.1016/j.erss.2015.12.014.

RCT. (2013). *Eagle Ford Shale Task Force Report*. Retrieved from: www.rrc.state.tx.us/media/8051/eagle_ford_task_force_report-0313.pdf

Rijksoverheid. (2012). Onderzoek schaliegas eind 2012 klaar. *Nieuwsbericht* [online]. 19 June 2012

Rootes, C. (2006). Explaining the outcomes of campaigns against waste incinerators in England: community, ecology, political opportunities, and policy contexts. In A. M. McCright & T. N. Clark (Eds.), *Community and Ecology* (vol. 10, pp. 179–198). Bingley: Emerald Publishing.

Stevens, P. (2012). *The 'Shale Gas Revolution': Developments and Changes*. Chatham House, London: Energy, Environment and Resources Dept.

Taebi, B., Correljé, A., Cuppen, E., van de Grift, E., & Pesch, U. (2016). Ethics and impact assessments of large energy projects. Paper presented at IEEE 2016: IEEE International Symposium on Ethics in Engineering, Science and Technology (ETHICS), 1–5.

Thibaut, J., & Walker, L. (1975). *Procedural Justice*. Hillsdale, NJ: Erlbaum.

Van de Graaf, T., Haesebrouck, T., & Debaere, P. (2017). Fractured politics? The comparative regulation of shale gas in Europe. *Journal of European Public Policy*, 1–18. doi:10.1080/13501763.2017.1301985.

Webler, T., Tuler, S., & Krueger, R. (2001). What is a good public participation process? Five perspectives from the public. *Environmental Management*, *27*(3), 435–450.

Whitton, J., Brasier, K., Charnley-Parry, I., & Cotton, M. (2017). Shale gas governance in the United Kingdom and the United States: opportunities for public participation and the implications for social justice. *Energy Research & Social Science*, *26*, 11–22. doi:10.1016/j.erss.2017.01.015.

Whitton, J., Parry, I. M., Akiyoshi, M., & Lawless, W. (2015). Conceptualizing a social sustainability framework for energy infrastructure decisions. *Energy Research & Social Science*, *8*, 127–138. doi:10.1016/j.erss.2015.05.010.

15 Shale gas development in England

A tale of two mineral planning authorities

Imogen Rattle, Tudor Baker and James Van Alstine

Introduction

The summer of 2016 was a tumultuous one for the United Kingdom. The vote to leave the European Union, after a campaign which many found both confused and confusing, revealed deep societal divides. The ramifications will take decades to manifest, but even as the national drama plays out, the wheels of the land use planning process continue to turn. Over the course of the year, two companies received planning permission to undertake exploratory hydraulic fracturing (fracking) for shale gas. These are the first planning consents for fracking in England for over five years. But even with favourable geological conditions, commercial production remains some years away and events to date suggest progress is unlikely to be smooth. The UK is a unitary state, retaining sovereignty and regulatory authority within central government, and this feature, combined with a property regime which vests hydrocarbon ownership in the Crown, gives national government a particularly prominent role in the national debate. The inherent contradictions between the centralizing tendencies of English shale gas policy and the Conservative Government's Localism Agenda is noted by Matthew Cotton (2016) in his review of the ethics and environmental justice issues of UK fracking policy. In this chapter, we expand upon this theme and show how the national systems of policy, planning and practice place communities opposed to shale gas development (SGD) in direct conflict with central government, a battle made manifest in the planning process. Drawing on an analysis of public submissions to two planning hearings, we find local identity and perceived democratic deficit form prominent themes in motivating local opposition. Analysis also reveals differences in the ability of communities to resist the centralizing tendencies of planning consultations, specifically highlighting direct historical experience with fossil fuel industries; the role of local MPs; and pre-existing civic capacity as factors which condition citizen responses and the ability of activists to mobilize citizens. We then undertake a comparative international analysis which illuminates how the systems of government and hydrocarbon ownership have shaped the evolution of national debate, and conclude with some remarks about the future prospects for shale gas in England.

Shale gas

Shale gas is predominantly methane, extracted via horizontal drilling into a shale bed followed by high volume slick-water fracturing. Alongside coalbed methane and tar sands, it forms one part of the trifecta known as 'unconventional hydrocarbons'. Large-scale discovery of shale gas in America was heralded as a game-changer for US energy policy (Gény, 2010), however, reports of damage caused by the industry are widespread. Local and global environmental concerns are well documented (Jackson *et al.*, 2014; Newell & Raimi, 2014) and as the industry matures, there is a growing body of evidence documenting negative health (McCoy & Munro, 2016) and social-psychological impacts (Jacquet & Stedman, 2014) on local communities. As a result, there is increasing local resistance to the industry and SGD is presently banned or under moratoria in parts of Canada, the US and Australia, and in the entirety of France, Germany and Bulgaria. In the UK, Scotland, Wales and Northern Ireland have likewise imposed moratoria, leaving England the sole home nation pursuing SGD. Here, activity is focused primarily on the Bowland shale, a geological formation running beneath the north of the country.

Development of the English debate

Cuadrilla Resources undertook the first fracking in England at Preese Hall, Lancashire, in 2011. The process caused two minor seismic events (Green, Styles, & Baptie, 2012), following which the government imposed a moratorium. An independent review concluded the process was safe if adequately regulated (Green *et al.*, 2012) and the following month then Prime Minister, David Cameron, announced his intention to 'go all out for shale' (Watt, 2014), a policy predicated on the national needs for energy security, economic growth and lower carbon emissions (DECC DCLG, 2015). While leaving the EU alters the institutional and legislative frameworks surrounding delivery of this ambition, as of 2018, the policy is unchanged. It is a stance increasingly at odds with public opinion, as support for shale gas dwindles, in part due well-publicized local protests against development (O'Hara, Humphrey, Andersson-Hudson, & Knight, 2016). Ministers hope opposition will ease once the industry is established, a position made explicit in a leaked Cabinet letter:

> One of the hurdles to overcome to develop a more favourable public attitude is that nobody in the UK has seen or experienced a fracking operation.... We need some exploration wells, to clearly demonstrate that shale exploration can be done cleanly and safely.
>
> (reported in Hope, 2016)

Obtaining approval for exploration wells, however, is no easy task. The first step in the process is for gas companies to obtain the appropriate consents from the regulatory authorities. The following section outlines the approval process for

SGD, shows how the characteristic features of the English system of central government limit opportunities for public engagement on this issue, and in doing so reveals why the planning process has become the main site of contention in the English debate.

Planning and regulation

There are four main bodies involved in the regulation of shale gas. In brief:

1. The Oil and Gas Authority (OGA), a government-owned company, assesses operator competence and financial capacity.
2. The Environment Agency (EA), a non-departmental public body under the Department for Environment, Farming and Rural Affairs, issues permits for emissions to air, soil and water.
3. The Health and Safety Executive (HSE), a non-departmental public body under the Department for Work and Pensions, considers well integrity and borehole legislation compliance.
4. Mineral Planning Authorities (MPAs) adjudicate on local issues, such as noise, transport and dust, using guidance issued by the Department for Communities and Local Government (DCLG).

These arrangements present several challenges to citizens seeking to influence national policy. First, there is the complexity of the system, neither easily understood nor navigated by those unfamiliar with the structures of Whitehall. Each of the regulators falls under a separate parent department and at present there is no central body to coordinate work. Perhaps counterintuitively, the Department for Business, Energy and Industrial Strategy – BEIS – plays no part in the day-to-day regulation of shale gas. This is a deliberate omission intended to ensure safety is not compromised by the political imperative to maximize energy production (Cullen, 1990), but also removes any obligation from BEIS to consult on the issue. The vertical division of responsibilities between parent departments, which deal with policy, and regulating bodies, which deal with implementation, provides a second barrier to citizens seeking to engage with policy-makers. This structure is intended to allow staff to focus upon core tasks but also serves to distance policy-makers from the effects of their policies (James, 2001). Finally, of all the regulatory bodies involved in SGD only MPAs, usually county councils, are locally situated and elected. Again, this is not a feature unique to shale gas; the UK has a century-long culture of centralism, of an extent unusual even among unitary states (Hestletine, 2012). It was in recognition of this imbalance of power that the Coalition Government of 2010–15 introduced the Localism Act (2011), with the stated intention of empowering local communities. As this chapter will detail, the progress of the shale gas debate is causing campaigners in the affected communities to express scepticism about the strength of this commitment.

Effectively barred from engaging at the national level, the public are left with three officially sanctioned routes to participate on SGD. These are illustrated in

Figure 15.1. The first is via operator-led consultation. The industry body, UKOOG, requires its members to 'identify and proactively address local issues and concerns' (UKOOG, n.d.), but the outcomes of these consultations have no binding force and the perceived vested interest of industry leaves their impartiality open to question. The second route is via EA consultation on the environmental permits issued to operators. Permits are issued following consideration of the specific characteristics of each well site, but the consultation is constrained to technical issues of pollution prevention (EA, 2015) which provides limited scope for layperson input. This leaves the planning process as the main forum for local communities to voice their concerns, but the scope of this consultation is tightly defined by nationally-issued planning policy.

Overarching planning policy for England is set out in the National Planning Policy Framework (NPPF), the stated aim of which is to empower local people to shape their surroundings in a sustainable manner. Ancillary to the requirement for sustainable development, however, the NPPF also advises MPAs to place 'great weight' on the benefits of mineral extraction (DCLG, 2012, p. 34). In further guidance specific to onshore oil and gas, DCLG advises MPAs to assume the regimes for regulating health and safety, and environmental issues will be implemented effectively and reminds them they 'should not consider demand for, or consider alternatives to, oil and gas resources' (DCLG, 2013, p. 15). Read in sum, therefore, planning guidance on SGD limits the role of MPAs to assessing material planning considerations, broadly defined as matters 'relating to the use and development of land' (DCLG, 2015 p. 14) and excludes matters of health, and local and global environmental effects, three of the areas where SGD is most controversial.

Even operating within these parameters, MPAs face no straightforward task. The complexity of the issues surrounding SGD means it is commonplace for gas companies to submit extensive documentation to support their case, and for opponents to submit a high volume of representations in response. The size and complexity of applications leave MPAs struggling to determine the cases within statutory timeframes. Frustrated by the continued delays, in August 2015 the Communities Secretary announced he reserved the right to determine shale gas applications in place of MPAs which repeatedly failed to meet deadlines, and would consider calling in appeals against planning decisions to refuse applications for SGD (DECC DCLG, 2015). It is against this backdrop of planning gridlock and increasing ministerial frustration, that the public hearings which form the subject of this chapter, took place.

Method

We undertook a qualitative thematic analysis of the public representations made to two planning hearings, through an inductive analysis of the webcast proceedings. These were the first planning determinations on fracking in England since the lifting of the moratorium in 2012. Details of the sessions are provided in Table 15.1. Members of the public had 3–4 minutes to present their

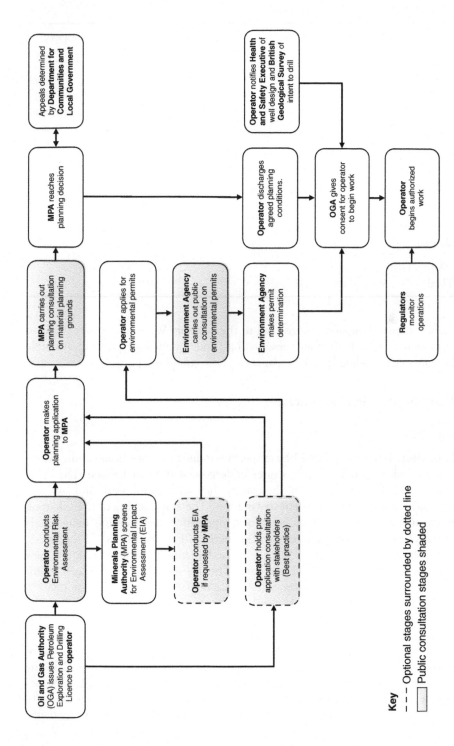

Key

Figure 15.1 Opportunities for public engagement within the approval process for shale gas operations.

Table 15.1 Details of planning hearings

Mineral Planning Authority	Lancashire County Council	North Yorkshire County Council
Applicant	Cuadrilla	Third Energy
Nature of application	To construct well pads, drill and frack up to eight wells at two sites – Preston New Road and Roseacre Wood	To frack one existing well at existing production site near Kirby Misperton
Nature of hearing	Appeal against decision to refuse planning permission	Planning hearing
Public sessions	17, 25 Feb; 8, 10 March 2016	20, 23 May 2016
Speaking in support of application	15	6
Neutral	3	2
Against	123	81
Total	141	89

views or have their submissions read to the hearing. We further contextualized our analysis with participant observation, and a review of publicly available documents, including local newspapers and government reports.

Planning decisions in context

The Fylde

Lancashire is a county shaped by extractive industries, once home to an extensive coal-mining industry, it has since undergone deindustrialization. The Fylde is a coastal plain to the west of the county. It is an affluent, semi-rural area and a popular tourist and retirement destination. The first fracking in the UK took place in Lancashire in 2011, and local opposition is becoming increasingly entrenched as the debate matures (Bomberg, 2015). In July 2015, the MPA, Lancashire County Council (LCC) refused planning permission for a new exploration site near Preston New Road. The decision was hailed by campaigners as a victory for local opinion, since it was made against the recommendation of the council's Planning Officer and despite legal advice that refusal could be appealed (LCC, 2015b).

In spring 2016, the Planning Inspectorate held an inquiry into the decision. It was clear from the outset the hearing was primarily symbolic since the Communities Secretary had previously announced he would call in the appeal on the grounds the decision had more than local significance (Boulton, 2015). Nonetheless, the public sessions were well attended. Those speaking in support of SGD were comparatively few in number. They focused on economic benefits, energy security, and the missed opportunity for Lancashire if it failed to adopt the industry. Those speaking against SGD often took a precautionary approach, focusing on the uncertain, and sometimes unknowable, risks of shale gas exploitation and the potentially serious consequences should an accident occur. Frequently mentioned concerns included health and local environmental effects; the stigma fracking would place on the local industries of farming and tourism; fears for future generation; visual impacts; and disruption to the rural way of life. In common with previous studies on locally unwanted land use (Devine-Wright, 2009), disruption to place attachment and place identity was a commonly cited factor prompting opposition. Concerns about energy policy, regulatory capacity and climate change also featured, but these were less frequently mentioned.

As the inquiry continued, two overarching themes emerged. One was the distributive justice implications of siting SGD in Lancashire, far away from London and the more affluent South. 'We're almost like disposable assets it seems to me, when I hear what's coming out of government. We're not considered. We're up North for starters, so we're disadvantaged there,' one business owner observed. The second was lack of democratic legitimacy. Residents expressed a profound sense of injustice that SGD would be forced on them despite the decision of their locally-elected councillors and contrary to the principles of localism. The chair of the Planning Committee which refused the original application, was forthright about the apparent double standards at play:

> The most important element for us councillors … is that we do not pre-determine the outcome of any application … I note that there is no such impartial approach within central government … [the Communities Secretary] has already made clear his views in support of fracking.

It was an observation which appeared justified when in October 2016 the Communities Secretary ruled to allow the application.

Ryedale

Across the Pennine Hills to Yorkshire, Kirby Misperton is a small village in the district of Ryedale. More sparsely populated than the Fylde, Ryedale is a rural, agricultural area and likewise home to an older population. Conventional gas wells have operated in Ryedale since 1995 and in May 2015, Third Energy, owner of the Kirby Misperton gas field, applied to the MPA, North Yorkshire County Council (NYCC), for planning permission to undertake exploratory fracking of its existing KM8 well. The final determination took place in May 2016.

Since the scope of both hearings were limited to material planning considerations, it is unsurprising that many of the arguments presented followed similar lines to those heard in Lancashire, however, there were some notable differences in emphasis. Speakers supporting SGD expressed scepticism about the motivations of anti-fracking groups, claiming their campaign would do more damage to Ryedale's reputation than fracking itself. A common theme was that much local opposition was due to misinformation rather than factually based. Several speakers referred to the uncontentious operation of the local gas field in support of this belief: 'What a difference the word "fracking" makes,' one industry consultant observed. Speakers against SGD focused on the effects on health, local businesses and the visual impacts on the countryside. They also expressed scepticism about the trustworthiness of government regulators, with the local MP receiving particular criticism for his perceived bias towards the industry. Themes of local empowerment were also present, but played a less prominent role than in Lancashire. The potential climate change effects of shale gas, however, formed a significant theme and the submissions included testimony from a former climate change diplomat. These arguments did not persuade the committee, whose chair had noted at the outset, 'it is not for us to decide county policy or even national policy on fracking', and they voted in accordance with their Planning Officer's recommendation to approve the application.

A tale of two mineral planning authorities

While these hearings provide only a snapshot of local concerns, a comparison between them nonetheless yields a number of insights into the progress of the English shale gas debate. It was apparent that while the 'bad governance' storyline identified by Bomberg (2015) was an important factor in motivating people to speak, particularly in Lancashire, many of the frames and narratives referred to by opponents to SGD were less like those detailed in the national level studies of Cotton, Rattle and Van Alstine (2014) and Hilson (2015) and more akin to the place-attachment narratives which frequently surround planning proposals (Vorkinn & Riese, 2001). Significantly, local people in favour of SGD, while fewer in number, also referenced place attachment in their arguments; in fact, both groups shared a goal: to improve, or protect, the local area. What differed was how they perceived SGD would help or hinder this endeavour. Age, sex, education, political affiliation and environmental attitudes all influence perceptions of SGD (Andersson-Hudson, Knight, Humphrey, & O'Hara, 2016; Boudet *et al.*, 2014; Veenstra, Lyons, & Fowler-Dawson, 2016) but the role of place identity appears complex and multilateral. An online survey of UK attitudes to SGD finds higher place attachment is correlated with a more positive assessment (Whitmarsh *et al.*, 2015), while a more recent survey of residents of the Marcellus Shale in the US suggests different in perceptions of SGD may be explained by differences in approach rather than values: those opposed seek to maintain their community in its present state, while supporters believe in using resources to promote the overall well-being of their community (Evensen, Stedman, & Brown-Steiner, 2017). The role of competing perceptions of place identity in influencing attitudes to SGD is at present under-explored in the English context, and we suggest it merits further study.

Our research also provided a number of insights into how local context may influence community responses to SGD. There are demographic similarities between the two communities of Ryedale and the Fylde. Both are rural, Conservative-voting constituencies, home to an educated population, and a higher than average number of retirees (ONS, 2011). It is an age-group which has limited interests in the jobs which shale gas might offer, and the time and resources to engage in the planning process, however, while the number of speakers at each hearing was broadly similar, the total number of written submissions received by each MPA in advance of its determination varied significantly – 4,000 in total in North Yorkshire (NYCC, 2016), 18,000 in opposition in Lancashire (LCC, 2015a). The widespread use of template emails limits the value of this metric as an absolute measure, nonetheless it provides some indication of the level of success local groups achieved in mobilizing public opinion. A second indicator is the willingness of councillors in Lancashire to go against the advice of their Planning Officer to reject a shale gas application, a course of action which councillors in North Yorkshire showed no signs of imitating. Our analysis of submissions to the planning hearings suggest three factors which may have contributed to the capacity of communities to mobilize anti-fracking support.

The first factor is familiarity and comfort with fossil fuel extraction. Research from the USA shows communities draw from a history of local extractive industries to frame the impacts of SGD (Ladd, 2014) and suggests living in an area with active oil and gas development can increase support for the industry (Boudet, Bugden, Zanocco, & Maibach, 2016). Two UK-based national surveys on attitudes to shale gas also support the proposition that prior knowledge of the industry is associated with more favourable attitudes (Stedman, Evensen, O'Hara, & Humphrey, 2016; Whitmarsh et al., 2015), findings which align with the wider risk management literature showing unfamiliar risks are perceived as more threatening (Covello, 1983). In the Fylde, whose residents frame their experiences of SGD in the context of the seismic events at Preese Hall, trust in the industry appears irrevocably lost. In Ryedale, where conventional gas wells have operated for decades with little controversy, familiarity may indeed increase acceptance.

A second factor is the presence or absence of local advocates for SGD. Here the different approaches of the local MPs appear noteworthy. Caught between his party's pro-shale gas policies and entrenched local opposition, Mark Menzies (Fylde) treads a cautious middle ground, not outright rejecting the industry but emphasizing the need for strong regulatory enforcement. By contrast, Kevin Hollinrake (Thirsk and Malton) is enthusiastic in his support for SGD and received repeated criticism for this perceived partiality at the North Yorkshire hearing. The lack of a pro-fracking advocacy coalition is one factor noted by Dufour, Bherer, and Rothmayr (2012) in their analysis of how environmental groups obtained a moratorium on SGD in Quebec and the lack of strong local voices in favour of SGD in the Fylde makes it difficult for supporters of the industry to counter the accusations of democratic illegitimacy.

Most important, however, is likely the role of civic capacity. Obach (2015) identifies the presence of pre-existing environmental groups and networks as a key factor in mobilizing the campaign which persuaded New York State officials to pass a moratorium on shale gas. The importance of civic capacity is likewise stressed by Vasi, Walker, Johnson, and Tan (2015) in their study of anti-shale gas mobilization in the Marcellus Shale and used by Eaton and Kinchy (2016) to explain the lack of collective mobilization against SGD by communities in Saskatchewan and Pennsylvania. Community groups in the Fylde began mobilizing against SGD in 2011 and have since amassed significant social capital experience in navigating the complexities of the regulatory system. Anna Szolucha's comparative analysis of the Lancashire case, in Chapter 16 in this volume, documents the extent to which local residents felt obliged to tailor their representations to planning hearings so they fell within the boundaries of material planning considerations. In Ryedale, organized opposition is relatively recent, dating from around 2014. The increased prominence of the climate change narratives presented at the North Yorkshire hearing may provide one indication that residents have less familiarity with the technical content of the planning guidance, which places such matters out of scope.

International comparison

As the contention around SGD continues, the topic is generating a growing academic literature documenting the effects of the industry on communities across the Global North, and their various strategies of dissent. Research from the US, Canada, and Australia reveals striking similarities in how local people report their experience of living in areas targeted for SGD: they speak of disempowerment, uncertainty, vulnerability and a way of life under threat (Sherval & Hardiman, 2014; Szolucha, 2016b; Willow & Wylie, 2014), narratives which we too heard in our research. Such accounts do not fit easily within the framework of English planning law, which favours a technical fact-based approach. Studies of the discourses used to frame unconventional hydrocarbons in the USA (Evensen, 2015) and Australia (Espig & de Rijke, 2016) show how debates in these countries have become similarly scientized, with calls to restrict discussion to emotionless, de-politicized facts. But an over-reliance on the primacy of facts has not always proved a successful strategy for shale gas advocates. One common finding across jurisdictions which have imposed moratoria is how anti-fracking groups used the scientific uncertainty about SGD to bring facts into question and argue for a precautionary approach (Dodge & Lee, 2015; Dufour et al., 2012; Metze, 2014; Stephan, 2016). This is not a change in emphasis which the government in England appears prepared to countenance; at present, there is no forum where the uncertainties of SGD form a legitimate topic of discussion, with the result, as Chris Hilson notes in a review of English planning law and practice, that the 'positive government framing of fracking inevitably wins through' (2015, p. 157). Denied a discursive space to contest this framing, it is unsurprising the lack of democratic legitimacy is becoming a prominent concern for local communities. Such accusations of heavy-handed central control are particularly difficult to rebut in the English context, where there is no buffering state-level layer to provide an intermediary; and they provide a sticky problem for a government committed to increasing local power and whose citizens recently voted to leave the EU under a campaign slogan of 'taking back control'.

Perhaps one of the greatest ironies of the English case is that the twin features of the unitary system of government and state ownership of hydrocarbons which provide central government the means and motivation to promote SGD, may also present it with its greatest hurdles in realizing this ambition. Research from the USA highlights the importance of the American private system of hydrocarbon ownership in generating community support for SGD (Kriesky, Goldstein, Zell, & Beach, 2013). Without it, the industry provides relatively little benefit to local residents, who are nonetheless expected to bear the associated risks for the national benefit. In Australia, which operates a similar hydrocarbon property regime to the UK, there are similar accusations of a lack of democratic legitimacy in the development of unconventional hydrocarbons (Curran, 2016) and, there too, local government has opposed unconventional gas development on behalf of its residents (Turton, 2015). But while in Australia, state-level governments in Victoria and Northern Territory have acted to impose moratoria on SGD, in England, there is no intermediate body with the authority to interpose on behalf of communities in Ryedale and the Fylde. Instead, lacking an attractive hydrocarbon ownership regime, central government is forging ahead in the hope familiarity will generate acceptance. It is far from clear this strategy will be successful. Even in Ryedale, a community which has hosted onshore gas extraction for over 20 years, there is significant local opposition to SGD, and in the Fylde it appears the government's actions have increased resistance rather than assuaging it – undermining trust in regulatory agencies and amplifying perceptions of risk on the part of local residents, as Anna Szolucha's work, in this volume, reveals. Further, if civic capacity is an important force in enabling communities to mobilize opposition to SGD, as our study suggests, then the national system of regulation may support them in this endeavour. A single system of law and policy allows the easy transfer of successful strategies of opposition between communities and could present central government with a national coalition of resistance far better resourced and densely networked than those faced by its federal counterparts.

Conclusion

What next for shale gas in England? At present, the battle continues with neither side willing to concede defeat. For a government facing significant economic uncertainty following Brexit and declining North Sea tax receipts, the prospect of new source of fossil fuel appears too enticing to ignore. A recent Treasury consultation proposing direct payments to households affected by SGD made explicit the economic imperative: 'The government is clear that local people should have greater control and say in decisions that affect them. More than this though, we are committed to delivering an economy that works for all' (HM Treasury, 2016, p. 3).

Meanwhile, having exhausted officially-sanctioned avenues for participation, campaigners are taking direct action, blockading gas companies and their suppliers. Such activities are designed to hit businesses in their pockets and ultimately the outcome may come down to brute economics. For local residents opposed to SGD, protest comes at a price – to their health and social well-being, but also in financial terms, as gas companies threaten litigation against them (Szolucha, 2016b). For MPAs too, refusing planning permission for SGD is not cheap. The Lancashire planning inquiry cost LCC more than £300,000 and this amount would have been significantly higher had the Communities Secretary not declined to award costs (Szolucha, 2016a). MPAs contemplating refusing shale gas applications in future, do so in the knowledge that he may not always be so lenient.

Given the imbalance of power and resources between local and national players, it is likely the will of national government will prevail, to the extent exploration fracking will take place during 2018. But SGD is not a done deal. The true costs of exploiting English shale gas are as yet unknown and may be considerably higher than in larger, less densely populated countries. Recent research suggests the amount of technically recoverable gas in the Bowland shale could be a quarter of original estimates due to the extent of above-ground infrastructure (Clancy, Worrall, Davies, & Gluyas, 2018). Combined with volatile world oil prices, the economic case for English shale gas remains unclear. The more expensive protesters can make it to extract shale gas, the less attractive the industry is to investors and the less likely shale gas will proceed to commercial production. Unanswered questions of poor governance and democratic legitimacy notwithstanding, SGD in England is unlikely to become politically unattractive until it becomes economically unviable. Until then, the war of attrition seems set to continue.

References

Andersson-Hudson, J., Knight, W., Humphrey, M., & O'Hara, S. (2016). Exploring support for shale gas extraction in the United Kingdom. *Energy Policy, 98*, 582–589.

Bomberg, E. (2015). Shale we drill? Discourse dynamics in UK fracking debates. *Journal of Environmental Policy & Planning, 19*(1), 1–17.

Boudet, H., Bugden, D., Zanocco, C., & Maibach, E. (2016). The effect of industry activities on public support for 'fracking'. *Environmental Politics, 25*(4): 593–612.

Boudet, H., Clarke, C., Bugden, D. *et al.* (2014). 'Fracking' controversy and communication: Using national survey data to understand public perceptions of hydraulic fracturing. *Energy Policy, 65*, 57–67.

Boulton, M. (2015). Town and Country Planning Act 1990 Appeals by Cuadrilla Bowland Limited, Cuadrilla Elswick Limited. from www.programmeofficers.co.uk/Cuadrilla/CoreDocuments/CD39/CD39.9.PDF

Clancy, S., Worrall, F., Davies, R., & Gluyas, J. (2018). An assessment of the footprint and carrying capacity of oil and gas well sites: The implications for limiting hydrocarbon reserves. *Science of the Total Environment, 618*, 586–594.

Cotton, M. (2016). Fair fracking? Ethics and environmental justice in United Kingdom shale gas policy and planning. *Local Environment, 22*(2), 185–202.

Cotton, M., Rattle, I., & Van Alstine, J. (2014). Shale gas policy in the United Kingdom: An argumentative discourse analysis. *Energy Policy, 73*, 427–438.

Covello, V. T. (1983). The perception of technological risks: A literature review. *Technological Forecasting and Social Change, 23*(4), 285–297.

Cullen, W. D. (1990). *The Public Inquiry into the Piper Alpha Disaster*. London: HMSO.

Curran, G. (2016). Social licence, corporate social responsibility and coal seam gas: framing the new political dynamics of contestation. *Energy Policy, 101*, 427–435.

DCLG. (2012). *National Planning Policy Framework*. London: TSO.

DCLG. (2013). *Planning Practice Guidance for Onshore Oil and Gas*. London: TSO.

DCLG. (2015). *Plain English Guide to the Planning System*. London: TSO.

DECC DCLG. (2015). Shale gas and oil policy statement. Available at: www.gov.uk/government/publications/shale-gas-and-oil-policy-statement-by-decc-and-dclg

Devine-Wright, P. (2009). Rethinking NIMBYism: The role of place attachment and place identity in explaining place-protective action. *Journal of Community & Applied Social Psychology, 19*(6), 426–441.

Dodge, J., & Lee, J. (2015). Framing dynamics and political gridlock: the curious case of hydraulic fracturing in New York. *Journal of Environmental Policy & Planning, 19*(1), 14–34.

Dufour, P., Bherer, L., & Rothmayr, C. (2012). Who governs? Changing the representation of the common good: the case of shale gas in Quebec. Paper presented at the Conference of the International Political Science Association.

EA. (2015). *Environment Agency Permitting Decisions: Preston New Road Exploration Site* (online No. EPR/AB3101MW/AOO1).

Eaton, E., & Kinchy, A. (2016). Quiet voices in the fracking debate: Ambivalence, non-mobilization, and individual action in two extractive communities (Saskatchewan and Pennsylvania). *Energy Research & Social Science, 20*, 22–30.

Espig, M., & de Rijke, K. (2016). Unconventional gas developments and the politics of risk and knowledge in Australia. *Energy Research & Social Science, 20*, 82–90.

Evensen, D. (2015). Policy decisions on shale gas development ('fracking'): the insufficiency of science and necessity of moral thought. *Environmental Values, 24*(4), 511–534.

Evensen, D., Stedman, R., & Brown-Steiner, B. (2017). Resilient but not sustainable? Public perceptions of shale gas development via hydraulic fracturing. *Ecology and Society, 22*(1).

Gény, F. (2010). Can unconventional gas be a game changer in European gas markets? Available at: www.oxfordenergy.org/publications/can-unconventional-gas-be-a-game-changer-in-european-gas-markets/

Green, C., Styles, P., & Baptie, B. (2012). *Preese Hall Shale Gas Fracturing Review & Recommendations for Induced Seismic Mitigation*. Available at: www.gov.uk/government/uploads/system/uploads/attachment_data/file/15745/5075-preese-hall-shale-gas-fracturing-review.pdf

Heseltine, M. (2012). *No Stone Unturned in the Pursuit of Growth*. London: BIS.

Hilson, C. (2015). Framing fracking: Which frames are heard in English planning and environmental policy and practice? *Journal of Environmental Law, 27*(2), 177–202.

HM Treasury. (2016). *Shale Wealth Fund: consultation*. London: TSO.

Hope, C. (2016). Ministers plot to foil anti-frackers. *Telegraph*. Retrieved from www.telegraph.co.uk/news/earth/energy/fracking/12130801/Ministers-plot-to-foil-anti-frackers.html

Jackson, R., Vengosh, A., Carey, J., Davies, R., Darrah, T., O'Sullivan, F., *et al.* (2014). The environmental costs and benefits of fracking. In A. Gadgil & D. M. Liverman (Eds.), *Annual Review of Environment and Resources*, vol. 39, pp. 327–362.

Jacquet, J., & Stedman, R. (2014). The risk of social-psychological disruption as an impact of energy development and environmental change. *Journal of Environmental Planning and Management, 57*(9), 1285–1304.

James, O. (2001). Evaluating executive agencies in UK government. *Public Policy and Administration, 16*(3), 24–52.

Kriesky, J., Goldstein, B., Zell, K., & Beach, S. (2013). Differing opinions about natural gas drilling in two adjacent counties with different levels of drilling activity. *Energy Policy, 58,* 228–236.

Ladd, A. (2014). Environmental disputes and opportunity-threat impacts surrounding natural gas fracking in Louisiana. *Social Currents, 1*(3), 293–311.

LCC. (2015a). Development Control Committee Minutes of the Meeting held on 23, 24, 25 and 29 June 2015, at 10.00 am, Council Chamber, County Hall, Preston (online).

LCC. (2015b). Preston New Road shale gas application advice note. Retrieved 2 April 2017, from www.lancashire.gov.uk/council/planning/major-planning-applications/shale-gas-developments-in-lancashire/shale-gas-application-advice-note.aspx

McCoy, D., & Munro, A. (2016). *Shale Gas: Risk and Benefit to Health.* London: Medact.

Metze, T. (2014). Fracking the debate: frame shifts and boundary work in Dutch decision making on shale gas. *Journal of Environmental Policy & Planning, 19*(1), 35–52.

Newell, R., & Raimi, D. (2014). Implications of shale gas development for climate change. *Environmental Science & Technology, 48*(15), 8360–8368.

NYCC. (2016). Planning and Regulatory Functions Committee, 20 May 2016. Available at: http://democracy.northyorks.gov.uk/FunctionsPage.aspx?dsid=77824&action=Get FileFromDB

Obach, B. (2015). A fracking fracas demonstrates movement potential. *Contexts, 14*(4), 72–75.

O'Hara, S., Humphrey, M., Andersson-Hudson, J., & Knight, W. (2016). *Public Perception of Shale Gas Extraction in the UK: From Positive to Negative*: Nottingham: University of Nottingham.

ONS. (2011). *2011 Area Classification for Local Authorities* (online). Retrieved from www.ons.gov.uk/methodology/geography/geographicalproducts/areaclassifications/2011area classifications/datasets

Sherval, M., & Hardiman, K. (2014). Competing perceptions of the rural idyll: responses to threats from coal seam gas development in Gloucester, NSW, Australia. *Australian Geographer, 45*(2), 185–203.

Stedman, R., Evensen, D., O'Hara, S., & Humphrey, M. (2016). Comparing the relationship between knowledge and support for hydraulic fracturing between residents of the United States and the United Kingdom. *Energy Research & Social Science, 20,* 142–148.

Stephan, H. (2016). The discursive politics of unconventional gas in Scotland: drifting towards precaution? *Energy Research & Social Science, 23,* 159–168.

Szolucha, A. (2016a, 3 Oct. 2016). Fracking and the price of democracy. Retrieved from http://repowerdemocracy.net/blog/2016/9/30/fracking-and-the-price-of-democracy.

Szolucha, A. (2016b). The human dimension of shale gas developments in Lancashire, UK: Towards a social impact assessment. Retrieved from www.repowerdemocracy.net/report

Turton, D. (2015). Unconventional gas in Australia: Towards a legal geography. *Geographical Research, 53*(1), 53–67.

UKOOG. (n.d.). Community Engagement Charter. v6. Retrieved 25 October 2016, from www.ukoog.org.uk/images/ukoog/pdfs/communityengagementcharterversion6.pdf

Vasi, I., Walker, E., Johnson, J., & Tan, H. F. (2015). "No Fracking Way!" Documentary film, discursive opportunity, and local opposition against hydraulic fracturing in the United States, 2010 to 2013. *American Sociological Review, 80*(5), 934–959.

Veenstra, A., Lyons, B., & Fowler-Dawson, A. (2016). Conservatism vs. conservationism: differential influences of social identities on beliefs about fracking. *Environmental Communication, 10*(3), 322–336.

Vorkinn, M., & Riese, H. (2001). Environmental concern in a local context: the significance of place attachment. *Environment and Behavior, 33*(2), 249–263.

Watt, N. (2014). Fracking in the UK: 'We're going all out for shale,' admits Cameron. *Guardian*, 13 January. Retrieved from www.theguardian.com/environment/2014/jan/13/shale-gas-fracking-cameron-all-out

Whitmarsh, L., Nash, N., Upham, P. *et al.* (2015). UK public perceptions of shale gas hydraulic fracturing: the role of audience, message and contextual factors on risk perceptions and policy support. *Applied Energy, 160*, 419–430.

Willow, A., & Wylie, S. (2014). Politics, ecology, and the new anthropology of energy: exploring the emerging frontiers of hydraulic fracking. *Journal of Political Ecology, 21*(12), 222–236.

16 Community understanding of risk from fracking in the UK and Poland

How democracy-based and justice-based concerns amplify risk perceptions

Anna Szolucha

Introduction

Europe has about 14 trillion cubic metres of unproven technically recoverable shale gas reserves (Andruleit *et al.* 2013). Yet, in 2016, there were no commercial shale gas wells on the continent. In fact, only three countries (Poland, the UK and Ukraine) had any shale gas wells scheduled for 2016. Shale gas spurred a lot of interest and enthusiasm among politicians and some citizens at the beginning of the decade. However, the 2011 assessment of shale gas resources prepared for the U.S. Energy Information Administration (Advanced Resources International, Inc. 2011) that was widely cited around the world, is very likely to have overestimated the reserves in Poland (Polish Geological Institute, National Research Institute 2012). In some countries, the potential of fracking has met strong local and international resistance. As a result, the fortunes of shale gas in Europe have been varied at best (Inman 2016). Fracking has been at least temporarily banned in states such as France, Bulgaria, Germany and Scotland. In the UK and Poland, which are two of the main champions of shale gas in Europe, the pace of drilling has also been quite varied. While 72 exploratory wells have been drilled and 25 hydraulically fractured in Poland ("Stan Prac w Polsce: Porozmawiajmy o Łupkach" 2017), gas companies in the UK are only beginning their activities.

Although more time and epidemiological studies are needed, researchers point to an increasing body of studies and evidence that suggest that the processes associated with shale gas exploration and production can negatively affect social well-being and health (Fischetti 2013). Water pollution can occur through: poor casing quality and compromised integrity of gas wells (Ingraffea *et al.* 2014), leaks through fractured rock and leakages and spillages during wastewater transport and disposal (Olmstead *et al.* 2013; U.S. EPA 2016). The fracturing fluids used in the process are known to contain methanol, ethylene glycol, naphthalene, toluene, ethyl benzene, formaldehyde and sulphuric acid, some of which are carcinogenic or toxic. The chemicals can negatively impact the sensory organs as well as the respiratory and gastrointestinal systems. Air pollution can occur as a result of many shale gas activities: from drilling and processing to the transportation of sand and chemicals (Pétron *et al.* 2012; Colborn *et al.* 2014; Shonkoff, Hays and Finkel 2014). Other significant impacts are related to noise and light pollution (Witter *et al.* 2013), the change in the character of the local area as well as the long-term climate change effects (Anderson 2016; Howarth 2014).

In the context of the potential impacts from shale gas production, Europe may seem an unlikely case for analysis since, as yet, there are no shale gas developments that have moved beyond the exploration phase. However, early studies suggest that even before shale gas exploration and production at scale begin, it can already have profound impacts on local communities (Grear *et al.* 2014; Szolucha 2016). These impacts stem from the social, psychological and political change processes engaged in the governing of shale gas in Europe. Indeed, the failure to consider the social impacts of fracking at each stage of its development significantly understates its actual and potential impacts and alters the governing balance in favour of development (Szolucha 2016).

To date, most shale gas impacts experienced by local residents in the UK and Poland have not emerged directly from development but rather from the social processes and interactions with energy companies and the local and national authorities. In this chapter, I draw on my ethnographic, participatory and documentary research in Lancashire, in North-west England, and the region of Grabowiec, in South-east Poland, to demonstrate the mechanisms and dynamics that have led to the disjuncture between community risk perceptions and the official evaluations of risk. I argue that the objections residents opposed to fracking have raised in the early stages of shale gas developments in Europe have to be understood not in a merely technical and factual way but as an expression of the limits of the planning and consultation processes, usually expressed as democracy- and justice-based concerns. By focusing on "material considerations" and compartmentalising development, the planning regimes artificially remove the social dimension of decision-making that pertains to the political questions of need, trust, justice and alternative visions of the social good.

By comparing case studies from Western and Eastern Europe, I highlight the similarities in how European governments and industry deal with resistance to shale gas developments despite the distinct legal, cultural and political contexts. The analysis underscores the role of citizens and community activism in shale gas governance. In the next section, I briefly summarise two local histories of shale gas developments in the UK and Poland.

The battle for local democracy in Lancashire, UK

The first planning permission for shale gas activities in Lancashire was granted in 2009 and related to the drilling of an exploratory borehole and testing for hydrocarbons near Preese Hall Farm. The application was submitted by the gas company – Cuadrilla, founded two years earlier and chaired by Lord Browne –

former chief of BP, President of the Royal Academy of Engineering and the UK Government Lead Non-Executive Director (2010–2015). The planning decision for Preese Hall was not made by county councillors but by a planning officer at Lancashire County Council. The development was not opposed by the local borough council. In 2010, another five permissions were issued to Cuadrilla for shale gas activities throughout Lancashire. In 2011, two small earthquakes occurred near Blackpool (of magnitudes 2.3 and 1.5 M_L). They were later linked to shale gas operations at Preese Hall (Green, Styles and Baptie 2012) and a temporary moratorium on shale gas exploration was introduced in the UK. Following these events, local opposition to fracking began to mobilise and raise awareness of the shale gas activities in the local area. The Localism Act (2011) was introduced in the same year. Its stated aim was to devolve more powers from central government to local representatives.

The "fracking moratorium" was lifted in 2012 and shale gas operations also resumed in other parts of the UK. The anti-fracking camp at Balcombe, Sussex, attracted wide public attention (O'Hara *et al.* 2013) and media coverage due to a large police presence and controversial arrests. A similar camp was organised at Barton Moss, Salford, and lasted from November 2013 to April 2014.

At the beginning of 2014, the then Prime Minister, David Cameron, declared that Britain was "going all out for shale" (Prime Minister's Office 2014), and Cuadrilla applied for two further planning permissions in Lancashire: for Preston New Road (PNR) and Roseacre Wood. A coalition of anti-fracking groups was formed under the banner of Frack Free Lancashire and residents led by "Lancashire Nanas" set up a temporary camp near the PNR site. Concerned local residents took an active part in the planning and consultation process, attending meetings, preparing formal representations to the Lancashire County Council, writing letters to relevant institutions and collaborating with environmental organisations. They claimed that the development was unsuitable for their area, a popular retirement and tourist resort. During a very tumultuous session of the Development Control Committee where county councillors were subjected to a significant amount of pressure to approve the applications (Short and Szolucha 2017), the County Council decided to refuse planning permission for exploratory drilling at both sites but approve seismic monitoring at Roseacre. Cuadrilla lodged appeals against the refusals. Before the end of 2015, the Secretary of State for Communities and Local Government called in the final determination of the fracking applications on grounds that the decision was of a national and not merely local significance. Thus, the decision was not going to be made by a County Planning Inspector as per the usual practice. The public inquiry was held in Blackpool, Lancashire, between 9 February and 16 March 2016, as described by Rattle, Baker and Van Alstine in Chapter 15 in this volume. On 6 October, the Communities Secretary announced that he was approving the PNR application. He was also "minded" to give planning permission to the site in Roseacre but was recalling a public inquiry before making his final decision. Soon afterwards, local residents announced that they disagreed with the way the determination overrode local democracy and launched legal challenges to the planning decisions.

Occupying Chevron in Żurawlów, Poland

In 2012, 111 shale gas licences were active in Poland covering approximately 30 per cent of its territory. Chevron (then Lublin Energy Resources) was granted a licence for the region of Grabowiec in 2007. Initial terms included the permission to drill four vertical exploratory wells and to conduct 2D and 3D seismic surveys. Between 2007 and 2013, the licence agreement between the corporation and the Polish Ministry of Environment was extended and amended several times. The Ministry asserted that the planned development would not significantly affect the environment and hence, did not require an environmental assessment.

In Poland, shale gas extraction has enjoyed wide public support (with 73 per cent claiming they are in favour of shale gas development) (CBOS 2011), making the sustained opposition to fracking in the Grabowiec region even more unexpected. The residents of this predominantly agricultural region became concerned about fracking in 2011, after the first seismic surveys. They claimed the surveys caused damage to their buildings and local roads as well as polluting water wells in the village of Rogów. Both the company responsible for the surveys and the Ministry of Environment denied that the surveys and the damage were in any way connected (Ministerstwo rodowiska 2011).

One of the turning points in the relationship between the gas corporation and the local residents was a public meeting in Żurawlów that was going to be the next site of shale gas development in the area. The meeting took place in January 2012 and was attended by Chevron's representatives, scientists, local authorities, residents, media as well as interested public, including members of environmental organisations. The presence of the latter was not welcomed by the corporation to the degree that its representatives left the meeting. The discussion and presentations continued, however, Chevron's exit made residents highly distrustful of the corporation. A few months later the company's contractors arrived in Żurawlów with heavy equipment. Notified by the residents, the police and local authorities intervened and the workers were forced to leave.

The corporation's subcontractors returned in June 2013 and tried to enter one of the fields leased by Chevron but encountered active resistance and direct action by local residents. They were concerned that shale gas developments in their area could negatively impact on one of the biggest underground aquifers in the country as well as on agriculture, which is the main source of income and employment for the local families. They set up a blockade, dubbed Occupy Chevron, that lasted for 400 days from 3 June 2013 to 7 July 2014 when the company left Żurawlów. In the meantime, however, the corporation sued local residents for their blockade. Some of the court cases continued well after Chevron had left the village, however, the residents were ultimately found not guilty.

The results of shale gas exploration in Poland have been disappointing due to difficult geological conditions. Most energy giants such as Chevron, Exxon Mobil and Total, that came to Poland during the period of "shale fever", left the country between 2013 and 2015. In 2015, the Polish and state-controlled companies owned the majority of the remaining 40 licences for exploratory shale gas activities. In early 2017, the number of active licences halved.

Methodology and research approach

Risk is a culturally perceived and socially constructed concept; an individual's understanding of danger can vary greatly (Jacquet 2014). There is often a disjuncture between the official and corporate evaluations of risk, on the one hand, and the community understanding of risk, on the other. What constitutes "evidence" and "impact" of shale gas developments is highly contested (Perry 2012) and similar to other resource extraction projects, citizens' concerns are often dismissed in favour of technical assessments based on probabilistic measures (Kasperson *et al.* 1988). However, research has shown that environmental impact assessments systematically underestimate the eventual impact of development and are rarely successful in making verifiable predictions (Sadler 1996; Lawrence 2013), which may result in a sustained and directional bias. Science sponsored by influential corporations may also be problematic for a host of reasons frequently reported in news media (Banerjee, Song and Hasemyer 2015) and academic publications (Kirsch 2014). A sustained research effort is required on the social and not merely technical or material aspects of shale gas developments. In this context, ethnographic and participatory research can improve the quality of risk assessments (Chase 1990; Checker 2007; de Rijke 2013a) and foster a better understanding of risk perception on the part of all stakeholders.

This chapter is based on participant observation and participatory research over a 20-month period in Lancashire, UK, and the Grabowiec region in Poland. I spoke to local residents, attended meetings and events of the local planning authorities, public inquiry hearings, court hearings, protests, the events of the local grassroots anti-fracking groups and national regulatory agencies. Some of the interviews and events were recorded and transcribed. The analysis has been complemented by documentary research involving primary documents such as official letters, legal acts, licence agreements, written evidence and submissions made during the planning process in addition to responses to public consultations. The data was imported into NVivo 11 Plus for coding and thematic analysis.

Findings

The discrepancy between how local residents, decision-makers and corporate stakeholders evaluate risk stems from how each actor assesses the adequacy of democratic arrangements that govern shale gas developments. In the recent academic literature, energy justice has emerged as a conceptual framework that aims to address the unequal distribution of risk by energy policy and development (McCauley *et al.* 2013; Sovacool *et al.* 2016; Jenkins, McCauley and Forman 2017).

In the following analysis, I examine how democracy-based and justice-based concerns have led to the amplification of risk perceptions (Kasperson *et al.* 1988) on the part of local residents by focusing on the two recurrent questions regarding energy justice that I encountered during research on shale gas developments in the UK and Poland:

1   Is regulation robust enough to guarantee the safety and security of all those affected by the development?
2   Is development activity carried out responsibly and according to the law by the operator?

Robust regulation

Planning decisions regarding shale gas developments are based on the assumption that the existing regulations are sufficient to ensure safety and adequate control. However, in the Grabowiec region, the argument that state bodies are solely responsible for controlling the planning process was used by local authorities to deny an environmental NGO the right to participate in the process. In Lancashire, this presumption was the main limitation to the planning process as Lancashire County Council is required to delegate matters within the purview of regulatory agencies such as the Environment Agency for them to address. The planning decision assumed that the agencies would adequately control shale gas developments and address emerging issues. Hence, the planning decision could only take into account the planning and material considerations such as the impact of the planned development on traffic, visual amenity, etc. (see Chapter 15 in this volume by Rattle, Baker & Van Alstine). This restricted the ability of the County Council and residents to successfully oppose fracking on the grounds of health, environment or climate. Local residents, who participated in the planning process at Lancashire County Council, understood these limitations and adapted their representations accordingly. However, they did not consider the situation to be just and felt that the presumption that regulators would act fairly was biased in favour of the gas company, as these quotes from the local residents demonstrate:

> The real difficulty in terms of the local councils and the appeals and the planning applications is that at the end of the day, those are about planning matters. So, I thought that the council did particularly well to listen to PNR's and Roseacre presentations where they brought in absolutely everything they possibly could but actually, not a lot of it relating to [material considerations] … [the councillors] were trying to make up their mind on what they could object [the application] on. So in actual fact, the objection is on landscape and visual intrusion so in a way that really narrows down

the field of objections ... I think that probably for a lot of the things that the planning committee deals with, limiting to just material considerations, is just fine. But I don't think it's fine with developing a new industry and industrialisation.

(local resident 1)

[T]hey [the regulators] are giving false assurances to the people in the country. They're saying that "we're one of the most regulated [countries]" but that's nonsense because there aren't any regulations. It's just self-regulation. I've got no confidence at all. In fact, this is something that cannot be done safely.... It's like the industry said about cigarette smoking: "You can't prove it that it's gonna cause you any harm."

(local resident 2)

Importantly, by limiting the planning process to "material considerations", the gas company could claim in the media that its applications for shale gas developments were not opposed on the grounds of health or environmental impact but only on the, relatively minor, aspects of visual impact or traffic. This clearly acts in the favour of Cuadrilla's image but misrepresents many residents' concerns.

It seems that residents opposed to shale gas in Lancashire do not trust the regulatory agencies. In their opinion, the regulators did not effectively deal with the noise issues caused by Cuadrilla's shale gas operations at Balcombe, a local cryptosporidium outbreak in 2015 or the 2011 earthquakes that were connected to shale gas activities. Public Health England, the government agency responsible for reviewing the impact of shale gas, is not trusted by those opposed to shale gas due to a highly criticised report (Law *et al.* 2014) on the potential public health impacts of exposure to chemical and radioactive pollutants from fracking. The report is cited by industry and the government to support shale gas exploration, concluding that the risk will "be low if the operations are properly run and regulated" (Kibble *et al.* 2014, p. iii). However, as researchers have noted:

The report incorrectly assumes that many of the reported problems experienced in the US are the result of a poor regulatory environment. This position ignores many of the inherent risks of the industry that no amount of regulation can sufficiently remedy, such as well casing, cement failures, and accidental spillage of waste water. There is no reason to believe that these problems would be different in the UK, and the report provides little evidence to the contrary, despite repeated assertions that regulations will ensure the safe development of shale gas extraction.

(Law *et al.* 2014, p. 1)

Despite UK Government assurances, researchers have identified significant gaps in national and European legislation, highlighting unsatisfactory shale gas governance (Hawkins 2015). Fears regarding the efficiency of shale gas regulations are not unfounded: a report by the Polish Supreme Auditory Office (NIK) ("NIK O Poszukiwaniach Gazu Łupkowego" 2014) highlights how the Polish Ministry of Environment failed to use even the little oversight powers that it had. It did not provide sufficient supervision of energy corporations regarding their compliance with environmental protection laws and did not follow up with the companies or hold them accountable when they failed to submit appropriate activity reports. Moreover, the corporations themselves failed to fulfil their obligations arising from the terms and conditions of their shale gas licences.

The presumption that regulation is robust has also been severely undermined in the eyes of local residents in Lancashire and Grabowiec due to the way shale gas developments are compartmentalised and legislation altered in a way that seems to favour gas companies. For example, in the UK and Poland, permission for exploration and then extraction had to be obtained separately. The initial stage of exploratory drilling is likely to generate fewer and less severe impacts than full-scale production. However, if exploration is approved and considered successful, the operator then applies for permission to extract gas. During this process, decision-makers will only consider the impact of the planned development as it is presented to them, i.e. permission cannot be refused on the grounds of potential future impacts from shale gas production. The exploratory activities, however, may establish a precedent or a principle of development, for example, by introducing an industry to formerly rural areas. By compartmentalising the permission process, the planning system precludes the consideration of long-term impacts of all stages of shale gas development on local communities and climate and, hence, is biased in favour of development. Furthermore, it seems that double standards apply regarding shale gas developments in the Polish and UK legislation regarding nationally significant infrastructure or development that is in the public interest. In this context, shale gas exploration and extraction are not considered separately but exploration is seen as being in the public interest precisely because it leads to production.

Changes in legislation introduced in anticipation of shale gas developments are also a cause for concern for local residents opposed to fracking. The new law seems to favour companies by removing potential barriers to development. In the UK, despite popular opposition, the Infrastructure Act (2015) represents a change in trespass law and provides drilling companies with automatic access rights to use the subsurface (below 300 m) for the purpose of exploiting petroleum. Furthermore, the Act obligates all future governments to maximise the economic recovery of UK petroleum. In Poland, a bill was proposed that would have allowed recalcitrant landowners to be expropriated if companies discovered shale gas under their land. Furthermore, the definition of a development that may significantly impact on the environment was changed in such a way that exploratory wells no deeper than 5,000 m (previously 1,000 m) did not require an environmental assessment. Despite regulations being in place, in practice, gas exploration companies continued to successfully evade the requirement to conduct environmental and social impact assessments. In 2016, the European Commission referred Poland to the European Court of Justice for the non-application of the EU rules concerning environmental impact assessment in shale gas developments (*European Commission vs Republic of Poland*, Case C-526/16).

Responsible development

Gas exploration companies produce literature and a narrative in which they aspire to be good neighbours in local communities as well as serving important national and global interest of ensuring energy security and mitigating climate change. From the perspective of the local residents opposed to fracking, however, the corporations use a range of unfair techniques and some of their activities may even constitute a socially divisive tactic (Wilber 2012; de Rijke 2013b; Szolucha 2016).

Residents involved in Occupy Chevron in Żurawlów claim it was concern regarding impacts on water resources and agriculture that stimulated involvement in the protest against shale gas. However, what kept them active was the shale gas companies' "colonial" attitude manifested in repeated attempts to begin shale gas activities without the appropriate permissions and licences. An analysis of the relevant documents confirms that at the time when Chevron entered Żurawlów with the intention to construct a fence around a field it was leasing in 2013, it could only carry out seismic surveys in the area. The company did not have permission to drill an exploratory borehole but still fenced off an area in preparation for it. The official correspondence between the local authorities and Chevron also records that although the authorities were originally in favour of the development, they too found themselves objecting to the corporation's methods when they attempted to bypass appropriate procedures to obtain relevant permissions.

Another justice-based concern for local residents is the way in which shale gas corporations deal with evidence of possible harm caused by shale gas activities. During one hearing at the Development Control Committee in Lancashire, a resident stated:

> They're playing a clever game. They call this temporary to underplay the impact especially if they know that the impact is awful. They have a pick-and-mix approach to evidence. They talk in averages, all clever stuff, but not very truthful.

Industry has also denied the possibility that fracking causes earthquakes and Cuadrilla's CEO said on the BBC in early 2016 that: "there isn't a single case in the US ... where *a public water supply* has been contaminated, interfered with or impacted by fracking" (BBC 2016). At the time these claims were made, they were not far from the truth but are misleading in that earthquakes were often caused by deep disposal of fracking's wastewater (Kerr 2012) rather than the process of fracking itself (in the popular discourse, both activities are often subsumed under the term of fracking). Water contamination has been found in domestic wells rather than public water supplies (DiGiulio *et al.* 2011). Studies published in 2016 confirm that earthquakes in Canada were "highly correlated in time and space with hydraulic fracturing, during which fluids are injected under high pressure … to induce localized fracturing of rock" (Atkinson *et al.* 2016, p. 631); and fracking can impact drinking water resources (U.S. EPA 2016).

Gas companies in the UK and Poland have threatened litigation, sued anti-fracking protesters and engaged in activities which had the effect of intimidating individuals and dividing communities (Szolucha 2016). The symbolic gestures of philanthropy and employing likeable representatives (such as a popular TV presenter as Chevron's spokesperson) were often treated with suspicion as an attempt to "sell shale gas" as this local resident in Lancashire recalls: "In the absence of the knowledge, people are going become sold, they're gonna think that it's wonderful … It's been sold to so many people as a prestigious thing to have in their area."

Conclusion

Robust regulation and responsible development are two aspects of energy justice comprising shale gas governance in Europe. However, in Lancashire and Grabowiec, it seems that both exploration companies and governments have fallen short of residents' expectations. There is a sense that they have undermined the democratic standards in the process of facilitating shale gas development.

To a large extent, the discrepancy between the official/corporate assessment of risk and the community understanding of danger from fracking stems from the pitfalls and faults of energy policy and planning regulations, which correspond to the triumvirate of tenets of the energy justice framework (McCauley *et al.* 2013). However, the local experiences of the interactions between the residents, authorities and energy companies are equally important. It is these experiences, rather than merely shale gas regulations and policy, that drive citizen participation and fuel protest.

As the discussion in this chapter demonstrates, risk is amplified not only when existing policies and regulations are ignored by the most powerful players or are considered to be inadequate to guarantee a balanced distribution of risk, but also when residents negatively assess the very ability and willingness of their democratic representatives and the energy companies to engage with them in equal and truthful dialogue. This demonstrates that various justice-based and democracy-based concerns, that extend beyond matters that can be remedied by adequate energy regulation and policy implementation, play a crucial role in amplifying risk perceptions. They act as a corrective mechanism for other, more technical, assessments of risk and bring them more in line with a broad range of actual risk factors (Kasperson *et al.* 1988).

Local residents in the UK and Poland have already experienced similar consequences from limiting the planning and environmental assessment process, the compartmentalisation of planning, the changes in legislation that aim to remove potential barriers to development, the double standards in law that may have the effect of undermining local democracy and the colonial attitude of some of the energy companies. In a way, there is nothing new in the fact that governments actively support domestic resource extraction as they have often used natural resources to redefine social problems as economic issues that could be remedied by timely development (Ferry and Limbert 2008). More research is needed that assesses the extent to which the understanding of risk by local residents stems from particular power relations that are articulated, enabled and prefigured by a specific technology of shale gas exploration and to what degree they are rooted in the longer history of state transformations and industrial relations.

Protests against shale gas exploration in Lancashire and Grabowiec demonstrate that in the absence of adequate regulations or poor implementation, citizens will strive for justice by other means, through organising and taking part in blockades and direct action, for example. It seems possible that so long as certain aspects of shale gas governance are perceived to actively support development and neglect social justice and popular democratic concerns, there remains a disjuncture in how those for development and those against understand risk.

References

Advanced Resources International, Inc. 2011. *World Shale Gas Resources: An Initial Assessment of 14 Regions Outside the United States*. Washington, DC: U.S. Energy Information Administration. Available at: www.adv-res.com/pdf/ARI%20EIA%20Intl%20Gas%20Shale%20APR%202011.pdf

Anderson, K. 2016. Proof of Evidence of Professor Kevin Anderson (PhD, CEng, FIMechE). For a Public Inquiry into Appeals by Cuadrilla Elswick Limited and Cuadrilla Bowland Limited Concerning Exploration Works at: 1) Roseacre Wood: 2) Preston New Road. Available at: bailey.persona-pi.com/Public-Inquiries/M4-Newport/Third Parties/M4

Andruleit, H., Bahr, A., Babies, H. G. et al. 2013. *Energy Study 2013. Reserves, Resources and Availability of Energy Resources*. Hannover: Federal Institute for Geosciences and Natural Resources. Available at: www.bgr.bund.de/EN/Themen/Energie/Downloads/energiestudie_2013_en.pdf;jsessionid=C007E5F81037A7F8BB4C7E3BDF2F0D0D.1_cid292?__blob=publicationFile&v=2

Atkinson, G. M., Eaton, D. W., Ghofrani, H. et al. 2016. Hydraulic Fracturing and Seismicity in the Western Canada Sedimentary Basin. *Seismological Research Letters*, 87(3): 631–47.

Banerjee, N., Song, L. and Hasemyer, D. 2015. Exxon's Own Research Confirmed Fossil Fuels' Role in Global Warming Decades Ago. *Inside Climate News*, September 16. Available at: http://insideclimatenews.org/news/15092015/Exxons-own-research-confirmed-fossil-fuels-role-in-global-warming

BBC. (2016, January 27). Chief Executive Cuadrilla Resources – Francis Egan, HARD-talk. Retrieved 18 October 2017, from www.bbc.co.uk/programmes/p03fzsw3

CBOS (Centrum Badania Opinii Społecznej). 2011. Wydobywać? Polacy O Gazie Łupkowym. BS/112/2011. Warsaw. Available at: www.cbos.pl/SPISKOM.POL/2011/K_112_11.PDF

Chase, A. 1990. Anthropology and Impact Assessment: Development Pressures and Indigenous Interests in Australia. *Environmental Impact Assessment Review*, 10(1): 11–23.

Checker, M. 2007. 'But I Know It's True': Environmental Risk Assessment, Justice, and Anthropology, *Human Organization*, 66(2): 112.

Colborn, T., Schultz, K., Herrick, L. and Kwiatkowski, C. 2014. An Exploratory Study of Air Quality Near Natural Gas Operations. *Human and Ecological Risk Assessment: An International Journal*, 20(1): 86–105.

DiGiulio, D. C., Wilkin, R. T., Miller, C. and Oberley, G. 2011. Investigation of Ground Water Contamination near Pavillion, Wyoming: Draft. EPA 600/R-00/000. Oklahoma: U.S. Environmental Protection Agency. Available at: www.epa.gov/sites/production/files/documents/EPA_ReportOnPavillion_Dec-8-2011.pdf

Ferry, E. E. and Limbert, M. E. 2008. Timely Assets: Introduction. In E. E. Ferry and M. E. Limbert (Eds.), *Timely Assets: The Politics of Resources and Their Temporalities* (pp. 3–24). Santa Fe, NM: School for Advanced Research Press.

Fischetti, M. 2013. Groundwater Contamination May End the Gas-Fracking Boom. *Scientific American*, August. Available at: www.scientificAmerican.com/article/groundwater-contamination-may-end-the-gas-fracking-boom/

Grear, A., Grant, E., Kerns, T., Morrow, K., and Short, D. 2014. *A Human Rights Assessment of Hydraulic Fracturing and Other Unconventional Gas Development in the United Kingdom*. The Bianca Jagger Human Rights Foundation. Bristol: UWE. Available at: http://eprints.uwe.ac.uk/26661/

Green, C. A., Styles, P. and Baptie, B. J. 2012. Preese Hall Shale Gas Fracturing: Review and Recommendations for Induced Seismic Mitigation. Department of Energy and Climate Change. Available at: www.gov.uk/government/uploads/system/uploads/attachment_data/file/48330/5055-preese-hall-shale-gas-fracturing-review-and-recomm.pdf

Hawkins, J. 2015. Fracking: Minding the Gaps. *Environmental Law Review*, 17(1): 8–21.

Howarth, R. 2014. A Bridge to Nowhere: Methane Emissions and the Greenhouse Gas Footprint of Natural Gas. *Energy Science & Engineering*, 2(2): 47–60.

Ingraffea, A., Wells, M. T., Santoro, R. and Shonkoff, S. B. 2014. Assessment and Risk Analysis of Casing and Cement Impairment in Oil and Gas Wells in Pennsylvania, 2000–2012. *Proceedings of the National Academy of the Sciences*, 111(30): 10955–60.

Inman, M. 2016. Can fracking power Europe? *Nature*, 531(7592): 22–24.

Jacquet, J. B. 2014. Review of Risks to Communities from Shale Energy Development. *Environmental Science & Technology*, 48(15): 8321–33.

Jenkins, K., McCauley, D. and Forman, A. 2017. Energy Justice: A Policy Approach. *Energy Policy*, 105(June): 631–4.

Kasperson, R. E., Renn, O., Slovic, P. *et al.* 1988. The Social Amplification of Risk: A Conceptual Framework. *Risk Analysis*, 8(2): 177–87.

Kerr, R. A. 2012. Learning How to NOT Make Your Own Earthquakes. *Science*, 335(6075): 1436–7.

Kibble, A., Cabianca, T., Daraktchieva, Z. *et al.* 2014. *Review of the Potential Public Health Impacts of Exposures to Chemical and Radioactive Pollutants as a Result of the Shale Gas Extraction Process*. Chilton: Public Health England.

Kirsch, S. 2014. *Mining Capitalism: The Relationship between Corporations and Their Critics*. Oakland, CA: University of California Press.

Law, A. Hays, J., Shonkoff, S. B. and Finkel, M. L. 2014. Public Health England's Draft Report on Shale Gas Extraction. *The British Medical Journal* 348(April): g2728.

Lawrence, D. P. 2013. *Impact Assessment: Practical Solutions to Recurrent Problems and Contemporary Challenges*. Hoboken, NJ: John Wiley & Sons, Inc.

McCauley, D., Heffron, R. J., Stephan, H. and Jenkins, K. 2013. Advancing Energy Justice: The Triumvirate of Tenets and Systems Thinking. *International Energy Law Review*, 32(3): 107–10.

Ministerstwo Środowiska. 2011. Informacja w sprawie nieprawdziwej informacji o zanieczyszczeniu wody w studniach w rejonie Rogowa i Ornatowic. Available at: www.mos. gov.pl/artykul/2427_sprostowania_poza_aktualnosciami/17197_15_11_2011_r_ informacja_w_sprawie_nieprawdziwej_informacji_o_zanieczyszczeniu_wody_w_ studniach_w_rejonie_rogowa_i_ornatowic_powiat_zamojski.html

NIK O Poszukiwaniach Gazu Łupkowego. 2014. *Najwyższa Izba Kontroli*. January 13. Available at: www.nik.gov.pl/aktualnosci/nik-o-poszukiwaniach-gazu-lupkowego.html

O'Hara, S., Humphrey, M., Jaspal, R., Nerlich, B., and Knight, W. 2013. *Public Perception of Shale Gas Extraction in the UK: The Impacts of the Balcombe Protests in July - August 2013*. Nottingham: University of Nottingham. Available at: http://nottspolitics. org/wp-content/uploads/2013/10/public-perceptions-of-shale-gas-in-the-UK-september-2013-1-2.pdf

Olmstead, S. M., Muehlenbachs, L. A., Shih, J.-S., Chu, Z. and Krupnick, A. J. 2013. Shale Gas Development Impacts on Surface Water Quality in Pennsylvania. *Proceedings of the National Academy of Sciences*, 110(13): 4962–7.

Perry, S. L. 2012. Addressing the Societal Costs of Unconventional Oil and Gas Exploration and Production: A Framework for Evaluating Short-Term, Future, and Cumulative Risks and Uncertainties of Hydrofracking. *Environmental Practice*, 14(04): 352–65.

Pétron, G. E., Frost, G., Miller, B. R. *et al.* 2012. Hydrocarbon Emissions Characterization in the Colorado Front Range: A Pilot Study. *Journal of Geophysical Research: Atmospheres*, 117(D4): D04304.

Polish Geological Institute, National Research Institute. 2012. *Assessment of Shale Gas and Shale Oil Resources of the Lower Paleozoic Baltic-Podlasie-Lublin Basin in Poland: First Report*. Warsaw. Available at: www.pgi.gov.pl/docman-tree/aktualnosci-2012/zasoby-gazu/769-raport-en/file.html

Prime Minister's Office. (2014, January 13). Local Councils to Receive Millions in Business Rates from Shale Gas Developments – GOV.UK. Retrieved October 18, 2017, from www.gov.uk/government/news/local-councils-to-receive-millions-in-business-rates-from-shale-gas-developments

Rijke, K. de. 2013a. Hydraulically Fractured: Unconventional Gas and Anthropology. *Anthropology Today*, 29(2): 13–17.

Rijke, K. de. 2013b. The Agri-Gas Fields of Australia: Black Soil, Food, and Unconventional Gas. *Culture, Agriculture, Food and Environment*, 35(1), 41–53.

Sadler, B. 1996. *Environmental Assessment in a Changing World: Evaluating Practice to Improve Performance* (final report of the International Study of the Effectiveness of Environmental Assessment). Ottawa: Ministry of Supply and Services. Available at: www.ceaa-acee.gc.ca/ Content/2/B/7/2B7834CA-7D9A-410B-A4ED-FF78AB625BDB/iaia8_e.pdf

Shonkoff, S. B., Hays, J. and Finkel, M. L. 2014. Environmental Public Health Dimensions of Shale and Tight Gas Development. *Environmental Health Perspectives*, 122, 787–85.

Short, D. and Szolucha, A. 2017. Fracking Lancashire: The Planning Process, Social Harm and Collective Trauma. *Geoforum*. Available at: https://doi.org/10.1016/j.geo forum.2017.03.001

Sovacool, B. K., Heffron, R. J., McCauley, D. and Goldthau, A. 2016. Energy Decisions Reframed as Justice and Ethical Concerns. *Nature Energy*, 1(May), 16024.

Stan prac w Polsce: Porozmawiajmy o Łupkach. 2017. Available at: http://lupki.mos.gov. pl/gaz-z-lupkow/stan-prac-w-polsce

Szolucha, A. 2016. The Human Dimension of Shale Gas Developments in Lancashire, UK: Towards a Social Impact Assessment. Available at: https://annaszolucha.wordpress. com/research/repower-democracy/report/

U.S. EPA. 2016. Hydraulic Fracturing for Oil and Gas: Impacts from the Hydraulic Fracturing Water Cycle on Drinking Water Resources in the United States (Final Report). EPA/600/R-16/236F. Washington, DC: U.S. Environmental Protection Agency.

Wilber, T. 2012. *Under the Surface: Fracking, Fortunes, and the Fate of the Marcellus Shale.* Ithaca, NY: Cornell University Press.

Witter, R. Z., McKenzie, L., Stinson, K. E. *et al.* 2013. The Use of Health Impact Assessment for a Community Undergoing Natural Gas Development. *American Journal of Public Health*, 103(6): 1002–1010.

17 Seeking common ground in contested energy technology landscapes

Insights from a Q-methodology study

Matthew Dairon, John R. Parkins, and Kate Sherren

Introduction

In the context of south-western Alberta, unconventional energy production, such as shale gas, almost never exists in isolation on the landscape. Often other energy technologies are present, including wind, solar, along with other land uses such as agriculture, urban development, protected areas and tourism. The presence of these diverse, complex, and often contested interests is now a common feature of rural landscapes across North America. As expected, planning and arrangements in these settings are fraught with challenges, often leading to serious conflict between stakeholders and associated policy gridlock (Dodge 2015). From the perspective of sustainability planning, Cowell (2013, p. 28) notes that:

> It is often when concepts of sustainable development are applied to decisions with ramifications for the use of land – the domain of planning – that irreversible choices become starkly apparent, consensus is prone to break down and sharply divergent values rise to the surface.

Yet within liberal democratic societies, scholars emphasize the demand for participatory governance arrangements, as expressed through a range of informal (e.g., local advocacy coalitions) and formal (e.g., land use planning) groups that have opportunities to influence the outcome of environmental policy decisions. Examining environmental governance arrangements in the Province of Alberta, Adkin et al. (2017, p. 304) express a sense that "liberal democratic politics do afford social interests space for using consultations and engagement exercises to push for meaningful engagement." Similarly, in New York State, Dodge (2015) emphasizes the possibilities for civil society to positively impact decisions on hydraulic fracturing.

In this complex governance environment, our aim in this chapter is to identify distinct discourses on energy development in the south-western region of Alberta and to identify areas of overlapping interest (common ground) that can serve as a focal point and a foothold for progress on participatory governance within this energy landscape. An energy landscape is defined as a large physical area comprising both natural and anthropogenic features, the most prominent of which is infrastructure for energy extraction or generation, which is the setting for resource decision-making, visual and environmental impact, and sometimes conflict. A discourse is defined as the avenues through which meaning is given to social and physical realities (Hajer 1995), with attention to the realities of energy landscapes in this chapter. To identify discourses, we draw on Q-methodology, involving the sorting of statements on energy production in Canada along with in-depth interviews. This method has value in highlighting points of divergence and convergence on energy production within the region, and our use of this method is consistent with other researchers in resource management settings (Clare et al. 2013; Cotton 2015). As a starting point for this work, the next section reviews the sociology of energy production as it relates to discourses on hydraulic fracturing and wind energy development.

Discourses on hydraulic fracturing and wind energy

Drawing on national research and case studies in North America, analysts claim that hydraulic fracturing (also known as fracking and hydro fracking) can provide benefits by increasing jobs, increasing property values, and providing additional sources of income for those who sign leases on private lands (Boudet et al. 2014). Fracturing is also associated with energy security (Finewood and Stroup 2012), via its framing as a key transition fuel in the fight against climate change (Stephenson et al. 2012), a view that is also identified in the UK (Cotton 2015). Contrasting these perceptions, opponents of hydraulic fracturing often structure their arguments around the social-environmental impacts, and the risks and uncertainties associated with the extraction method (Davis and Fisk 2014; Howarth et al. 2011), with particular attention to negative impacts on water (Colborn et al. 2011; Gordalla et al. 2013).

Looking specifically at scholarship from the United Kingdom and Europe, authors identify several discourses that characterize these perspectives on fracking. In the UK, Bomberg (2015) describes two opposing discourses representing views held at the polar ends of the debate termed as the "Pro-shale Coalition and the 'Opportunity' Storyline," and the "Anti-shale Coalition and the 'Threat' Storyline." Through the use of interview data in the UK, Cotton et al. (2014) come to a similar conclusion, but highlight slightly different arguments in the process. In addition to the two polarizing discourses, working in Germany, Schirrmeister (2014) classifies a third discourse that includes views concerned with the risks and threats of hydraulic fracturing, but do not wish the technology to be prohibited. Instead, these voices call for further research and risk assessment before development is permitted to continue. Additionally, drawing on work from Australia, De Rijke (2013) describes public discourse which focuses on arguments that frame hydraulic fracturing as a clean transitional source of energy. Although De Rijke (ibid.) categorizes these views as a separate discourse, scholars such as Cotton et al. (2014) have deemed such views part of the pro-hydraulic fracturing discourse.

Compared to hydraulic fracturing, wind energy is equally contentious but for very different reasons. Those who support wind energy often cite the environmental benefits associated with the technology. Based on research from the UK, such benefits include a lower carbon footprint (Mander 2008). Research from Texas also highlights the economic benefits (Brannstrom et al. 2011; Jepson et al. 2012). Against the views and arguments of wind energy proponents, opponents of wind in Europe, Canada and Mexico focus on the negative environmental impacts (Carneiro et al. 2013) and also highlight ways in which the technology can potentially adversely impact individual and social well-being (Baxter et al. 2013; Pasqualetti 2011). It is also argued that because wind energy development is often sited in rural areas, the potential exists for pre-existing rural-urban tensions to be reignited due to the perceived unfairness of project siting (Warren et al. 2005).

In an attempt to understand the arguments made for and against wind energy, scholars have classified several wind-related discourses, drawing on a variety of sources, such as interviews, the published literature, and policy documents to conduct their discourse analysis. Drawing on insights from research in the UK, Denmark, and France, Mander (2008), Jessup (2010), and Szarka (2004) present additional discourses to describe the views held by wind energy opponents and proponents. Although each author describes different findings, there is significant overlap so we focus primarily on three British and European-based discourses described by Szarka (2004). The first, "pro-wind coalition," focuses on the arguments made by wind proponents. The second discourse, "dilemma and dissent," presents a cautionary tale by stating that when moving forward with wind energy development, long-term sustainability issues need to be balanced with the immediate impacts caused by such development. Such views can be seen as similar to those described by Bell et al.'s (2005) "qualified supporter." The final discourse presented by Szarka (2004) is characterized as "anti-wind" and describes the perspectives of wind opponents. Studies such as Jepson et al. (2012, p. 851) in the United States also provide nuanced descriptions of discourses that are relatively unique to localized populations. For example, in Sweetwater, Texas, a unique perspective – described as "not taking the pledge" – was identified that captured "a view that accepts the economic products, processes, and policy innovations advocated by ecological modernization without accepting the core claim that innovations are required to adapt to environmental change." These studies demonstrate that energy discourses within a relatively localized region are diverse and complex, and that a careful examination of these discourses can provide a more nuanced understanding of local points of view and associated governance challenges.

The study region

As with much of southern Alberta, conventional oil and gas development is a prominent feature in the Cochrane region. At a provincial scale, Alberta has a long history of hydraulic fracturing for oil and gas with more than 179,000 wells fractured since the 1950s (Government of Alberta 2016; Marsh et al. 2013). Over the past four or five years, as conventional sources of oil and gas become scarce, hydraulic fracturing technologies have been increasingly used in the area to gain access to unconventional sources of oil and gas. In response to this development, some residents living near the local hydraulic fracturing wells have voiced their concerns about the environmental and health effects they have experienced. In contrast to this conventional energy landscape, a second region, Pincher Creek, is a historically gas-producing region that began transitioning toward wind energy production in the early 1990s (Town of Pincher Creek Alberta 2014a). There are approximately 270 wind turbines in the region that have the potential to produce a total of 291 megawatts of energy (ibid.). Other forms of energy are also produced in the region, including hydroelectricity from the Oldman River dam (Town of Pincher Creek Alberta 2014b) and natural gas from the Shell Canada Waterton Gas Complex (Town of Pincher Creek 2014c). These two regions represent some of the diversity of energy production landscapes in Alberta.

Research methods

Q-methodology (referred to here as Q-method) provides a structured platform for qualitative examination and comparison of subjective states by measuring quantifiable responses to various stimuli (Wolsink and Breukers 2010). In Q-method, stimuli represent discrete value positions within a given discourse and usually take the form of textual statements. One strength of the Q-method is its ability to identify less familiar discourses that may be overshadowed by more dominant or well-established societal points of view (e.g., jobs versus the environment). This subtlety in identifying discourses makes Q-method a valuable technique for exploring the complex and diverse "rationales, narratives or perspectives" associated with different points of view in discourses (Wolsink and Breukers 2010, p. 538).

Purposive sampling was used to identify participants who are influential in advocating diverse points of view related to local energy development (Maxwell 2013). In total, eight residents from Pincher Creek and 25 residents from Cochrane participated in Q-method procedures. These individuals were selected as residents and business people with direct interests or experiences with energy production. For this study, the Q-set of 48 statements was developed by Parkins et al. (2015) and reflects a 'balanced' and non-technology-specific set of items from which multiple discourses can be identified. Reflecting the diversity of energy production technologies in the study region, the use of this Q-set is beneficial because it taps into a wide range of energy development issues and principles without simply polarizing around energy sources. Research participants were invited to arrange the statements from strongly disagree to strongly agree on a Q-sort board (Table 17.1). The list of 48 statements is provided in Table 17.2.

Q-sort data from both communities was analyzed together using principal component analysis (PCA), followed by Varimax factor rotation, using freely available software designed specifically for Q-methodological studies (PQmethod version 2.35, Schmolck and Atkinson 2014). Here we define "minority discourse" as a discourse that is less commonly held in our observed data and in the related literature. In addition to in-depth interviews with all participants after

Table 17.1 Q-sort configuration based on force choice set from strongly disagree to strongly agree

	Strongly disagree				Neutral					Strongly agree
Column ranking	–5	–4	–3	–2	–1	0	1	2	3	4	5
Statements per column	1	2	4	6	7	8	7	6	4	2	1

the initial Q-sort was completed, we also conducted follow-up interviews with participants associated with minority discourses to gain greater understanding of the deeper meanings behind these factors.

Results

Using factor analysis techniques provided in the PQMethod software, a PCA four-factor solution was extracted as an accurate reflection of the dominant and nuanced aspects of the sorts collected in this study. Follow-up interviews were conducted with the four participants who contributed to the definition of the two minority discourses, factors 3 and 4. After reviewing the descriptions of all the identified factors, all four participants confirmed that the factor they identified with accurately described their view on energy development. To help provide context as to how the factors were interpreted, the statement number and its related scoring are provided in parentheses, for example, statement number 36 in Table 17.2 is "Climate change poses a grave and urgent threat to our planet." This statement is identified with Factor 1 in the section below, with a factor score of +5 (i.e., 36: +5). Refer to Table 17.2 for a full list of the statements used in the Q-sort.

Factor 1: climate-concerned citizen

The views held under factor 1 in Table 17.2 are primarily motivated by concerns about the dangers of climate change (36: +5) and anthropogenic impacts that are pushing the global environment beyond a self-correcting state (17: –5). Energy development is viewed as having a prominent role in the disruption of natural systems, as both living and energy systems are considered to be interconnected (26: +2). While describing their concerns about climate change and nature's ability to self-correct, participants made statements, such as:

> There are a lot of people that really think that global change is not imminent, global change isn't going to really affect them, sitting in the middle of Alberta. They are not worried about the oceans rising and stuff like this. But I actually think that, just from knowledge that I have gathered, that we are drastically losing arable land. I think that glaciers, which I would relate to as a water source, are receding. I think that our groundwater is becoming polluted.

Table 17.2 Q-statements, factor arrays and averages scores for each statement

No	Statement	Factor				Avg*
		1	2	3	4	
1	Companies must take responsibility and pay for the pollution they produce	4	2	1	5	3.0
2	Canadians have a duty to be global leaders by reducing our own energy consumption	3	1	3	−4	0.8
3	Our energy problems will be solved in the future through new technology and innovation	0	3	1	2	1.5
4	Consuming too much energy is immoral	1	−3	5	−3	0.0
5	Compared to citizens of other countries, Canadians consume an obscene amount of energy	1	−2	−1	−1	−0.8
6	A high level of energy consumption is part of the good life	−2	2	−4	−1	−1.3
7	The current fad for "going green" will accomplish nothing	−3	−1	0	1	−0.8
8	Canada's commitment to democracy makes it an ethical supplier of energy	−3	0	2	0	−0.3
9	Fossil fuels should not be burned … they should just be left in the ground	−2	−4	−3	−1	−2.5
10	Energy structures, like transmission towers, hydroelectric dams or wind turbines, can be beautiful	−1	2	−5	−3	−1.8
11	Market forces, not incentives or taxes, drive development and conservation of energy	0	1	1	−5	−0.8
12	Energy infrastructure is part of our modern Canadian identity	0	3	2	2	1.8
13	No energy source is perfect; there are trade-offs between economic development and environmental protection	2	3	−2	−1	0.5
14	Small and distributed energy sources are more resilient than centralized production	0	−1	3	0	0.5
15	NIMBYism (Not In My Back Yard) poses a real threat to becoming a cleaner and greener society	1	1	−3	−1	−0.5
16	Our national energy resources should be used in Canada for the benefit of Canadians	0	−1	−1	4	0.5
17	Nature will be fine no matter what humans do; it is a robust, self-correcting system	−5	−5	1	−2	−2.8
18	Growth in energy production is key to Canada's economic progress	−2	5	1	0	1.0

continued

Table 17.2 Continued

No	Statement	Factor				Avg*
		1	2	3	4	
19	Current trends in energy consumption are clearly unsustainable and must be reduced immediately	3	−2	4	−2	0.8
20	Canada should brand itself as renewable energy innovators	1	1	−2	1	0.3
21	Improved power grid technology will help us manage energy better	1	1	−1	2	0.8
22	Renewable energy options are too expensive right now	1	0	1	0	0.5
23	Only the world's poorest people will suffer from climate change	−3	−3	−1	−2	−2.3
24	Canada's prosperity is based on ample supplies of affordable energy	0	4	3	3	2.5
25	We need to find ways to develop untapped resources for renewable energy	4	1	0	−1	1.0
26	Energy systems are interconnected with all living systems	2	1	3	0	1.5
27	Most Canadians are well aware of the environmental impacts of energy development	−3	0	−3	−4	−2.5
28	Large facilities and concentrated production is the smartest way to provide energy	−2	0	−2	0	−1.0
29	Renewables cannot generate enough energy to significantly reduce greenhouse gases	−2	−1	−2	0	−1.3
30	Energy, not money, is the vital essence that flows through human societies	−1	2	1	1	0.8
31	Energy infrastructure does not belong in our cherished landscapes	−1	−4	−1	2	−1.0
32	All forms of energy should be more expensive	−1	−3	−2	−2	−2.0
33	Increased investment in clean energy will boost our economy while improving the environment	3	2	−1	4	2.0
34	Our standing in the global economy depends upon maximizing fossil fuel energy exports	−2	3	2	−2	0.3
35	We should have more energy choices at the household level	2	−1	0	3	1.0
36	Climate change poses a grave and urgent threat to our planet	5	−2	−4	−1	−0.5
37	Scientific experts should decide how resources should be developed	0	−2	−3	2	−0.8
38	Canadians would conserve more energy if it saved them more money	1	−1	2	0	0.5

Table 17.2 Continued

No	Statement	Factor				Avg*
		1	2	3	4	
39	The local community should decide on the energy systems that are best for them	−1	−2	2	1	0.0
40	Energy from dirty sources should be more expensive for consumers	2	−3	0	−2	−0.8
41	People accept energy projects when there are benefits to the local community	0	2	−2	1	0.3
42	Environmentalists are standing in the way of economic development	−4	0	−1	−3	−2.0
43	Renewable energy options like wind, solar or geothermal should be placed only where the potential is greatest	−1	0	2	3	1.0
44	Canada's greenhouse gas emissions are justified because they are tiny compared to other countries	−4	0	0	−3	−1.8
45	Any energy source that produces close to zero carbon emissions (wind, solar, hydroelectric, nuclear) is urgently needed	2	−2	0	2	0.5
46	The government should provide incentives to support clean energy development	3	0	0	1	1.0
47	Canada's energy resources make it a powerful global leader	−1	4	4	3	2.5
48	We need to reduce pollution and consumption, not find ways to develop more resources	2	−1	0	1	0.5

Note
* Average factor score per statement.

When addressing the role of energy development in Canada, the views held in factor 1 are not supportive of Canada's prosperity and economy being strongly reliant on fossil fuel development (18: −2; 34: −2; 24: 0). Instead, participants want diversification and progress of the Canadian economy to one that is no longer reliant on fossil fuel development and exportation (20: +1). Supporting this notion, one community resident stated:

> You know they are stuck in a box, this province is a stunning example of that. Putting all their eggs in one basket: when are you guys going to wake up? ... it doesn't matter if it's energy or what it is, when are you going to wake up and say, we have to diversify this thing?

To achieve a shift away from Canada's current dependence on fossil fuels, factor 1 participants suggest that governments provide incentives to support clean energy technology (46: +3; 21: +1) and tap new resources to advance renewable energy development (25: +4). As climate change is seen to be a threat of grave importance, the shift to clean energy technologies that produce close to zero carbon emissions is viewed as urgently needed (45: +2). Additionally, the excuse that no action is needed to reduce greenhouse gas emissions due to Canada's "tiny" contribution to global emissions is not accepted (44: –4). They disagree with arguments that are used to justify the continued rapid extraction of resources and high levels of carbon dioxide, such as "Canada's commitment to democracy makes it an ethical supplier of energy" (8: –3). Methods to achieve this reduction that are supported in factor 1 include placing monetary penalties on dirty sources of energy (40: +2) and providing more energy options, such as renewables, at the household level (35: +2). Other actions to reduce pollution and consumption, such as "going green," are also viewed as important contributions to improved outcomes (7: –3).

Factor 2: energy and prosperity

The views represented by factor 2 primarily focus on the relationship between energy development and Canada's prosperity and economic progress (18: +5; 24: +4). Canada's ample fossil fuel resources are viewed as key to this prosperity, as fossil fuels offer an affordable source of energy for citizens (24: +4; 40: –3) and position Canada as a powerful global leader (47: +4). As one participant put it: "If you are going to have an economy, you are going to have an energy source, and it has to be affordable." For Canada to continue experiencing economic progress and secure its standing in the global economy, it is believed that fossil fuel resources should continue to be extracted (9: –4) and exported (34: +3; 16: –1). The continued development of energy resources is embraced in factor 2, as it is viewed as an important part of Canada's modern identity (12: +3), with energy infrastructure being looked upon positively as something that can be beautiful (10: +2).

When addressing advances in the hydraulic fracturing industry, one participant stated:

> I think mankind is very innovative: if forced to come up with new technologies they will be doing that. I spent this summer [working] for a company that is in the oil and gas industry and they were talking about how they are using Debolt [saline water] to inject into the fracking wells instead of freshwater/potable water. That's really new, and it's at the forefront.... So that's innovation....

Advances in technology are thought to assist not only in the continued development of fossil fuel resources but also in renewable energy resources (25: +1). Investments in clean energy are viewed as the way which Canada will be able to boost the economy and improve the environment (33: +2). However, the implementation and transition to energy sources that produce close to zero carbon emissions are not viewed as urgently needed (45: −2). It is understood that no energy source is perfect, and that there are trade-offs between economic development and environmental protection (13: +3). These trade-offs include a "polluter pay" approach to mitigating pollution (1: +2). Additionally, the views held in factor 2 recognize a limit to nature's robustness and ability to correct itself and therefore energy development does have the potential to have long-lasting effects on the environment (17: −5). This indicates that although energy development is of great importance, humans need to be aware of the interconnection of energy systems with all other living systems (26: +1). The views represented by this factor strongly embrace the notion of trade-offs, which also includes support for siting energy infrastructure in landscapes that may be considered by some to be off-limits (31: −4). To exclude such areas from development could lead the prioritization or favoring of particular communities over others.

Factor 3: overconsumption and local sustainability

Views held within factor 3, the first of the identified minority discourses, are orientated around the topic of consumption and the view that current rates of energy consumption are unsustainable and have reached immoral levels (4: +5; 19: +4; 2: +3; 6: −4). Although this factor identifies overconsumption as a concern, it is not suggesting that Canadians rid themselves of all modern comforts. It is instead indicating that unnecessary energy consumption is becoming prevalent in Canada, and has led to unsustainable energy development practices. As one participant stated: "I like the modern conveniences but I don't feel it's my right to use everything. I feel that what I use in one way or another should be in a sustainable manner."

One unique feature that separates factor 3 from factor 1 is that the desire to reduce energy consumption is not driven by concerns associated with climate change (36: −4). This is because concerns of climate change are questioned and are seen as exaggerated, with issues of overconsumption being viewed as a much higher priority. Although climate change is not a primary concern within factor 3, the effects of energy development on the landscape are not overlooked, as the interconnection between energy systems and other living systems is recognized (26: +3). Further, there is a concern that overconsumption is leading to unsustainable energy development and industrialization of landscapes (10: −5). Instead of being concerned about global sustainability issues such as climate change, there is a greater focus on local sustainability. It is also thought that the current use of large concentrated energy production is unsustainable and results in unnecessary adverse effects (28: −2). For instance, transmission lines and other energy infrastructure are viewed as aesthetically ugly (10: −5), or as one participant indicated, a form of "environmental ruin." Small and distributed localized forms of energy production are seen as the way to allow local communities to decide on the energy system that is best for them (39: +2), enabling them to maximize the benefits and reduce the costs of the chosen energy source (13: –2; 43: +2). As local energy development should be directed to address local needs and limitations, decisions relating to local energy development should be made by locals and not by outside experts (37: –3). Along these lines of thinking, one participant stated:

> I wouldn't even want to make a preference for renewables or gas or biofuels or anything. [It depends on] what works best for the region, what works best for the community, what keeps transmission to a minimum, because I think my energy future would be getting away from large conglomerates like the large utilities and basically move power generation into the hands of the community. They decide and they manage their own power generation.

Factor 4: power inequality

The views held in factor 4, the second of the two identified minority discourses, are centered on concerns over power inequities that are associated with energy development in Canada (1: +5; 11 –5). These views are balanced by the recognition of the importance of Canada's energy resources to the prosperity of the country (47: +3; 24: +3; 9: –1). However, in factor 4, the view is that the benefits of energy development are not being fairly distributed. As one participant stated: "[T]he energy that we use and that drives the development and conservation of energy should benefit all classes of citizens in Canada and right now it doesn't, it only benefits the very rich...."

The primary power inequality issues on which factor 4 focuses are those related to companies' responsibility for pollution and adverse impacts produced during energy production. Views shared in factor 4 suggest that currently energy companies (particularly oil and gas companies) are not held responsible by the government and its regulatory bodies for all the pollution produced during energy production (1: +5). Instead, participants associated with factor 4 are of the opinion that the responsibility and cost of pollution, including the cost of proving the pollution is harmful, are placed upon the individual. For instance, one participant stated:

> I know that I need gas, but make oil companies responsible for any faults or problems that come from [them]. They say. "Well, you have to prove that your water is going to be unsafe." Well, there is no way that I can prove it; I am not a scientist ... I went to [the] government to get them to set up a program where if the oil company did something wrong that they pay for the mistakes so I don't have to, but that is not the case.

The transfer of responsibility for pollution to the individual is associated for this factor with the fact that market forces no longer dictate how energy resources are developed or conserved (11: –5). Instead, the desire of the elite to acquire further profits determines how energy resources and their impacts are managed. At the local level, the prioritization of profit is viewed as having taken away an individual's power to adequately voice their concerns, or to influence how energy is produced in their community.

According to the views expressed in factor 4, one reason why local and national environmental and social issues continue to be overlooked is the general population's limited awareness of the environmental impacts of energy development and how these impacts affect people (27: –4). Canadians' limited awareness of environmental and community impacts is partly a result of the separation of the general public from energy development. As the majority of the Canadian population lives in urban environments they are seen as seldom coming into contact with, or directly impacted by, resource extraction activities and energy development. This limited interaction allows the majority of Canadians to separate themselves from the impacts of energy development, thus continuing to allow inequitable power distributions to exist.

One solution to the power inequalities identified in factor 4 is seen as increased investment in, and development of, clean and efficient energy technologies. By using clean and advanced energy technologies, Canadian energy development could be managed in a way that prioritizes benefits to Canadians (21: +2; 16: +4), while also employing more people and boosting the Canadian economy (33: +4). However, for the implementation of clean energy technologies to be conducted properly, the maximization of affordable energy production, although important (43: +3), must not be the only variable considered.

Toward common ground

Although our analysis highlights the difference between these four discourses, and sources of tension within the governance of natural resources, we can also identify important areas of overlapping agreement across the factors. Areas of commonality are reported in Table 17.3.

In addition to these areas of alignment expressed in Table 17.3, the views on climate change expressed in factors 1 and 4 are different, but both factors voice concerns over power inequalities that exist between local communities and the energy industry. Similarly, while factors 1 and 3 have conflicting views on climate change and the solutions for how to address it, they share the opinion that energy consumption and development should be practiced more sustainably – particularly in relation to local impacts. While comparing the different factor arrays during the follow-up interview, and discussing their experience on a local committee, a factor 3 participant reflected on the relationship between factors 1 and 3 by stating:

> The more I was on the committee with [name of a committee member], and over the course of time, the more I realized that even though I didn't agree with what he was saying, we both had the same long-range goals in mind. It was just that we had come at it from total different aspects.... So the same

Table 17.3 Areas of commonality between factors

No	Statement	Factor				Avg*
		1	*2*	*3*	*4*	
1	Companies must take responsibility and pay for the pollution they produce	4	2	1	5	3.0
24	Canada's prosperity is based on ample supplies of affordable energy	0	4	3	3	2.5
47	Canada's energy resources make it a powerful global leader	−1	4	4	3	2.5
17	Nature will be fine no matter what humans do; it is a robust, self-correcting system	−5	−5	1	−2	−2.8
9	Fossil fuels should not be burned … they should just be left in the ground	−2	−4	−3	−1	−2.5
27	Most Canadians are well aware of the environmental impacts of energy development	−3	0	−3	−4	−2.5

Note
* Average factor score per statement.

here. I look at it from a totally different perspective than factor 1 but in the end game we want long-term sustainability, it's just how we look at arriving at that. So the factor 1 people, I don't agree with them, but I understand what they want to achieve.

Similarities can also be found between the two most opposing discourses identified within the study: factors 1 and 2. For instance, factors 1 and 2 have opposing opinions when it comes to climate change and the relationship between fossil fuel development and Canada's prosperity. However, despite these differences, both factors were found to describe the self-correcting characteristics of nature as having limits – limits that, if put under enough pressure, can be compromised by human activities. Additionally, participants who represent these factors agree that companies should take responsibility for the pollution they produce. These similarities demonstrate that factors 1 and 2 are not as polarized as they first appear.

Conclusion

Our aim in this chapter is to identify distinct discourses on energy development in the south-western region of Alberta and to identify areas of overlapping interest (common ground) that can serve as a focal point for more harmonious governance of energy resources. We identify this common ground through Q-method and four specific energy-related discourses. Factors 1 and 2 resemble the opposing discourses that are common among opponents and proponents of energy projects. Similar to the discourses described by Bomberg (2015) and Cotton et al. (2014) in the UK, factor 1 focuses on the deleterious impacts associated with energy development, while factor 2 tends to emphasize the economic benefits. More specifically, Cotton (2015) notes substantial agreement on negative local impacts from fracking in the UK, such as increased road traffic and reduced property values. These concerns for local sustainability are also expressed in several of the discourses noted above. The recurrence of these polarizing discourses in this study does not come as a surprise. As other scholars have noted, information presented by proponents of hydraulic fracturing and wind energy development is often framed in the language of economics, while opponents use frames related to the environment, health and climate change (Brannstrom et al. 2011; Finewood and Stroup 2012; Bomberg 2015), with growing recognition of local impacts ranging from increased road traffic to the upheaval of transmission lines.

The identification of overlapping views between dominant and minority discourses not only furthers our understanding of the spectrum of views present in the south-west region of Alberta, but also demonstrates potential areas in which local organizations, such as the Synergy Alberta (2017) organization for community participation in energy resource development, can build from common ground between groups that are normally in conflict with each other. With insights from the Q-method results, those who associated with the identified discourses have a common thread established between them. This commonality can be described as the desire to improve upon how energy development is conducted within Alberta. Although the end goal and the manner in which change is achieved may be defined differently, the common desire for improvement provides a footing on which constructive conversations can be established.

Separating our findings from a conventional understanding of these polarizing perspectives (e.g., jobs versus the environment) involves attention to the commonalities between discourses. The identification of dominant and minority discourses also helps to illuminate nuances between discourses, while at the same time bringing to light areas of contention and pathways for change that may be under-examined within this context. Such findings can help those who are engaged in energy debates better understand what motivates particular points of view, thereby helping to uncover common threads between viewpoints on which understanding and dialogue can germinate.

References

Adkin, L. E., Hanson, L. L., Kahane, D., Parkins, J. R., and Patten, S. 2017. "Can public engagement democratize environmental policymaking in a resource-dependent state? Comparative case studies from Alberta, Canada." *Environmental Politics*, 26(2): 301–321.

Baxter, J., Morzaria, R. and Hirsch, R. 2013. "A case-control study of support/opposition to wind turbines: Perceptions of health risk, economic benefits, and community conflict." *Energy Policy*, 61: 931–943.

Bell, D., Gray, T. and Haggett, C. 2005. "The 'social gap' in wind farm siting decisions: Explanations and policy responses." *Environmental Politics*, 14(4): 460–477.

Bomberg, E. 2015. "Shale we drill? Discourse dynamics in UK fracking debates." *Journal of Environmental Policy & Planning* (ahead-of-print),1–17.

Boudet, H., Clarke, C., Bugden, D. et al. 2014. "'Fracking' controversy and communication: Using national survey data to understand public perceptions of hydraulic fracturing." *Energy Policy*, 65: 57–67.

Brannstrom, C., Jepson, W. and Persons, N. 2011. "Social perspective on wind-power development in West Texas." *Annuals of the Association of American Geographers*, 101(4): 839–851.

Carneiro, F. O. M., Barbosa Rocha, H. H. and Costa Rocha P. A. 2013. "Investigation of possible societal risk associated with wind power generation systems." *Renewable and Sustainable Energy Reviews*, 19: 30–36.

Clare, S., Krogman, N. and Caine, K. J. 2013. "The 'balance discourse': A case study of power and wetland management." *Geoforum*, 49: 40–49.

Colborn, T., Kwiatkowski, C., Schultz, K. and Bachran, M. 2011. "Natural gas operations from a public health perspective." *Human and Ecological Risk Assessment: An International Journal*, 17(5): 1039–1056.

Cotton, M. 2015. "Stakeholder perspectives on shale gas fracking: A Q-method study of environmental discourses." *Environment and Planning A*, 47(9): 1944–1962.

Cotton, M., Rattle, I. and Van Alstine, J. 2014. "Shale gas policy in the United Kingdom: An argumentative discourse analysis." *Energy Policy*, 73: 427–438.

Cowell, R. 2013. "The greenest government ever? Planning and sustainability in England after the May 2010 elections." *Planning Practice & Research*, 28(1): 27–44.

Davis, C. and Fisk, J. M. 2014. "Energy abundance or environmental worries? Analyzing public support for fracking in the United States." *Review of Policy Research*, 31(1): 1–16.

De Rijke, K. 2013. "Hydraulically fractured: unconventional gas and anthropology." *Anthropology Today*, 29(2): 13–17.

Dodge, J. 2015. "The deliberative potential of civil society organizations: Framing hydraulic fracturing in New York." *Policy Studies*, 36(3): 249–266.

Finewood, M. H. and Stroup, L. J. 2012. "Fracking and the neoliberalization of the hydro-social cycle in Pennsylvania's Marcellus Shale." *Journal of Contemporary Water Research & Resources*, 147(1): 72–79.

Gordalla, B. C., Ewers U. and Frimmel, F. H. 2013. "Hydraulic fracturing: A toxicological threat for groundwater and drinking-water?" *Environmental Earth Sciences*, 70(8): 3875–3893.

Government of Alberta. 2016. *Unconventional Resources – Shale Gas*. Edmonton. AB: Alberta Energy. Available at: www.energy.alberta.ca/OurBusiness/944.asp

Hajer, M. A. 1995. *The Politics of Environmental Discourse: Ecological Modernisation and Policy Process*. Oxford: Clarendon Press.

Howarth, R. W., Ingraffea, A. and Engelder, T. 2011. "Natural gas: Should fracking stop?" *Nature*, 477(7364): 271–275.

Jepson, W., Brannstrom, C. and Persons, N. 2012. "'We don't take the pledge': Environmentality and environmental skepticism at the epicenter of US wind energy development." *Geoforum*, 43(3): 851–863.

Jessup, B. 2010. "Plural and hybrid environmental values: A discourse analysis of the wind energy conflict in Australia and the United Kingdom." *Environmental Politics*, 19(1): 21–44.

Mander, S. 2008. "The role of discourse coalitions in planning for renewable energy: a case study of wind-energy deployment." *Environment and Planning C: Government and Policy*, 26(3): 583–600.

Marsh, R., Parks, K. and Crowfoot, C. (eds.). 2013. *Alberta's Energy Reserves 2012 and Supply/Demand Outlook 2013–2022, ST98–2013*. Calgary, AB: Energy Resources Conservation Board.

Maxwell, J. A. 2013. *Qualitative Research Design: An Interactive Approach*, 3rd ed. Thousand Oaks, CA: Sage.

Parkins, J. R., Hempel, C., Beckley, T. M., Stedman, R. C., & Sherren, K. 2015. "Identifying energy discourses in Canada with Q methodology: Moving beyond the environment versus economy debates." *Environmental Sociology*, 1(4): 304–314.

Pasqualetti, M. J. 2011. "Opposing wind energy landscapes: A search for common cause." *Annals of the Association of American Geographers*, 101(4): 907–917.

Schirrmeister, M. 2014. "Controversial futures-discourse analysis on utilizing the 'fracking' technology in Germany." *European Journal of Futures Research*, 2(1): 1–9.

Schmolck, P. and Atkinson, J. 2014. PQMethod (Version 2.35). Computer software and manual. Available at: schmolck.userweb.mwn.de/qmethod/ (accessed June, 2014).

Stephenson, E., Doukas, A. and Shaw, K. 2012. "Greenwashing gas: Might a 'transition fuel' label legitimize carbon-intensive gas development?" *Energy Policy*, 46: 452–459.

Synergy Alberta. 2017. *Synergy Alberta: Our Community. Our Future*. Available at: www. synergyalberta.ca/synergy-groups (accessed May 18, 2017).

Szarka, J. 2004. "Wind power, discourse coalitions and climate change: Breaking the stalemate?" *European Environment*, 14(6): 317–330.

Town of Pincher Creek Alberta. 2014a. "Wind energy." Available at: www.pinchercreek. ca/business/wind_energy.php (accessed June 20, 2014).

Town of Pincher Creek Alberta. 2014b. "Irrigation and hydroelectricity." Available at: www.pinchercreek.ca/business/hydro.php (accessed June 20, 2014).

Town of Pincher Creek Alberta. 2014c. "Natural gas." Available at: www.pinchercreek. ca/business/natural_gas.php (accessed June 20, 2014).

Warren, C. R., Lumsden, C., O'Dowd, S. and Birnie, R. V. 2005. "'Green on green': Public perceptions of wind power in Scotland and Ireland." *Journal of Environmental Planning and Management*, 48(6): 853–875.

Wolsink, M. and Breukers, S. 2010. "Contrasting the core beliefs regarding the effective implementation of wind power: An international study of stakeholder perspectives." *Journal of Environmental Planning and Management*, 53(5): 535–558.

18 Scientized and sanitized

Shale gas in the context of New Brunswick's political history

Kelly Bronson and Tom Beckley

Introduction

In government discourses, the practice of hydraulic fracturing (fracking) is often celebrated as a technique for boosting local and national economies and mitigating climate change; according to some measures, burning natural gas emits roughly half as much carbon dioxide as coal (see Miller et al., 2015). According to other accounts, shale gas extraction has a higher greenhouse gas footprint than coal (Howarth et al., 2011; Wigley, 2011). As well, many citizens, especially those in communities situated close to sites where natural gas is extracted, raise serious concerns about the effects of the practice on society, the environment and human health (Perry, 2013). Uptake of these concerns by policymakers has been mixed at best, with activists charging that local and state-level agencies protect the interests of industry over the public (e.g., Cook, 2015; Hudgins and Poole, 2014).

These contrasting and competing discourses play out in interesting ways in the eastern Canadian province of New Brunswick. In Canada, fracking for shale gas is regulated at the provincial and territorial levels and regional differences exist in the legislation surrounding its use. In New Brunswick, subsurface rights reside with the provincial government and recent provincial governments saw the potential in the royalties fracking would produce, as a means to create jobs and reduce growing budget deficits. While shale gas exploration is currently being carried out in several Canadian provinces (Canadian Association of Petroleum Producers, 2013), an indefinite moratorium on the practice of fracking in New Brunswick came into into effect in June 2015 after intense public controversy on the issue. The deep apprehension about fracking shared by many New Brunswick citizens (see New Brunswick Commission on Hydraulic Fracturing, 2016) is fueled by a wider mistrust of government and long-standing relations with industry characterized by workforce exposure to hazards and the operation of monopoly corporations.

The New Brunswick provincial government has only furthered public mistrust for governance processes through its treatment of the fracking debate. Drawing on documents analysis and inductive textual analysis of transcribed audio-recordings of three formal public engagement sessions (August 21, 2013;

October 21, 2013; and March 28, 2014), we argue that governments under-appreciated that many citizens, perhaps especially First Nations residents, viewed the development of shale gas as a moral and political issue; instead two separate provincial governments have focused governance efforts on investigating royalty rates and environmental risks. Government seems to have mistakenly believed that if citizens understood the risks and rewards better, then concern over the practice would dissipate. As such, this is a case of government actors assuming a knowledge deficit model: "If regular citizens knew and understood what the expert/bureaucrat knows, then they would have the same values position on the issue" (Brossard and Lewenstein, 2010). With this mindset, the government scientized and sanitized the fracking debate in this province, talking past the issues at root of public concern, particularly concern about the democratic process.

Although New Brunswick is a hotbed of political controversy surrounding fracking, it has until now played a very minor role in the social science research on this topic (cf. Bronson, 2016). This chapter brings attention to this jurisdiction, focusing on particular public engagement initiatives around fracking as they illuminate government understandings of the public as ultimately misinformed on technical matters (see also de Saille, 2015; Welsh and Wynne, 2013). This chapter also turns attention to something of broader theoretical significance. Interestingly, we show how citizens involved in roundtable dialogues fail to challenge the technocratic framework given to them by government actors. Ultimately, then, this chapter fits within recent critical social science on public engagement in governance, which calls for attention to the role of publics in sticky governance relations (e.g., Hess, 2015).

We begin by descriptively sketching the contours of the fracking debate in New Brunswick as it relates to the province's unique political culture. We then draw on empirical material collected from specific public engagement exercises hosted by government to reveal moments where decision-makers narrowly defined the limits of deliberations to overemphasize technical issues related to fracking at the expense of social, political, and cultural concerns raised by activists in the province.

Context

New Brunswick's shale deposits

New Brunswick is a small province by Canadian standards, both by population and geographic area. Located in eastern Canada, just south of Quebec, north of Nova Scotia and east of the US state of Maine, it is comprised of roughly 7.3 million hectares of land, and has a population of roughly 750,000 residents as of 2014. Like much of Canada, its economy is export-driven and focused on natural resource extraction. Forestry has been the dominant sector for more than two centuries, but mining and fishing have been important as well. In the rest of Canada, 80% of the population live in urban areas, however, New

Brunswick has three small metropolitan areas that account for roughly half the province's population with the remainder rural. This rural population distribution is partly what makes the New Brunswick shale gas story unique in Canada.

In recent times, there has been a significant contraction in many resource sectors. Forestry, for example, generates significant overall wealth, but it no longer generates significant jobs or as much income for individual woodlot owners as it once did. For over one century, rationalization and mechanization have reduced the number of high-paying natural resource jobs across many resource sectors in the province.

Unlike the downturn in other sectors like forestry and mining, shale gas exploration in the province has increased. Some oil and gas development has existed in New Brunswick since 1859 (Park, 2012). Relatively recently, the Frederick Brook shale deposit came under scrutiny for its shale gas potential and a combination of directional drilling and exploratory hydraulic fracturing has resulted in estimates that this reserve might contain as much as 80 trillion cubic feet of natural gas (Canadian Association of Petroleum Producers, 2013; National Energy Board, 2009; Tutton, 2013). Geographically, the potential shale resource is concentrated in the central and south-eastern portions of the province and covers less than one-quarter of the total area of New Brunswick. This means that health and environmental concerns over the development of the industry would be concentrated while the benefits (through royalties to government) would be shared across the province. Another unique feature of New Brunswick's shale resource is that the deposits lie deeper underground than in many other jurisdictions (e.g., Marcellus), and it has a relatively thick vertical profile. The geologic formations where the potential for shale gas is present supply many rural residents who rely on wells to provide their domestic water supply but also, and uniquely, the urban areas surrounding Fredericton, the provincial capital, and Moncton, the second largest city in the province.

Fracking controversy in New Brunswick

As political theater, the fracking controversy in New Brunswick has it all. A key report on the health effects of shale gas from the previous Chief Medical Officer of Health was only released to the public after intense public pressure on government (Office of the Chief Medical Officer of Health, 2012). Initial public "consultations" were conducted throughout the province by a long-time consultant with Canadian provincial and federal governments, Louis LaPierre (LaPierre, 2012). A recommendation coming from these processes was that there existed a need to create an unbiased, third party Energy Institute that would both engage public and technical expertise in energy decision-making. Two months after Louis LaPierre was chosen by the government to initiate the Energy Institute, he was effectively forced to resign because it was discovered that he had doctored his academic credentials. In 2013, five police vehicles were burned and 40 protesters were arrested in Rexton, New Brunswick. The Alward government suffered a legitimation crisis after these events and were voted out in a near referendum on shale gas in the provincial election of 2014. Citizens charged the Alward government with being more concerned about supporting private over public interests.

The governance of New Brunswick's natural resources has historically been characterized by a privileging of the province's political and economic elite. In the nineteenth century, the politically and economically powerful actors were one and the same. The timber barons, who were the chief capitalists of the era, also served in the provincial legislature. In contemporary New Brunswick, government and private sector elites are not necessarily the same individuals, though there is a notable "revolving door" from government to industry (and back). There is widespread public recognition that the economic capital in New Brunswick is highly concentrated, largely in the hands of one very powerful family – the Irving family (Poitras, 2014).

The tendency toward oligopoly manifests into a governance of the resource sector in New Brunswick wherein there exists mutual distrust between decision-makers and citizens. It appears that many citizens believe that the majority of economic policy decisions are made behind closed doors and in consultation with the economic elite, while government actors distrust the electorate's ability to process complex technical information enough to make informed decisions (New Brunswick Commission on Hydraulic Fracturing, 2016). The distrust between citizens and government cross-cuts political party lines. For generations there has been a two-party political culture with left-moderate Liberals and right-moderate Progressive Conservatives. Exploration of the province's shale gas deposits was initiated by a Liberal Party led by Premier Shawn Graham in the late 2000s. The Graham government invited external companies with unconventional gas development experience to assess the viability of the resource in New Brunswick. Initially, the Progressive Conservatives, then in opposition, appeared skeptical about shale exploration. The Graham Liberal government was unelected in 2010, largely due to controversy over the proposed sale of the provincial utility and all its assets. Once in power, the Progressive Conservatives under the leadership of Premier David Alward, expressed new enthusiasm for the potential to use shale gas royalties toward bringing down budgetary deficits. It is widely acknowledged that the Alward government lost to Premier Brian Gallant's Liberal government in the fall of 2014 due to the former's unabashed pro-shale gas stance. In December 2014, Liberal Premier Brian Gallant introduced the *Prohibition Against Hydraulic Fracturing Regulation*, which, when passed in June of the following year, placed a moratorium on fracking in the province.

There are many actors involved in the fracking debate in this province beyond politicians and bureaucrats who formally discourage or encourage corporate activity (say, through tax incentives). Various interest groups have been trying to influence the conversation on fracking, one obviously being the exploration and development corporations themselves: Corridor Resources, a resource extraction corporation, who has been fracking in the province, and SWN – both of whom are interested in wide-scale resource exploration. Another broad interest group is the research community, which contains varying and often competing interests: engineers and biologists, many of whom appear cautiously in favor of fracking investment (Al et al., 2012); medical researchers and professionals, including New Brunswick's Chief Medical Officer of Health, who are concerned about the possible socio-economic and health impacts of boom-and-bust industrial development (Office of the Chief Medical Officer of Health, 2012); social scientists concerned principally with engaging ordinary citizens in the imagination of the province's energy futures (Beckley, 2014; Beckley, Parkins and Sheppard, 2007; Bronson, 2016). Other groups outside of the research community include New Brunswick tradesmen and women, who have vocally supported potential job creation from government investments in the industrial sector, including the shale gas industry. There are members of the public and non-profit groups, who have been vocal about provincial policy directions. There are well-established environmental groups (e.g., Conservation Council of New Brunswick) and unaffiliated environmental activists, who have expressed concern about the possible environmental and health impacts of fracking because it is a relatively new technical practice with dynamic technologies and methods, an unclear regulatory structure and what they describe as inconclusive scientific evidence to support it (Conservation Council of New Brunswick, 2013; Hubner et al., 2013). However, the shale gas controversy did not play out as many previous environmental controversies have with clear leadership from established environmental NGOs. Rather, a loosely but effectively coordinated agglomeration of community and watershed-based groups have arisen principally due to this particular issue. The website of the New Brunswick Anti-Shale Gas Alliance, for example, lists 19 distinct supporter groups, many of which have names depicting a distinct focus on shale gas development. First Nations (especially the Elsipogtog) have a parallel but unique stance against shale development, centered largely around a custodial orientation toward freshwater resources.

Value-based citizen concerns, misguided government response: the New Brunswick Energy Institute

Activists in New Brunswick have raised a number of value-based concerns related to a possible fracking industry in the province. For one, many activists suggest there are inherent inequities in the shale gas industry – egregious profiting for large, foreign corporations at the expense of community and environmental health. Members of First Nations share these concerns and have additional and significant cultural, and land rights concerns (Howe, 2015). In fact, indigenous activism around fracking culminated in Rexton, New Brunswick, on October 17, 2013, in a violent stand-off between members of the Elsipogtog First Nation (a Mi'kmaq people) and the US-based SWN Corporation who wanted to prospect for shale gas and industrial development on untreatied land (for more details, see ibid.).

This confrontation between police and First Nations was partly a response to concern over a lack of meaningful consultations on the subject of fracking; just before it occurred, the Alward Conservative government had attempted to restrict the controversy to its technical dimensions with the establishment of the New Brunswick Energy Institute (NBEI). By the establishment of the NBEI, government thought that both scientific data and "a ... dialogue was needed to determine the viability and safety of a shale gas industry and other energy development in the province" (New Brunswick Energy Institute, 2014; see Figure 18.1). The provincial government initially funded the NBEI, but the Institute soon after attained independent status as a non-profit in May of 2013. The original Chair of the NBEI, Louis LaPierre, himself a government appointee, selected and appointed the other roundtable members (see Table 18.1). Louis LaPierre was chosen based upon his experience as a consultant to governments – both federal and provincial – on the environmental impacts of large infrastructure projects.[1]

The NBEI came about in the context of complex public debate over a possible fracking industry in New Brunswick and also as a direct result of two significant governance documents. In 2011, the Conservative provincial government released the *Energy Blueprint*, which was meant to provide policy direction and a three-year action plan for the energy sector in New Brunswick (Department of Energy, 2011). One of the key objectives outlined in this

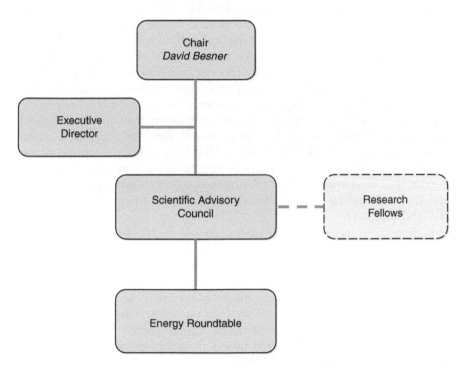

Figure 18.1 Organizational structure of the New Brunswick Energy Institute.
Source: The Institute.

Table 18.1 Membership and affiliations of the New Brunswick Energy Institute Roundtable

Name	Affiliation
Josee Albert	Agricultural Alliance of NB
Richard Blais	Worksafe NB
Glen Cleland	University of NB
Leandre Desjardins	Citizen
Phil Desroisiers	Citizen
Frederick Dions	Association Francophone
Jamie Gormon	Tobique First Nation
Susan Holt	NB Business Council
Kathy Lambert	Esgenoopetitj First Nation
Donald MacPhale	Geologist/Economist
Stephanie Merrill	Conservation Council NB
Denna Murphey	Corridor Resources
Chad Peters	SWN Resources Canada
Sylvain Poirier	NB Community College
Michel Savoy	Ecologist (Independent)
Dan Yturralde	NB Medical Society

governance document was to gather stakeholder input (defined as input from citizens, industries, and other interest groups) in the production of another "blueprint," this time more precisely dealing with oil and natural gas. That oil and gas investments in the province were an area of controversy became obvious during these input-gathering processes, which ended with the release of the *Oil and Natural Gas Blueprint* that outlined guiding principles for the development of oil and natural gas policy decisions: environmental responsib- ility, effective regulation and enforcement, community relations, First Nations engagement, stability of supply, and economic development. The Conser- vative government founded the NBEI in May 2013 with the intention that it would further these policy objectives in the following mandate: (1) the pro- duction of a solid evidence base relating to the benefits and risks of fracking; and (2) by providing "a public forum for debate on energy development in NB" (NBEI, 2014).

Curious given its mandate, our analysis reveals the NBEI roundtable deliber- ations were structured to privilege discussions that turned on economic gains and potential environmental risks presented by a potential fracking industry in the province (see also Bronson, 2016). As such, the NBEI roundtable makes little to no epistemic space for the complex historical, social, political, and cul- tural issues related to fracking that have been raised by activists during informal political processes (such as demonstrations). This attempted public engagement on fracking arguably only furthered historic relationships of mistrust between citizens and government in New Brunswick.

Clearly the Executive of the NBEI was aware of the deep democratic issues confounding the debate around fracking in New Brunswick. At the first meeting, the then-Chair of the NBEI, Louis LaPierre, outlined the mandate of the Institute, describing it as a mechanism for delivering citizens the kinds of truths they expect to receive but are not getting from government:

> The NBEI emerged from a recommendation I made to government and they accepted, and we are here today. NBEI was initiated after a listening tour across the province.... One of the main issues [that arose during the listening tour on fracking] is government integrity. Many citizens of NB don't believe that government will do what it says it's going to do [laughs] ... they are convinced of that. What I did say [to government] is if there is a potential for a shale gas industry in New Brunswick, then we should try to understand it.

Interestingly, this single quotation speaks to the fundamental misunderstanding between government actors and citizens over fracking in New Brunswick: citizens have moral and political concerns that government actors register and address on a technical level. LaPierre suggests that providing information on a potential shale gas industry will remedy citizen mistrust in government (and provincial democratic processes). A member of the Council of Canadian Academies makes similar assumptions about the fracking debate in his speech to roundtable member at the first meeting:

> So, what I learned, the literature was dominated by what I've been telling you [has just been talking about *GasLand*], and there has been little credible research concerning shale gas and environmental impacts. So, based on a scientific debate, the general public has good reason to distrust the industry and government, there is no doubt about that.... How can public trust be established? Fairness and transparency in a science-driven approach.

Similarly, a bureaucrat from the provincial Department of Energy and Mines spoke to the roundtable members at this first meeting, reducing the debate around fracking to the technique's technical complexity:

> As we all know, many developments in the energy and oil and gas sectors like fracking are technically complex and certainly not without debate where it comes down to the need for environmentally sustainable development and effective regulation around these projects.

He continues:

> It became clear to the [Conservative] government that in order to move forward, particularly for the development of the oil and gas resources in our province, independent research was needed in order to provide factual science-based and truthful information to both the public and government. Hence, the creation of the Energy Institution.

Not only does the bureaucrat's wording in the above quotation speak to a fundamental misstep on the part of government actors regarding fracking – reducing widespread political and social concern to technical ignorance – but it also suggests policy priorities were set in advance of deliberation, and the perceived route to legitimate those priorities is thought to be providing the public with "science-based" or "truthful information" via the roundtable members. Roundtable members are told by the Executive, over the course of several meetings, that the NBEI's scientific body (the Scientific Advisory Council, see Figure 18.1) will "examine the science on fracking" in order to "understand the possibilities involved with shale gas industry," and that roundtable members are to communicate the findings to members of the public. As LaPierre puts it:

> We would expect that most of you go back and share with your constituents ... this is not confidential information but information you should share, you can get the information from the website. So, this is part of our mandate.... We do have a responsibility for conducting research and providing a flow of understanding to the public.

A focus on moving a fracking industry "forward" is all the more curious, given that the Institute was by definition an independent non-profit charged with thinking through energy developments at large. Fueling a perceived legitimation crisis, the government continued to actively promote the idea of fracking development before any formal reporting had come from the NBEI.

Ultimately the NBEI roundtable discussion was limited by its Executive not only to one on fracking but, moreover, to a narrow set of issues surrounding the technique. The parameters of the discussion were themselves never deliberated upon by roundtable members but instead were pre-decided by the NBEI Executive as discussion about the future of a fracking industry, hinging on managing its technical risks. As Louis LaPierre puts it during the first roundtable: "Then there is a screening and assessment of the risk; ... if there's no risk, the project is accepted, the components of the project are accepted, we move forward."

The structure of the roundtable meetings was such that NBEI members were spoken *to* by expert presenters (invited by the Executive), with space made at the end of presentations for clarifying questions. The audio-recordings of roundtable meetings show no evidence of deliberation among roundtable members and the closed nature of the meetings (not open to general public) closed off the possibility of wider democratic conversation. The majority of expert presenters discussed the known environmental risks associated with fracking – notably risks of groundwater contamination. NBEI members were thus pre-empted from discussing the risks associated with fracking that can less easily be made sense of as scientific. For example, one citizen concern that was not brought into the roundtable dialogue, is the possible cultural risks associated with fracking, such as those the First Nations have raised regarding the possible threat fracking poses to water's cultural role for Indigenous peoples in the province. In fact, roundtable members appear to have shared the assumption that water is a "resource" with an economic value in its competing industrial and recreational uses. Cultural descriptions of water (e.g., as life force) – those that have been raised by Indigenous activists – never appear in the roundtable dialogues.

There is no evidence of conversation about bringing the energy needs of New Brunswickers, as articulated by citizens themselves, into these dialogues. For example, green energy technologies, like those being advocated for by local environmental activists (e.g., Coon and Couture, 2007), are never explicitly made the topic of roundtable discussion. During the October 2013 roundtable meeting, one roundtable member does initiate a discussion on renewable energy technologies. The NBEI Director, now David Besner, shifts the conversation toward one about the limitations of renewables (specifically energy storage technologies):

MEMBER: I'm just thinking ... maybe gas isn't necessarily what we should be putting all of our money into ... because we're actually in the center ... you know Quebec is selling energy for nothing to the States and we do have a nuclear power in NB ... maybe we're putting too much on gas.

DIRECTOR: That's entirely possible ... Maurice [Desault] discussed yesterday a bit about some new research going on in energy storage and the limitations of this technology, which is something we need in order to use renewables ... because the wind doesn't always blow, the sun doesn't always shine. Maurice, I don't know if you want to mention....

As this meeting, this particular conversation about renewables goes no farther. While the NBEI was debating the finer points of the safety of fracking, at this precise time (October 2013), First Nations protesters were literally taking up arms at Rexton.

Discussion

Our chapter focusing on the public debate around fracking in the Canadian province of New Brunswick is instructive on broader governance concerns around public engagement, legitimacy, social license, and ultimately what is an appropriate role of government in promoting resource development. The shale gas controversy in New Brunswick both springs from and perpetuates deep and long-standing mistrust between citizens and the government, which should remind government actors to make themselves aware of long-standing and complex relationships as these inform tensions over current policy issues. For years, government actors in New Brunswick have attempted to persuade citizens to agree to government's energy policy goals with promises of jobs and community royalty sharing regimes. Moreover, governments led by both major parties have simultaneously and untenably acted as boosters for exploration and development as well as "honest brokers," making evidence-based decisions on energy technologies (Pilke, 2003). The Liberal government of Shawn Graham

(2006–2010), and the Progressive Conservative government led by David Alward (2010–2014), were both unabashed boosters of shale gas exploration. While exploration was already underway, putative public dialogues turned on how much development would be appropriate, who would do it, under what rules and conditions, with what economic benefits to New Brunswickers and with what protections for local citizens in the impact zones. As with other resource developments in the province, the New Brunswick government appears to have fundamentally underestimated the possible role of publics in actually formulating the decisions on energy in New Brunswick, leaving little to no space for the incorporation of citizens' social and political public concerns into policy directions.

Multiple provincial governments in New Brunswick have been unable to create inclusive policy development and public engagement on various resource files from forestry to electrical energy, instead attempting to appease citizens by leveraging scientific facts that support already-established policy commitments. Government actors appear to assume that the issues surrounding policy decisions are merely technical and that "the public" will get on board with policy decisions that are supported by scientific information. These assumptions were exemplified in the New Brunswick Energy Institute roundtables. The NBEI Executive appeared to view "the public" as misinformed on the technical matters related to fracking and they structured the dialogue around environmental risk and economic gain. The appeals to science as an arbiter of truth by the NBEI Executive (and by many guest presenters, like the DOE visitor) also resonate with dominant discourses in the oil and gas industry that frame debates about fracking in almost exclusively technical terms. In this reasoning, the technical is privileged "above all else" (Schneider, 2013) and the "problem" of fracking is that the "uninformed" public does not understand the true risks and rewards. Within such deficit framings, the solution and resolution to the public conflict are merely to educate the public, which is what the NBEI ultimately understood as the primary role for roundtable members. It is possible that the NBEI roundtables were doomed to failure before they even began. These public engagement processes were led by Louis LaPierre who had previously consulted with members of the public in order "to obtain feedback from New Brunswickers on the proposed regulations [for fracking] which were released on May 17th, 2012" (LaPierre, 2012). From these early consultations made with 200 citizens, Lapierre expressed frustration that not many had taken the opportunity to familiarize themselves with the new regulations. Citizens, on the other hand, publicly expressed frustration with the narrow mandate of these early meetings (discussion of royalty and regulatory structure) and many spoke to their opposition to shale gas development as one that included political and social concerns.

The New Brunswick government's vision for the role of science in democracy – a scientific approach to democracy as opposed to a democratic approach to science (Sarewitz, 2009) – is premised upon normative assumptions about science as value-neutral (see Merton, 1942). In the common view, science is supposed to cut through self-interest and rhetoric and short-term thinking because science seeks truth. According to this way of thinking, scientists take a "view from nowhere" – the so-called "God's eye view" (Haraway, 1988). Sarewitz describes the common assumptions behind scientized debates this way:

> If politics is the arena of the irrational, then science is the only rational player in the game and scientific truth must be a guiding parameter for wise political decision making. According to this perspective, science could resolve a multitude of thorny political problems that confront people and nations if only humanity would rely on facts instead of perception of the facts.
>
> (2009: 72)

Unfortunately, scientized energy policy-making is unlikely to ever result in policies that achieve social legitimacy and public support. Welsh and Wynne (2013) point out a danger in appealing to science in controversies such as the fracking debate in New Brunswick because this ignores the uncertain aspects of scientific investigation and can lead to science-based value judgments, wherein "science is given authority well beyond its ostensible role of providing best available facts and information ... to one where science is also allowed to declare which information is salient and which is not" (ibid.: 544). Numerous case studies (see, notably, Wynne, 1992) suggest that controversies with technical underpinnings, like the fracking debate in New Brunswick, cannot be resolved solely by technical means, through consideration of scientific information, or by so-called experts acting alone (Sarewitz, 2009: 385). For one, there are almost always social, political, and cultural issues that cannot be addressed when the controversy is dealt with only on a technical register. Schneider writes:

> Of course, there may be technical misunderstandings – there often are. But clarifying those – whether by calling for revised science education or publishing another fact sheet debunking the documentary movie *GasLand* – does not mean someone will end up agreeing with you. Because, fundamentally, you may be disagreeing not about information, but values.
>
> (2013: 26)

Furthermore, treating a debate as if it is about technical matters alone actually works to make invisible the value commitments necessarily embedded within conversations that appear to turn on value-neutral science (Sarewitz, 2004). How the NBEI dealt with the technical details about water, for example, depended upon how water was conceptualized in the first place; in other words, factual treatment of water data is actually premised upon particular value commitments, like the commitment to treat water as a resource. Thus, not only are expressions of social, cultural, and political ideas, issues, needs, and concerns suppressed in a scientized debate, but value-based commitments – say, to monopoly industries – remain beyond reproach, hidden behind the perception that the debate is being carried out in unbiased terms. That a limited range of (fossil fuel-based) energy solutions to the economic problems of New Brunswick dominated the attention of the NBEI is problematic because these happened at the expense of other possible solutions (i.e., fracking versus renewables); but this limiting is made further problematic by the fact that these commitments were hidden through the Institute's scientization, and are thus removed from the democratic scrutiny that the Institute purports to further. It is, after all, these democratic issues which have stood stand at the center of public discontent over resource governance in New Brunswick for over a century.

While we highlight the failure of technocratic policy processes in this chapter, we are mindful of David Hess's (2015) suggestion to acknowledge the public's role in participating in the acceptance or rejection of government visions – of the public, of proper decision-making – in such analyses. Hess notes that citizens often contest the assumptions of official visions held by governing elites (ibid.: 77). Similarly, Welsh and Wynne (2013) argue that the increase in public critique of science-led policy in the 1970s altered government perceptions that "the public" was a passive and compliant entity. There are contemporary examples, even in reference to fracking (see Kinchy et al., 2014), where members of the public use science in an attempt to shift policy directions (e.g., through citizen-derived science), thus fundamentally challenging a vision of "the public" as a deficient and misinformed entity (Endres, 2009, 2012). In the New Brunswick case, members of the public arguably were already always disengaged from official governance processes such that they never attempted a contestation with the visions set within formal political dialogues. Instead, activists remained active outside of these formal processes, pushing the fracking debate out of the technical and into the political realm through direct (and sometimes violent) action, as happened at Rexton.

Conclusion

On June 26, 2016, the current (Liberal) provincial government imposed a moratorium on shale gas development (NB Commission on Hydraulic Fracturing, 2016) and said they would not open the door to additional exploration or development until several conditions were met:

- A social license is in place.
- Clear and credible information is given about the impacts of hydraulic fracturing on health, the environment and water, allowing the development of a country-leading regulatory regime with sufficient enforcement capabilities.
- A plan that mitigates on the public infrastructure and that addresses issues such as wastewater disposal.
- A process in place to respect obligations under the duty to consult First Nations.
- A mechanism in place to ensure the benefits are maximized for New Brunswickers, including the development of a proper royalty structure.

Then the new government charged an independent New Brunswick Commission on Hydraulic Fracturing with determining whether and how these conditions could be met. The Commission's report, released in February 2016, identified an impassable public controversy on which a shale gas industry is hamstrung. They write: "Despite government efforts, the end result has been two solitudes – those who wholeheartedly support shale gas, and those who do not" (2016: 4). Most significant for this chapter, the Commission identified the root cause of the rift on fracking as being a deep public mistrust of government – one problematically remaining, regardless of what happens with shale gas.

The broken relationship between New Brunswick citizens and government is historical, with shale gas activists merely beneficiaries of over two decades of decision processes that have failed to substantively engage citizens on a variety of natural resource files. Arguably, the persistent failure to meaningfully engage citizens in governance processes has to do with assumptions made by government actors that citizens are incapable of participating substantively in energy decision-making because they lack technical know-how, and that citizen concerns around energy policy are merely technical, rather than political, social, and cultural. Public engagement efforts in New Brunswick or any other political jurisdictions that focus on the technical dimensions of energy policy-making alone are doomed to fail, when citizen concern about energy technology is inevitably socio-technical. Citizens have a right to broader and more comprehensive conversation with governments about our shared energy futures.

Note

1 LaPierre was removed from the position of Chair of the Energy Institute after it was revealed that he had actively falsified his credentials for the 40 years of his active science advisory career.

References

Al, T., Butler, K., Cunjak, R., and McQuarrie, K. (2012). *Opinion: Potential Impact of Shale Gas Exploitation on Water Resources*. Fredericton, NB: University of New Brunswick. Available at: www.unb.ca/initiatives/shalegas/shalegas.pdf (accessed March 17, 2016).

Beckley, T. (2014). "Public Engagement, Planning and Politics in the Forestry Sector in New Brunswick, 1997–2014." *Journal of New Brunswick Studies*, 5, 41–65. Available at: https://journals.lib.unb.ca/index.php/JNBS/article/view/22337 (accessed March 17, 2016).

Beckley, T. M., Parkins, J. R., and Sheppard S. R. J. (2006). *Public Participation in Sustainable Forest Management: A Reference Guide*. Edmonton, Alberta: Sustainable Forest Management Network.

Bronson, K. (2016).). "(Re)producing Power: A study of the New Brunswick Energy Institute" *Journal of New Brunswick Studies*, 7(2): 71–91.

Brossard, D. and Lewenstein, B. (2010). "A Critical Appraisal of Models of Public Understanding of Science." In L-A. Kahlor, and P. Stout (eds.) *Communicating Science: New Agendas in Communication* (pp. 11–39). New York: Routledge.

Canadian Association of Petroleum Producers. (2013). Industry across Canada – New Brunswick. Available at: www.capp.ca/canadaIndustry/naturalGas/ShaleGas/Pages/default.aspx (accessed October 8, 2016).

Chief Medical Officer of Health. (2012). *Chief Medical Officer of Health's Recommendations Concerning Shale Gas Development in New Brunswick.* Fredericton, NB: Government of New Brunswick.

Conservation Council of New Brunswick. (2013). "The Risky Business of Shale Gas Fracking." Press release, October 26. Available at: www.conservationcouncil.ca/our-programs/freshwater-protection/shale-gas-alert/ (accessed March 17, 2016).

Cook, J. J. (2015). "Who's Pulling the Fracking Strings? Power, Collaboration and Colorado Fracking Policy." *Environmental Policy and Governance, 25,* 373–385.

Coon, D. and Couture, T. (2007). "Roadmap to a Self-Sufficient Energy Future." *Conservation Council of New Brunswick,* November 2007. Available at: www.conservation-council.ca/wp-content/uploads/2013/02/energy-roadmap-nb-2007-11.pdf   (accessed March 17, 2016).

Department of Energy. (2011). *The New Brunswick Energy Blueprint.* Report produced by the Department of Energy, October 19, 2011. Available at: www2.gnb.ca/content/dam/gnb/Departments/en/pdf/Publications/201110NBEnergyBlueprint.pdf   (accessed March 17, 2016).

Endres, D. (2009). "Science and Public Participation: An Analysis of Public Scientific Argument in the Yucca Mountain Controversy." *Environmental Communication, 3,* 49–75.

Endres, D. (2012). "Sacred Land or National Sacrifice Zone: The Role of Values in the Yucca Mountain Participation Process." *Environmental Communication: A Journal of Nature and Culture, 6,* 328–345.

Haraway, D. (1988). "Situated Knowledges: The Science Question in Feminism and the Privilege of Partial Perspective." *Feminist Studies, 14*(3), 575–599.

Hess, D. (2015). "Publics as Threats? Integrating Science and Technology Studies and Social Movement Studies." *Science as Culture, 24,* 69–82.

Howarth, R. W., Santoro, R., and Ingraffia, A. (2011). "Methane and the Greenhouse-Gas Footprint of Natural Gas from Shale Formations." *Climate Change Letters, 105,* 5.

Howe, M. (2015). *Debriefing Elsipogotog: Anatomy of a Struggle.* Halifax, NS: Fernwood Publishing.

Hubner, A., Horsefield, B., and Kappe, I. (2013). "Fact Based Communication: The Shale Gas Information Platform, SHIP." *Earth and Environmental Sciences, 70,* 3921–3925.

Hudgins, A. and Poole, A. (2014). "Framing Fracking: Private Property, Common Resources, and Regimes of Governance." *Ecology, 21,* 222–348.

Kinchy, A., Jalbert, K., and Lyons, J. (2014). "What Is Volunteer Water Monitoring Good for? Fracking and the Plural Logics of Participatory Science," In F. Scott and D. Hess (Eds.), *Fields of Knowledge: Science, Politics and Publics in the Neoliberal Age* (pp. 259–289). Bingley: Emerald Group Publishing Limited.

LaPierre, L. (2012). "The Path Forward." Available at: www2.gnb.ca/content/dam/gnb/Corporate/pdf/ShaleGas/en/ThePathForward.pdf (accessed October 17, 2016).

Merton, R. (1942 [1973]). "The Normative Structure of Science." In N. Storer (Ed.) *The Sociology of Science: Theoretical and Empirical Investigations* (pp. 267–278). Chicago: University of Chicago Press.

Miller, C. A., Richter, J., and O'Leary, J. (2015). "Socio-Energy Systems Design: A Policy Framework for Energy Transitions." *Energy Research & Social Science, 6,* 29–40. doi:10.1016/j.erss.2014.11.004.

National Energy Board. (2009). *A Primer for Understanding Canadian Shale Gas – Energy Briefing Note*. ISSN 1917–506X. September 25. Available at: www.neb-one.gc.ca/clf-nsi/rnrgynfmtn/nrgyrprt/ntrlgs/prmrndrstndngshlgs2009/prmrndrstndngshlgs2009-eng.html› (accessed October 16, 2016).

New Brunswick Commission on Hydraulic Fracturing. (2016). *Volume I: The Findings.* Fredericton, NB: Government Printing Office.

New Brunswick Energy Institute. (2013). Scientific Advisory Council Members, Fellows to Energy Institute Named. Press release.

New Brunswick Energy Institute. (2014). NBEI website. March 14, 2014. Available at: www.nbenergyinstitute.ca/

Office of the Chief Medical Officer of Health, NB. (2012). *Chief Medical Officer of Health's Recommendations Regarding Shale Gas Development in the Province.* Public Report, September, 2012. Available at: www2.gnb.ca/content/dam/gnb/Departments/hs/pdf/en/HealthyEnvironments/Recommendations_ShaleGasDevelopment.pdf (accessed March 17, 2016).

Park, A. (2012). "Shale Gas in New Brunswick: Promise, Threat or Opportunity?" *Journal of New Brunswick Studies*, 3, 14–23.

Perry, S. L. (2013). "Using Ethnography to Monitor the Community Health Implications of Onshore Unconventional Oil and Gas Developments: Examples from Pennsylvania's Marcellus Shale." *NEW SOLUTIONS: A Journal of Environmental and Occupational Health Policy*, 23, 33–53.

Pilke, R. Jr. (2003). *The Honest Broker*. Cambridge: Cambridge University Press.

Poitras, J. (2014). *Irving vs. Irving*. New York: Penguin Books.

Saille, S. de (2015). "Dis-inviting the Unruly Public." *Science as Culture*, 24, 99–107.

Sarewitz, D. (2004). "How Science Makes Environmental Controversies Worse." *Environmental Science & Policy*, 7, 385–403 (accessed March 17, 2016).

Sarewitz, D. (2009). *Frontiers of Illusions: Science, Technology, and the Politics of Progress.* Philadelphia, PA: Temple University Press.

Schneider, J. (2013). "Barriers to Engagement: Why It Is Time for Oil and Gas to Get Serious About Public Communication." *Oil and Gas Facilities*, April: 25–27.

Tutton, M. (2013). "N.B. Energy Minister Says Some Shale Gas Opponents Are Ignoring Facts." *The Canadian Press*, October 1, 2013. Available at: http://atlantic.ctvnews.ca/n-b-energy-minister-says-some-shale-gas-opponents-are-ignoring-facts-1.1478566 (accessed October 11, 2016).

Welsh, I. and Wynne, B. (2013). "Science, Scientism and Imaginaries of Publics in the UK: Passive Objects, Incipient Threats." *Science as Culture*, 22, 540–566.

Wigley, T. M. (2011). "Coal to Gas: The Influence of Methane Leakage." *Climate Change*, 108, 601.

Wynne, B. (1992). "Misunderstood Misunderstanding: Social Identities and Public Uptake of Science." *Public Understanding of Science*, 1(3), 281–304.

Index